Calvin Coolidge

The Presidency and Philosophy of a Progressive Conservative

M.C. Murphy

McFarland & Company, Inc., Publishers
Jefferson, North Carolina

Frontispiece: Calvin Coolidge, President of the United States, August 2, 1923, to March 4, 1929, shown here ca. 1924 (Harris & Ewing Collection, Library of Congress).

LIBRARY OF CONGRESS CATALOGUING-IN-PUBLICATION DATA

Names: Murphy, M.C., 1962– author.
Title: Calvin Coolidge : the presidency and philosophy of a progressive conservative / M.C. Murphy.
Description: Jefferson, North Carolina : McFarland & Co., Inc., Publishers, 2023. | Includes bibliographical references and index.
Identifiers: LCCN 2023021107 | ISBN 9781476691244 (paperback : acid free paper) ♾
ISBN 9781476649979 (ebook)
Subjects: LCSH: Coolidge, Calvin, 1872–1933. | Coolidge, Calvin, 1872–1933—Political and social views. | Presidents—United States—Biography. | United States—Politics and government—1923–1929.
Classification: LCC E792 .M877 2023 | DDC 973.91/5092—dc23/eng/20230503
LC record available at https://lccn.loc.gov/2023021107

BRITISH LIBRARY CATALOGUING DATA ARE AVAILABLE

ISBN (print) 978-1-4766-9124-4
ISBN (ebook) 978-1-4766-4997-9

Front cover: Official presidential portrait of Calvin Coolidge

Printed in the United States of America

McFarland & Company, Inc., Publishers
Box 611, Jefferson, North Carolina 28640
www.mcfarlandpub.com

To my parents,
John and Constance

Acknowledgments

This work was made possible in large part by material available through the Library of Congress in Washington, D.C.; the Calvin Coolidge Memorial Foundation in Plymouth Notch, Vermont; and the Forbes Library in Northampton, Massachusetts. The staff at all three locations provided invaluable research assistance, with special thanks to Cynthia Bittinger, former executive director of the Calvin Coolidge Memorial Foundation, and Julie Bartlett Nelson and the late Lu Knox, the current and former archivists, respectively, at the Coolidge Museum at Forbes Library. Two of the leading scholars and writers on the Coolidge presidency, Jerry Wallace and David Pietrusza, provided insights and guidance on the manuscript, although any mistakes are mine alone. I also wish to thank McFarland for outstanding support throughout the publication process.

Contents

Preface

This portrait of Calvin Coolidge looks at his presidency and his philosophy of practical idealism in opposing the unprecedented pressures of the 1920s to grow the federal government. He did so without a reliable party caucus but with a well-trained mind, a subtle knack for publicity, and more political experience than perhaps any president in history.

The narrative derives in large part from primary sources, including diaries, eyewitness accounts, letters, memoirs, newspapers, periodicals, press conferences, research collections, and speeches, to immerse the reader as much as possible into the Coolidge presidency and the politics of the 1920s as they were. The abundance of primary sources allows such an approach, even though our 30th president destroyed most of his private papers after leaving office and even though he was the last president not to have a presidential library. The discovery of some of his remaining papers in Vermont and the availability of the unpublished biography of former assistant White House physician Joel T. Boone, through the Manuscript Division of the Library of Congress, have been important additions in recent years, providing valuable insights into the political and personal aspects of the Coolidge White House.

The literature on Coolidge provides many comprehensive accounts of his life and presidency. Among biographies, *Coolidge* by Amity Shlaes (New York: HarperCollins, 2013) set the most recent standard in fine fashion; *Calvin Coolidge: An American Enigma* by Robert Sobel (Washington, D.C.: Regnery, 1998) and *Calvin Coolidge: The Quiet President* by Donald R. McCoy (Lawrence: University of Kansas Press, 1967) provide balanced and thorough accounts on their subject; and *Calvin Coolidge: The Man from Vermont* by Claude M. Fuess (Boston: Little, Brown, 1940) is an invaluable work on his youth and his rise in Massachusetts politics in particular. Among the histories of the Coolidge administration, *Calvin Coolidge* by David Greenberg (New York: Henry Holt/Times Books, 2006) and *The Presidency of Calvin Coolidge* by Robert H. Ferrell (Lawrence: University of Kansas of Press, 1998) are decidedly informative works.

The publication of *The Tormented President: Calvin Coolidge, Death, and Clinical Depression* by Robert E. Gilbert (Westport, CT: Praeger, 2003) and his related works have been influential in forming academic and popular perceptions of Coolidge and his presidency. The premise, in short, is that Coolidge, having suffered the early loss of his mother and his sister and having been prone to melancholy as a result, slipped into what appeared to be a clinical depression following the death of his youngest son in the summer of 1924 and turned into an inactive, largely ineffective president after a promising start in office. The task Dr. Gilbert undertook is highly difficult, and anyone attempting to write about Coolidge will have to take his work into full consideration and weigh the evidence for themselves.

Many of the key accounts of and information available on Coolidge belie the notion that he was a different president after his son died than he was beforehand, particularly considering his efforts to shape legislation on agriculture relief, flood relief, naval cruisers, and other large spending measures during his full term in office, from 1925 to 1929. The transcripts from his press conferences reveal a president with a strong, highly detailed understanding of the issues at hand throughout those years, despite his sorrow.

This author benefited from these and other books and literature on Coolidge in attempting to consider his place in history and his relevance today. Now that we have all the primary material on the subject that we are likely to have, besides miscellaneous additions from time to time, we can only think about him within his era and within our own.

Introduction

The move toward a pervasive federal government in the United States, more than a response to the economic troubles of the 1930s, began to take shape during the middle and late 1920s.

- The first attempt to subsidize an economic sector—agriculture—occurred during the latter part of the decade and nearly succeeded.
- The first scheme to have the federal government cover the relief and recovery costs of a natural disaster followed the Mississippi River flood of 1927 and partially succeeded.
- The first bill to provide federal funds for old age pensions appeared in 1928 and provided the basis for the historic Social Security Act of 1935.
- The push for unemployment insurance, underway at the state level by the early 1920s, picked up momentum at the national level in the late 1920s.
- Other initiatives during the decade included the first federal subsidies for social programs and an unprecedented benefit for war veterans.

Proponents of such measures held that state and local governments, charities, and volunteer associations were inadequate to address the needs and inequities of an industrialized, urbanized society. In Europe, strong central governments had been prevalent for centuries and cradle-to-grave social programs had been in place since the late 19th century. In the United States, two developments made such a transition possible: the adoption of the federal income tax in 1913 and the prosperity that began in the 1920s. Previously, most federal revenue came from customs duties and excise taxes, limited sources that limited the growth of government. The income tax provided the capacity to collect unprecedented revenue from individuals, families, and businesses. The prosperity, following the emergence of the United States as an economic and financial power after the Great War, provided the means to do so. This convergence led to rising appropriation proposals and claims on the Federal Treasury during the middle to late 1920s, with legislators, lobbyists, and special interest groups supporting programs and policies to give the federal government more authority in national affairs.

Calvin Coolidge, the first president to face such pressures, was no reactionary or ideologue. He reviewed proposals by considering their impact on budgets, debt, and taxes and their validity as proper functions for the federal government under the Constitution.

He was a fiscal conservative and a progressive conservative at that.

On budgets, he achieved reductions by cutting waste and line item appropriations, pushing department and bureau administrators to produce savings year to year, and making constructive economy the highest priority of his presidency and the dominant issue in national politics during his years in office. He produced balanced budgets each year without imposing austerity or slashing government services, while signing into law many large expenditures. "I am not advocating parsimony," he said in a speech in 1924. "I want to be liberal."[1]

On debt, he believed in regular redemption schedules to avoid overburdening contemporary or future generations and to maintain good credit for the government while returning additional surplus revenue to individuals and businesses through tax cuts to keep money in circulation and promote strong markets in goods and services. "Debt reduction is tax reduction," he said in one speech.[2] Many at the time thought his administration redeemed the $22 billion debt too hastily. Others thought the reductions should be accelerated as he attempted to strike a balance between contemporary and future needs.

On taxes, he believed that their purpose should be to raise revenue rather than to address income disparities and that reductions in rates should be preceded by budget surpluses. "The collection of any taxes which are not absolutely required, which do not beyond reasonable doubt contribute to the public welfare, is only a species of legalized larceny," he declared at his inauguration in 1925.[3] The notion that tax cuts could increase revenues by spurring economic growth, which began to emerge in the 1920s and became known as supply-side economics in the 1980s, was never more than a theory to him. The fact that revenues went up following his tax cuts did not prove a correlation. In 1926, 1927, and 1928, he opposed large tax cut proposals from Republicans and Democrats because they might produce a budget deficit, given estimates for a small surplus and uncertainties about business conditions. "It is far better to have no tax reduction than to have too much," he said at a budget meeting in 1928.[4] In speeches, press conferences, and other statements throughout his presidency, he stressed the same message. In addition, he and his Secretary of the Treasury, Andrew Mellon, supported the progressive income tax as the backbone of the federal revenue system and never attempted to flatten rates despite concerns that fewer people were paying more revenue and many were paying nothing because of exemptions. Both opposed sporadic efforts to supplement or replace the income tax with a national sales tax.

On the proper role of the federal government, Coolidge supported initiatives that advanced the country as a whole, such as funding the development and regulation of commercial aviation and radio, but he opposed attempts to benefit special interest groups, provide social services, or infringe upon the powers and responsibilities of the states through loose interpretations of the general welfare clause in Article I of the Constitution. The Framers, for the most part, intended to limit general welfare to the 18 defined powers cited in Article I. They did not mention social spending in writing or during discussions on the Articles of Confederation, the Constitution, or the *Federalist Papers* or during the state ratification conventions. Congress took a broader interpretation of the clause to fund internal improvements during the early days of the republic, leading Monroe to veto the Cumberland Road bill in 1822, Jackson to veto the Maysville Road in 1830, and Polk to veto the Bill for the Benefit of the Indigent Insane in 1854, among other presidential actions to check the legislature. Throughout the history of the country, Congress had asserted the right to determine the general welfare, the executive branch had pushed back at times, and the Supreme Court had avoided ruling on the matter. The push for spending that emerged in the 1920s would soon challenge this impasse and force the three branches to address the question of whether the federal government could provide a social benefit at the national level without an amendment to the Constitution as proponents of the income tax and prohibition did to clear the way for controversial and legally questionable measures.

Three months before Coolidge became president, in May 1923, the Supreme Court issued two landmark decisions that backed the constitutionality of federal subsidies to the states for maternity care and suggested a broad interpretation of the general welfare clause. The first, *Massachusetts v. Mellon,* involved a claim by the state that Congress had assumed a power reserved strictly to the states under the Tenth Amendment and that the subsidy exceeded the spending powers enumerated in Article I, Section VIII, Clause I of the Constitution. The second, *Frothingham v. Mellon*, involved a suit by a private citizen asserting that federal expenditures on health services violated the Fifth and Tenth amendments and that her property—her tax money—had been taken without due process of law. In reviewing the cases simultaneously, the Supreme Court determined that it lacked clear jurisdiction. In *Massachusetts v. Mellon*, the Court found unanimously that the means of addressing the legislation were available through Congress and state legislatures, that state participation in the subsidy program was voluntary, and that a state had no power to institute judicial proceedings to protect citizens from the operation of federal statutes. In *Frothingham v. Mellon*, the Court laid down the controversial, precedent-setting principle that no taxpayer or group of taxpayers had the standing to challenge a legislative appropriation because their contribution was "comparatively minute and indeterminable."[5] The rulings, by inferring that the high bench would not interfere with attempts to use federal tax revenue for economic and social purposes usually within the domain of the states, would make it difficult, if not impossible, for the courts to check spending by the legislature.

The two cases advanced the cause of national supremacy and contributed to calls for a more activist federal government. This became a rallying cry of sorts for progressives, who, for all their divisions and disparate priorities in the 1920s, began to redefine their movement around economic redistribution and social welfare.

Coolidge had his own interpretation. "More work and better work for a smaller outlay of the money of the taxpayer is the real test of a progressive administration," he said during the summer of 1926, the peak of his popularity.[6]

The emphasis on good government was essential to progressivism in the late 19th and early 20th centuries, along with the many political and economic reforms that Coolidge backed during his rise in Massachusetts politics from city councilman in 1898 to governor in 1918. It was not so much that he became less progressive as president but that he thought most reforms should be done at the state and local level and that the shift in progressivism, from promoting a more direct democracy and correcting problems in industry to supporting certain constituencies, was imprudent from a fiscal and constitutional standpoint. This put him at odds with some Republicans and most Democrats on subsidies to farmers, bonuses and pensions to veterans, assistance to natural disaster victims, and insurance to older citizens and unemployed workers during his presidency. Coolidge lamented the influence of special interest groups on Capitol Hill: "It is because in their hours of timidity the Congress becomes subservient to the importunities of organized minorities that the President comes more and more to stand as the champion of the rights of the whole country."[7] In appealing to his fellow citizens, he urged them to recall the ideals and founding principles of the country, to preserve local and state privileges, and to maintain the virtues of independence and self-support against encroachment.

The Coolidge administration, from 1923 to 1929, reduced federal spending to under $3 billion for the first time since before the war; slashed the national debt from $22.35 billion to $16.93 billion; achieved debt settlement plans with European countries through shrewd pressure tactics; produced a federal budget surplus every year, totaling nearly $2 billion or more than the combined surpluses of Harding, Wilson, Taft, Roosevelt, McKinley, Cleveland, Harrison, Garfield, and Hayes; and lowered federal income tax rates on three occasions. These achievements were made possible, in part, by strong economic growth. Still, Coolidge kept a tight rein on fiscal matters through full implementation of the Budget and Accounting Act of 1921, twice-weekly meetings with his budget director, pressure on his cabinet, consultations with legislative leaders, vetoes, reductions in military spending proposals, and appeals to the public through speeches and press conferences. No administration has produced such a fiscal record before or since.

The growth in federal spending and borrowing since the 1920s, following broad interpretations of the general welfare by the Supreme Court in the 1930s, has led to the formation of formidable special interests that promote entitlements and hinder reform. To be determined is whether such growth is sustainable without tax increases and currency debasements that undermine prosperity and the constitutional principle that personal rights and property rights are essentially the same.

Chapter One

The Thirtieth President

The telegram from San Francisco arrived at the Western Union office at White River Junction, Vermont, at about 10:30 p.m. Eastern standard time, August 2, 1923, an unusually warm evening. President Warren Harding was dead at age 57.

The operator, knowing Vice President Calvin Coolidge was with his father in Plymouth Notch, in the Green Mountains, 30 miles away, tried to reach the general merchandise store there. No one answered. Then he called the switchboard operator at Bridgewater, where W.A. Perkins took the message and drove at such high speeds that he broke his speedometer on a straightaway before the steep hill leading up to Plymouth Notch. It was near midnight as he arrived at the small hamlet and knocked on the door of the Coolidge house, a simple white-framed, black-shuttered place with an attached barn, shouting, "Hallo!"

John Coolidge appeared in a nightshirt, carrying a kerosene lamp. He read the message, thanked Perkins, and turned toward the stairs, calling for his son. "Calvin!"[1]

The vice president sensed the urgency: "I noticed that his voice trembled. As the only times I had ever observed that before were when death had visited our family, I knew that something of the gravest nature had occurred."[2]

Coolidge knelt in prayer before retrieving a bucket of cold water from the kitchen, shaving without soap, and donning a blue serge suit, a hard-starched white shirt with a detachable collar, a blue tie, and high-laced black button shoes. Meantime, his secretary, Edwin C. Geisser, and his chauffeur, Joseph McInerney, had arrived at the scene. Representative Porter H. Dale, railway mailman L.L. Lane, and local reporter Joe Fountain had arrived as well, having heard the news. "Good morning," Coolidge said as he and his wife, Grace, came down the narrow staircase. He went into the study with Geisser to dictate a telegram to Mrs. Harding and a public statement to the country. Then Dale took him aside, speaking with urgency, saying he ought to take the presidential oath promptly and that his father, as public notary, was eligible to administer it. Coolidge found the oath inside a copy of the *Revised Statutes of Vermont* and told Geisser to prepare three copies on a typewriter.

* * *

Hours earlier Coolidge had taken a break from raking hay with a neighbor to tell reporters that Harding seemed to be through the crucial phase of his illness—acute indigestion and a possible heart attack—based on the latest updates from the West Coast.[3] Some reporters had gone home, thinking the crisis was over.

* * *

A little past 2:30 a.m. on August 3, Coolidge and the others gathered around a round table in the sitting room, its low ceiling charred by the stove, its rug worn, illuminated by a kerosene lamp. Coolidge faced his taller father, who had put on a black suit and bowtie. Coolidge raised his right hand and repeated the oath:

> I, Calvin Coolidge, do solemnly swear that I will faithfully execute the office of the president of the United States and will, to the best of my ability, preserve, protect, and defend the Constitution of the United States. So help me God.

No one spoke except Dale, who, removing a gold watch from his pocket, said, "It is exactly two forty-seven!" The elder Coolidge fumbled through some books, catalogues, and papers on his desk, and pulled out his public notary seal impresser and applied it to each copy of the oath. The president signed them in his neat, slanted script. Moments later another reporter, accompanied by a photographer, arrived and asked the president whether he would kindly stand with his father beside the table to make a photographic record of the event. Normally quite willing to pose for photographs, he declined. "No," he said. "It is too sacred a thing." No appeals by others in the room could persuade him.

Then came employees of the Southern Vermont Telephone Company, sent by the Secret Service to install temporary service at the house. Coolidge watched intently as they laid a black line from the parlor through the front door and placed a clunky black telephone on a chair since his father would not let them hang it on the wall. Once the line was connected to the trunk line between White River Junction and Bellows Falls, with a circuit to provide direct service to Washington, the president called Secretary of State Charles Evans Hughes—the lone cabinet officer in the capital—to report the transition of power was complete. Then he went upstairs, back to sleep, he said, while workers installed a telephone on a tree outside the store for reporters to use. The nearest Secret Service agent, in Boston, four hours away, was on the way.[4]

Later that morning, Coolidge greeted neighbors outside and invited his father to Washington, to which he replied, "I think that my place is at home."[5] The president and first lady slid into a black sedan and began their long trip, stopping at the hillside cemetery where his mother was buried, and heading north by northwest, across the mountains to the Rutland train station at 15 miles per hour, nearly swerving off the road when some pigs ran in front of their vehicle.

* * *

John Coolidge sat on his stoop that morning, talking to neighbors and newspapermen, his big knotty hands across his knees, the fifth man to live long enough to see his son become president.

Born in 1845, he came from old Yankee stock, dating back to the Normans who went to England after 1066 and the early settlers of Massachusetts and Vermont. He became a storekeeper at 22 and made about $1,200 a year, bartering with freight wagon operators and traveling to Boston twice a year on purchase runs, taking the midnight train from nearby Ludlow and returning the same day to avoid a hotel bill, walking home 12 miles in darkness. He also did credit checks, insurance policies, bookkeeping, masonry, blacksmithing, tinsmithing, plumbing, carpentry, carriage-making, coffin-making, horse-mending, dentistry, and legal work, and he usually wore a business suit with a white dress shirt, unlike his neighbors with their outer garments of brown or blue drilling and their colored shirts. A Republican in Republican Vermont, he had been voted into many local offices, like his father, despite not serving in the Civil War after turning 18 in March 1863, old enough to enlist but two years shy of conscription. "You tell Mr. Coolidge to keep John home never let him go to war," a neighbor wrote Mrs. Coolidge in September 1862, after fighting in the battle at Baton Rouge, Louisiana.[6] Instead her only son volunteered as a state militia officer and received the honorary title Colonel Coolidge.

Calvin had been his first-born after four years of marriage to neighbor Victoria Moor and born on a holiday no less, July 4, 1872, in the clapboard cottage behind the store across the street. Two months later the Colonel had been elected to the state legislature, serving three terms before returning home to take over a 200-acre farm from his father and give up the store business but not the store building, which he leased. In 1876, he bought the house that would become known as the site of the midnight inaugural.

Colonel Coolidge raised his boy with expectations, not rules, figuring the more rules, the more rules to break[7]; likewise his daughter, Abigail, or Abbie, who was born behind the store in 1875. To be sure, he was determined that they receive proper training and he was demanding. They were a religious people and he ran the village church, down to where people sat at funerals. They never had a regular minister but he made sure Calvin received a daily reading from the Bible at a young age. For chores, he had Calvin fill the wood box, feed the chickens and pigs, drive the cows to pasture at dawn and retrieve them at dusk, cut and husk corn, and plow with the horse-drawn mowing machine once he turned 12. Whenever possible he took his son to court hearings and town meetings, where everything was put to a vote, from hiring a teacher to setting tax rates. At tax collection time they went from house to house as farmers handed over their cash. Calvin kept a personal account book of all sums received and spent, balancing them out to the penny.

They had been through a lot. In 1885, the Colonel lost his wife and Calvin his mother when Victoria, a striking woman inclined toward literature and gardening, died at 39, after being weakened by a carriage accident and possibly tuberculosis. Two years later Abbie succumbed to appendicitis at age 12.

Colonel Coolidge thought his son, though slightly built and prone to allergies and respiratory ailments, might one day take up his work at the family homestead.[8] To provide him an education beyond the one-room schoolhouse in the village, he sent him at 13 years old to Black River Academy at Ludlow, paying about $150 a year in tuition and room and board. When Calvin appealed for more education several years later, the Colonel agreed to send him to Amherst College in western Massachusetts, making him the first in the family to pursue a higher education. Though he struggled initially, failing to make a fraternity and falling near the bottom of his class in weight, in lung capacity, and in the number of push-ups and pull-ups he could do, he graduated cum laude in 1895, with much enthusiasm for the lectures of historian Anson Morse and philosopher Charles E. Garman, who encouraged students to differentiate between the accidental and the essential, to guide themselves by general principles and not lose themselves in particulars, to become men of vision and not visionaries, to follow the truth, and to serve.

The elder Coolidge then supported his son as a law clerk at a firm in Northampton, eight miles from Amherst, sending $30 a month for room and board. When Calvin was admitted to the Massachusetts bar in 1897, the elder Coolidge recommended an opening at an established firm, but Calvin wanted his own practice and opened an office in a new building on lower Main Street in Northampton after considering Boston, Montpelier, and a couple of other towns.[9] The Colonel sent him a monthly check for two more years.

Now 78, he was a handsome man with a fine forehead, small eyes, flattened cheekbones, and a strong nose, who went bareheaded year-round and never took alcohol or tobacco. A second wife had come and gone, taken by cancer several years earlier. As he sat on his stoop that August morning, he told a reporter that his son had been a quiet, conscientious boy who did his schoolwork and chores and never played much or showed any remarkable abilities: "I told Calvin always to do his job well and he always did."

The reporter asked how he thought his son would do as president.

Looking straight ahead, he took his time to reply. "I think he'll do fairly well. He did fairly well as Governor and I guess he'll do fairly well as President." Then he went inside to make sure workers removed the temporary telephone.[10]

* * *

George L.R. French, general superintendent of the Rutland Railroad, offered to run a special train that morning, but Coolidge declined. Instead he had a private car attached to the regular train departing at 9:35 a.m.

As the 12-hour ride began, Coolidge could see small crowds gathered along the way. At Troy, New York, he and his party switched to the New York Central line, rumbling down the Hudson Valley to Manhattan and pulling into the lower level at Grand Central Station shortly after four in the afternoon, amid heavy security, including a hundred plain-clothes policemen. Benjamin Felt, his aide, and Frank Stearns, a Boston department store owner and longtime supporter, were there with his silk hat in a box. Edward Clark, his secretary, was there, having taken the first train from Washington. To avoid the crowd at the Park Avenue entrance, bodyguards led Coolidge up a freight elevator to the Forty-Fifth Street entrance where he took a motorcar to Pennsylvania Station at Thirty-Third Street, with mounted police and motorcycles leading the way through rush-hour traffic. As the luggage was transferred to the new train, a reporter asked Coolidge whether he would repeat the oath before a justice of the Supreme Court.

"No, indeed," he replied. "Any person authorized to administer an oath can swear in a President of the United States."[11]

* * *

Of the five men who previously succeeded to the presidency on the deaths of incumbents, four had taken the oath from a federal judge. When William H. Harrison died of pneumonia in April 1841, John Taylor was at home in Williamsburg, Virginia, where a messenger found him in the street, playing marbles with his sons, and took him to Washington to take the oath in a hotel from the chief justice of the district supreme court. When Zachary Taylor died of cholera in July 1850, Millard Fillmore took the oath from the same judge in the chamber of the House of

Representatives. When Abraham Lincoln was killed in April 1865, Andrew Johnson took the oath from the chief justice of the Supreme Court in a hotel. When William McKinley was assassinated in September 1901, Theodore Roosevelt was found hiking in the Adirondacks, followed by a wild dash through the mountains and a train ride to Buffalo, where he took the oath from a United States district court judge in a private home.

The exception was Chester Arthur, who, following the assassination of James B. Garfield in September 1881, took the oath from a New York Supreme Court judge shortly past midnight at his posh Lexington Avenue townhouse in Manhattan. Two days later he took a second oath in Washington with Chief Justice Morrison R. Waite of the Supreme Court to make it official.

* * *

Aboard the train to Washington, Coolidge, Mrs. Coolidge, Stearns, Felt, and Clark dined on chicken broth, striped bass, roast lamb, new peas, new beans, creamed potatoes, salad, cheese, crackers, and ice cream, while watching a violent thunderstorm out the window. Two Secret Service men stood at opposite ends of the car. "A quiet meal, always remembering what had happened in San Francisco as well as thinking of what lay ahead," Felt wrote in his diary, having known Coolidge since the latter was a state representative. "As we sat there it was impossible not to think of the new power that had come so suddenly to this man."[12]

They made two stops—Philadelphia and Baltimore—where the president and first lady appeared on the rear platform and bowed to small crowds. As the train rolled south, he talked to reporters and posed for photographs, some sitting, some standing, some alone, some with Grace, who wore a brown traveling dress with a lace waist and collar.

"God be with you," said a photographer.[13]

Arriving at Union Station shortly past nine in the evening, Coolidge encountered a silent crowd, stunned by events. Men raised their hats as he walked by, but no one applauded. The president and his party drove away in a short line of limousines, past the impressive Capitol dome under newly installed flood lights and down dusky Pennsylvania Avenue, lit by gas lamps, like most streets in the city, to the famed Willard Hotel, where he had lived for the past two years, former haunt of Calhoun, Clay, Webster, Hawthorne, Douglas, Lincoln, McClellan, Grant, Whitman, Morse, Twain, and Dewey, with a Beaux Arts exterior, rich carpets, marble columns, oak woodwork, glittering chandeliers, and palm trees in the lobby. Upstairs, in his two-room suite, he met with Secretary of State Charles Evans Hughes and a military aide to plan a state funeral and write a proclamation for a national period of mourning.

"It was interesting to see the President after he had been on duty five minutes," Stearns wrote. "No one seeing him would have supposed he had not been there fifty years in the same place. He was unusually cordial to everyone but said little more than he usually says. Everything he said took the form of orders."[14]

At 51, the slight, sandy-haired Vermonter, standing five feet, nine inches, weighing 160 pounds, had reached the highest office with ample preparation. When someone later asked what went through his mind when he learned he was president, he said, "I thought I could swing it."[15]

* * *

Northampton had been ideal for young Coolidge, large enough to hold various interests, small enough for him to advance despite his laconic ways. Settled by Englishmen in 1654 in the fertile Connecticut River Valley, alongside meadows formed by centuries of flood deposits, with Mount Tom to the south and the Holyoke Range to the southeast, the former frontier post had grown to 17,000 residents. There were farmers, lawyers, bankers, clerks, professors, insurance agents, salesmen, tradesmen, shopkeepers, artisans, gravel miners, and manufacturers recovering from the depression of 1893 and producing baskets, butcher knives, bricks, buttons, brushes, caskets, hats, hosiery, mirror backs, revolver boxes, sewing machines, screw drivers, socks, stoves, tableware, silk, and the first toothbrushes made in the country. Downtown Northampton had broad tree-lined avenues, sidewalks, lanterns, electric street cars, and brick mercantile buildings, two to three stories high. The Boston and Maine Railroad connected the city to the state capital.

"I was full of the joy of doing something in the world," he relates, learning the law by day and reading his small collection of histories, literature, orations, and poetry by night, taking time to translate Cicero from the original Latin.[16]

In the evening he dined at a local establishment where he and other patrons discussed politics, automobiles, and the philanthropic efforts to kill the beetles that were destroying the trees on Elm Street, among various topics. The most notable trait in Coolidge was his ability to concentrate, observed a Smith College professor. "As to clothes, he was always well dressed; but he was not what you might call a natty dresser; he was neat; he was inconspicuous." That Coolidge might one day become famous never occurred to him.[17]

No sooner had Coolidge arrived in 1895 than he became involved in Republican politics in what was still a mostly Republican town, handing out ballots, writing articles, attending meetings, never saying much but making a modest impression. "There were already four or five Vermont fellas trying to get into Northampton politics, and the local politicians resented it," remarked one resident. "And here was Cal trying to hop in, too."[18] To his Republican legal mentors, John C. Hammond and Henry P. Field, he was reliable and circumspect.[19] To attorney and local party leader Richard W. Irwin, he had potential and ought to get into politics despite his shyness and reluctance to have his picture taken. "Because you can do it," Irwin told the young lawyer.[20] So he began—city councilman, city solicitor, court clerk, and local party chairman—running his own campaigns and hoping to please and honor his father as much as anything else. In 1905, a month after he was married to neighbor Grace Goodhue, a teacher at the Clark Institute for the Deaf and a native Vermonter, he lost a close contest for school board in which one voter said someone seeking such a position ought to have children. "Might give me time," he replied.[21] That was the last time he lost. In 1907, he was elected to the Massachusetts House of Representatives. In 1908, he was reelected by 36 votes. In 1909, he was elected mayor of Northampton. "I wanted to gratify you," he wrote his father.[22] The following year he was reelected on a record of tax cuts and budget cuts and proceeded with plans to lay down concrete sidewalks in the city without a bond issue or new levies. In 1911, he was elected to the Massachusetts Senate, serving four terms and rising to the presidency of that body. "I am sure you would be gratified if you saw the place I hold here," he wrote his father, who was serving in the Vermont Senate.[23]

Though not one to make a rousing speech or slap a man on the back, Coolidge had a reputation for integrity and the innate appeal of a vote-getter, who avoided controversial issues unless or until he needed to address them and promoted the broadest public interest. He seldom said "yes" or "no" right away. He also had strong support among Irish Democrats such as shoemaker Jim Lucey, baker Jim Maloney, brick mason Ed Lynch, lunch wagon operator Johnny Prokup, tavern keeper Johnny Dewey, bookseller Cliff Lyman, blacksmith Phil Gleason, and innkeeper Dick Rahar. They all had stories about him. When Maloney needed a lawyer one night to write a will for his dying mother, Coolidge returned to his office, retrieved the necessary paperwork, and hurried to her bedside, charging only $5 for his services. As Lyman was wrapping books in his shop one evening, Coolidge stopped by to talk and, observing the procedure, suggested a new method that saved the bookseller time and money. When two Democratic ward leaders approached Gleason to ask whether he was still a Democrat, given his support for Coolidge, he replied, "So I am and always will be, but I just figured how Coolidge was about the best Democrat we had in the city."[24] Coolidge was known to live modestly, paying $28 a month to rent half of a two-family house at 21 Massasoit Street, with a sagging porch, a party line telephone, and no electricity. He never had a retainer from any client and never made more than a few thousand dollars in a single year or had a car.[25]

"I am not wholly lacking in liberal views as to legislation and some other things," he told a supporter in 1913; he knew the world moved and wished to move with it.[26]

In the legislature, he backed female suffrage, an anti-discrimination bill, an anti-monopoly bill, an eight-hour workday for children, a minimum wage for female workers, public aid for needy mothers, pensions for the widows and orphans of deceased firemen, compensation for injured workers, pensions for public school teachers, legalized picketing, licenses for barbers, protection for tenants, regulations for the practice of optometry, direct primaries and direct elections for the United States Senate, and two new amendments to the state constitution—one to establish a state income tax and the other to allow women to serve as public notaries. Most conservatives fought the tax, but he supported it as long as it was levied at the same rate for all taxpayers. He opposed the death penalty as an option for juries in murder trials. This progressive record put him in line with the reformist traditions of Republican Massachusetts, the first state to adopt the Australian ballot, child labor legislation, a factory inspection system, a railroad commission, pure food laws, and free libraries.

A fellow legislator described him as "uncomfortably progressive for some of his constituents in Northampton."[27]

Still, Coolidge was cautious. In fiscal matters he favored low taxes and balanced budgets. In legislative matters he wanted to know how bills would be implemented and enforced before he backed them.

"It is more important to kill bad bills than to pass good ones," he wrote his father in 1910, during a tense legislative session on Beacon Hill.[28]

"Give administration a chance to catch up with legislation," he said in 1914, in his inaugural address as president of the state senate.[29]

Stearns provided further insight on the political philosophy of Coolidge: "He told me once that when he first went into the legislature he supposes he was considered a radical, especially along the lines of legislation in favor of social betterment. There came a time about the middle of his legislative experience when he came to the conviction not that his previous ideas were wrong but that Massachusetts, at any rate, was going too fast. As he put it, legislation was outstripping the ability to administer."[30]

As one who knew the law and the rules and procedures of the legislature, who attended meetings and hearings, who studied bills and consulted with experts, who seldom missed a vote, Coolidge rose steadily. A veteran reporter says he did not stick out much but was an excellent source: "He could tell you about a bill—what was in it, what was around it, what was underneath it."[31] At night he retired to a dingy, badly furnished, dollar-a-day room at the Adams House on Washington Street, near the State House, sipping green tea, reading the *Evening Transcript* and the *Manual of the General Court of Massachusetts* or some history or biography. Against Democratic governor David I. Walsh, he kept the senate in check and legislation at a minimum for two years.

"Men do what I tell them to do—why, is a great mystery to me," he wrote his father in 1915. "Whatever you may read of good or ill I am just the same as when I was a boy at home and am at my best when I am most like you."[32]

Up the escalator system of Massachusetts Republican politics he went with support from two key figures, Senator W. Murray Crane and party leader William Butler, from lieutenant governor in 1916 to governor in 1919. A Harvard professor, observing him, wrote, "A small, hatched-faced colorless man with a tight-shut, thin-lipped mouth, very chary of words but with a gleam of understanding in his pretty keen eye."[33]

Coolidge was an active, progressive governor, dealing with some 200,000 war veterans returning to Massachusetts amid housing shortages, state debt, unemployment, inflation, and an influenza outbreak. "Let there be a purpose in all you legislation to recognize the right of man to be well born, well nurtured, well educated, well employed and well paid," he said in his inaugural address on January 2, 1919, setting the tone for his administration.[34]

To protect tenants against landlords trying to exploit housing shortages, he sponsored laws that gave the courts power to stay evictions in some cases, prohibited rent increases above 25 percent, and penalized landlords who reneged on utility service agreements. Against the wishes of the 1,500 member-companies of the Associated Industries of Massachusetts, he supported and signed into law a bill reducing the maximum workweek for women and minors from 54 to 48 hours, the first such law in the nation. To promote public health and welfare, he approved regulations on the licensing of daycare nurseries, the sale and cold storage of fresh fish, and the use of airplanes. To protect railway workers, he ordered that all trains carry first-aid equipment and lifting jacks with sufficient power to hoist the heaviest steel car, so that workers pinned beneath cars would have a chance to survive, which had seldom been the case with the small calibered jacks used in the past. To promote education, he increased funding for public colleges and scholarships and signed a bill allowing Massachusetts to disburse revenues to communities based on how much they paid their teachers, prompting many municipalities to increase salaries. To protect textile mill workers from swindling management practices, he signed a bill requiring mill owners to furnish a price list for specified work done by weavers. Among other reforms, he backed female suffrage, approved absentee ballots by mail, authorized the reforestation of 100,000 acres of wasteland, developed easier filing procedures for small claims courts, granted additional home rule to towns and municipalities, condemned racial discrimination, authorized a two-platoon system for firemen to reduce their hours, empowered the Insurance Commission to require insurance firms to deposit with the State Treasury sufficient cash to meet outstanding obligations, vetoed an act that would have required all motion pictures to pass censorship, initiated a $2.5 million public works scheme to alleviate postwar unemployment, approved two weeks of annual vacation for state workers, appointed a bipartisan commission to consider a pension system for public servants, and increased the maximum payment for injured workers from $14 to $16 a week.

The vetoes of his governorship were no less significant or indicative of his political philosophy. When the legislature passed a measure to widen L Street in South Boston, he turned it down with a statement that "the functions of the City Hall ought not to be performed by the State House."[35] When the legislature enacted a measure to suspend civil service regulations in favor of veterans, he rejected it to ensure the commonwealth would maintain the highest standard in hiring those entrusted to protect public health and safety. When the legislature passed a bill allowing the sale of beer or wine with a 2.75 percent alcoholic content, in apparent violation of the Eighteenth Amendment, he rejected it, blaming special interest groups and declaring, "We have had too much legislation by clamor, by tumult, by pressure."[36]

The widespread postwar labor unrest of 1919 began in Massachusetts with a Lawrence mill strike, a telephone operator strike, and a Boston Elevated Railway Company strike. These were resolved in arbitration with minimal disruption.

Coolidge was barely eight months in office when trouble began with the Boston police, who in 1906 had formed an unofficial union, whimsically named the Boston Social Club, to seek higher wages, better stations, a fairer promotion system, and shorter shifts. Similar entities operated in 43 cities, including Cincinnati, Fort Worth, Los Angeles, Terre Haute, Topeka, Vicksburg, and Washington, but no force had a more peculiar legal status than the Boston police, who served the city but were considered servants of the commonwealth, whose wages were paid by the city treasury but whose wage rate was set by the state legislature. In May, the legislature approved a $200 raise, which, though twice that given to other city workers, left policemen, on average, earning less than streetcar operators, with a pay scale of $1,100 to $1,600 annually. When the largest union in the country, the American Federation of Labor—the AFL—announced in June that it would grant charters to police in a bold move to unionize public servants, the Boston police, along with cohorts in several cities, began the process.

Police Commissioner Edwin U. Curtis, a Boston Brahmin who ran the predominantly ethnic Irish department in a heavy-handed manner, with petty rules such as forbidding on-duty officers from frequenting fruit and peanut stands in the streets, issued a general order stating that union membership was inconsistent with the sworn duty of police officers. Twelve days later the police applied for, and received, an AFL charter. With support from Coolidge, Curtis charged 19 union leaders with insubordination and placed them on departmental trial, but, after finding them guilty, postponed sentencing as Boston mayor Andrew J. Peters formed a bipartisan committee to review the state of the department. The committee, led by investment banker James J. Storrow, met with union leaders several times and made little progress before recommending another delay. Curtis agreed to postpone sentencing until September 8 as all parties turned to the governor.

Yet Coolidge had no authority over the internal affairs of the police department and no inclination to serve as a mediator. There was nothing to arbitrate, not the rules of the force, not the authority of the commissioner, not the public safety. Butler advised him to do nothing under the circumstances. Coolidge agreed: "I fully expected it would result in my defeat in the coming campaign for reelection as Governor."[37]

A day before the deadline the Storrow Committee proposed a compromise that would prevent a police walkout, prevent further punishment of the officers on departmental trial, and allow the police to have an unaffiliated union and take grievances to an impartial board. Peters blessed the plan. The newspapers, besides the *Evening Transcript*, were favorable, and the police were ready to accept on advice from counsel. Curtis, however, refused to drop charges against the 19 officers to maintain discipline for the future.

More than two-thirds of 1,544 Boston policemen abandoned their posts, exceeding predictions and leaving the sixth largest city in the country without sufficient authority to enforce law and order. A force of citizen volunteers had been preparing for the strike, but Curtis declined to use them because he could not arm them. Peters neglected to call out the Boston state guard regiments for reasons unknown. As darkness fell, small crowds gathered near the seedy flophouses and taverns of Scollay Square in South Boston, prowling the streets, breaking windows, looting stores, robbing pedestrians, and blocking traffic at main intersections, but other neighborhoods remained calm. North End, East Boston, Charlestown, West End, Jamaica Plain, Mattapan, Hyde Park, and Beacon Hill were remarkably quiet.

Coolidge received updates that evening and seemed empathetic toward the police. "They are misguided," he told his bodyguard. "They are making a grave mistake."[38]

The following morning Peters used a dubious old statute to remove Curtis from office, called out the Boston state guard, and released a statement that he had "received no co-operation from the Police Commissioner and no help or practical suggestions from the Governor." The day passed without further incident but gave way that evening to violence in Scollay Square where steel-helmeted guardsmen were hit with glass, stones, and bricks before opening fire on their assailants, killing three and wounding dozens as striking policemen incited the mob in the worst violence the city had seen since the draft riots of the Civil War.

Thursday morning, September 11, Coolidge met with former attorney general Herbert Parker and William Butler, who implored him to take over the situation by calling out the full militia and seizing control of the police affairs of Boston. Parker agreed. So advised, Coolidge issued a proclamation calling out the state guard and every citizen "to aid me in the maintenance of law and order" and issued an executive order restoring Curtis to office by means of an old statute he found on the books that authorized him to request any police officer in the state to assist him.[39] Then he asked Democratic president Woodrow Wilson to prepare to send military troops if necessary, prompting the War Department to place 10,000 troops on short notice.

That evening brought little violence, looting, or vandalism, and Coolidge awoke the next day a national figure, his name and stern countenance on front page newspaper stories across the country. This was the year of the strike, involving one in five workers, five times more than the average prewar year. Unions, released from wartime no-strike pledges and wage restraints, faced with competition from soldiers and immigrants, determined to reassert themselves, led by the Industrial Workers of the World, the United Mine Workers, and the National Labor Party, which called on workers to "take control of their lives and their government." In New York, dockworkers, dressmakers, actors, and actresses went on strike. In Seattle, a five-day general strike nearly brought the city to a halt. In West Virginia, the governor and state militia smashed a coal miner strike, citing wartime regulations. In Boston, the dramatic turn of events caught national attention like none other.

That morning he met with local and national reporters who had arrived on the scene to cover the still volatile development. Having met with Boston reporters on a daily basis as governor, he was at ease with the press, but this would be his first encounter with outsiders. A *New York Times* reporter asked for an update on the strike.

"The present situation should not be called a strike," Coolidge replied. "There is no strike on. These men are public officials, not employees. The affair is improperly referred to as a strike."

"May we ask how you draw the distinction?" someone asked.

"A strike is generally considered to be an act of employees seeking to gain better conditions from a private employer. These police officers were officials, representing not any private employer, but the whole public."

"What do you call their act of leaving their positions?"

"Desertion of duty."[40]

The following day, September 13, Coolidge received a telegram from AFL boss Samuel Gompers, asking him to reinstate the strikers since they had withdrawn from the union. Responding in the negative, he wrote, in words that reverberated across the country, "There is no right to strike against the public safety by anybody, anywhere, any time."[41]

Coolidge won reelection that autumn by 125,101 votes, nearly eight times his margin of victory the previous year, leading a Republican sweep of state offices and receiving thousands of split-ticket votes from Democrats. No gubernatorial candidate in the state had ever received more votes, and newspaper editorials across the country praised the outcome, including the *Atlanta Constitution*, the *Baltimore American*, the *Buffalo Courier*, the *Hartford Courant*, the *Indianapolis Star*, the *Memphis Commercial-Appeal*, the *New Haven Journal Courier*, the *New York Sun*, the *New York Times*, the *New York World*, the *Philadelphia Public Ledger*, the *Philadelphia Record*, the *Pittsburgh Gazette Times*, the *Providence Journal*, the *Seattle Post-Intelligencer*, the *St. Paul Pioneer Press*, the *Syracuse Post Standard*, and the *New Orleans Times-Picayune*. To the *Literary Digest*, "Such an impressive victory in a doubtful state and upon what is becoming a great national issue has naturally thrust Governor Coolidge in the limelight for the Republican nomination for President in 1920."[42]

Coolidge ruled out a formal declaration of candidacy and refused to enter any presidential primaries or travel around the country because of his duties as governor but allowed supporters to open offices in Chicago and Washington to pursue uncommitted delegates from the 28 states without primaries. The race was open, without a clear frontrunner following the sudden death of Theodore Roosevelt in 1919. When one of the favorites, former Rough Rider and New Hampshire native General Leonard Wood, won six of the 30 delegates at stake in Massachusetts, Coolidge backers had to explain why he lacked a unanimous endorsement from his own state—a prerequisite for most serious candidates. That and the failing health of his mentor, Senator Crane, hurt his prospects at the nominating convention in Chicago, where 529 out of 984 delegates were up for grabs and newspapers put his odds against winning at 15 to one. Coolidge was uncertain to say the least. "Things are shifting very rapidly and I think in my favor but no one can know what will happen there," he wrote his father five days before the convention began. Three days later he wrote with considerably less optimism: "You know there is no chance for me except when it may appear none of the leaders can get it."[43]

The favorites were General Wood, Senator Hiram Johnson of California, and Governor Frank O. Lowden of Illinois, but when none broke through in early balloting, Senator Warren Harding of Ohio began to emerge as a compromise candidate. The conservative former schoolteacher, insurance salesman, and editor-publisher of the *Marion Star* surged through the seventh, eighth, and ninth ballots, and secured a stunning victory on the tenth.

In a room beneath the Chicago Coliseum brokers met to select a vice presidential nominee and chose moderate senator Irvine L. Lenroot of Wisconsin to balance the ticket politically. This might have gone through but for Oregon, whose chairman, John L. Rand, a transplanted New Englander, like many Oregonians, had heard Coolidge speak at a dinner six months earlier and read his collection of published speeches, messages, and proclamations titled *Have Faith in Massachusetts*. Never mind what the brokers wanted, he wanted Coolidge.[44] The others agreed, and delegate-at-large Wallace McCamant stood on a chair in the rear of the auditorium, waving his arms, shouting, and receiving the floor for an impromptu nominating speech before the roll call vote began. Delegates, wanting to wrap up business after a long week in a hot auditorium without air conditioning, and having been pressured and instructed on how to vote throughout the proceedings, began to take the initiative in a slight murmur. Coolidge, the law-and-order governor, the man who broke the police walkout, had enough appeal to catch on, each delegate having received a pamphlet that week containing excerpts from his speeches, as arranged by Stearns. The shouts began, "Coolidge! Coolidge!" Men leaped on their seats and waved flags, and an elderly delegate who had voted for Lincoln and attended every convention since 1856 said he had never seen a more spontaneous and enthusiastic tribute to a nominee for president or vice president. As Maryland, North Dakota, Kansas, Connecticut, Pennsylvania, and Massachusetts seconded the nomination, the chant "We Want Coolidge!" arose from the benches, louder by the minute. Faced with a rare uprising, leaders began the balloting and Coolidge won easily.

The news reached Coolidge by telephone, in Boston, with Grace at his side. "Nominated," he said after he hung up.

"Oh, you don't mean it," she said, thinking he was joking.

"Indeed, I do," he replied.[45]

Inside the Adams House he began to receive more calls and visitors offering congratulations on one of the more astounding developments in the annals of political conventions.

"I hope you will not be disappointed," he wrote his father the next day, describing how federal office holders had denied him the top nomination in favor of one of their own, against the wishes of the delegates, when in truth he had never been a serious alternative at any point in the balloting.[46]

"I am happily disappointed that Cal got the nomination for Vice President," the elder Coolidge told a reporter. "I did not expect that he would be selected for either office."[47]

Republicans, with the most conservative ticket since McKinley and Hobart in 1896 and a platform favoring low taxes, flexible tariff rates, an executive budget, and strict economy amid a severe postwar depression, won by a landslide with 60 percent of the vote, ending an eight-year absence from the White House and increasing their seats in the House of Representatives from 240 to 303 and in the Senate from 49 to 55. It was the most decisive presidential election in a century.

As vice president, Coolidge presided over the Senate, attended cabinet meetings, delivered speeches, represented the administration at ceremonies and functions, delivered speeches, backed the party line, studied legislation, and impressed most observers as imperturbable and highly competent and knowledgeable on the issues. Yet he seemed destined to become another Hannibal Hamlin of Maine, elected with Lincoln in 1860 and dropped from the ticket four years later in favor of Andrew Johnson to appeal to War Democrats. Western progressives sought to replace Coolidge with Theodore Roosevelt, Jr., the young assistant secretary of the navy, in part to weaken the New England hold on the party, represented by Coolidge, Speaker of the House Frederick H. Gillett, Senate Majority Leader Henry Cabot Lodge, and Secretary of War John Weeks, all of Massachusetts. Not since the Virginia court with George Washington as president, Thomas Jefferson as secretary of state, and Edmund Randolph as secretary of war had a single state held such a place in the high affairs of the nation. New England as a whole, accounting for only 7 percent of the national population, had a disproportionate influence as the base of the majority Republican Party, which held all 12 Senate seats and 29 out of 32 House seats in the region, including many "safe seats" that allowed representatives to obtain seniority status and secure key committee slots, while promoting fiscal conservatism. Indeed Lodge had been in Congress since 1887, or longer than Arizona, Idaho, Montana, New Mexico, North Dakota, Oklahoma, Washington, and Wyoming had been states in the union.

The population center of the country had moved westward from census to census, from 23 miles east of Baltimore in 1790 to 18 miles west of Baltimore in 1800, and onward, past Virginia, West Virginia, Ohio, and Kentucky, to a 40-acre farm at Owen County, Indiana, in 1920. Nearly three in 10 citizens lived beyond the Mississippi. The population of California increased by 65.5 percent from 1910 to 1920, adding more than a million residents, primarily through immigration and westward migration from other states. Los Angeles, the former mudflat, grew by 80 percent during the decade, passing Detroit and Buffalo to become the tenth largest city, thanks to farming, the film industry, and the promotion of health benefits from having warmth and sunshine. Arizona increased by 30.4 percent during the same span, with new communities and businesses made possible by mining and advancements in irrigation and water supply lines. Texas increased by 24.8 percent, with modern skyscrapers shooting upward in Dallas, Fort Worth, and Houston, built with oil revenues in the new automobile age. Oregon increased by 21.6 percent, with prosperous local industries, lumber, fishing, and fruit farming. Washington increased by 18.1 percent, with Seattle becoming the 20th largest city in the country as the gateway to trade with the Alaska territory and Asia. New England on the whole increased by only 12 percent. Vermont lost population for the first time in state history. Maine and New Hampshire barely grew.

For Republicans, the 1920 elections marked a turning point, with the west producing almost every new senator and securing control of the upper legislature. Most Republican senators now represented states bordering upon or lying west of the Mississippi. Some were conservative, notably Lawrence C. Phipps of Colorado, Francis E. Warren of Wyoming, and Reed Smoot of Utah. Most were progressive on farm relief, tariff rates, income taxes, federal subsidies, railroad regulation, public utilities, and pensions, in line with western sentiment that the eastern capitalists who had financed the railroads, mines, lumber mills, packing houses, and grain elevators since the Civil War had received from Congress favors that restricted competition and increased private fortunes, such as high tariff rates and tight money supplies.

Western Republicans thought Roosevelt would balance the ticket in 1924 by appealing to former supporters of his beloved father out west.[48] At 34, he had never held or sought elective office, but his name was enough.

Like any skilled politician, Coolidge responded to the Roosevelt boom by seeking the upper hand. "The office of the Vice President does not greatly appeal to me," he told the *Evening Transcript* in April 1923. "Massachusetts will elect a senator in 1924 to succeed David I. Walsh, who, I have been told, I can beat. To sit in the Senate would be pleasanter by far than to sit up aloft looking over the Senate without saying a word."[49] Several days later he released a statement: "I believe the people will demand the renomination and re-election of President Harding because of the great record of accomplishment of his leadership. I have no announcement to make at this time of my own plans for the future."[50] By the time he arrived in New England that summer he had lost interest in the Senate race, telling the governor of Massachusetts that he would run for reelection for vice president or nothing at all.[51] He made a similar comment to longtime supporter and mentor William Butler.[52] But such are the whims of fortune.

Chapter Two

"Minimum of fanfare"

As the nation rallied around Coolidge, he wore a black mourning arm band and struck a calm manner in conducting his new duties. Saturday, August 4, he worked a full day at the Willard and added four rooms to his suite for his secretaries, stenographers, bodyguards, and telephone and telegraph operators, while reporters roamed the hallways, trying to learn more about him and receiving an audience that afternoon. One noted that his "prodigious nose" looked larger in person than in photographs.[1] That evening the president and first lady took a ride to escape the heat since the hotel had no fans or air conditioning. On Sunday he took Holy Communion at the First Congregational Church of Washington at 10th and G Street, for, though reared on the Bible and a regular churchgoer in Northampton, he had hitherto kept to his nondenominational upbringing:

> Among other things, I had some fear as to my ability to set that example which I always felt ought to denote the life of a church member. I am inclined to think now that this was a counsel of darkness.[2]

Monday, August 6, he worked alongside longtime supporter William Butler, who had hurried down from Cape Cod to be with him. Twelve years older than Coolidge, with close-cropped white hair, rimless glasses, a barrel-like chest, and a taut chin, he had gone into law and business and made a fortune in cotton mills, street railways, and life insurance, placing him among the wealthiest men in New England. Like Coolidge, he had served as president of the state senate. Then he had gone back to business, while keeping his hand in politics through donations and committee work, and serving as a de facto adviser to Coolidge during his gubernatorial years, particularly during the police walkout. Among the callers that Monday was none other than their former nemesis, labor boss Samuel Gompers, to discuss an impending coal strike in Pennsylvania and to wish the president well. That evening Coolidge wrote on black-bordered mourning stationery a short note to Northampton shoemaker Jim Lucey, who provided advice while he was wooing Grace and who in 1907 saved his reelection to the Massachusetts House of Representatives by rallying Irish-Democrat voters to help produce a 36-vote victory:

> My Dear Mr. Lucey:
>
> Not often do I see you or write to you, but I want you to know that if it were not for you I should not be here. And I want to tell you how much I love you. Do not work too hard and try to enjoy yourself in your well earned hour of age.[3]

The following morning he took a walk down F Street, stopping to look into shop windows and receiving scant notice from other pedestrians. Back in his drawing room, decorated in olive green and wood brown, with chairs covered in green satin damask and lamps shaded in bronze silk, he began to receive the visitors waiting in the hallway to pay respects and offer their support. Many party leaders and cabinet officers, having returned from summer recess to attend the funeral, appeared throughout the day in a procession that lasted 11 hours.

Chief Justice William H. Taft arrived from his summer cottage at Murray Bay in Canada, the only man to have held the highest perch in the executive and judiciary branches. The presidency, for him, had been a "nerve-racking" job, requiring eleven-hour work days and constant decisions with little time to think through problems or consult with others; he never liked party politics; he never ran for office before the presidency; he never wanted to be president so much as others wanted him to be; his lone term ended in the disastrous party split of 1912 that produced the first Democratic presidential victory in 20 years; and he had discouraged efforts to enlist him as a draft candidate to regain the White House in 1916.[4] The court, by contrast, was given to contemplation and inquiry, allowing him to work mornings at home on Wyoming Avenue, where he could see from his third-floor study distant views of the Washington Monument and the Capitol, before strolling up to Capitol Hill for his daily noontime session. As president he had taken short vacations interrupted by paperwork, visitors, meetings, and telegrams. Now he took a daily walk and long vacations each summer, having lost 90 pounds since leaving the White House and looking years younger. Coolidge he barely knew, but they shared the opinion that private property had come under assault during the progressive era and would need protection against further encroachment. They also shared an admiration for the late Senator Crane, that most silent of politicians who never gave an interview and made but one speech in the Senate chamber, a brief eulogy to his predecessor. Taft thought the new president "looked cool and self-possessed."[5]

That evening Coolidge went to Union Station to meet the Harding funeral train, which had traveled 3,000 miles, coast to coast, with millions of mourners lining the tracks, forcing police to clear the way at times, delaying arrival by nine hours. A band played "Nearer My God to Thee" as the crepe-covered train backed up to the platform.

Next morning a military escort took the casket up Pennsylvania Avenue, from the White House to the Capitol as temperatures exceeded 100 degrees at street level, causing nearly 200 pedestrians and 44 marines to seek medical attention. A Boy Scout, standing at his post along the route, fell unconscious, severely injuring his face. At the fountain outside the Library of Congress, boys filled glass bottles with water to sell for a nickel apiece, taking advantage of a temporary ban on street vendors. All 937 city policemen were on duty to assist the Secret Service and prevent a reoccurrence of the McKinley funeral, during which hundreds of grievers had been hurt in a crush at Capitol plaza. Coolidge, plainly suffering from the heat and humidity, led a cortege of official mourners to view the body under the dome of the rotunda.

On Monday, August 13, Coolidge took over the executive offices at the White House, telling Mrs. Harding to stay in the residential rooms as long as necessary and holding a two-hour meeting with budget director Herbert M. Lord. He read through the spending estimates from the various departments, pausing repeatedly to ask questions and instructing that expenditures should be "cut to the bone." He told Lord that their goal should be to cut federal spending below $3 billion a year, exclusive of debt payments and postal expenditures, which were handled separately.[6]

The new administration began to take shape that week. The president held his first cabinet meeting and his first press conference, promising to meet regularly with reporters, responding to questions with verve and precision, and receiving applause. He kept the Harding cabinet in place with Hughes at State, Andrew Mellon at Treasury, Herbert Hoover at Commerce, Henry Wallace at Agriculture, Harry Daugherty at Justice, John Weeks at War, Edwin Denby at Navy, James Davis at Labor, Hubert Work at Interior, and Harry New as Postmaster General. The favorite for presidential secretary was Edward Clark, the Northampton-bred Amherst graduate and Boston attorney who had been with him since 1921, a thin, hard-working, energetic, nervous type with large blue eyes. Instead Coolidge made him assistant secretary and chose C. Bascom Slemp, a millionaire coal operator, lawyer, landowner, and former congressman from mountainous southwestern Virginia, in a surprise move that struck newspapers and pundits as a sign that Coolidge meant to run for president in 1924. The Democratic National Committee foresaw the "first step to round up the delegates from the Southern States."[7]

Born at Turkey Cove, Virginia, in 1870, Slemp attended the Virginia Military Institute, studied law at the University of Virginia, and practiced law before replacing his father as the representative from the Ninth District from 1907 to 1923 and the lone Republican congressman from Virginia. Two years older than Coolidge, at 53, he was a bachelor, thin and vain, with a military posture, a narrow forehead, a long nose, and a mask-like countenance, willing to serve through the election at $7,500 a year, in what many saw as a step down for such an estimable figure. No doubt he saw the position as a stepping stone to a cabinet position, like John Hay, secretary to Lincoln and later secretary of state, or George Cortelyou, secretary to Roosevelt and later secretary of the treasury. The appointment was controversial. Democrats pointed to his past involvement in patronage and fund-raising shenanigans, including the alleged sale of post office appointments, and the Republican-dominated NAACP issued a statement that "Mr. Slemp has betrayed the confidence of that race in trying to put into power a 'Lily White' Republican Party in his State of Virginia, as well as elsewhere."[8] Disappointed with missed opportunities under the Harding administration, such as the inability to pass anti-lynching legislation, the lack of political appointments, and the failure to eliminate segregation in federal agencies, black Republicans were losing faith in their longtime party allegiance. At the annual NAACP meeting in September, leaders told members to be politically independent.

In dealing with Coolidge, the Virginian set the tone early. The first time Coolidge spoke brusquely to him, he took him to task, warning it must not happen again. Coolidge apologized, saying he smoked too much the day before and was "hard to get along with."[9]

* * *

After the Attorney General advised that Colonel Coolidge, as a state official, may have been ineligible to administer a federal oath of office, the president had him arrange at the Willard on August 17 a second oath with Justice A.A. Hoehling of the Supreme Court of the District of Colombia. The ceremony occurred at 3:45 p.m. during a thunderstorm and lasted five minutes. They used a hotel Gideon Bible as a bodyguard stood in the hallway. No publicity was given to the event lest it embarrass his father and take away from the drama of the first oath, which had captivated the nation.

* * *

All through August the Coolidge boys stayed in Massachusetts, where they had been on the night their father became president. John, 16 years old, was attending a civilian military camp. Calvin, 15, was picking tobacco for $3 a day in Northampton and preparing for the coming school year.

"The papers have said very nice things about you, father," wrote the younger boy. "I hope you are well."[10]

To which the president replied, "We are all right and always glad to hear from you, but I am too busy right now to say anything other than we want you to keep on in being a good boy and doing your school work."[11]

* * *

When a Treasury Department messenger delivered to Coolidge his first paycheck as president, he looked at the amount—six times more than he made as vice president—and signed the voucher, saying, "Come again."[12]

* * *

Tuesday afternoon, August 21, three days after Mrs. Harding left the White House, the new occupants arrived with their possessions packed into eight trunks, coming up the graveled driveway to the north portico on such short notice that no reporters or cameramen were present to record the scene and the housekeeper lacked provisions for supper. No one had expected them until Wednesday. "As we passed through the open doorway to the columned corridor, the sun was shining in at the south windows and a soft breeze stirred the leaves of the evergreen magnolia outside," wrote Grace Coolidge, at 44 years old the youngest chatelaine of the mansion since Frances Cleveland.[13] Vivacious and high-spirited, she was the only child of the late Andrew Goodhue and Lemira Barrett Goodhue of Burlington, Vermont, with an old New England lineage, a strong religious upbringing, and a degree from the University of Vermont, where she participated in glee club and acted in Shakespeare plays. An attractive woman, standing five-four with firm muscle tone, large brown eyes, olive skin, a wide mouth, and thick dark hair pinned up in a mass of curls, she never bothered with cosmetics but kept in fashion, favoring a sporting look with flapper-style dresses, foulard skirts, and the like. This was only her third time in the White House. The first had been as a chaperone for Northampton High School students in 1905, when a policeman chided her for touching the gilded piano in the East Room. The other occasion had been as the wife of the vice president, but she had never seen the private quarters.

The second floor had a wide corridor that ran east to west, lined with old prints on the walls and sofas and straight-back chairs from the Lincoln years, covered in black horsehair that had seen better days. There were eight bedrooms, a study, a drawing room, and a sitting room, with 19-foot ceilings but few closets or storage areas. Indeed the manse was an old-fashioned place, lacking in modern conveniences. The laundry room had no electric washing machine or electric iron; all washing was done by hand, all ironing by flat irons. Every day was washing day. The kitchen had no dishwasher or electric refrigerator, which cost about $450 each and were beset by leaky tubes, malfunctioning compressors, and broken motors and thermostats. Victuals went into an ice box. There was no air conditioning. The executive office was kept cool by a box-shaped receptacle beneath the floor, 12 feet wide, eight feet high, with galvanized iron rack shelves for holding huge blocks of ice brought in daily from a nearby plant. The White House used as much as three tons of ice a day in hot weather, with power fans circulating the cold air into the room through pipes. Many an apartment in the city had more amenities, and better furniture too.

The president instructed head usher Irwin "Ike" Hoover to keep tourists and callers downstairs. "I want things as they used to be—before!" he snapped, alluding to the looser atmosphere of the Harding years.[14] Then he had Stearns placed in the Lincoln Bedroom in the southeast corner of the mansion, a token of thanks to the portly Boston dry goods merchant who had long supported him, raising money, paying for pamphlets, recruiting campaign volunteers, attending the Republican national convention in 1916 to promote the then little-known lieutenant governor, working with Houghton Mifflin Co. to publish in 1919 a collection of his speeches titled *Have Faith in Massachusetts*, and distributing some 65,000 copies of the book to libraries, newspapers, and individuals.

Grace Coolidge (shown here ca. 1924), former teacher, the first presidential spouse to hold a college degree, and a most popular figure throughout her public years and beyond (Harris & Ewing Collection, Library of Congress).

* * *

The threat of a Pennsylvania anthracite coal strike on September 1 by the 155,000-member United Mine Workers put Coolidge to an early test. With mine owners resisting demands for a wage increase of 20 percent, better working conditions, and the automatic withdraw of union dues from worker paychecks, politicians and editorialists urged him to mediate the dispute—or to seize the mines—before it disrupted industry and rail transportation and caused heat shortages in homes that winter, particularly in the populous northeast, where the long-burning, high-heat coal remained preeminent despite the greater use of bituminous coal and oil elsewhere. Advocates of federal intervention cited Cleveland in the 1894 Pullman Strike, Roosevelt in the 1902 anthracite strike, and Wilson in the 1919 coal strike. Representative Frederick W. Dallinger of Massachusetts told the president that the strike presented "a wonderful opportunity to render a great service" for the nation and for the party.[15] Many legislators implored him to summon a special session of Congress, which was not scheduled to meet until December. Republican newspapers encouraged him to take control of the situation as in the Boston police walkout.

Coolidge balked at such suggestions. "It is commerce within the state and not commerce between the states," he told reporters four days before the strike deadline.[16]

Secretary Hoover suggested using the United States Coal Commission, established by Congress in 1922 to investigate a similar dispute, albeit without meditative authority. Coolidge agreed and met with members to request their assistance. Then he consulted Daugherty, who advised he was not authorized to act before the strike took place. Coolidge promptly rang for temporary secretary George Christian.

"Mr. Christian," he began, looking out the window, smoking a cigar, "it is about time for many people to begin to come to the White House to discuss different phases of the coal strike. When anybody comes, if his special problem concerns the state, refer him to the Governor of Pennsylvania. If his problem has a national phase, refer him to the United States Coal Commission. In no event bring him to me."[17]

Nonetheless, Governor Gifford Pinchot of Pennsylvania, a Roosevelt Republican and prospective presidential candidate in 1924 following his stunning victory against the state party machinery in 1922, repeatedly pressed Coolidge to intervene as the strike deadline approached. On August 15, the first day of Coal Commission talks with union and company representatives in New York, Pinchot recommended a special arbitration board to mediate the dispute. After talks quickly fell apart over mine owners rejecting the pay increase and mandatory union dues withdraw, Pinchot dined at the White House and learned Coolidge had no plans except to promote anthracite substitutes to alleviate shortages. Indeed Coolidge encouraged him to handle the situation as a state matter. The mines were in Pennsylvania. The mining was governed by Pennsylvania laws, which required that miners be licensed and stipulated that they work other jobs at the mines for a prescribed length of time before receiving a license, thus discouraging the use of imported nonunion labor to replace strikers and impeding federal intervention.

Pinchot set aside all other business to meet daily with union and company representatives, proposing a wage increase of 10 percent, an eight-hour workday, full recognition of the union, and a compromise on union dues, whereby union leaders would be present at the time and place of payment of wages but not receive dues through automatic paycheck withdraw. The proposal, while unable to prevent a strike on September 1, was accepted a week later.

"One of you gentlemen has brought me a bit of very pleasing news," Coolidge opened his press conference that afternoon, naming the correspondent. After praising Pinchot for the settlement, he said, with a sly grin, "I assume of course that the news is reliable and authentic."[18]

Coolidge sent Pinchot a telegram lauding his efforts in the "very difficult situation in which I invited your cooperation," which the latter saw as a ploy to take partial credit for the settlement.[19] It was all Pinchot could do to release the telegram to the public, as customary.

Some prominent politicians thought Coolidge had made a tactical political error in turning over the settlement to a potential rival, but the Pinchot boom subsided as the price of coal rose within 48 hours of the settlement. Pinchot hoped producers, shippers, and retailers would absorb the 60 cent per ton increase in production costs caused by the settlement, but instead they passed on costs to consumers. When he asked the administration to help control prices, Coolidge ordered the Federal Trade Commission to investigate anthracite profiteering, but mostly left the governor to manage the situation he created.

"Mr. President," a friend said after the strike, "you seem to be standing the strain well."

"Haven't been under any strain yet," he replied.[20]

To former classmate Dwight Morrow, a Wall Street attorney who arrived in Washington on the day of the settlement, Coolidge said, "I am not going to make the mistake that lots of them make. I am not going to try and be a great President."[21]

* * *

The main concern abroad that autumn was in Mexico, where revolutionary forces threatened to disrupt the transition from outgoing leader Alvaro Obregon to the duly elected Plutarco Calles. Mexico called on the United States to lift its arms embargo and encourage bankers to lend money for arms purchases. Coolidge agreed. "We'll be the laughing stock of the world if we don't send guns to Mexico," he said privately. "Look what happened when Wilson refused to support Huerta. If we allowed Obregon to be overthrown, we shall be put in a ridiculous position as we have already rendered him some aid and are committed to his cause."[22] The administration lifted the embargo, and U.S. financiers helped Obregon buy enough weaponry to crush the rebellion within several months.

* * *

"There is a zip about Coolidge that we didn't have before," said a White House reporter. "He gives you the feeling that there is going to be something doing."[23]

Awake by six most mornings, he took a walk on the Mall or down F Street to the shopping district, posture straight, nose pointed forward, homburg squarely on top of his head, wearing a business suit rather than the formal morning coat adorned by most previous presidents. Before McKinley was shot in 1901, presidents could take walks or carriage rides alone. Lincoln was apt to decline protection, walking between the White House and the War Department late at night and riding horseback through the city streets, where he was shot at more than once. Grant and Harrison took walks along the main thoroughfares, looking into shop windows and chatting with acquaintances. Arthur took carriage rides. Cleveland, the first president to request a plain-clothes bodyguard from the metropolitan police department, which protected the executive mansion, was criticized for doing so. McKinley declined protection—except for special occasions—and removed the ugly sentry boxes his predecessor installed on the front lawn of the White House to protect his young family. "I have never done any man a wrong, and believe no man will ever do me one," he said.[24] But after a lone gunman killed him in Buffalo, Congress made the Secret Service bureau of the Treasury Department responsible for protecting the president, and none since had been allowed to leave the White House without at least two men at his side or several paces behind. The vice president, cabinet members, and congressmen had to fend for themselves, but the president was under constant surveillance.

Coolidge, following his 30-minute walk, had breakfast with his wife and read the New York and Washington newspapers before heading to the mailroom where the attendant sorted out correspondence and checked suspicious packages by listening for ticking noises, opening them at the end of a pole or dunking them in oil. Hastily, Coolidge carried his mail to his oval-shaped office, painted in tones of pale and dark green, with a mahogany desk, leather-cushioned chairs, a brown rug, a blue-shaded lamp, a fireplace, built-in bookcases, and three windows facing south toward the Mall and the Washington Monument. There he read letters and dictated responses to his secretary or annotated them with comments, often "yes" or "no" in a bold black hand. Then he had appointments with legislators, cabinet officers, newspaper editors, publishers, businessmen, labor leaders, educators, and others, seeking information and sometimes advice but seldom committing to a position.

When young Theodore Roosevelt suggested a plan to strengthen prohibition with a special tax that would provide a billion dollars a year, he listened patiently. "Colonel, never go out to meet trouble," he said at last. "If you see ten troubles coming down the road, you can be sure that nine will run into the ditch before they reach you."[25]

At half past noon, Monday through Friday, Coolidge had a 30-minute handshaking session with the public. This event, dating back to Thomas Jefferson, separated the White House from the residences of other leaders around the world, surrounded as they were by gates, walls, and sentries to keep out the public. European diplomats marveled at the open atmosphere of the White House and the duties of the president as ceremonial and administrative head of state. "No European statesman could stand the strain of his routine functions," said one ambassador.[26] Nor could the typical European, without credentials or proper introduction, hope to enter a royal or presidential residence. At Buckingham Palace in London, high iron rails, detectives, and sentries in scarlet coats and bearskin bonnets protected King George and his family. At 78 Wilhelmstrasse in Berlin, sentinels in dull gray uniforms kept the public away from the presidential palace, save for three official dinners and two annual beer evenings. At the royal palace in Madrid, sentinels wearing steel helmets and carrying spears stood in two rows outside the quarters of dashing King Alfonso and his family. At the Chigi Palace in Rome, guards at three checkpoints kept unwelcome visitors from Benito Mussolini. At the Kremlin in Moscow, well-manned checkpoints and drab red walls ensured that only visitors with appointments and documents could see Lenin in his windowless office.

At the White House, the front gates were always open and anyone could walk or drive up to the manse, day or night, to see the grounds or peer through the windows on tiptoes as two or three policemen kept watch. Thousands of people a day came during visiting hours, wandering from room to room on the first floor, purloining souvenirs, such as little silver trays and the tassels on the draperies, and wearing out the carpets, which were replaced annually. Two servants stood at the front door, and Secret Service men kept watch as visitors waited to meet the president, their loud voices carrying into his office. At one handshaking session a little lady in a black silk dress with lace collar and cuffs approached Coolidge, bowing and curtsying like someone from long ago. "You know, Mr. President," she said, "I am from Boston," to which he replied, "Madam, you will never get over it."[27] An English advertising man said Coolidge was the first man he had seen in the United States whose shoes were shined.[28]

After lunch and sometimes a nap, Coolidge turned to the 80 or so documents that came across his desk daily for signature: alien property claims, consular postings, court martial orders, diplomatic correspondence, extradition warrants, extraordinary expenditures, legislative acts from the Philippines Islands, military commissions, municipal ordinances from Puerto Rico, naval officer retirement requests, pardons, postmaster nominations, proclamations, and others. This review took two to three hours a day. The only documents requiring presidential approval that he did not have to sign personally were land grants, thanks to a 19th-century provision that permitted a clerk to handle the tedious task, amounting to as many as 100,000 documents per year. "They say at the office that he is the first president since Grover Cleveland who reads and considers every word of every little thing he signs," wrote his housekeeper.[29]

Slemp had never seen such discipline: "He concentrates more intensely and more continuously than any man I have ever known."[30]

Responsibility for keeping the paperwork in order fell to executive clerk Rudolph Forster, a lean, inscrutable Washington native, 51 years old, who wore dark, heavy-rimmed glasses and could handle dictation with unrivaled speed and accuracy, and knew the routines, customs, and procedures of the White House, having been there since his agency loaned him to McKinley for a few days in 1897. McKinley, Roosevelt, Taft, Wilson, Harding, and Coolidge, he had served six presidents in 26 years. None had been more efficient at reviewing documents than Wilson, the former professor, but Coolidge was close. "The little fellow wades into it like Wilson," Forster said privately, noting that Harding, by comparison, had struggled with paperwork, leaving a messy pile of documents on his desk each evening, requiring his clerks to work uncompensated overtime.[31] Coolidge kept a clean desk with no papers, folders, memoranda, knick-knacks, or scratchpads. Newspapers were stacked on a stand to his left. Pencils were lined in formation before him, beside a jar of smelling salts and a daguerreotype of his mother.

"The universal testimony of those who knew him is that he is always thinking," wrote a magazine editor who spent a week with Coolidge. "Not mind-wandering, casual consciousness, but hard, disciplined, purposeful thinking upon his problems. He is, they say, forever thinking ahead. That is why he is never caught off guard, never excited when the moment for decision and action comes."[32]

The executive office had no telephone, despite having been wired for one since 1879. Harding had been the first president to use the telephone regularly for business purposes. Wilson had largely ignored the instrument and instructed White House switchboard operators never to call him. Taft had made periodic local and long-distance calls, mainly to relatives. Roosevelt had considered the telephone a barbaric invention, to be used only in emergencies, and banned them from his summer White House at Oyster Bay. McKinley, Cleveland, Harrison, and Hayes had used them sparingly. Coolidge occasionally made calls from a private booth and his study, speaking to cabinet officers and his budget director, among others.

The new president seldom worked at night. Indeed his approach was simple: "In the discharge of the duties of the office there is one rule of action more important than all others. It consists in never doing anything that some one else can do for you."[33] One evening he and his bodyguard, Colonel Edmund Starling, noticed a light burning in the top-floor office of Secretary Denby as they walked along Pennsylvania Avenue.

"He must be an excellent man for the job," Starling remarked.

"I wouldn't say that," Coolidge replied. "I don't work at night. If a man can't finish his job in the day time he's not that smart."[34]

Coolidge, to be sure, kept shorter daily office hours than Taft, Wilson, and Harding, but worked weekends and seemed to be always "thinking, thinking."[35] With only 40 employees, mostly clerks crammed into five offices in the west wing of the mansion, he was his own counsel, press secretary, and legislative liaison. Once an avid reader—histories, biographies, Cicero, Webster, McCauley, Kipling, Carlyle, Dante, Milton, Hawthorne, Longfellow, Whittier, Shakespeare, Tennyson, and Dante—he now had little time to read anything beyond the issues at hand. To subordinates seeking advice, he would usually tell them to do what the law required.[36] Twice a week, Tuesday and Friday, he met with the cabinet, sitting at a long mahogany table in black leather chairs and asking whether anyone had issues for his consideration. The meetings were allotted two hours on his schedule but seldom lasted an hour and sometimes only 15 minutes. "There are many things you gentlemen must not tell me," he told his officers. "If you blunder, you can leave, or I can invite you to leave. But if you draw me into all your departmental decisions and something goes wrong, I must stay here. And by involving me you have lowered the faith of the people in their Government."[37] Whereas Harding regretted he could not hold a cabinet meeting daily, Coolidge preferred to see people alone, extracting information in a more confidential setting. Harding often held two-hour cabinet meetings. Coolidge kept them to 15 minutes sometimes.

Massachusetts Governor Channing Cox was astonished at the businesslike schedule at the White House. "With all the people you see," he told Coolidge, "you don't seem to be pressed for time, while I'm always fighting to get through so I can do some real work."

"Channing, the trouble is that you talk back to them."[38]

Democrat Bernard Baruch sat with him in his book-lined study one evening, smoking cigars and discussing at length the railroad industry, agriculture, taxes, and other issues.

"You know, Mr. President, everybody says you never say anything."

"Well, Baruch, many times I only say 'yes' or 'no' and even that winds them up for twenty minutes more."[39]

Slemp kept things on schedule by handling congressmen and other visitors who came in with candidates for postmaster, customs officer, consular officer, patent officer, military academy, and the like. The best secretary in two decades, some said, he had a clever knack of convincing visitors he would tend to their business without disturbing the president and then insisting they greet him on the way out, so as to make them feel important without bothering Coolidge more than a moment. The president stood the whole time to discourage any notion that he had time sit down and talk.

Coolidge also set a new standard for presidential press conferences. Cleveland and Harrison loathed reporters and would not see them. McKinley met with them, but disliked publicity and divulged little information. Roosevelt held sporadic conferences, while inviting favored reporters on a whim, promising a "bully story" for their publication, or sometimes bursting into the press room and interrupting reporters playing checkers games to provide information. Wilson held one a week before the war, evasive and ill at ease for the most part; he stopped once hostilities began; indeed he closed the White House gates and tried to censor the press. Harding had two a month but, despite his newspaper background, struggled to provide a coherent message or storyline. Coolidge had two a week, Tuesday and Friday, with a set routine. Correspondents, numbering a dozen or so, arrived 30 minutes early and submitted a small stack of written questions from which Slemp chose five to 20 for use. Then Coolidge received everyone in his office at noon, rising from his desk, putting out his cigar in an ashtray. Sometimes he would glance through the questions, let the slips of paper flutter down to his desktop, one by one, without answering them, look at the reporters, and say, "I have no questions today." Sometimes he would pretend to lose certain questions. Oftentimes he replied at length, speaking as long as 15 minutes without notes, trying to sway public opinion on legislation and other matters, promoting economy, and showing humor. Asked to comment on a controversial lecture by the writer Rupert Hughes, who described George Washington as a vain, irreligious man prone to gambling, dancing, foul language, cards, and whiskey—no small matter in prohibition times—he turned to look out the window at the white marble shaft rising above the trees on the Mall and said, "His monument is still there."[40]

The only stipulation he made is that correspondents not publish the content of unanswered questions or cite direct quotations in their stories to prevent misquotes, leaving them to create a "White House Spokesman" for attribution purposes. When *New York Herald-Tribune* boss Frank A. Munsey encouraged him to allow direct quotes, like the prime minister of England did, he replied he did not think the president of the United States should be in the newspapers quite that often.[41] As it was, his off-the-record statements were sent by wire across the country and overseas to London, Paris, and other European capitals, where they were closely monitored for content on debt negotiations, arms talks, and various policies.

* * *

Within 30 days of taking office Coolidge had emerged as the hands-down favorite to win the Republican presidential nomination in 1924 in a remarkable turn of events. After his ascension to the office, most politicos had predicted an open race featuring aspirants from the 1920 campaign, notably Senator Johnson, Governor Lowden, and Secretary Hoover, who had risen from an orphan childhood in Iowa to prominence as an international mining engineer with offices in New York, San Francisco, London, St. Petersburg, and Paris, and a personal fortune estimated at $10 million. The two senators from Ohio, Simeon D. Fess and Frank B. Willis, were seen as possibilities, given the past successes of candidates from their state. So was Senator James E. Watson of Indiana. *New York Times* political correspondent Richard V. Oulahan, in a piece published on August 4, titled "Party Chaos Left by Loss of Harding," all but dismissed Coolidge as a contender. Now, one month later, even some Republicans who had opposed a second Harding term thought his successor would be nominated and elected. Senator George Moses of New Hampshire led the way. Having defied Harding on numerous issues, he had been expected to support an intraparty challenge in 1924, but instead became the first Republican legislator to publicly back Coolidge, appealing to New England to unite behind the first New England president since Franklin Pierce in the 1850s. Cabinet officers Mellon, Work, and Davis endorsed the president. Taft quietly backed him. Others wanted to see how he dealt with Congress when it reconvened in December, but agreed he had done well.

The only accidental president to have been nominated by his party and elected to his own term had been Roosevelt. The other four had fallen short. Tyler, Johnson, and Arthur had not been nominated by their respective parties. Fillmore had been nominated by the fading Whig party but not elected to his own term. Coolidge, like Roosevelt in 1901, had taken office with his party in the ascendancy and his country strong and prosperous following a victorious war.

The new president made an impression on the public by working hard and declining to speak publicly or call a special session of Congress during his first month in office. After the Wilson reforms, the war, the League of Nations quarrel, the Red Scare, the postwar depression, and the Republican legislative agenda, which kept Congress in session almost continually from March 1921 to March 1923, the country needed a break from politics. The people wanted "a minimum of fanfare," he told assistant White House physician Joel T. Boone.[42]

* * *

In observance of the 30-day period of national mourning, the president and first lady held no entertainments and mostly stayed to themselves at night, reading, writing, listening to radio shows, and retiring early. Momma and Poppa they called each other; they never talked politics. "What knowledge I had of public affairs," she admitted, "I obtained from the daily papers and other sources of information open to everybody."[43] Having taken to Washington during their vice presidential years, reveling in the parks, the trees, the architecture, the people, the parties, the theater, and even the weather, which everyone had warned about, she now had a private office, a social secretary, a housekeeper, 18 domestic servants, and a full daily appointment book, with barely enough time for a brisk afternoon walk to the Lincoln Memorial, where she could see children swimming in the reflecting pool during the last days of summer. Previously she had hosted a weekly tea party and attended functions with little notice. Now she faced the pressures of protocol in a city that had become a world capital since 1900, leaving behind the provincialism of men wearing sombrero hats and shoes without socks, slicking down their hair with bear grease, and spitting tobacco on the streets. The number of embassies and consulates had more than tripled in two decades. The number of newspaper correspondents assigned to Washington had doubled.

"This is a beautiful old house, Ivah, rich in memories and traditions," she wrote college classmate Ivah Gale. "Those who live here are of necessity very much hemmed in by form and circumstance but there are many compensations."[44]

Their first overnight guests were Mr. and Mrs. Richard W. Irwin of Northampton, fittingly enough. It was he who had convinced Coolidge to run for city council in 1899 and advised him through his first campaign, and who, when Coolidge was elected to the state legislature in 1906, had written a letter of introduction to the speaker-elect, with the splendid line "Like the singed cat, he is better than he looks."[45] Fifteen years older than Coolidge, the former machinist, watch maker, city solicitor, probate court clerk, state representative, state senator, district attorney, militia captain, army lieutenant, volunteer fireman, bank vice president, and band leader had once been mentioned for lieutenant governor or governor but the honors had gone elsewhere and he had been appointed to the Superior Court of Massachusetts in 1911. Coolidge had had similar aspirations back then: "I fully expected to become the kind of country lawyer I saw all about me, spending my life in the profession, with perhaps a final place on the Bench."[46] Yet he had kept winning elections and taking advantage of opportunities that never came to Irwin in quite the same way.

Chapter Three

"I am for economy"

The war had brought unprecedented federal expenditures, from $713 million in 1916 to $18.5 billion in 1919. Before the war, expenditures had never exceeded 2.4 percent of Gross National Product. During the war they reached 12.5 percent. The Harding administration had cut spending to $3.7 billion in 1923, through demobilization and stricter departmental accountability, but further reductions would be difficult because most annual expenditures were fixed, including $1 billion in interest on the war debt, $400 million in mandated debt reduction payments, and $700 million in benefits and services for veterans and dependents. That left about $1.6 billion in discretionary spending, half for the military and half for agriculture, commissions, federal salaries, reclamation, reservations, road construction, rivers and harbors, and tax collection.

The war was to blame, most agreed.

Yet spending pressures had been rising since a loose coalition of Democrats and Republicans from western states pushed through the Sixteenth Amendment in 1913, leading to a federal income tax in 1913 and expanding the reach and authority of the federal government more than any act since the Civil War. Before 1913 most federal income came from internal revenue and customs duties, limited sources that limited what government could do. The income tax was intended to compensate for the low tariff rates of the Wilson administration, rather than to increase revenue. Proponents insisted the tax would be small and blocked efforts to add a provision to the Sixteenth Amendment in 1913 to limit the top rate to 10 percent. Republican senator William E. Borah of Idaho went so far as to assert that the direct nature of the income tax would promote retrenchment in that "it would be a teacher of economy in public expenditures."[1]

This underestimated the sentiment growing among German-trained political economists and within farmer-laborer movements since the late 19th century, mostly in the southern and western states, to reduce local and state tax burdens by collecting and redistributing more of the wealth of the industrialized northeastern states. These elements pushed for more progressive rates and higher rates than those enacted in 1913, with support from the Wilson administration and consent from the Supreme Court.

Now—10 years later—the new fiscal state had produced a steady increase in tax rates, tax revenue, and government activity. Take the Treasury Department. Before 1913, it had been limited to keeping records of government receipts and expenditures, printing money, minting metal, overseeing the national banks, and collecting revenue through the Internal Revenue Bureau and the Customs Service. Since 1913, this venerable institution had been entrusted with such miscellaneous tasks as printing liquor permits, enforcing prohibition, supervising farm loans, protecting the president, maintaining homes for lepers, surveying rural sanitation, and patrolling the southwest border, and its budget had tripled from $34 million to more than $100 million, led by a sixfold increase in the Internal Revenue Bureau. Indeed the cost of collecting a dollar in revenue had risen from less than one-half cent in 1913 to more than a cent in 1923, mostly because income taxes were harder to enforce than customs duties.[2]

In 1913, the federal government had six independent bureaus: the Interstate Commerce Commission, the Civil Service Commission, the Smithsonian Institution, the National Museum, the Victory Memorial Commission, and the Commission of Fine Arts. By April 1917, before the United States entered the war, 10 more were in existence: the Federal Trade Commission, the Federal Reserve Board, the Tariff Commission, the Shipping Board, the Federal Board for Vocational Education, the Employees Compensation Commission, the National Advisory Committee for Aeronautics, the American Section of the Inter-American High Commission, the Council of National Defense, and the Meade Memorial Commission. The war brought others. Some were eliminated afterward, but five survived, including the Housing Corporation and the Interdepartmental Hygiene Board, boosting the tally to 21 independent bureaus. This increase had less to do with the war than with the income tax, which raised $18 billion from 1914 to 1923, exceeding the total government revenue during the preceding 25 years.

The bureaus had been created with no clear lines of authority: some reported to Congress, some to the president, some to neither. Each Congress had added to their duties, leading to more employees and higher budgets, surrounded by what one politician described as a "protecting influence" of legislators and lobbyists, thwarting attempts at reform.[3]

The income tax also gave rise to the "50–50" system of federal aid to the states, much like the education subsidy program in Switzerland that began in the 1830s and the grant-in-aid system in England that began with agriculture in 1846 under Sir Robert Peel and soon led to subsidies for education, police, public health, roads, poverty alleviation, and housing, in steadily increasing amounts despite efforts by William Gladstone to put a halt to them during the 1880s. More recently, Belgium, France, and Germany had adopted similar programs and extended them for various purposes.

In the United States, this contrivance began with the Smith-Lever Agricultural Extension Act of 1914 and an appropriation of $480,000 to be divided equally among the states on condition that they establish a coordination agency, follow guidelines, and provide a matching amount for educating citizens in agriculture and economics. Like many fundamental changes in federal policy that begin with a small measure or appropriation, the bill had been approved with little opposition or debate in Congress or the press. Two years later Congress had approved the Federal Aid Roads Act of 1916 with a $5 million subsidy to the states, reflecting greater support among farmers in the good roads movement, the rise of the automobile, and the Supreme Court ruling in *Wilson v. Shaw* in 1907 that found Congress had the power to create interstate highways under the commerce clause of the Constitution. This placed Washington in road construction for the first time since before the Civil War and discouraged legal challenges by presenting the aid as consistent with the constitutional power to fund post roads. Then came the Smith-Hughes National Vocational Education Act of 1917, the Chamberlain-Kahn Venereal Disease Act of 1918, the Industrial Rehabilitation Act of 1920, and the Sheppard-Towner Maternity Act of 1921. By 1922, the subsidies totaled $118 million annually. By 1924, they reached $144 million annually, led by $80 million for road and highway construction and $12 million for agricultural programs. Notably, from a political standpoint, they were funded on a continuing or automatic basis so that Congress would have to vote to stop them, effectively entrenching them within the budget.

The subsidies, while small on a budgetary scale, had changed the dual nature of federalism into a cooperative federalism that was still developing. To supporters, they had multiple advantages. First, they allowed states with low per capita revenues or sparse populations spread over spacious areas to provide better services through indirect funding from the wealthier states. Second, they provided a national minimum standard to promote good highways and other services in an increasingly mobile society in which people traveled and moved to other states for work and pleasure. Third, they avoided the need for a centralized bureaucracy. Fourth, they encouraged cooperation between corporations, trade associations, private groups, localities, and states. Fifth, they preserved the sovereignty of the states by making participation voluntary.

The disadvantages subsidies were less apparent but no less compelling. First, they increased debt levels by encouraging states and municipalities to pursue "easy money" from Washington to get their fair share or more. Second, they increased federal authority over the states, for they came with stipulations and oversight, effectively turning some state officials into agents of the federal government in certain capacities. Third, they expanded Washington into new aspects of economic and social life, with the Chamberlain-Kahn Venereal Disease Act and the Sheppard-Towner Maternity Act marking the first federal public health programs, nearly a hundred years after the Supreme Court ruled in *Gibbons v. Ogden* in 1824 that health laws were not within the powers granted to Congress and thus fell to the states under the Tenth Amendment to the Constitution. Chamberlain-Kahn included a provision that required participating states to enact legislation concerning the travel of infected persons within their borders, an aspect of intrastate commerce clearly reserved to the states. Sheppard-Towner had survived two constitutional challenges in 1923, with *Massachusetts v. Mellon* and *Frothingham v. Mellon.*

By contrast, federal aid to the states during and after the Civil War, such as the Morrill Land Grant Act of 1862 to promote the establishment of agricultural and mechanical colleges, the Hatch Act of 1887 to fund such colleges, and the National Forest Fund Act of 1907, had been provided with few conditions or federal involvement. The new subsidies had unlimited potential to expand into other areas, posing a potential threat to the financial state of the country and the balance between the federal government and the states, with legislators and lobbyists clamoring for more money and more programs, particularly in education and social welfare, which had been the function of local and state governments. Opponents feared that the programs in place marked a first step toward a permanent shift from local to federal control, positioning the federal government to coerce the states into taking certain positions by threatening to withhold money.

The progressive rates of taxation behind such spending also marked a break with the past. At the Constitutional Convention of 1789, participants said taxes should be fair and uniform, or "common to all." As Madison wrote: "The moment you abandon the cardinal principle of exacting from all individuals the same proportion of their income or their profits you are at a sea without a rudder or compass and there is no amount of injustice and folly you may not commit."[4] Throughout the 19th century, the Supreme Court interpreted this to mean the same rate for everyone. The first income tax, which Congress imposed in 1861 to support the war effort and abandoned 10 years later, had a 3 percent rate on incomes above $800 a year. The second, which Congress enacted in 1894 with a flat rate of 2 percent on incomes above $4,000 a year and progressive rates on estate inheritances, had been declared unconstitutional that same year as a breach of the prohibition against direct taxes. "The present assault on capital is but the beginning," wrote Justice Stephen J. Field in his concurring opinion. "It will be but the stepping-stone to others, larger and more sweeping, till our political contests will become a war of the poor against the rich; a war constantly growing in intensity and bitterness."[5] Nonetheless, representatives from the southern and western states had continued to submit income tax bills every year, hoping to collect and redistribute some of the vast wealth in the northeastern states.

The third income tax, enacted in 1913, followed a constitutional amendment that limited judicial review. Indeed the Supreme Court approved the progressive aspects of the tax in the case of *Brushaber v. Union Pacific R.R.* in 1916, opening the door to compensatory rates on high incomes and redistribution schemes. Wilson, like Gladstone in England, promoted high surtaxes as a wartime expedient and, like his fellow liberal, largely kept them in place afterward despite recommending rate reductions. The revenue proved irresistible.

Harding had lowered the maximum surtax from a world-highest 65 percent to 50 percent, but the progressive income tax remained the backbone of the modern fiscal state, accounting for nearly two-thirds of federal revenue, compared with less than 16 percent in 1916, before the war. Once the national economy recovered from the postwar depression of 1920–1922, the prosperity boom provided unprecedented peacetime revenue and heightened spending pressures on Capitol Hill to assist farmers, provide a bonus to war veterans, raise pension payments for all veterans, increase federal subsidies to the states, and initiate public infrastructure projects, in particular.

Meantime, the progressive income tax disproportionally placed the burden of supporting the federal government on wealthy individuals and wealthy states, partly because of the high personal exemption for income earners. In 1924, less than 10 percent of all taxpayers accounted for 70 percent of federal income tax revenues.[6] In 1923, the five states of Illinois, Massachusetts, Michigan, New York, and Pennsylvania, containing barely one-quarter of the population of the country, accounted for about 60 percent of federal revenue.[7] Nearly 40 states contributed less per capita than the average for the country, giving the vast majority of states and citizens a stake in maintaining the status quo. No wonder that most subsidy supporters came from southern and western states. Nevada, for example, contributed two-hundredths of 1 percent of all federal taxes and received more than 1 percent of federal subsidies. New York, by contrast, contributed nearly 25 percent of federal taxes and received about 5 percent of federal subsidies.[8] With nine out of 10 congressmen representing districts or states that paid less than they received, the incentive to tax and spend was stronger than ever on Capitol Hill. This stood in contrast with the more equitable consumption taxes that most industrialized countries had adopted during or following the Great War, based on the principle that everyone would pay the same rate and that such taxes were easier to collect than income taxes.

Coolidge, well trained in finances as a former mayor, lieutenant governor, and governor, took a greater interest in taxing and spending than any other issue and oversaw the federal budget in a way that would have been impossible three years earlier.

The historic Budget and Accounting Act of 1921 had given the United States for the first time a comprehensive budget system and had given the president the ability to coordinate and largely control the fiscal affairs of the executive branch of the federal government. The previous system of "budgeting without a budget" developed during colonial times and continued following independence, in line with Anglo-American political traditions that dated back to the Magna Carta and placed the power of the purse in the representative body closest to the people, as stated under Article I of the Constitution. This arrangement led to corruption and a lack of long-term planning and accountability, particularly during the late 19th century as the country and the government grew. Before 1921, the forty-odd departments of the executive branch submitted their annual budgets to the Treasury Department, which sorted, printed, and submitted "the book of estimates" to Congress without further review, covering some 5,000 spending items. On Capitol Hill, the book had been divided and distributed to eight committees in each chamber, encouraging alliances between the spending departments and their committee counterparts and further removing the White House from the process, unlike the open budget process in the British Parliament and the French Chamber of Deputies. There had been no balance sheet, no statement of assets and liabilities, no comparison of expenditures and revenues. Indeed President Monroe had learned from a legislator, rather than his own secretary of the treasury, that his administration had run up a deficit for the first time in 1822.

Now, thanks to the new law, the president submitted to Congress an annual federal budget and a statement of expected revenue, allowing the White House to review, coordinate, and revise department estimates, and impose discipline over expenditures. The law had three other important aspects: it created a Budget Bureau within the Treasury Department and conferred to the president the power to appoint the director and assistant director; it prohibited federal agencies from trying to influence the budget determinations of Congress save at legislative request, prompting the House and the Senate to reduce from eight to one the number of committees responsible for appropriations; and it established a Comptroller General and a General Accounting Office to review all expenditures against government laws and regulations and to conduct routine audits. Thus the United States had become the last great nation to adopt a budget system.

Coolidge gave authority to Budget Bureau Director Lord to interact directly with department heads without going through Secretary Mellon, making him the second most powerful figure in the executive branch. Mellon tried to rein in his bureaucratic subordinate by recommending to the president that Lord submit all spending estimates to the Treasury Department for review and approval before dissemination to the White House, the Congress, and the public. In a letter to Coolidge on October 23, he presented his grievances and complained, "While General Dawes was Director of the Budget he worked in close cooperation with the Treasury at the suggestion of President Harding, but General Lord has not pursued this policy."[9]

Coolidge had the letter sent to Lord, who proceeded to reach agreement with Mellon on a coordination process that maintained the operational independence of the Budget Bureau within the executive. This formidable officer had earned the trust of the president during his early weeks in office.

Born in 1859 at Rockland, Maine, Lord attended Colby College, walking 55 miles to and from campus each semester, and worked as a schoolteacher, a reporter, and a clerk with the House Ways and Means Committee, learning finances, budgets, audits, taxes, loans, and capital, before enlisting in the army. There he served as paymaster in Cuba in 1899, handling more than $24 billion in wartime payouts in 1918 and being promoted to chief financial officer in 1920 with the rank of Brigadier General. As the second director of the Budget Bureau, following Charles G. Dawes in 1922, he inherited an established entity that had been through three budget cycles with routines, procedures, and only 20 staff officers, including generals, colonels, and majors. A sprightly, nonsmoking, nondrinking Christian Scientist in his mid–50s with brown eyes, round wire-rimmed glasses and thinning hair, he lived in the Woodley apartments near Connecticut Avenue, hiked in Rock Creek Park at five most mornings, and worked long hours at his plain desk on the third floor of the Treasury building, chewing gum and breaking into song as he poured over estimates from the various agencies, holding daily hearings with department supervisors, searching desk drawers after hours for extra pencils and other items, and insisting on amounts to the penny. "Fine! Fine!" he would exclaim when he received positive news.[10] This was nothing less than a "great economy crusade" by the administration, in his view.[11] Twice a week he met with Coolidge, sometimes more. No other adviser saw Coolidge so often.

In studying the government balance sheet, Coolidge was disturbed by the far-reaching impact of the national debt, which, after holding steady at about $1 billion annually since 1888, had risen to $25.9 billion during the Great War. The numbers were startling. In 1914, the debt had been $1 billion. By 1923, interest payments alone exceeded $1 billion. On a per capita income basis the debt was smaller than the Revolutionary War debt and the Civil War debt, but the sudden increase received widespread attention in a country accustomed to low debt. In Europe, most nations carried large perpetual debts before the war, some dating back to the 18th century, mostly relating to previous wars. Germany applied 6.6 percent of its prewar budget to debt service, England 11.6 percent, Russia 12.6 percent, France 18.0 percent, Italy 19.7 percent, and Belgium 27.0 percent. In the United States, that figure had been only 2.3 percent.[12]

Alexander Hamilton, the first secretary of the treasury, perceived utility in the debt as a stimulus—albeit an artificial one—to promote capital formation but dismissed the European notion that public debts are public benefits and insisted that the assumption of debt must be accompanied by a payoff plan. And so the new republic, with its meager resources and weak revenue system, had redeemed its $77 million debt despite considerable borrowing for the Louisiana Purchase of 1803 and the War of 1812. The last payment installment had been made in 1834, a remarkable feat in the annals of national finances. Since then the United States had followed a policy of debt redemption, interrupted by heavy borrowing for the Mexican War, the Civil War, and the Spanish War.

The current debt was not a constructive debt like that incurred to pay for the Panama Canal or railroad construction, reducing transportation costs and promoting trade and commerce. It was mainly a war debt used to finance loans to military allies and to purchase war-related materials at home that had been consumed or destroyed with no discernible economic benefit. The last of the Civil War bonds had been called for redemption in April 1907, only 16 years ago. Now the country faced another 40 years of war bonds incurred in 1917 and 1918, with the Treasury Department employing thousands of accountants to handle the bonds, adding to the waste. In 1919, Congress had mandated a permanent sinking fund appropriation of 2.5 percent of the debt toward redemption, less the amount of obligations of foreign governments held by the United States. As Harding had applied the proceeds from the liquidation of wartime assets as well as small amounts of surplus revenue to the debt each year, lowering the balance to $22 billion by 1923, Coolidge intended to reduce the debt by at least $400 million annually to meet the Congressional mandate and to pay off the full amount in 25 years, using additional funds that might otherwise have been used for tax cuts or other purposes. This would be the most ambitious reduction since Jefferson in 1801–1809.

To Coolidge, debt reduction was necessary to maintain the credit of the United States Government at a high level to finance its obligations at the lowest possible interest rates. This came down to faith within the lending market that the country could and would manage its debt and expenditures. Private individuals and businesses could secure low rates through mortgages and other collateral. Governments could not. The two options for debt reduction were to retire obligations and to refinance outstanding securities bearing a high rate of interest into securities bearing a lower rate of interest. These methods involved intricate bookkeeping within the Treasury Department to keep track of transactions and maturity dates and to ensure sufficient funds to meet obligations to individuals, banks, businesses, the Federal Reserve, and other entities buying and selling short-term and long-term securities. The total volume of transactions at the New York Federal Reserve Bank alone approached $2 billion a day.[13]

After a review of federal expenditures and efforts by the Budget Bureau to reduce the cost of many of the more than 5,000 items submitted by the departments, Coolidge proposed a $3.3 billion budget for fiscal year 1925, excluding debt reduction payments and postal expenses. This was the lowest since before the war, with reductions across the board. The Veterans Bureau was to be reduced from $431 million to $349 million, the Army from $349 million to $336 million, the Navy from $297 million to $278 million, Interior from $325 million to $299 million, Agriculture from $85 million to $69 million, the Shipping Board from $50 million to $30 million, Labor from $7.5 million to $6.7 million, and the Interstate Commerce Commission from $5.2 million to $4.2 million. Federal subsidies to the states were to be held in check. The national debt was to be reduced by $400 million. The goal was to produce a budget below $3 billion by 1925.

The surpluses for fiscal year 1924 and fiscal year 1925 were estimated at $329 million and $395 million, respectively. This made a tax cut "possible" as long as Congress avoided any large expenditures, Coolidge noted. This would be his first of many declarations as president that budget surpluses were a prerequisite for tax reductions.

In submitting the budget to Congress, the president wrote:

> The executive instructions governing the preparations of these estimates called for a substantial reduction as compared with the appropriations for 1924. This was essential to a continuation of the policy of strict and drastic economy.[14]

The most contentious issue in Washington was how to divide the surplus between bonus payments for Great War veterans and income tax cuts. Both sides agreed that the fate of one hinged on the fate of the other.

Bonus advocates had been pushing their cause since the American Legion emerged in 1919 to promote patriotism and the rehabilitation of veterans. Their demand for "adjusted service compensation" for all veterans, rather than a pension for disabled or older veterans, marked a break with precedent. The first national pension law, enacted by the Continental Congress in August 1776, promised half pay for life to every officer and every disabled soldier and seaman. In 1818, half payments were extended to those who served at least nine months. In 1832, full payments were offered to those who served two years and proportionate pay to those who served more than six months. In 1836, pensions were granted to widows who had married veterans within a certain period. In 1848, pensions were extended to all Revolutionary War widows, the last of whom died shortly before the Great War. This pattern of increased benefits and widened coverage had been repeated during and after the War of 1812 and the Mexican War, in contrast with England and other European countries that confined payments to disabled veterans.

The Civil War produced more than twice as many veterans as all previous conflicts put together and resulted in massive federal spending for decades. In 1862, the federal government adopted a pension for soldiers who suffered disabilities or death connected with their service. In 1866, the year after surrender, Union veterans established the Grand Army of the Potomac, which became the largest and most effective lobbying organization for a particular interest group in history. Two years later the states ratified the Fourteenth Amendment, which contained a significant but little noticed clause to prevent judicial interference: "The validity of the public debt of the United States, authorized by law, including debts incurred for payment of pensions and bounties for services in suppressing insurrection or rebellion, shall not be questioned." Thus Civil War pensions become legal and unquestionable, with consent from the Supreme Court in *U.S. v. Hall* and *U.S. v. Teller*. Congress soon responded to pressure from the Grand Army of the Republic by steadily increasing benefits, adding widows and children as recipients, and expanding coverage from physical disabilities suffered in war to disabilities related to age, culminating in the Dependable Pension Act of 1890, the first social welfare legislation in U.S. history. Roosevelt went so far as to unilaterally increase pensions to Union veterans, a controversial and highly political move on the eve of the 1904 election. All told, Civil War pensions accounted for as much as 40 percent of federal spending during the late 19th century and early 20th century, and resulted in widespread patronage and corruption.

More recently, Congress enacted an elaborate system of pensions for Spanish War veterans even though the Fourteenth Amendment applied only to veterans of civil conflicts. No other country in the world provided such generous benefits to veterans.

When the United States entered the fighting in Europe in 1917, Congress tried to break the pattern of ever-escalating pensions by adopting an insurance policy for all soldiers and sailors upon their return from duty. The Selective Service Act of 1917 ruled out a bonus, but the following year Congress granted a one-time $60 payment to every man on his discharge, establishing a precedent that encouraged the American Legion to seek more.

With some 700,000 members and 11,000 local posts across the country, the Legion proposed to provide some 4.5 million veterans with cash payments of $50 for certain beneficiaries and adjusted service certificates for others, payable in 20 years or upon death. This amounted to $1.25 per day for each day of overseas service and $1.00 per day for each day of home service, in excess of 60 days of service. Individual payments were not to exceed $625 for overseas service and $500 for home service. Total costs were estimated at nearly $4 billion, the largest single expenditure in American history. Annual costs were estimated as high as $135 million, including more than 5,000 clerks to handle some 167 million documents in five million case files, with about 50,000 Smiths, 40,000 Johnsons, 29,000 Browns, and 28,000 Williamses, sorted into five miles of metal cabinets that occupied three floors at the old Washington Barracks and weighed 1,100 tons, enough to fill 54 freight cars.[15] Nearly one-quarter of potential applicants could neither read nor write the English language, requiring interpreters and further complicating matters. Notwithstanding efforts by the Legion to promote the bonus as "compensation" for the "economic loss" incurred by soldiers during the war, the lowest enlisted man had received $1,287 annually during his service, more than most farmers and factory workers made back home. Veterans had also received $650 million in federal discharge payments and state bonuses, exceeding the combined efforts of England and France for their respective troops, even though they had served as many as four years during the combat, compared with one year, seven months, and four days for American troops. More to the point, Congress had offered subsidized insurance policies to all servicemen in 1917 on the grounds that such provision would relieve the government of further obligation. The government had distributed some $500 million on these policies, with nearly $3 billion more outstanding.

Harding had blocked the bonus in 1922, but only because Congress failed to provide a means of payment. Thus he gave away the issue. If the money was due, the plea of economy had no validity and the debt was irrelevant. To make matters worse, four senators who backed the Harding veto and provided the margin of victory had been defeated by pro-bonus candidates in the midterm elections of 1922. Those four votes alone would be enough to override another presidential veto. With 50 veterans of the war in the House and five in the Senate, the veteran bloc was stronger than ever and even conservatives regarded the bonus as inevitable.

The case for tax cuts fell to Secretary Mellon, who proposed in November a $323 million reduction that would absorb most of the surplus. The plan was to reduce rates for most taxpayers, lower the maximum rate from 50 percent to 25 percent, and reduce the inheritance tax. Eastern financial interests and business associations were supportive, but the American Legion disputed his figures and noted he had killed the bonus in 1922 by reporting a probable deficit of $600 million that turned into a surplus of $300 million. Various bonus backers cited the "billion dollar error" as evidence that Mellon and his aides could not be trusted to provide accurate estimates on what the country could and could not afford.[16]

"Mr. Mellon is using his position as a Cabinet officer to lobby against a measure which the great majority of people favor," said the head of the American Legion. "He is maintaining this lobby by manipulation of Treasury Department figures."[17]

In private talks with legislative leaders, Coolidge backed the tax cuts over the bonus, but he said little publicly before his first annual message to Congress on December 6. Most newspapers and political observers assumed Mellon would not have publicized his plan without presidential approval. When party stalwarts pressured the president to state his position to counter political maneuvering by Republican insurgents and Democrats, he met with Senator Lodge on November 18 and let him divulge to reporters afterward that the message to Congress would include support for the Mellon plan and opposition to the bonus.[18]

* * *

Now more than 100 days in office, Coolidge had declined speaking invitations because the country was in mourning. This had the effect of heightening anticipation for his message to Congress, which he was to deliver in person like Wilson and Harding, rather than by messenger like other presidents since Jefferson. The speech was to be broadcast by radio—the first presidential address to a national audience and the first time microphones had been placed in the House chamber. This was no small achievement, requiring weeks of advance work to coordinate links between radio stations and telephone lines and set up amplifiers at certain locations to compensate for weakened reception at distances from Washington. Twenty stations scattered from Boston to Kansas City agreed to carry the speech, but stations west of the Missouri River declined to participate because of the expense of using and, in some cases, laying land wire services over vast distances.

Determined to keep secret the contents of the speech, Coolidge met with party leaders to get their input but wrote alone, editing in his study at night, rehearsing in his bedroom behind closed doors for three weeks, telling his secretary to limit appointments to those of necessity. Dr. Boone noticed he was testy over the impending task, and when he saw a newspaper story at breakfast one morning about Grace taking riding lessons at Fort Meyer across the river, replete with a smart ensemble from a local haberdashery, he snapped, "I think you will find that you will get along at this job fully as well if you do not try anything new."[19]

Three days before the speech, White House aides told reporters that the president would be an active candidate for the Republican nomination, with campaign offices in every state. This increased interest in what he would have to say to Congress.

At noon, December 6, he went before the opening session of the 68th Congress, his thin hands trembling as he held his address, his slightly high-pitched, nasally voice carried to more than one million listeners.[20] No voice in history had been heard by more people. In Washington thousands stood on the Capitol lawn to hear the message through amplifiers on the Capitol steps. In other cities people gathered at radio stores and businesses with loud speakers, drawn by the novelty of hearing a president speak live. Harding had spoken on radio a few times, but to small regional audiences before the radio craze. The number of households with sets had increased from about 60,000 in 1922 to about 400,000 in 1923, and chain systems now carried transmissions from the East Coast to as far as Kansas and Texas. Listeners a thousand miles away could hear Coolidge turning the pages of his manuscript, thanks to recent advances in carbon-based microphones.

As expected, Coolidge took his lead from the 1920 party platform. In foreign affairs he reiterated that the United States would remain outside the League of Nations: "The incident, so far as we are concerned, is closed." He endorsed membership in the World Court of Justice, listed conditions for the resumption of normal relations with communist Russia, opposed the cancellation of war debts, supported the renegotiation of debt terms, and defended high tariffs.

Turning to domestic matters, he advocated reductions in spending and income taxes and stipulated the former would need to match the latter:

> The taxes of this country must be reduced now as much as prudence will permit, and expenditures must be reduced accordingly. High taxes reach everywhere and burden everybody. They bear most heavily upon the poor. They diminish industry and commerce. They make agriculture unprofitable. They increase the rates on transportation. They are a charge on every necessary of life.

He favored promoting farm exports, regulating aviation and radio, strengthening the diplomatic corps, reforming the civil service, tightening restrictions on immigration, passing an anti-lynching law, selling the Muscle Shoals water power project that began under Wilson, selling the merchant marine fleet put together during the war, regulating coastal water pollution and the Alaskan fisheries, enacting a minimum wage for female workers, reviewing freight rates, increasing reforestation, and enforcing prohibition, for "it is the duty of a citizen not only to observe the law but to let it be known that he is opposed to its violation." He supported more hospitals and better hospitals for veterans, along with rehabilitation therapy and vocational training.

"But I do not favor the granting of a bonus," he stated.[21]

* * *

As Coolidge spoke, the man who had done more than anyone in recent years to place him in such august circumstances sat alone in the back office of a Boston department store, listening by radio. When an employee stopped in and began to make casual remarks about the speech, Frank Stearns held out his hand and appealed, "Mr. Blank, please be quiet—I feel as if that were my son talking."[22]

* * *

In the library of a Federalist-style brick home at 2340 S Street, Northwest Washington, a fashionable area near Embassy Row, across town from the Capitol, sat the man who had revived the practice of personally delivering the annual message to Congress, the high-minded idealist whose rhetoric had stirred millions and taken him from Princeton University to the White House, despite having the least practical political experience of any president since Grant. Alone, he listened to Coolidge by radio.

Woodrow Wilson, now 66, bore faint resemblance to the man who appeared before Congress in December 1913 to deliver his first annual message in dramatic fashion, or the figure whose presence in Milan in 1918 inspired thousands of Italians to break through thick lines of soldiers into the Piazza del Duomo and run to his balcony at the Palazzo Reale, shouting "god of peace." Though partly recovered from the stroke that nearly killed him during his ill-fated fight for the League of Nations, he walked with a cane, leaned to one side, and needed assistance at times; his hair had turned white and thinned out; his mouth twisted into a half-smile when he spoke; he stayed home for the most part, receiving massage treatments, reading books and newspapers, dictating correspondence, and seeing select visitors. As the first former president to make Washington his permanent residence, save John Quincy Adams and William H. Taft, who returned for official duties, he drew considerable local press coverage, tour buses, and curiosity-seekers who gathered outside his house each day to see him pull away in his limousine for his daily drive, his hair whisking unkemptly about his ears. Public appearances were kept to a minimum besides a forceful two-minute radio address on Armistice Day, one month earlier, which had surprised politicos and served notice that he meant to reopen the League of Nations debate during the coming presidential campaign. The issue remained his obsession lest anyone think he accepted the landslide of 1920 as a referendum on his cherished institution. "It occupies him to the exclusion of practically every other thought," said one Democratic insider.[23]

To hear the practical-minded Coolidge dismiss the League as an issue of the past must have appalled his predecessor. Liberalism was in retreat. Conservatism was in the ascendancy.

Two hours later a news ticker reported that Wilson had died, causing newspapermen to rush to his residence. Not so, said his secretary, he had taken a ride around the city that afternoon and felt "as fine as ever."[24]

The following day Wilson gave his verdict on Coolidge to a newspaper editor and longtime intimate: "The message did not breathe one human hope."[25]

* * *

Newspapers praised the president for his directness and common sense, and radio listeners sent thousands of letters and telegrams to their representatives—90 percent in favor of tax reduction—in what many observers described as the quickest public reaction in years.[26] Fiscal conservatives rallied around his single sentence on the bonus.

* * *

The White House social season began with a diplomatic reception, a brilliant affair with ambassadors from around the world, Marine Corps trumpeters in scarlet uniforms, bright floral arrangements, the first lady in a gown of white brocaded satin, and ice water as the lone beverage. Washington society praised the formal but friendly atmosphere. A few days later the Coolidge boys arrived on Christmas break from Mercersburg Academy in Pennsylvania, where they had been since 1921. After decorating the White House in wreaths, hollies, and trees, they went to a local haberdashery with White House valet Arthur Brooks to select suits and hats. Afterward the president inspected the suits in silence. "You will take that one, John," he said at last, pointing at a suit. "Calvin, you will take that one." Then he went through the same procedure with the hats, instructing Brooks to return the remaining items.[27] Indeed he took a keen interest in all matters relating to his sons, insisting they wear suspenders rather than belts, don tuxedos for dinner, and say their prayers at bedtime, very strict and rigid with them.

On Christmas Eve Coolidge and his sons walked down F Street, mingling with other last-day shoppers and making several purchases. That evening he went to the ellipse behind the White House to touch an electric button that lit the first national Christmas tree, whereupon Grace invited the public to sing carols with the chorus of the First Congregationalist Church on the White House grounds, a joyous scene with 10,000 revelers. Christmas Day the family gathered around a small tree in the Blue Room to exchange gifts with their guests, Frank and Emily Stearns, before visiting wounded veterans at Walter Reed Hospital.

The first day of 1924 brought nearly 5,000 visitors to shake hands with the president in a time-honored reception introduced as an invitation-only affair by John Adams and opened to the public by Andrew Jackson. By tradition the first couple received cabinet members and diplomats before admitting the general public at 11:00 a.m., led by J.W. Hunefeld of Northeast Washington, who had taken his customary position outside the manse early that morning. For five hours they stood in the Blue Room, shaking hands and greeting their fellow citizens, who braved cold winds and long lines in their finest clothes to wish them well. The president later received medical attention for a swollen wrist from all the grabbing and gripping.

The following day Coolidge looked ahead to the campaign with cautious optimism, having been told he had enough delegate support to win the nomination by at least 40 votes, with commitments from Alaska, Alabama, Colorado, Delaware, the District of Colombia, Hawaii, Kansas, Missouri, Nevada, New Mexico, New York, North Dakota, Oklahoma, Puerto Rico, Texas, Utah, and Wyoming, and solid support in New England and the southern states.

"We cannot now see that anything can prevent my nomination on the first ballot at the Republican convention," he wrote his father, "but one never knows what will happen in politics."[28]

* * *

Three weeks later, on a Monday evening, the president went to Memorial Continental Hall, a stately white-marble structure off the White House ellipse, to address the semiannual meeting of the Business Organization of the Government. Established in 1921 to promote economy and efficiency along corporate lines, as made possible by the Budget and Accounting Act, the meetings went by a set routine with the president delivering introductory remarks and the budget director providing the latest fiscal and managerial developments in a fervent manner that brought a revivalist atmosphere to the proceedings. To further liven up the scene, the United States Marine Band played music at intervals. For most senior government managers, budget officers, and disbursement officers, attendance was mandatory.

Coolidge stressed economy and efficiency through coordination among the federal agencies and used the occasion to warn Congress against supplemental appropriations during the legislative session to protect an estimated surplus of $328 million for fiscal year 1924. This would be necessary to support a reductions in tax rates. "There is scarcely an economic ill anywhere in our country that cannot be traced directly or indirectly to high taxes," he declared.

Then he addressed a budget item that was small fiscally but important politically as a threat to good government and the proper constitutional balance between federal and state authorities:

> I take this occasion to state that I have given much thought to the question of Federal subsidies to the state governments. The Federal appropriations for such subsidies cover a wide field. They afford ample precedent for unlimited expansion. I say to you however, that the financial program of the chief executive does not contemplate expansion of these subsidies. My policy in this matter is not predicated alone on the drain which these subsidies make on the national treasury. This of itself is sufficient cause for concern. But I am fearful that this broadening of the field of federal activities is detrimental to both the Federal government and the state governments. Efficiency of Federal operations is impaired as their scope is unduly enlarged. Efficiency of the state governments is impaired as they relinquish and turn over to the Federal government responsibilities which are rightfully theirs.[29]

* * *

The lead political variable of 1924 was a scandal over the leasing of two naval oil reserves, Teapot Dome in Wyoming and Elk Hills in California, which had been transferred to the Interior Department under Harding. Former interior secretary Albert B. Fall admitted to leasing them to private firms under a 1920 law promoted by conservationists and western politicians as a practical use of excess reserves. The Wilson administration had signed similar leases. Fall insisted his leases had been legal. He denied any personal gain. Navy Secretary Denby and Mammoth Oil Company president Harry F. Sinclair, who leased one of the fields, provided corroboration. Thus the so-called Teapot Dome investigation was near collapse in January 1924 when Fall told investigators that to purchase land and make improvements to his ranch in New Mexico he had borrowed $100,000 from *Washington Post* publisher Edward B. McLean, which would have been acceptable had the latter not denied it. This put Fall in the awkward position of having to admit to another source of funds without divulging it. The press drew parallels to the Ballinger affair of 1910–1911 in which the

Taft administration had tried to open public lands in Wyoming, Montana, and the Alaskan territory to private exploitation.

Coolidge was determined to avoid hasty decisions despite pressure from Democrats and Republican insurgents. Asked to comment on the scandal at a press conference on January 18, he said, "That is under investigation, I think, by a senatorial committee, and of course no action is contemplated by any other arm of the government so far as I know."[30] Six days later hearings produced hearsay evidence that Fall had received money from Mammoth Oil president Sinclair, followed by testimony from Pan-American Petroleum president Edward Doheny that he had loaned $100,000 to Fall after leasing an oil reserve in California. The following day Coolidge directed the Justice Department to observe the hearings in case evidence should emerge requiring legal action.

That weekend Coolidge returned from a river cruise to learn Senate investigators were about to request the appointment of two special prosecutors, one Republican and one Democrat, to investigate the matter, prompting him to announce an identical plan in a midnight press release:

> Counsel will be instructed to prosecute these cases in court, so that if there is any guilt, it will be punished; if there is any civil liability, it will be enforced; if there is any fraud, it will be revealed; if there are any contracts which are illegal, they will be cancelled.[31]

Back at the White House, a visitor remarked on the scandal as the president stood near a window in his study, facing toward Virginia less than two miles away. "They say Lincoln could look out that window and see a Rebel flag flying," he replied. "Well, I guess nobody since Lincoln has had that much to worry about."[32]

Soon he had on his desk a Senate resolution, backed by 10 Republican senators, demanding the dismissal of Denby for negligence in transferring the oil fields to the Interior Department without consulting staff officers or the General Board of the Navy. The transfer was deemed illegal for ignoring a Congressional act that placed the reserves under the jurisdiction of the Navy. Coolidge, citing the precedents of James Madison, who at the Constitutional Convention of 1789 blocked a provision that would have allowed Congress to veto presidential dismissals, and Grover Cleveland, who resisted pressure to discharge an assistant, declared that any dismissal of a public official other than by impeachment was "exclusively an executive function." There would be no senatorial meddling. Newspapers around the country, by and large, backed the president.

"I continue to be very proud of you," wrote Richard Irwin from Northampton, noting that all the lawyers he knew thought the Denby resolution was unconstitutional.[33]

Denby insisted the oil lease contracts were legal even as the administration, through special counsel, prepared to annul them because they were made outside the authority of the law. This led to his resignation on February 18 and his replacement with Curtis D. Wilbur, a California Supreme Court Justice.

The pressure to remove Daugherty for having upheld the legality of the leases increased as Borah demanded his dismissal and Democratic senator Burton K. Wheeler of Montana sponsored a resolution calling for his resignation. Coolidge, though compelled to protect his constitutional prerogatives, hoped Daugherty would leave. In August 1923, he had sent Chief Justice Taft to seek a resignation from the attorney general, who insisted on his innocence.[34] Now, six months later, Coolidge thought Daugherty showed signs of mental unbalance and discussed the matter with Dr. Boone, who replied that while Daugherty suffered from high blood pressure, nervous tension, and the effects of a recent stroke, his psychological state was another matter, requiring a full examination. When Coolidge sent him to see Daugherty, the latter refused to cooperate.[35] Frustrated, Coolidge invited Daugherty and Borah to the White House and listened to them argue for nearly an hour, the former claiming to be the victim of a political vendetta, the latter asserting he should resign because the public had lost confidence in him. When Daugherty stormed from the room, showing a bit of his well-known temper, Coolidge said, "Senator, I reckon you are right."[36] Yet he was reluctant to dismiss the attorney general or anyone appointed by Harding, while filling out his term.

The decisive moment came in late March when Daugherty refused a Senate request to open various files at Justice Department for inspection and Coolidge wrote, "I do not know how you can be acting for yourself in your own defense in this matter, and at the same time and on the same question acting as my attorney general."[37] Daugherty resigned the following day. H.L. Mencken of the *Baltimore Evening Sun*, being less than impressed with Coolidge, wrote, "He opened fire upon poor Daugherty only after the man was dead and the smell of carcass unbearable."[38] Slemp said in private that Coolidge had no consideration for others and would sacrifice anyone for political gain, but most Republicans commended his handling of the matter.[39]

To fill the vacancy, Coolidge considered Chief Justice Arthur P. Rugg of the Massachusetts Supreme Court but decided not to encourage the western perception that "Massachusetts was in the saddle."[40] Instead he turned to former schoolmate Harlan F. Stone, who, though reared in Massachusetts and educated at Amherst, had had the good fortune to be born elsewhere, in distant New Hampshire. Coolidge invited a group of senators to have breakfast with Stone, who had recently resigned as dean of

Columbia Law School to work on Wall Street for a salary of $100,000 a year. "Gentlemen, this is Mr. Stone," he said without mentioning the cabinet vacancy. After the legislators left, he took Stone into his study for a smoke without discussing the post until they were about to part, saying, "Well, I think I will send in your name!" Stone, though reluctant, felt bound to accept and relinquish his lucrative career for a cabinet salary of $12,000.[41] Confirmed less than a week later, he began to reorganize and restore the stature of the department in haste.

The appointment came as a surprise to Representative Bertrand H. Snell of New York, who had recommended Stone to the president more than once, with little response. The congressman met with Coolidge on another matter several days later and brought up his surprise. "I thought you would probably find out about it," Coolidge replied.[42]

* * *

With the scandal fading from newspaper headlines, Coolidge was happy to have his sons back for spring break in late March. John, a senior, standing five feet, 11 inches, 140 pounds, was sober and responsible, sensitive about criticism from his father regarding his clothes, music, and other matters. Calvin, a junior, five feet, 10 inches, and thin at 118 pounds, was a more whimsical lad, a runner, tennis player, violinist, and voracious reader taking on *The Three Musketeers* that spring; he liked history and politics and hoped to run a department store in Boston one day, like Frank Stearns.[43] Both were taller than their father. Despite a week of wet, blustery weather, they went walking on the Mall, horseback riding in Rock Creek Park, and boating on the Potomac, making the most of their vacation. Dr. William M. Irvine, their headmaster, arrived midweek to stay several nights at the behest of the president, who thanked him for instilling discipline and hard work into his boys, while keeping the press away. One evening young Calvin got into a billiards game in the basement with his mother, another player, and Dr. Irvine, who consistently posted the lowest scores of the foursome. "Well, Doctor," he said at last, "you give splendid evidence of not having wasted your youth."[44]

Sarah Pollard of Proctorsville, Vermont, the recently-widowed aunt of the president, also came to visit. Now 83, she delighted in seeing Washington for the first time, riding in the presidential limousine, cruising on the river, listening to a Senate debate on immigration, and seeing the S Street residence where Woodrow Wilson had died two months earlier.

Coolidge, who often stayed with her and her family during his boarding school days, was glad to please. "What men owe to the love and help of good women can never be told," he wrote, sentimentalist that he was.[45]

* * *

President and Mrs. Coolidge with their two sons, Calvin Jr. (to their right) and John, June 30, 1924 (National Photo Company Collection, Library of Congress).

Having eluded ill-founded rumors of involvement in Teapot Dome, the president practically clinched the nomination by March, before the first primary vote. His support among state party organizations provided enough delegates to win a first ballot victory by 200 or more votes, barring a complete collapse in the 19 states with primaries that might prompt committees in other states to switch their support to an alternative candidate with momentum. Numerous favorite-son candidates had opted not to seek the nomination, leaving Hiram Johnson and Senator Robert M. La Follette of Wisconsin as the lone challengers.

Johnson, with his progressive voter base, had a chance to embarrass Coolidge in certain western primaries. That was all. Regular Republicans still blamed him for his role in splitting the party and handing the election to Wilson in 1912, and then failing to deliver the California vote in 1916 to prevent a second term for the Democrat.

La Follette, born in 1855 on a farm in southern Wisconsin and left fatherless before his first birthday, had worked his way through college and law school before winning a seat in Congress at age 30. After losing his reelection bid, he ran against the state party machinery and became governor in 1900, fighting to regulate and tax the railroads, among other progressive measures. Then he ran for the Senate, winning election in 1905 and presenting 13 planks to the Republican National Convention of 1908, including the direct election of United States senators, the regulation of telegraph and telephone rates, and the creation of a Tariff Commission and a Department of Labor. All 13 were rejected. All, except one, were later enacted. A man ahead of his times, said supporters. In 1912, he entered the primaries against Taft and suffered a breakdown during a speech that ruined his campaign. Now, at 69, with a massive gray pompadour and a history of mental breakdowns, he prepared to run against the "reactionary" Coolidge administration, but his decision to enter only the Wisconsin and North Dakota primaries made his candidacy less threatening.

The primaries began with Coolidge taking North Dakota, Johnson winning a thousand-vote upset victory in South Dakota, and Coolidge rebounding in Michigan with a decisive victory. From there the president won Illinois, Nebraska, Oklahoma, New Jersey, Ohio, and California, where he dispatched one-time resident Herbert Hoover to split the progressive vote, hold on to conservatives, and help defeat Johnson in his native state by 54 percent to 46 percent.

All told, Coolidge won two-thirds of the ballots cast in the primaries, securing 572 of the 616 delegates up for grabs. He also claimed most of the 493 "instructed" delegates from states without primaries, in part because Slemp managed to restore the delegate counts in Georgia, Mississippi, and South Carolina, following a rule in 1920 that reduced their numbers because of the small Republican voter base in all three states.

* * *

As the 68th Congress prepared to vote on legislation, Republicans held advantages of 51 to 43 in the Senate and 225 to 205 in the House, but their ranks numbered western insurgents who were disinclined to support the party platform or their accidental president despite his popular message in December. These elements had held the balance of power in both chambers since the midterm elections of 1922, when Republicans lost seven seats in the Senate and 70 in the House, most of them stalwart members. In the Senate, La Follette, Borah, Johnson, Smith W. Brookhart of Iowa, Magnus Johnson and Henrik Shipstead of Minnesota, George W. Norris of Nebraska, Edwin Ladd and Lynn Frazier of North Dakota, and Peter Norbeck and William McMaster of South Dakota tended to thwart party leaders and support government ownership and income redistribution. Once the parties had disciplined senators by controlling the nomination process at the state and local level, but the Seventeenth Amendment in 1913 had changed that by adopting the popular vote and making senators hypersensitive to public opinion. In the House, where the 1910 revolt against Speaker "Uncle Joe" Cannon transferred power to the committees and weakened party discipline, Representative John M. Nelson of Wisconsin led a faction of 17 insurgent Republicans from his own state and neighboring states, who succeeded in placing him on the House Rules Committee, which controlled the legislative schedule, by threatening to vote for a Democrat. This gave the committee eight Republicans and four Democrats, but in reality, five regular Republicans against three insurgent Republicans and four Democrats. The same obstructionist tactics altered House rules by allowing more amendments to bills during floor debates.

The result was some $12 billion in spending bills against an estimated $4 billion in revenue. Many bills were introduced "by request" and not expected to survive committee review, but, put together, showed unprecedented spending pressures on Capitol Hill. The bonus bill was only the beginning. There was a $305 million bill to stabilize wheat prices, a $100 million bill to buy and sell farm products, a $100 million bill to establish a department of education, a $75 million bill to promote self-supporting agriculture, a $30 million bill to buy wheat, a $30 million bill to build roads, a $10 million bill to create a National Department of Highways, and a $1 million bill to relieve drought-stricken farmers. There were bills calling for 795 new post office buildings in various congressional districts. There were dozens of bills to improve harbors, rivers, and public buildings. "The introduction of these bills is the greatest raid on the Federal Treasury in the history of our national life," concluded an analysis for the National Budget Committee.[46]

Coolidge threatened to use his veto against the bonus and tried to rally public sentiment. "One of the disturbing factors of the present time to me is the large number of bills pending in Congress calling for tremendous appropriations," he told reporters in late February.[47] To promote better relations with the legislature in what was sure to be a contentious session, he introduced the White House breakfast, inviting eight to 10 congressmen at a time and listening to their views on legislation and other matters.

Mellon told the House Ways and Means Committee and other audiences that each of the two preceding years had produced surpluses greater than $300 million, that the next few years seemed likely to bring similar results, that the revenue encouraged reckless expenditures such as the bonus, and that high tax rates pushed individuals into tax-exempt public securities at a rate of $1 billion a year instead of productive investments such as corporate stocks. He also used press conferences, press releases, speeches, tax clubs, and a book, published in April, to support the bill. He stated that the sole purpose of the income tax should be to raise revenue without attempting to redistribute wealth. The *Saturday Evening Post* and the *Literary Digest*, the two largest publications in the country by circulation, ran numerous articles and editorials in favor of the plan, but detractors challenged Mellon on his facts and figures. They argued that high rates encouraged corporate investment and expansion rather than taxable dividend payments, and that municipality bonds promoted the construction of schools, libraries, hospitals, parks, highways, streetcars, rail lines, bridges, dams, police stations, waterworks, and sanitation plants. They opposed reducing the high-income surtax in particular. Democrats, with support from insurgent House Republicans, proposed an alternate bill with a maximum surtax of 44 percent on incomes and larger reductions for other income levels than those in the Mellon bill, hoping to win favor in the November elections.

Republican legislative leaders knew the Mellon proposal to reduce the surtax to 25 percent was lost once Chairman William R. Green of the House Ways and Means Committee endorsed a higher rate. They agreed to make a stand for 35 percent but would accept 37 percent or even 40 percent to muster a majority vote.

On February 29, the House voted, 216 to 199, to accept a compromise bill setting the surtax at 37.5 percent and adopting the low Democratic rates on other income levels, with amendments to increase inheritance taxes to a maximum of 40 percent on amounts above $10 million, enact a gift tax with similar rates, and make public the amounts of taxes paid by individuals and corporations. Disappointed, Reed Smoot, Chairman of the Senate Finance Committee, said the bill would have to be rewritten to prevent a deficit of $100 million or more. This former businessman and bank president was known as the most powerful committee chairman and the purse-protector of the Senate, notwithstanding his efforts to support the bonus, to place veterans of the Utah Indian wars on the pension rolls, and to initiate a Salt Lake City–Los Angeles airmail route at a cost of $460,000 to federal taxpayers. The son of a polygamist, he had been the first Mormon elected to the Senate, in 1902. Now in his fourth term, tall, lean, immaculate, with short gray hair, round glasses, and a mustache, he was the hardest working man in the Senate, routinely putting in 16-hour days; when his son was married at nearby Rockville, Maryland, he sent best wishes but missed the ceremony to attend hearings.[48]

Coolidge reiterated support for his proposal, and Mellon attacked the surtax, the increase in inheritance tax rates, the gift tax, and the publicity provision approved by the lower chamber. Smoot and the Senate Finance Committee, by a partisan vote of eight to seven, endorsed the Mellon bill.

The stalemate on taxes continued as Congress voted to give priority to the bonus despite opposition from Coolidge and Mellon, demonstrating the strength of the American Legion to produce a barrage of letters to Capitol Hill, even though its membership had declined from 800,000 in 1920 to 600,000 in 1924 and represented only one-sixth of Great War veterans. Head lobbyist John T. Taylor had learned politics as secretary to the late senator Boies Penrose of Pennsylvania, a cold-blooded Republican tactician, and learned them well. In his office near Capitol Hill he kept 60 green-covered volumes with records of every bill, resolution, hearing, and report pertaining to veterans during the past decade, and 20 more with details on how every congressman voted on such measures. He knew the rules and procedures. He knew the committee chairmen and the clerks who set the schedule from day to day and would allow him to attend closed conferences where most deals took place. No lobbyist in Washington could compare to this tough, sharp-eyed, prematurely gray-haired attorney and former lieutenant colonel, who pushed Congress to approve the payments and secured nearly unanimous support from the veteran bloc on Capitol Hill.

In early May, Congress passed the bonus by a whopping margin of 355 to 54 in the House and 67 to 16 in the Senate, as compared with 333 to 70 in the House and 47 to 22 in the Senate in 1922. This increase in support would be enough to override another presidential veto.

Coolidge, though ill with a bronchial cold that made him cancel other engagements and receive chlorine gas treatments, invited to breakfast six Republican senators who had voted yea and one who had been absent. To sustain a veto, he would need to pick up nine votes in the upper chamber. As the senators finished their pancakes and maple syrup, he asked in a husky voice whether they would stand by their party. Henry W. Keyes of New Hampshire, William B. McKinley of Illinois, Lawrence C. Phipps of Colorado, and Thomas Sterling of South Dakota said they would do so. The other three were silent. Coolidge, knowing he had lost, pushed back his chair and thanked everyone for their time.[49]

Coolidge returned the bill to Congress on May 15 with a terse message that some predicted would cost him the election. From a practical standpoint, he argued that many veterans opposed the bonus, that all volunteered for service, that all received $60 at discharge, that most received state monies, that the federal government had spent $2 billion for the care and rehabilitation of wounded veterans, that subsidized insurance policies had been offered to all servicemen in 1917, and that the annual expenditure of $140 million to finance bonus certificates through Treasury loans would limit tax reductions for years and possibly cause deficits. "We have no money to bestow upon a class of people that is not taken from the whole people," he declared. "Our first consideration must be the nation as a whole."

Whereas Harding would have signed the bonus under better financial conditions, Coolidge opposed the payments on principle:

> We owe no bonus to able-bodied veterans of the World War. The first duty of every citizen is to the nation. The veterans of the World War performed this duty. To confer upon them a cash consideration or its equivalent for performing this first duty is unjustified. It is not justified when considered in the interests of the whole people; it is not justified when considered alone on its own merits.
>
> The gratitude of the nation to these veterans cannot be expressed in dollars and cents. No way exists by which we can either equalize the burdens or give adequate financial reward to those who served the nation in both civil and military capacities in time of war. The respect and honor of their country will rightfully be theirs forevermore. But patriotism can neither be bought nor sold. It is not hire and salary. It is not material, but spiritual.
>
> It is one of the finest and highest of human virtues. To attempt to pay money for it is to offer it an unworthy indignity which cheapens, debases and destroys it. Those who would really honor patriotism should strive to match it with an equal courage, with an equal fidelity to the welfare of their country, and an equal faith in the cause of righteousness.[50]

The message was received in silence in the House chamber, followed by raucous applause as second-term Democrat congressman and war veteran John E. Rankin of Mississippi said the veto language "goes out of its way to offer a gratuitous insult to the ex-servicemen."[51]

Congress, under pressure from the American Legion in the form of a million letters and telegrams from every district in the country, a petition with three million signatures, and the wide distribution of pro-bonus publications, such as the *Legionnaire* and the *Service Record*, took up the veto less than a week later on May 19, before packed galleries in both chambers. "Vote! Vote!" cried pro-bonus legislators as administration forces tried to postpone the proceedings a few days. Senator Lenroot of Wisconsin, the man who would have been president but for the spontaneous Coolidge nomination in 1920, took his seat for the first time in weeks, following an illness, and cast his pro-bonus vote. Senator Frank D. Green of Vermont made a surprise appearance to vote no, two months after being severely wounded while passing an alley during a shootout between bootleggers and prohibition agents on Pennsylvania Avenue. The roll call continued on, with pro-bonus forces winning by a margin of 313 to 78 in the House and 59 to 26 in the Senate. Thirty Republican senators opposed Coolidge, including the majority leader, the whip, the president pro tem, and the chairman of the Appropriations Committee. The vote lasted 20 minutes and marked the first time in American history that an organized lobby had succeeded in obtaining legislation over a presidential veto. To begin the payments, Congress appropriated $100 million per annum.

Meantime, Coolidge blocked two other initiatives—one to raise annual pension appropriations for war veterans by a total of $58 million and one to increase postal worker salaries by a total of $68 million.

The pension bill, put forward by Republican Holm O. Bursum of New Mexico, proposed to increase by 25 percent payments to veterans and dependents of the War of 1812, the Mexican War, the Civil War, the Indian conflicts, and the Spanish War, and to extend the service limit of Civil War veterans from April 1865 to August 1866, so that those who served during those 16 months of peace were eligible for the same benefits as those who fought during the war. This was consistent with past efforts to liberalize pension and disability programs, while steadily increasing payment amounts, in response to pressure from veterans and their supporters.

In vetoing the Bursum bill, Coolidge wrote:

> The need for economy in public expenditures at the present time cannot be overstated. I am for economy. I am against every unnecessary payment of the money of the taxpayers. No public requirement at the present time ranks with the necessity for the reduction of taxation. This result cannot be secured unless those in authority cease to pass laws which increase the permanent cost of government. The burden on the taxpayers must not be increased; it must be decreased.[52]

This took some pluck considering he declined to enlist in Company I of the Second Massachusetts Volunteer Infantry in 1898, when he was 26, healthy, and a bachelor. "I am sorry I did not go," he had written home after watching the sunburnt troops return from Cuba to a heroic welcome at the Northampton train station, minus the eight who died in the war and one who died from yellow fever on the way home.[53] The lack of military service had never hurt Coolidge politically, but during the Boston police walkout, the policemen had criticized him for calling them deserters and traitors when, in fact, many had served in Cuba while he was practicing law. To the extent he thought about his personal history in regard to the Bursum bill, he probably considered it irrelevant to the issue at hand. Delegates from the United Spanish War Veterans lobbied him to sign the bill, but neither they nor the press mentioned his record in 1898.

The vote to override the veto took place on May 13, in high drama. Veterans, many in uniform, arrived early to get seats in the Senate gallery or gathered in the hallway outside the chamber. Supporters of the bill figured they had enough votes to win once Republican stalwarts Fess, Lenroot, Lodge, Watson, and Willis indicated they would break with the president. As the process began, however, several Democrats from southern states cast their votes against the measure. They were less than enthusiastic about a pension for Civil War veterans from the northern states only, and many agreed with Coolidge on economy. In fact, more Democrats than Republicans voted against the bill that afternoon. The final tally: Democrats, 19 yea and 16 nay; Republicans, 32 yea and 12 nay; independents, two yea and no nay. The veto was sustained by a single vote when Republican John W. Harreld of Oklahoma switched from the yea to the nay column.

This infuriated bill supporters, as Democratic senator Matthew M. Neely of West Virginia called for retribution at the polls: "Since President Coolidge has taken the position that it will be too costly to the country to provide the beneficiaries of the Bursum bill pensions of $72 a month, I hope that our veterans and the widows and orphans of soldiers will decide that it will be too costly to pay Mr. Coolidge $205 a day to be President for the next four years."[54]

On the postal bill, Coolidge noted that the 375,000 postal workers had received three raises since 1918 and were paid better than the average federal employee and comparable private sector workers at a time when living costs were steady. Indeed the Civil Service list had 6,000 eligible candidates waiting to fill government vacancies and another 25,000 applicants under review.

When Republican senator James Couzens of Michigan insisted that a postman could not raise a family on $1,500 a year, Coolidge replied, "In Northampton, Massachusetts, you can have a first-rate home to live in for $30 a month."

Couzens was flabbergasted: "That's no argument! All of our postal employees can't live in Northampton, Massachusetts!"

"I had an uncle in Northampton," Coolidge went on, nonplussed. "He sent his children through high school and college and he never made more than $1,500 a year in his whole life."

"That's the trouble with you, Mr. President. You have a Northampton viewpoint, instead of a national viewpoint."[55]

After the Senate passed the bill by a massive 70-vote margin, Coolidge issued a veto statement, noting the lack of increase in parcel post or other rates to meet the additional outlay, despite warnings that he was committing "political suicide."[56] Republican Senate leaders managed to postpone a second vote that would have certainly resulted in a veto override and embarrassment to the administration in an election year.

These spending pressures prompted Director Lord to use a little-known provision within the Budget Bureau to tighten control over department spending and views on legislation. Issued in December 1921, Circular No. 49 mandated that all agency proposals for legislation or views on pending legislation be submitted to the Bureau before presentation to Congress, or what was known as "legislative clearance." The agencies had resisted implementation as a broad and rather vague imposition on their activities and their access to the president, and Harding had abandoned this sweeping instrument of administrative authority. Lord, with support from Coolidge, activated it and demanded implementation across the federal government during the early months of 1924, using investigations, warnings, threats, and formal complaints to achieve compliance. This allowed the White House to assess the financial impact of each spending proposal and hold up any legislation "in conflict" with the budget or, for that matter, the policies and priorities of the president unless the funding request was deemed as necessary.[57]

"As the situation stands today," Lord wrote Coolidge on May 24, "I am satisfied that your approval of the Tax Bill will not prevent the Budget being balanced for the fiscal year 1925 or the fiscal year 1926."[58]

And so, thanks to spending discipline and reductions in bonus implementation costs by transferring other funds and personnel to the undertaking, Coolidge and Mellon pushed ahead with tax reduction, albeit less than their original proposal of $323 million. After much wrangling on Capitol Hill, the two chambers agreed on May 26 to a bill that appeared to fall within the parameters of the surplus, despite the bonus, but came as a disappointment to the administration and supporters. All taxpayers were to receive a 25 percent reduction, placing the maximum surtax at 40 percent vice 25 percent. The corporate tax remained at 12.5 percent, and the inheritance tax increased from 25 to 40 percent on amounts above $50,000. A gift tax was enacted with the same rates and provisions as the inheritance tax. A credit on "earned income" of $10,000 favored middle and low income earners. A publicity provision required the Internal Revenue Service to make public the amounts of taxes paid by individuals and corporations. No other country in the world published such information.

The federal tax code was made more intricate with new guidelines on gains and losses in corporate mergers and reorganizations, gains and losses from the sale of capital assets, depletion allowances on natural resources, the calculation of inventories, and other corporate bookkeeping practices. "The lawyers in Congress certainly did a good thing for their fellow-lawyers," said one tax practitioner with glee.[59]

In reluctantly signing the bill on June 2, Coolidge wrote: "A correction of its defects may be left to the next Congress. I trust a bill less political and more economic may be passed at that time. To that end I shall bend all my energies."[60]

Meantime, Coolidge suffered other setbacks. Insurgent Republicans blocked his plan to privatize Muscle Shoals, a Wilson scheme to produce hydroelectric power and nitrates along the Tennessee River in Alabama, barely one-third completed despite $100 million in public funds. Southern Democrats blocked an anti-lynching bill in the House. Members of both parties defied the president by adding a ban on Japanese migrants to a bill restricting the number of admissions allowed to any nationality annually to 2 percent of the number from that country in 1890. Secretary Hughes began negotiations with Japan to voluntarily limit emigration to 250 persons annually, but then blundered by asking Ambassador Masanao Hanihara to prepare a background statement to help Congress sort out the issue, leading to cries of foreign intrusion into a domestic matter. The House passed the bill with the ban by a vote of 326 to 71. As the Senate began deliberations, Ambassador Hanihara warned of "grave consequences" if the 250-person quota was not approved, leading to much outrage.[61] Coolidge discussed with immigration committee members a two-year delay to cool tempers and allow time to negotiate a voluntary halt, but received scant support, even from progressives such as Borah, Johnson, La Follette, Norris, and Wheeler. Then he tried a one-year delay to no avail. With the previous bill due to expire on June 30, he had little choice but to sign the Immigration Act of 1924.

Many presidential recommendations were blocked in committee or ignored, such as a minimum wage for female workers and a proposal to enter the World Court. Only two of the 33 legislative items in his address to Congress were approved: a bill to spend an additional $6.8 million on hospital facilities for veterans and a bill to combine the consular and diplomatic services into a new foreign service.

Republican newspapers and other outlets blamed Congress for thwarting the president. "The Congress that nobody liked," proclaimed *Time Magazine*.[62] "The Republican party is in power in all branches of the government—except when it comes time to vote," wrote the lead political columnist for the *Washington Post*.[63] Democrat William Randolph Hearst, whose thirty-odd publications tended to support Coolidge, visited the White House and liked him. The president was no ultraconservative, he said.[64]

* * *

Indeed the press was mostly favorable toward him and his administration. "I suppose that I am not very good copy," he told reporters. "The usual and ordinary man is not the source of very much news. But the boys have been very kind and considerate to me, and where there has been any discrepancy, they have filled it and glossed it over, and they have manufactured some."[65] Frank Kent, writing in the progressive *American Mercury*, accused Washington correspondents of creating a "Coolidge myth" to interest readers when, in truth, the president was dull. "No man ever had a better press," he wrote.[66]

Acutely publicity conscious since his early days in politics, Coolidge took advantage of the new mass media—radio, magazines, motion pictures—to strengthen his public image, giving him an edge over previous accidental presidents Tyler, Fillmore, Johnson, Arthur, and Roosevelt, in that people could hear his voice, see his attractive family, and identify with him personally in a way that would have been unthinkable previously. He would even encourage the Secret Service to slip anecdotes to the press. "Better tell that one to the newspaper boys," he would say when a certain incident cast him in a favorable light, but within limits, not wanting to overdo it.[67]

He was more willing than any of his predecessors to pose for photographers, who, with the advent of mass-circulation magazines and tabloid newspapers, had become ensconced in the presidential entourage. Cleveland, McKinley, Roosevelt, Taft, Wilson, and Harding, for the most part, had limited photographs to public appearances. When a cameraman took a candid shot of Roosevelt entering his carriage one morning at Oyster Bay, a Secret Service man retaliated by knocking him to the ground with a violent blow. When a photographer snapped a picture of Wilson and his daughters cycling in Bermuda, hair disheveled, the president charged at him in double-fisted anger; he hated having his picture taken and avoided it as much as possible. Coolidge, by contrast, submitted to the cameras at private moments and allowed his wife to be photographed more than any first lady in history, well aware of her popularity and photogenic qualities. Few newspaper readers had known what Mrs. McKinley, Mrs. Roosevelt, and the others looked like, but Mrs. Coolidge was familiar to all. "Mrs. Coolidge is one of the finest women I ever photographed—lots of personality and always gives perfect cooperation," said a local cameraman.[68] Oftentimes the president called in photographers with their tripods and boxes to take pictures of a bill ceremony or delegation visit, waiting patiently for them to set up. The lone restriction he put on them was not to shoot him smoking, lest he set a poor example for the youth of the country.

With the number of household radios increasing from about 400,000 in 1923 to nearly 10 million in 1924, or one in every two or three households, the administration planned a series of appearances over the airwaves. An estimated five million people heard Coolidge speak at the Lincoln Day Dinner in New York on February 12. Several million heard his tribute to George Washington 10 days later, delivered from the White House study in the first presidential address made exclusively for radio. Several million heard him speak to the Associated Press in March and the Daughters of the American Revolution in April. More people probably heard him speak during the early months of 1924 than heard Theodore Roosevelt in some 1,300 speeches spanning three decades. Slemp and others ensured the largest possible audience by promoting the speeches in advance and providing the chain to regional stations in New York, Providence, Washington, St. Louis, Kansas City, and Dallas, to relay to smaller stations by short-wave transmission.

White House clerk Judson Welliver helped with research, but Coolidge wrote nearly all his addresses, putting a strain on his temperamental nature as he labored to find the right words, the right tone, without a mistake, working as much as 200 hours on a single speech.[69] "I let him alone as much as possible," Grace told Dr. Boone during one such preparation.[70] The speeches were nonpartisan, almost nonpolitical, replete with history, homilies, moral themes, and language and allusions from the Scripture. They were practically devoid of first-person references. His voice came across the airwaves strong and succinct, less nasally than in person, and his steady delivery, precise pronunciation, short sentences, and knack for phrasemaking made him a natural radio speaker, unlike La Follette, Borah, and other old-time orators, who struggled with the concept of having to stay in one place and lean into a microphone rather than walking about the stage and gesturing to their audience, much less keeping their speeches to the 15-minute slot allotted for radio rhetoric.

* * *

In Vermont, John Coolidge listened to his son speak whenever possible by walking up the road to visit neighbor Dick Brown, who owned a radio set. The old gentleman might have had his own, he said, but his housekeeper did not want to be "bothered with it."[71]

Chapter Four

Settlement of War Debts

Coolidge, like Wilson and Harding, opposed proposals to cancel or reduce the principal of the $10.1 billion in wartime debts that the former allies owed to the United States, led by England at $4.3 billion, France at $2.0 billion, and Italy at $1.0 billion. The United States Treasury loaned a large percentage of the proceeds of domestic wartime bond issues to the European allies in 1917 and 1918, primarily to purchase food for their armies and civilian populations, cotton for uniforms, horses, guns and munitions, and cigarettes. The loans also served to sustain the franc, the lira, the pound, and other currencies, which otherwise would have depreciated and raised prices for European governments and consumers. The intent had been to use repayment from those countries to redeem the war bonds held by more than 11 million Americans, who bought them in response to the greatest government publicity campaign in history, with bonfires, parades, speeches, and modern advertising. The loans had been made at 3.5 percent interest. The bonds were to be paid at 3.5 percent interest. Any default on the loans would have to be paid by American taxpayers, who had their own national debt to redeem; in other words, bond holders would essentially have to provide for their own interest earnings through their income tax payments.

Neither political party backed the cancellation or reduction of foreign loans for those reasons, and many legislators took the position that payments on them would help cover the costs of the bonus program. Congress, in establishing the World War Foreign Debt Commission in 1922, provided strict guidelines for negotiations with debtor countries, led by prohibiting the cancellation of any debt, prohibiting the extension of maturity dates beyond 25 years, and prohibiting any interest rate below 4.5 percent. Congressional approval was required for any settlements outside those parameters.

Coolidge, not only bound by law to pursue repayment, agreed from a historical and practical standpoint because "unless money that is borrowed is repaid, credit cannot be secured in time of necessity."[1] This fundamental principle had formed the basis of trade and commerce since the nation state emerged in the 17th century. Instead he was willing to rewrite the loans on more favorable terms to European nations, following the precedent set in the Anglo-American debt settlement of January 1923 in which England funded its debt over a period of 62 years at an average interest rate of 3.3 percent. That restructuring cost the United States more than $1 million a day in deferred interest payments and put the onus on American taxpayers to make up the difference, but was widely seen as acceptable at a time when average annual debt payments, $204 million, amounted to only 6 percent of annual federal revenue and one-quarter of 1 percent of national income. The second such settlement, with Finland, was near agreement in 1924. The settlements were an admission of sorts that debt had hindered economic recovery in Europe and U.S. exports, as asserted by domestic banking, business, and agricultural concerns.

"The American producer needs these debt settlements," remarked Secretary Mellon. "The entire foreign debt is not worth as much to the American people in dollars and cents as a prosperous Europe as a customer."[2]

"The prosperity of the United States largely depends upon the economic settlements which may be made in Europe," claimed Secretary Hughes.[3]

The problem was that, whereas England had the gold and financial reserves to make a deal without guarantees of reparation payments from Germany, many debtor nations insisted that their ability to repay the United States hinged on reparation payments, and Germany insisted that such payments were beyond its means. The postwar system of international finance was at risk, with British economist J.M. Keynes and others calling for a cancellation, partial cancellation, or postponement of all wartime debts.

* * *

The debts accumulated during the Great War had been the largest fiscal transactions in history between governments. The allied countries, Belgium, England, France, Greece, Italy, Portugal, Romania, Russia, and Serbia, had borrowed in total more than $16 billion to finance their efforts. England and France had been lenders and borrowers. The United States, a debtor nation before 1914, had become the leading creditor nation in the world after European rushed to sell their bonds on the New York market in response to wartime demands. Germany had waited until 1917 to raise taxes and had largely financed the war by selling bonds to German citizens, after falsely assuming it would win a speedy victory and collect tributes from its vanquished enemies. The debts could not be settled by transfers of funds between government treasuries or large banks, but rather by a constant exchange of goods, services, and currency between creditor and debtor countries. Take France. In order to make debt payments to the United States, the French government had to collect the necessary francs through taxes or duties and then convert the francs into dollars, which could be done only by French individuals and companies selling goods or rendering services to U.S. buyers and receiving payment in dollars, or by selling goods or rendering services to third parties able to pay with dollars obtained from U.S. buyers through separate transactions.

The debts had a political aspect as well. In the early months of the war, the foreign ministers of France and Germany had publicly stated that the enemy would be held liable for damages. This stance, which followed precedents set during the Napoleonic wars and the Franco-Prussian war of the 19th century, contributed to the widespread demand for reparations following the German surrender in 1918. The "khaki election" in England one month later strengthened public opinion in favor of making Germany pay for the war, as the government began to prepare for peace settlement talks with the other allied countries.

The Treaty of Versailles, signed in 1919, had imposed upon Germany the obligation to make reparation for the damage done by its aggression to the civilian populations and properties of the allies, without setting an amount. This task was given to a Reparation Commission, which would also collect payments and distribute them among the allied countries. France and Belgium soon made their claims for homes, public buildings, roads, railways, factories, mines, livestock, and other assets destroyed by German troops. France had been hit hardest, losing 3.3 percent of its population and having some 6,000 square miles laid to waste. England, largely unscathed by the war at home, insisted on including the pensions paid to veteran soldiers and the separation allowances paid to civilians during the war, despite protests from Germany and the United States until President Wilson capitulated to Prime Minister Lloyd George. This more than doubled the amount Germany would owe, even though the United States declined to seek payments for pensions and medical care provided to war veterans. The final amount, determined at a conference in London in May 1921, was set at $33 billion. Germany was to pay $375 million annually from 1921 to 1925 and then about $900 million annually, along with 26 percent of the proceeds of its exports and certain amounts of coal and other materials, known as payments in kind.

The German Reichstag had accepted the ultimatum within a week, without conditions or reservations, despite domestic protests that the terms were punitive and unrealistic.

The first payment installment had been on schedule, with Germany remitting $250 million by printing marks and selling them for foreign currency on the open market, and the Reichsbank accepting the monthly treasury notes from the government to cover the budget deficit. This policy led to rising prices and a falling exchange rate, as German leaders blamed conditions on reparations. Germany pursued such an ill-fated approach in large part because of its heavy spending at the national, state, and city level, which took about one-third of gross national product, including subsidies and other support for industries, farmers, and unemployed workers. Germany struggled financially for other reasons as well. The country had a poor balance of trade, which predated the war and worsened in its aftermath. The loss of Alsace-Lorraine, Posen, and Upper Silesia in the Versailles settlement had included regions with large supplies of iron ore, potash, coal, metallic ores, and grain, requiring Germany to import more raw materials and foodstuffs. The reduction in merchant marine capacity under Versailles, from 5,500,000 tons before the war to 400,000 tons, had removed a steady source of foreign revenue. German exports had also been hurt by domestic restrictions on exports and by foreign barriers on imports, including high tariffs in Central Europe and the United States. Without a surplus of exports, goods, and services to produce foreign currency, Germany would be hard pressed to make reparation payments.

By early 1922, Germany had been unable to stabilize the mark or keep pace with the reparation schedule, leading to partial payments, delays, moratoriums, and finally a temporary suspension of cash payments and a reduction in payments in kind in August. The two main recipient countries, England and France, soon fell into disagreement on how to respond. England was willing to provide some accommodation, having achieved a balanced budget and stabilized the pound. France was unwilling to relent on reparations, needing coal deliveries to address shortages caused by wartime damages to French mines and insisting on monetary payments on schedule to meet its own obligations as the largest debtor country in the world and to prevent German rearmament. This stalemate had continued until January 1923, when the Reparation Commission, by a vote of three to one, with England voting alone, declared Germany in default on agreed-upon coal deliveries. Two days later French and Belgian troops had marched into the Ruhr district of Germany, home to 75 percent of German coal and coke output and 80 percent of German steel production, site of the Essen and Krupps works and the principal source of wealth for Imperial Germany, with enough natural reserves to last a thousand years.[4] Foreign troops seized all mining operations and mineral resources, as permissible under the noncompliance terms of the Versailles Treaty.

The occupation led to nine months of passive resistance in which Germany printed marks to pay workers in the Ruhr not to work and put a halt to nearly all reparations payments, while the previously little-known

Hitler emerged as the most vocal nationalist demagogue in the country. The Deutsche mark fell precipitously in currency trading. The French franc followed in short order, causing incalculable losses.

* * *

This impasse remained in effect as Coolidge took office, followed by another change in national leadership 10 days later that gave some hope for progress between France and Germany. The election of Gustav Stresemann as Chancellor of Germany in August led to abandonment of passive resistance in September and soon made France more or less amenable to negotiations, even though Germany did not resume reparations payments. Secretary Hughes, sensing an opportunity, recommended the creation of two international committees of experts, with no connection to the Versailles Treaty, to assess what Germany could pay and how it could best meet its obligations. The other parties agreed in November. Hughes, with consent from Coolidge, selected three prominent American financiers as unofficial advisers to the committees, while making clear that they were to serve as private citizens and to make recommendations only. By not sending them in an official capacity, the administration hoped to keep the talks on economic matters and avoid the political wrangling that had beset so many postwar negotiations, even as State Department and Commerce Department provided data and technical assistance through the U.S. commercial attaches in London, Paris, and Berlin. Coolidge met with two of the unofficial advisers, former budget director Charles G. Dawes and General Electric chairman Owen D. Young, in late December to discuss their pending trip to Europe.

"The general drift of the conversation was that they did not know yet exactly what would be required, and were prepared to study the situation and make the best recommendations they can," the president told reporters.[5]

In the early months of 1924, Coolidge kept tabs on the committee work through Hughes and others and told reporters that the administration was not even paying the travel and living expenses of the private citizens serving as advisers.[6] In March, Hughes reported to the cabinet that the work was near completion and would almost certainly result in a new settlement on reparations.[7]

In April, the committee approved and released a report that recommended reducing the amount of payments for the following year, increasing the amount in increments until Germany could get back on schedule, and stating that Germany would be able to raise the agreed-upon $33 billion by achieving a stable currency and a balanced budget. Coolidge endorsed the report in a public speech, Hoover issued a statement on the potential trade advantages, and Hughes departed on a tour through Europe to pressure leaders to accept the so-called Dawes plan. In France, he told Premier Edouard Herriot that his cabinet "must endorse" the plan. In Germany, he warned the foreign minister that failure to adopt the plan would mean the United States "was finished" trying to mediate the problem.[8]

The plan, adopted in July and implemented in August, proposed that Germany collect the necessary taxation revenue to make reparation payments to a reparation agent, who would then transfer the money to the allies, in their own currencies, within the limits of the German balance of international payments. If such transfers were not possible, the accumulating sums were to be held in Germany until they could be disbursed. This would avoid the burden of the allies having to convert Deutsche marks into British pounds and French francs. The allies might also take deliveries-in-kind such as German coal, coke, dyestuffs, fertilizer, machinery, wood, and other products, as stipulated by the Versailles Treaty. France and Belgium agreed to withdraw their troops from the Ruhr within a year.

An infusion of U.S. capital would be necessary to revive the German economy and give the Dawes plan a chance to succeed, albeit as a short-term stimulant. This was accomplished by lowering the discount rate from 4.5 percent to 3 percent through the New York Reserve Bank, convincing Wall Street colossus J.P. Morgan and company to issue a $110 million loan, and promoting the loan subscriptions through an intense publicity campaign by business and political leaders. In response, Americans purchased the loan subscriptions for the entire $110 million in 15 minutes, a frenzied flow of capital to Germany that soon became large enough to concern the same policymakers who had encouraged the investments in the first place.

The boom market for German bonds on Wall Street would eventually total $2.5 billion, which Germany used to make some reparation payments and which the former allies used to make some loan payments to Washington, in a triangle of payments that was never intended by those who devised and supported the Dawes plan. Nor did the credit infusion solve the German debt problem, such as determining the schedule of repayment or the rate of interest. Yet the Dawes plan brought a temporary end to German financial woes and some stability to European currency markets and bilateral trade, providing a "breathing space" as Keynes wrote.[9] If the plan failed to produce a long-term solution, Germany deserved blame for not achieving a balanced budget or a stable currency, as recommended by the report. Had the republic done so, it would have attracted more foreign capital to help make reparation payments. France, by comparison, responded to its war debts by cutting expenditures and raising taxes, reaching a surplus by 1925, not counting the "extraordinary" expenses it kept separate from "ordinary" expenditures. England also reduced its debts.

Coolidge was pessimistic that the former combatants would ever meet their obligations. "A lot of people think the war is over," he told Dwight Morrow. "The war ain't over till the debt is paid."[10]

* * *

The $250,000 that Moscow owed Washington was by far the smallest debt of the main combatants, and the least likely to get paid. This debt, incurred by the Provisional Government of Russia in 1917, after the overthrow of Tsar Nicholas II and before the Bolshevist revolution, had been repudiated by the Soviets in 1918 as an obligation of one capitalist government to another, despite a longstanding international legal principle that a government succeeding power assumes all the obligations of its predecessor.

Nonetheless, Coolidge came under pressure during the early months of 1924 to restore diplomatic ties to the Soviet Union, particularly after England granted official recognition without any commitments from the regime on debt repayments. The most vocal proponents of recognition were legislators from out west, representing farmers who wanted to sell wheat and other crops to the communist regime. Other proponents insisted that the Soviet Government and the Communist International were separate entities and that the former bore no responsibility for the propaganda and subversive activities of the latter. On January 21, Secretary Hughes responded by making available to the Senate Committee on Foreign Relations a vast amount of material showing Soviet-directed propaganda disseminated in the United States and aimed at overthrowing the institutions of the United States. Later that day the world learned that Soviet leader Vladimir Lenin had died of a massive stroke at age 53.

Coolidge, at a press conference the following day, made a short statement, withholding any criticism, as appropriate. He ended with a well-worded message on the ruthless figure who had outlawed law with a single decree in November 1917 and invented the modern concentration camp: "Let us hope that the work he did, though it is difficult to see just how it did, worked for the benefit of Russia and for the betterment of civilization."[11]

The administration continued to insist on three requisites for any change in the 1917 policy of nonrecognition: first, that U.S. citizens deprived of their personal property through confiscatory decrees must be compensated; second, that the regime agree to recognize the national debts of the previous government; third, that it cease anti–U.S. propaganda. When Moscow indicated a willingness to negotiate, Secretary Hughes replied that the demands were nonnegotiable and continued the policy of nonrecognition even as visa travel and trade increased between the two nations, led by Du Pont, Ford, General Electric, and Standard Oil.

Coolidge, for his part, was more philosophical than antagonistic toward the regime:

> Communism will fail because what it attempts is against human nature. No man will provide me with food and other necessities of life unless he is a gainer by it in some way.[12]

* * *

The protectionist policies of the United States brought criticism from Europe and other sources as unsuitable for a creditor nation and a drag on global economic recovery and debt repayment. To Coolidge and most Republicans, the Fordney-McCumber Tariff Act of 1922 had been a laudable achievement, reducing the number of commodities on the free list, increasing rates on farm products, empowering the president to raise or lower rates as much as 50 percent on goods that foreign competitors were found to produce at lower costs due to subsidies or cheap labor, and authorizing the Tariff Commission to recommend rate adjustments, pending presidential approval. The intent had been to remove politics and special interests from tariff-making in favor of experts and a scientific process, but the ability to determine differences in production costs between domestic and foreign manufacturers had proved impossible, and pressures from special interests had swayed many decisions. The result had been to reverse the low tariff of the Wilson years and restore rates to those prevalent under McKinley, Roosevelt, and Taft.

To Coolidge, who as a boy in the mid–1880s had seen low rates hurt Vermont sheep growers and mill workers, this was primarily a domestic issue, falling under the broad Republican policy of protecting free labor, beginning with the movement against slavery in the 1850s and continuing with restrictions on immigrants and duties on imports derived from cheap foreign labor. He did not perceive high rates as unsuitable for a creditor nation or an impediment to trade.[13] U.S. imports were increasing at an annual average of more than $350 million, mostly led by demand for sugar, coffee, rubber, and silk from developing countries, rather than European goods. U.S. exports were increasing as well, resulting in a record $757 million surplus of exports over imports in fiscal year 1924. This balance-of-trade surplus had developed since the 1870s and reflected self-sufficiency in the U.S. economy and international trade patterns across most manufacturing and agricultural sectors, as much as it did high tariff rates. Overall, he agreed to raise the rates on 33 items and reduce them on five: mill feeds, live quail, paint brush handles, cresylic acid, and phenol.

Chapter Five

"The most conservative country"

"The only hope of the party is in Coolidge," Chief Justice Taft wrote as the president took control of the party apparatus in the spring of 1924, selecting Cleveland for the convention site, accepting the resignation of chairman John T. Adams, and replacing him with William Butler, who applied business management tactics, discipline, strict accounting, and mass marketing to promote the president.[1] Most political observers agreed that Coolidge, with his reputation for personal integrity, would allow the party to move past the oil scandals and head toward November with confidence, even though few used the term Coolidge Republicans, like the Blaine Republicans and Roosevelt Republicans of yesteryear.

"With all this loyalty to Coolidge, there was a curious lack of enthusiasm for him," wrote Theodore Roosevelt, Jr., running for governor of New York in his first political campaign. "They accepted him as logical, inevitable; a good man, but one whom they did not particularly warm to."[2]

The 18th Republican National Convention opened on June 10 without bands or ballyhoos or many of the old guard senators who had dominated events four years earlier. Murray Crane of Massachusetts and Boies Penrose of Pennsylvania had died. Medill McCormick of Illinois had lost in the primaries. Hiram Johnson and William Borah had stayed home. Chauncey E. Depew of New York, who had attended every convention since 1860, remained home at age 90, suffering from the grip. Henry Cabot Lodge, the Boston Brahmin, the frail, thin, gray-haired "scholar-in-politics" who had written a dozen books, who had been convention chairman in 1900 and 1920 and chairman of the committee on resolutions in 1916, who had attended every convention for the past 40 years except in 1912, learned he would be merely an at-large delegate this time. Perhaps he should have seen it coming. For years he had been losing influence to intrastate rivals Crane, Butler, and Coolidge, who differed with him temperamentally as much as politically. In 1920, he had angered them by reneging on an offer to nominate Coolidge at Chicago and subsequently giving the nod to Harding when party leaders met at the Blackstone Hotel to discuss events during a pivotal moment, with the nomination up for grabs. Still—despite all that—despite his votes against the administration on the bonus, postal salaries, immigration, and the World Court—Lodge was surprised by his fallen status. "But they can't do that to me!" he allegedly cried out.[3]

The convention promised to be a dull affair as compared with 1920, much less the Republican convention of 1912 when Roosevelt and followers bolted from the party, or the Democratic convention of 1912 when Wilson snared the nomination despite losing the delegate vote to Champ Clark. In Cleveland, Lodge appeared on the first morning, smiling, taking his seat in the front row of the Massachusetts delegation, almost hidden under the black platform. "Without blinking an eye, or moistening his lips, he stared politely before him and gave his foes no sign of his pain at the performances," wrote an observer.[4] When reporters inquired as to the political implications of his demise, he replied calmly, "There is no fight."[5] Old guard remnants scattered about the new 13,000-seat auditorium, some in the balconies, some in their delegations. Many grumbled of having been reduced to distributing tickets and the like.

All sorts of delegates complained about Cleveland, proudly hosting its first major political convention, having surpassed Cincinnati as the largest city in Ohio, with some 796,000 residents. In the mid–19th century, Cincinnati had been the "Queen City of the West" and more vital than Chicago and St. Louis, much less Cleveland, a fledgling city at the time; but geography had proved to be destiny. Cleveland, located at the terminus of the best lowland route from Lake Erie to the Pittsburgh coal fields and blessed by an easy grade for rail lines running east to west, with more diverse industries and faster immigration growth than its intrastate rival, had become the fifth largest city in the country. None of this mattered to delegates as a hard cold rain forced them to don overcoats during the first day of the convention, and the main attractions were the last-place Indians baseball team, a vaudeville show, the Home Town Glee Club, and a small theater district featuring *The Demi-Virgin* and *So This Is London!* Many downtown buildings were covered by soot from the Cuyahoga Valley, where blast furnaces poured out some 2,000 tons of iron per year. Among the smoke-blackened structures near the convention stood one with a plaque that read: "1858—Old Courthouse. 1924—Same Old Courthouse." If that were not enough, additional federal, state, and municipal authorities were on duty to enforce prohibition. A drug store on Superior Avenue advertised "Coolidge highballs" for 25 cents, consisting of ice, pineapple juice, grape juice, and an egg.

"The city is opening up the churches now and having services so the delegates and visitors can go and hear some singing or excitement of some kind," quipped Will Rogers, humorist and Coolidge Democrat, in his syndicated column.[6]

Northampton shoemaker Jim Lucey arrived by train, his first vacation in 12 years after working all night to finish his orders. A stocky, thick-haired, mustached man in his late 60s, with blue eyes and iron-rimmed spectacles, the Irish shoemaker had apprenticed at 15, married at 21, and emigrated from County Kerry at 23, following his brother to western Massachusetts. By working six days a week, 14 hours a day, and earning about $4 a day, he could support his wife and eight children, and live happily at that. By working alone he knew every shoe was done properly, hand sewn in places where machine stitching caused stiffness, and made with right and left heels, which, though more expensive than same-heeled shoes, were necessary for a proper fit. He was a shoemaker, not a cobbler, he corrected the head of the Smith English Department one evening.[7] Former Northampton residents living as distant as Philadelphia and Detroit still sent in orders, including Coolidge, whom he had known since the fall of 1893 when the then college sophomore came into his basement shop at 18 Gothic Street with a torn shoe, and began to visit whenever he went to town, talking history and politics with the well-read immigrant. "I always had an idea he was lonely," Lucey relates; he never mentioned fraternities, sports, drinking, or women, other than to praise his stepmother for pushing him to do well scholastically; he seemed about average in intelligence but wise beyond his years. The shoemaker had long predicted that Coolidge would rise to prominence, even as local politicians and other residents thought he had peaked at various points along his ascendancy.[8]

No sooner had Lucey arrived at the convention, weary from travel, than a newspaperman approached him to hear about his famous customer. Lucey said Coolidge wore only the best shoes—a sure sign of character.[9]

The first day featured speeches, platform debates, and roll calls, as delegates strolled in and out, and Butler, Stearns, and Slemp sat calmly on the stage in black morning clothes, having arranged, nay controlled, the proceedings like no convention in history. The keynote speech fell to former Cleveland mayor Theodore E. Burton, who demanded a Republican Congress with members "tried and true who will stand united," as men stood in the galleries, shouting, "Down with Lodge!" and "Put Lodge out!"[10] The other speakers included Addison G. Proctor, the last survivor from the Republican convention of 1860, who left his family in Massachusetts in 1857, at age 19, to take part in the struggle to make Kansas a free state, and who became the youngest delegate at the fabled wigwam in Chicago three years later. Now, 64 years later, he described how the main issue before the party in 1860 had been to save the western territories from slavery and how the delegates had selected a former one-term congressman from Illinois after Cameron, Chase, Seward, and other luminaries failed to secure the nomination.

"In the nomination of Lincoln it seems to me we builded better than we knew," he deadpanned to applause.[11]

The platform was simple: economy, tax reduction, high tariffs, lower freight rates, cooperative marketing for farmers, an amendment against child labor, honest government. As to the resurgent Ku Klux Klan, which boasted some three million members and influenced gubernatorial races in Alabama, California, Georgia, and Oregon in 1922, while recruiting heavily in the Middle West in response to postwar black migration, Coolidge reportedly wrote the following plank: "The Republican Party reaffirms its undying devotion to the Constitution and to the guarantees of civil, political, and religious liberty therein contained."[12]

In what was essentially the first modern political convention, with 20 radio stations broadcasting the proceedings from New York to Kansas City and 100 Western Union operators in the basement, working 12-hour shifts and typing some 700,000 words a day, the news was minimal. At past conventions reporters had loitered in hotel lobbies and bars at all hours, talking politics and politicians, but, with little to discuss and less to drink this time, they were more interested in arranging tee-times at local courses. Many had written their stories in advance, knowing that Coolidge would win on the first ballot and that his managers would stamp out any controversy. "He could have been nominated by postcard," wrote Will Rogers.[13] Photographs were transmitted by wire for the first time in history, while flashlight originals were flown daily to New York, dropped by parachute near the Statue of Liberty, and delivered by motorboat to a newspaperman waiting ashore.

The ballots were cast and Coolidge received 1,065 out of 1,109 votes as he listened to the radio amplifiers temporarily installed in the White House, courtesy of the C. and P. Telephone Company. In Vermont, his father listened by radio, wearing a suit and tie, his eyes watering up with pride.[14] Invited to Cleveland as an honorary guest, he had sent the following message: "Telegram received. Thanks. I cannot see my way clear to go to the convention."[15] He had been late planting potatoes.

Then came choosing a vice presidential candidate with Coolidge instructing party managers to secure a moderate to conservative nominee but otherwise abstaining from the process, telling Dwight Morrow the last convention made a pretty good selection on its own and so would this one.[16] As proceedings began, he wandered in and out of the State Dining Room, where Grace and Dr. Boone listened by radio, before leaving to take a nap. Moments later Edward Clark arrived with news that the convention had chosen Governor Lowden. "I must confer with the President immediately," he said, leaving Grace to perform the unenviable task. Coolidge appeared, half asleep, slumping into a large chair and listening to the news without response. Gently prodded by his secretary, he dictated a short message to Lowden and returned to bed, but no sooner had Clark sent the telegram than Lowden turned down the nomination, the first such declination since 1844, when the Democratic convention chose Senator Silas Wright of New York to run with James K. Polk. This led delegates to tap Charles Dawes, the slim, gray-eyed banker and former budget director who had served on the reparations committee earlier in the year. Again Clark rushed to the west wing. "Asleep," said Grace, pointing to the door, but hearing the news, she reluctantly awakened the president. Coolidge returned, listless and drowsy, and lit a cigar as Clark told him about Dawes. Again he had no response.

John Calvin Coolidge, father of the 30th president of the United States and a longtime office holder in state and local Vermont politics. Date unknown (Bain News Service Collection, Library of Congress).

"Mr. President," said Clark, "you now have to send General Dawes a message of congratulations."

"Send the same message I sent Lowden."[17]

The telegram went out and the convention ended after three days, the shortest since 1904.

* * *

That weekend Coolidge took several guests on a cruise aboard the *Mayflower*, the 10-bedroom, white presidential yacht that came complete with a Navy crew, a band, a physician, a chaplain, a radio set, and daily newspaper deliveries from a hydroplane. The weather was most pleasant with temperatures in the low 80s and a light breeze as they left the Navy Yard in Southeast Washington on Saturday morning and steamed down the Potomac, observing the lush banks and the sun glittering off the water. The president, in a plain yachting cap and white duck pants, had become enamored of his yacht, watching the crewmen, walking the deck, talking to 70-year-old pilot William E. Luckett, who knew the river like no one else, having hiked and fished along its banks as a boy and navigated its waters for half a century from Georgetown to Norfolk. "He could smell his way up and down the Potomac," relates Dr. Boone, who had seen him motor through the heavy fogs of Pamunkey and Occoquan on many occasions.[18] Captain Luckett had taken every president since Roosevelt on the river, but none so often as Coolidge, who seemed quiet but content that morning, passing the once-vibrant port of Alexandria, halting for the customary all-hands salute at Mount Vernon, and continuing toward the Chesapeake Bay.

Yet even at this moment of triumph the nominee was not completely at ease, summoning Dr. Boone to report immediately on Sunday morning and complaining that the newspapers were an hour late.[19] Notwithstanding the fine weather and happy circumstances of the cruise, he was agitated without his papers—without something to occupy his mind.

Back at work Monday, Coolidge found Slemp waiting with a letter of resignation over tensions with Butler in Cleveland. The president refused to accept and remained behind closed doors with him for nearly two hours, convincing him to stay through the election, before turning to a pile of congratulatory letters and telegrams. Later that week his sons arrived on summer break. John had been accepted at Amherst College for the fall term. Calvin, now tallest in the family, had one more year at Mercersburg. They were to stay a few weeks before taking civilian military training in Massachusetts, for the president did not want them idle in Washington all summer under media scrutiny.

Again Coolidge invited his father to visit, telling him about a new daily train from Montreal that stopped at White River Junction:

> If you will let me know when you can come, I will arrange a reservation for you, and you would find the ticket and reservation waiting for you at the White River Junction ticket office. The boys have come home, and I am sure we should think it very pleasant to have you here on the Fourth of July.[20]

Colonel Coolidge had not been to Washington since the inauguration in 1921, but he declined the offer, for he disliked being away more than a night at a time, even though tourists had become such a distraction that he had to rise at four each morning to do his chores before they arrived in motorcars and horse carriages, eager to see the oath room, the family Bible, and the famous kerosene lamp he bought in Boston in 1867 at age 22. The Colonel would invite them inside and lead them around in his deliberate way, letting them hold the pen his son used to sign the oath and showing them the lamp. Still aggravated by a newspaper article on how the lamp looked the morning his son took the oath, he told one visitor, "It's old enough, but it wasn't greasy, that morning or any morning."[21]

Among the visitors that summer was Justice Hoehling from the District of Columbia, who had administered the secret second oath to the president. As Colonel Coolidge proudly showed him the historic sitting room, Hoehling said nothing of the second oath.

Another visitor inquired, "How did you know you could administer the presidential oath to your son?"

"I didn't know that I couldn't," he replied.[22]

With reporters, the Colonel spoke of bygone days when people made their clothes by shearing their sheep, combing and carding the wool, wheeling it, spinning it, and weaving it. For shoes they cut strips of leather for an itinerant shoemaker, who came around annually to take their measurements and make their boots while staying in their homes. When someone took ill, neighbors took turns sitting up all night with that person until he or she improved. While reluctant to discuss politics, girls in knickers, prohibition, and other changes since his heyday, he was appalled by those who borrowed money or mortgaged their homes to buy an automobile. Personally he traveled by foot or horse carriage, though he could afford a car.[23]

* * *

On Monday evening, June 30, the president went to Memorial Continental Hall to address the semiannual meeting of the Business Organization of the Government, with his cabinet and more than 2,000 managers, budget officers, clerks, and disbursement officers in attendance. He began by stressing the need to avoid any unnecessary taxation:

> A government which lays taxes on the people not required by urgent public necessity and sound public policy is not a protector of liberty, but an instrument of tyranny. It condemns the citizen to servitude. One of the first signs of the breaking down of free government is a disregard by the taxing power of the right of the people to their own property. It makes little difference whether such a condition is brought about through the will of a dictator, through the power of a military force, or through the pressure of an organized minority. The result is the same. Unless the people can enjoy that reasonable security in the possession of their property, which is guaranteed by the Constitution, against unreasonable taxation, freedom is at an end.

The latest numbers were disturbing. In the fiscal year ending that evening, expenditures had declined to slightly above $3 billion, excluding debt reduction and postal expenditures, the lowest amount since before the war and barely above the goal he set during his first days in office. The national debt had been pared-down more than $1 billion to $21.2 billion, saving some $120 million in interest payments. In the fiscal year ahead, however, the addition of $132 million in annual bonus payments had reduced the estimated surplus to $25 million. He called on attendees to find another $83 million in spending cuts. There were too many government publications and travel orders. He also warned them not to share their budget estimates with Congress in advance. The budget act of 1921 stipulated that the executive branch was to send the estimates to Congress all together in a single document. "I herewith serve notice again, as chief executive, that I propose to protect the integrity of my budget," he stated.

In concluding his remarks, he used language familiar to all by now, yet distinctive enough to grab headlines in newspapers the next morning: "I am for economy. After that I am for more economy. At this time and under present conditions that is my conception of serving all the people."[24]

* * *

Three days later Dr. Boone arrived for a tennis match with the Coolidge boys and learned Calvin did not feel well enough to play. Entering the Lincoln Bedroom, Boone saw him in bed, felt his warm forehead, took out a thermometer, and found he had a 102 degree fever, not a cold, as the family thought. Further examination showed no signs of inflammation in his throat or appendix, but then Boone discovered enlarged glands in the groin area. He suspected an infection.

"Yup," replied Calvin, he had a blister on the big toe of his right foot from playing tennis without socks a few days earlier; he had been in a hurry, he said.

It was a dark blister, about the size of a thumbnail. Boone noticed faint red streaks on his leg and "knew we were in trouble." After sending a culture to the Naval Medical School laboratory for priority handling, Boone informed the president and first lady, who had been through a health scare with Calvin in 1913 when he caught pneumonia and empyema—a deposit of pus that involved a risky surgical procedure and a slow recovery with a tube stuck in his back.[25]

That evening Calvin had a restless sleep, his fever worsening. Friday morning, July 4, test results revealed evidence of staphylococcus aureus organisms, for which, like other infections, no antibiotics were available. The president delivered a speech to educators but canceled a weekend river cruise and instructed Edward Clark to inform reporters of the illness. As

Calvin became more lethargic, White House physicians consulted experts in Washington, Baltimore, and Philadelphia, hoping a new treatment or procedure might emerge. The president took some lettuce and, crawling on his hands and knees in the garden, captured a rabbit to show his ailing son, who could barely manage a smile.

"Calvin is very sick so this is not a happy day for me," Coolidge wrote his father that afternoon, his 52nd birthday.[26]

The following afternoon Calvin was taken to Walter Reed Hospital by ambulance and began to drift into periods of unconsciousness and hallucination as physicians vainly administered an autogenous vaccine and tried to relieve his pain. Dr. John B. Deaver of Philadelphia examined the patient by making an incision over his left tibia, chiseling away some bone, and confirming the presence of staphylococcus aureus in the cultures. The president and first lady stayed by Calvin, stunned by his sudden illness.

As Calvin slipped into delirium on Monday, July 7, he seemed to be on a horse leading a cavalry charge in battle. "Come on, come on, help, help!" he shouted as a thunderstorm raged outside. For a while he thought he was sitting backwards on his horse and asked to be turned around. Finally he relented, "We surrender! We surrender!" Dr. Boone said, "Never surrender, Calvin." To which he replied, "Yes," and lost consciousness.[27] The president stood tense, almost motionless, watching the doctor use his stethoscope, before asking permission to listen to the failing heart sounds. Then he sat beside his 16-year-old son, clasping his hand, stroking his forehead and sandy hair, until he was gone.[28]

The first radio bulletins went out almost immediately. Colonel Coolidge heard a report around 10:00 p.m., and, hoping it might not be true, walked to the store and awakened the proprietor to find out by telephone whether neighbors with radio sets had heard the news in the same way. When the sad tidings were confirmed, he returned home to look up details connected with the family lot in the village cemetery.[29]

The remains of Calvin were placed in a rose-bedecked coffin and carried to the East Room at the White House the following day. Dr. Boone was leaving the manse that evening when he saw the president slip downstairs in a dressing gown and stand beside his son, stroking his head in tender caress.[30]

Funeral services were held there with sun streaming through the tall windows as the president sat beside Grace and John, arms linked together, showing no outward emotion. They went by train to Northampton, stopping at their home of 18 years, the narrow frame dwelling at 21 Massasoit Street, painted white with a green screen door, green blinds, and green lattice below the front porch, leading to a tight entrance hall, a parlor, a dining room, a kitchen, a pantry, three bedrooms, and one bathroom. Here

Calvin had been born and raised in a pleasant neighborhood with turn-of-the-century gabled houses set close together, delivering newspapers, raking leaves, playing, and attending local schools. Now housekeeper Alice Reckahn lived there with Mrs. Lemira Goodhue, who moved in after her husband died in 1923, at the behest of her daughter. Services were held at Edwards Congregationalist Church, a vine-covered brick structure on Main Street. From there the family took the train to Vermont, switching to automobiles at Ludlow and traveling north by northwest for 12 miles, past lakes and dark wooded hillsides, to the gravel road to Plymouth Notch, so steep that cars were set 100 feet apart and sent up one by one in low gear. At the top they turned down a dirt road to the small hillside cemetery where the body was laid to rest under blue skies. The president barely moved during the ceremony, standing beside his wife and father, who swallowed hard once and pressed his lips tight together. Grace looked straight at the pastor. "As we stood beside the grave, the sun was shining, throwing long, slanting shadows and the birds were singing their sleepy songs," she later wrote. "I came away with a peace which passeth understanding, comforted and full of courage."[31]

At the house, Coolidge said his son had been weakened by a recent growth spurt, pointing to a series of height marks drawn on the door jam of the front porch each summer that showed Calvin had been five inches shorter than John in 1922 and only two inches shorter in 1923. Then he measured John and, trembling slightly, wrote above it a mark labeled, "C.C. if alive."[32]

In Washington the next morning Coolidge looked drawn but worked a normal schedule, holding a cabinet meeting and reading documents that had piled up on his desk. Stoic though he was in his bereavement, he was distraught and guilt-ridden:

> We do not know what might have happened to him under other circumstances, but if I had not been President he would not have raised a blister on his toe, which resulted in blood poisoning, playing lawn tennis in the South Grounds.
>
> In his suffering he was asking me to make him well. I could not.
>
> When he went the power and glory of the Presidency went with him.[33]

In ordering a gravestone for his son, he purchased a second stone for himself and had a blank space left for his own death.

Colonel Coolidge stayed a fortnight in Washington after the funeral, sitting in the executive office each morning, responding to queries from reporters with a simple "yes" or "no," and seldom venturing outside as daytime temperatures hovered at about 90 degrees. To escape the city heat, they took a weekend cruise aboard the *Mayflower*, father and son sitting on deck, observing the broad sweep of the river and discussing the price of sheep back home. The elder Coolidge had been in the sheep business since the Civil War when wool brought in $1000 a pound because of the loss of southern cotton and the demand for wool uniforms for the northern troops. Nowadays he made about $50 a year raising sheep, and his son could not understand why farmers and small property owners in Virginia, still recovering from the Civil War in many respects, neglected the sheep business.[34] On the first night of the voyage, Colonel Coolidge found spread on his bed a tuxedo, a dress shirt, cuff links and studs, and a black bow tie, provided by his son for dinner. With assistance from Dr. Boone, he put on the unfamiliar attire and strode up to the deck without so much as a glance in the mirror. The president took delight in his handsome, trim appearance, but never said a word about it as they stood on deck, admiring the Potomac at sunset.[35]

"They are just alike, only the old gentleman is more so," said a Secret Service man.[36] Everyone regretted his return to Vermont, but he was glad to get home. It was haying time.

Reporter John T. Lambert called at the White House a short time later to offer condolences. "I am sorry," he said. "Calvin was a good boy."

The president looked away, his eyes brimming with tears. "You know, I sit here thinking of it, and I just can't believe it has happened," he said. "I just can't believe it has happened."

When he looked out the window, he said, he could still see his boy playing tennis.[37]

Grace turned his bedroom into a small shrine with fresh flowers beside the bed and pictures of him on the wall. One day she was in there with friends, knitting and chatting, when she received a letter with a snapshot of young Calvin on his bicycle in Northampton. Much to their surprise, she hastily picked up a tack, removed her shoe, and used its high heel to hang the photograph on the wall.[38]

* * *

The presidential campaign of 1924 featured the first three-way contest since 1912, with a breakaway Republican leading the third party again. Democrats, in a tumultuous convention, fraught with tension over the Klan and sectional differences, nominated former West Virginia congressman and Wall Street lawyer John W. Davis, after 17 days and 102 ballots failed to break a deadlock between two favorites in a party divided between its emerging northern urban element and its conservative southern element. The third party candidate was none other than La Follette. Most pundits gave the edge to the majority Republican Party. The last Democratic candidate to win with a majority of the popular vote had been

Pierce in 1852 with 51 percent. The rest, including Cleveland and Wilson, had been elected by mere pluralities.

The states almost certain to back Coolidge tallied 135 electoral votes, including all of New England, Illinois, Michigan, Oregon, Pennsylvania, and Utah. The solid south behind Davis tallied 147 votes, including Alabama, Arkansas, Florida, Georgia, Louisiana, Mississippi, North Carolina, South Carolina, Texas, and Virginia, which had voted Democratic in every election since 1880. The only state conceded to La Follette was Wisconsin with 13 votes. This left 23 competitive states with a total of 238 votes to decide the election. In the Middle Western states of Indiana, Iowa, Kansas, Minnesota, Missouri, Nebraska, North Dakota, and South Dakota, representing 106 votes, La Follette had a chance to pick up votes or hurt Coolidge enough to help Davis. In populous Maryland, New Jersey, and New York, representing 67 votes, Coolidge was favored to win, but all three states had Democratic governors.

Coolidge and Davis were fiscal conservatives within their respective parties and the two platforms were similar on the issues—excepting the tariff and the surtax—but the La Follette progressives were far more radical than the Roosevelt progressives of 1912. They did not represent the sort of factional bitterness that doomed Republican candidates in the past, such as Blaine in 1884 and Taft in 1912, nor the single-issue discontent that drove most third parties in history, such as the Know-Nothings of the 1850s and the Greenbacks of the 1870s. They were farmers, union members, veterans, socialists, and radicals who had been active in labor and agrarian parties since the war, and thought, like members of the Labor Party in England, the Radical Socialists in France, the Social Democratic Party in Germany, and the Fascisti in Italy, that vocationalism was the future basis of politics.

"There were no corrupt bosses, no professional ward politicians, only simple people, serious and rather boring," wrote one observer as this somber crowd convened in Cleveland and endorsed La Follette as an independent candidate without bothering to form a third party.[39] The platform called for nationalization of railroads, farm aid, strong labor laws, public ownership of water power, high surtaxes, a ban on monopolies, public construction of a St. Lawrence seaway, a child labor amendment to the Constitution, the direct election of the president, the election of judges, the right of Congress to overrule Supreme Court decisions, a popular referendum before Congress could declare war, and the abolition of conscription.

The progressives had faint prospects to win because election laws kept La Follette off the ballot in several states and the legislative successes of the bipartisan farm bloc since 1921 negated the need for a third party to represent agricultural interests, as in the late 19th century. The only hope was to prevent Republicans or Democrats from securing a majority in the Electoral College and thus throw the election into the House of Representatives, where a hodgepodge progressive coalition might prevail.

"The issue will be Coolidge versus La Follette, and Davis will fade away," said Butler.[40]

Coolidge took exception to the widespread notion that La Follette and his followers would carry the progressive banner. "As a matter of fact all the political parties are progressive," he told reporters. "I can't conceive of a party lasting for any length of time that wasn't progressive, or of leadership being effective that wasn't progressive."[41]

The campaign began, in a way, on August 11, with Coolidge recording on the South Lawn of the White House a message on fiscal rectitude, using the latest sound-on-film technology as the first president to appear on sound film. He looked careworn, speaking in a monotone for several minutes before removing his spectacles and walking away from the camera without a parting line.

The following week he went to Vermont with his secretary, stenographer, physician, two clerks, and 18 bodyguards, who scattered about in hotels, cabins, and tents, happy to escape a heat wave that softened the asphalt and wilted trees along Pennsylvania Avenue, prompted hundreds of Washingtonians to sleep in parks or public beaches along the Potomac, and forced the early closure of the temporary, low-ceilinged, wartime government buildings on and around the Mall three days in a row. "They say it is a good plan for a person to go back as often as they can into the atmosphere in which they were born and brought up," Coolidge told reporters on a brisk 60-degree day in Plymouth Notch, 1400 feet above sea level. "I always get refreshed by coming up here. Naturally I feel rested and revived."[42] He set up office in the vaulted room above the store, with four desks made from plain boards resting on trusses, a wall clock, two telephones, and four kerosene lanterns hung from the ceiling. This is not to suggest he worked at night; he usually left at noon, slipping out the back to avoid tourists, past the kerosene barrels, leaving his secretary and stenographer to man the telephones during the afternoon while he sat on his veranda, listening to the clack-clack of mowing machines and looking toward the hills.

The president was about to retire on the evening of August 22 when Slemp delivered news that Davis, in his first address of the campaign, denounced the Klan and challenged Coolidge to do so. For Davis, having been endorsed by the Klan, this was a necessary maneuver to appeal to doubtful states in the northeast. Slemp discussed the matter with Coolidge and told reporters that the president had nothing to say in reply.[43] Coolidge had recently praised the many contributions of black citizens and promised to safeguard their constitutional safeguards in a commencement address at Howard University; publicly rebuked a New York Republican for suggesting he, as president and party leader, should use his influence to prevent the nomination of Charles D. Roberts, a black dentist, as the Republican candidate from the Twenty-First District of New York; and wired a laudatory message to the annual convention of the National Negro Business League. Thus he saw no need to reiterate his position.

The following day brought newspaper headlines and hundreds of calls and telegrams urging him to speak out. Again he met with Slemp, who then told reporters the president would respond in time, perhaps in a speech to the Holy Name Society in September.[44] As letters and telegrams poured into Washington and Vermont, some called for a forceful anti-Klan statement, others encouraged him to ignore the Democratic bait. "SILENCE IS GOLDEN INSOFAR AS THE SOUTH IS CONCERNED," wrote an admirer in Natchez, Mississippi.[45]

Charles Dawes arrived from making an anti-Klan speech in Maine to discuss campaign tactics as John Coolidge ate silently at the kitchen table. When the elder Coolidge went back outside to work, reporters surrounded him and inquired whether the Klan had been mentioned inside.

"My hearing ain't as good as it used to be," he deadpanned.[46]

All the while tourists arrived by the hundreds daily, parking their vehicles along the road and walking up to the Secret Service "dead line" in front of the Coolidge home. Roosevelt, Taft, and Wilson had selected summer vacation sites surrounded by grounds and easily protected, but anyone could get within 100 yards of the Coolidge place beside the road. Normally John Coolidge would have invited them inside and recorded their names in a series of notebooks he kept by the door—he had received an astonishing 26,732 visitors during the previous 12 months—but the Secret Service put his home off limits to strangers while his son was there. Still, tourists came in droves from all over the country, bringing an economic boom to the village. Ruth Aldrich, daughter of the village cheesemaker, opened the "Top of the Notch Tea Room and Gift Shop" across from the store and made enough money in three days to buy a new motorcar. Storekeeper and post mistress Florence Cilley, who usually made about $50 annually selling stamps at the post office, made $1,500 that summer, mostly from postcard buyers.[47] Others set up souvenir and soft drink stands. Henry Ford, Thomas Edison, and Harvey Firestone came to endorse the president and discuss campaign issues, sitting outside, admiring the scenery, as photographers snapped away with their tripod cameras. Coolidge gave Ford an old maple sap bucket that belonged to his ancestors, and which housekeeper Aurora Pierce had scrubbed with all her might, still smarting from the newspaper story that described the lamp used in the midnight inaugural as greasy.

"The United States is lucky to have Calvin Coolidge," Edison declared.[48]

Back in Washington, Coolidge, one of 13 "oudens" in the Amherst class of 1895, learned his son had made a fraternity, Phi Gamma Delta, no less, and responded with strict guidance:

> I have already indicated that I want you to stay in Amherst and study, and not be running to Northampton. If anybody invites you to go out evenings or anything of that kind, you will tell them that it is all you can do to take care of your work at college. You are going to be there four years, and there will be time enough to do visiting after this first year.[49]

As bodyguard Edmund Starling came to the White House one morning he saw a small boy standing at the fence and asked why he was up so early.

"I thought I might see the President," he said. "I heard that he gets up early and takes a walk. I wanted to tell him how sorry I am that his little boy died."

"Come with me," Starling replied. "I'll take you to the President."

They walked on to the grounds and waited momentarily until Coolidge appeared. The boy, overwhelmed with awe, could barely speak, leaving Starling to deliver his message.

Coolidge had trouble controlling his emotions. Afterward he told Starling: "Colonel, whenever a boy wants to see me always bring him in. Never turn one away or make him wait."[50]

* * *

As the presidential campaign began in September, the *Washington Post* ran an editorial titled "Coolidge or Chaos" on the specter of a deadlocked election.[51] Written by new editor George Harvey, a Vermont native and Coolidge supporter, the piece reverberated in newspapers across the country and helped to check the third candidate movement as "Coolidge or Chaos" became the conservative mantra everywhere.

Amid widespread discussion of the Klan issue, Coolidge felt pressure to respond. "They put the Klan in politics; now they want me to take it out," he told Dwight Morrow.[52] Hoping to end the matter once and for all, he had Slemp release to the public a letter to a newspaper editor with the following passage: "Concerning the Ku Klux Klan, the President has repeatedly stated that he is not a member of the order and is not in sympathy with its aims and purposes."[53] Two weeks later, Sunday, September 21, he addressed 100,000 members of the Holy Name Society on the grounds near the Washington Monument, in a plea for religion and tolerance, widely seen as a backhanded criticism of the Klan:

> Something in all human beings makes them want to do the right thing. Not that this desire always prevails; oftentimes it is overcome and they turn towards evil. But some power is constantly calling them back. Ever there comes a resistance to wrongdoing. When bad conditions begin to accumulate, when forces of darkness become prevalent, always they are doomed to fail as the better angels of our nature are roused to resistance.[54]

Coolidge declined to take a speaking tour, despite pressure to appear before the voters like his two opponents. Instead he released a book of his speeches titled *The Price of Freedom* and used radio to reach vast audiences that autumn, with the party securing airtime at $5,000 per hour for national broadcasts. To improve his use of the new medium—the most important change to campaigning since the extension of the railroad in the 1860s—he received special training in "microphone manners" from a local broadcaster.[55] "I am fortunate that I came in with the radio," he told Senator James E. Watson of Indiana. "I can't make an engaging, rousing, or oratorical speech to a crowd as you can, and so all I can do is stand up and talk to them in a matter-of-fact way about the issues of the campaign; but I have a good radio voice, and now I can get my messages across to them without acquainting them with my lack of oratorical ability or without making any rhetorical display in their presence."[56] As the leaves began to drop that autumn, the summertime static went away and radio listeners had clear reception throughout the country.

At the unveiling of a statue of Francis Asbury, the first American bishop of the Methodist Episcopal Church, in mid–October, Coolidge spoke of his religious convictions:

> Our government rests upon religion. It is from that source that we derive our reverence for truth and justice, for equality and liberty, and for the rights of mankind.
>
> The government of a country never gets ahead of the religion of a country. There is no way by which we can substitute the authority of law for the virtue of man.
>
> We cannot depend on government to do the work of religion. We cannot escape a personal responsibility for our conduct. We cannot regard those as wise or safe counselors in public affairs who deny these principles and seek to support the theory that society can succeed when the individual fails.[57]

In speaking engagements that fall, he kept remarks concise and nonpolitical without making promises or mentioning his opponents by name. To reporters he recalled that no candidate "ever injured himself very much by not talking."[58]

To supervise campaign speeches, radio talks, and newspaper statements, Coolidge appointed an advisory publicity board led by former campaign manager James B. Reynolds, former naval censor George Barr Baker, publicist Frederick W. Hume, and newspapermen R.B. Armstrong of the *Los Angeles Times* and George Ackerson of the *Minneapolis Tribune*. The board resided within the Republican National Committee under Chairman Butler, who instructed spokesmen to stick to the Coolidge record of budget cuts, tax cuts, debt reduction, and prosperity, and monitored compliance through a daily review of newspapers from New York, Washington, and Chicago. No campaign in history had gone to such lengths to stay on message. Even the illustrative Secretary Hughes submitted his speeches in advance. When Secretary Wilbur submitted a speech to be delivered in Denver at an impromptu appearance, Butler read the contents, which mentioned the League of Nations, Teapot Dome, and other indiscretions, and had Edward Clark show a copy to the president. Coolidge read a few pages and threw it down in disgust, saying, "Wire that man to return to Washington immediately!"[59] As the press picked up the story, Democrats belittled the administration for censoring a cabinet officer, and Coolidge insisted the recall was related to budgetary issues—namely to discuss a reduction in the naval allowance—which had the merit of partial truth.

The only departure in campaign policy was to condemn La Follette for his proposals to hold elections for federal judges and to allow Congress to overrule Supreme Court decisions. "The Socialist-Third Party is pledged to the destruction of the Constitution—the destruction of the Supreme Court," fumed Butler. From then on, Republican orators were instructed to refer to La Follette as the "Socialist-Third Party Candidate."[60]

In the Middle West, where La Follette was strongest, Coolidge received significant support. When he asked Senator Arthur Capper of Kansas to make one speech in Minnesota, one in Iowa, and one in Nebraska, the popular legislator responded by making two in each state, predicting "safe majorities" in all three and supporting Coolidge in his farm periodicals and newspapers, which had some three million readers, stretching from Texas to Pennsylvania.[61] Another prominent Kansan, progressive newspaper editor William Allen White, wrote a series of pro-administration pieces and sent copies to the White House with a note promising "to make Coolidge votes."[62]

Western Republicans, for the most part, stayed with the administration despite differences on taxes, tariff rates, and farm relief, while Democrats failed to resonate in the region. This baffled a political reporter from the *New York Times*, who went there to better understand popular sentiment. "Wheat is Republican," explained a young farm paper editor in South Dakota. "Cotton is Democratic."[63] Western farmers were loath to support any third-party entity that might help the main opposition.

"I think Coolidge will be able to buy the election," Hiram Johnson told reporters, still bitter about his defeat in the primaries. "The amount of money behind him will be greater than in all previous campaigns during our lives."[64] Republicans would spend less in 1924 than in 1920 but outspend Democrats by a wide margin nonetheless. The fact is, Republicans outspent Democrats in every presidential campaign between 1860 and 1924, except for 1884, 1892, and 1912, three of the four Democratic victories during that span. La Follette raised $171,824, as compared with $552,368 for the Democrats and $3,742,962 for the Republicans.[65]

All signs pointed to a Coolidge victory. Industrial output shot up in September and was higher than normal through October, as stocks rebounded from a spring slump. Grain prices rose through late summer and autumn. "There never has been but one political issue in this country since the Civil War," said one Democrat off the record. "That is good times. We are having good times right now. Mr. Coolidge gets the credit."[66] More than 50 supporters of the Progressive Party in 1912 issued a statement urging their former cohorts to vote Republican, and Butler predicted the ticket would receive at least 350 electoral votes.[67]

"The outlook appears to be promising, but as I have often told you elections are very uncertain," Coolidge wrote his father. "I hope this is the last time that I shall ever have to be a candidate for office."[68]

At a press conference the following day he declined to make predictions: "My reports indicate that I shall probably carry Northampton. That is about as far as I can go into details. That is based more on experience."[69] Since losing to insurance agent John Kennedy for school board in 1905, he had won 15 consecutive elections and knew when a campaign was going well. Not only were party leaders and precinct workers pressing hard around the country, but the opposition was weak, with Davis failing to captivate Democratic activists and La Follette speaking only 20 times in 13 states, missing the ballot in some states, and running under confusing labels in others. The latest *Literary Digest* polls showed Coolidge with a two-to-one margin over either opponent, receiving at least 372 electoral votes and capturing the bellwether states of New York, Maryland, Kentucky, Missouri, and Kansas.[70]

On October 26, Coolidge made a telephone address to the Federation of Jewish Philanthropic Societies of New York, praising their efforts to help the poor without undermining self-reliance, lauding their application of business principles to charitable work. He compared their pragmatic approach to his economy in public expenditures, a "sort of obsession with me."[71]

Two days later he told reporters he was done with his campaign, having set forth his attitude on the positions of the day.[72] As he and Grace filled out their absentee ballots on the south lawn of the White House, photographers recorded the event.

On November 3, Election Eve, Coolidge skimmed through a small stack of telegrams on the political situation amid reports that the western states were turning his way, including Minnesota, where La Follette was slipping. The president took a nap and wrote a short speech to be delivered by radio at 10:00 p.m. In a brilliant bit of political theater, he spoke for 15 minutes to a record 30,000,000 listeners, stressing the importance of voting without mentioning his candidacy and ending on a touching note: "To my father, who is listening in in my old home in Vermont, and to my other invisible audience I say, 'Good night.'"[73]

Election Day, November 4, the president worked a normal schedule and dined in private with Grace, who wore a lucky necklace with seven ivory elephants strung together, before repairing to a sitting room to receive returns by radio and telegraph with Frank and Emily Stearns, sipping green tea. The first bulletin showed young Theodore Roosevelt carrying Buffalo by 10,000 votes over incumbent governor Al Smith, who had taken the city by 16,000 votes in 1922. "Looks as if Roosevelt will be elected," Coolidge said, smiling.[74] The next bulletin, from Massachusetts, stated that Speaker of the House Frederick H. Gillett had been elected to the Senate by a wide margin over Democrat David I. Walsh, an Irish Catholic and popular former governor. This pleased the president, who had convinced Gillett to enter a tough three-way Republican primary that summer. By the time Eastern polls closed at 8:00 p.m., Coolidge knew he had swept every state from Maine to Maryland, with a weak showing by Davis in Democratic urban areas. By 10:15 p.m., many newspapers and wire services proclaimed Coolidge the president-elect. By the time he retired at 12:45 a.m., he knew he had secured a tremendous victory.

All told, Coolidge polled 15,725,016 votes to 8,386,624 for Davis and 4,831,470 for La Follette, winning an impressive 54 percent of the vote. In the Electoral College, he received 382 ballots against 136 for Davis, who won the south, and 13 for La Follette, who won only Wisconsin and received less than one-third of the votes cast in the Middle West. In the Senate, Republicans added five seats. In the House, they added 22. It would be a "Coolidge Congress" wrote the *Literary Digest* since regular Republicans would outnumber the coalition of insurgent Republicans and Democrats that had repeatedly thwarted the administration to date.[75] Three of the senators who had led the fight for the bonus had lost. Seven who had voted against the bonus had won.

In New York, the man who might have been vice president during a second Harding term, the candidate who many thought would follow his father to the White House, Theodore Roosevelt, Jr., lost by 112,179 votes, despite Coolidge winning the state by more than 900,000 votes and Republicans sweeping every other statewide contest and taking the state senate. The difference was an overwhelming vote for Governor Smith in all five boroughs of New York City.

A letter postmarked Northampton arrived at the White House. "You are not given to becoming pouter-pigeon-chested, when things come your way," wrote Richard Irwin, "but you are now entitled to bulge a bit."[76]

* * *

Voters had elected the most fiscally conservative presidential candidate in decades. "It was a famous victory, and one most useful in the lessons to be drawn from it, one of which is that this country is no country for radicalism," Chief Justice Taft wrote a friend. "I think it is really the most conservative country in the world."[77]

* * *

In Europe, by comparison, socialists had been viable since the 1870s, through trade unions, political parties, newspapers, and cooperatives. This went back to medieval times, when guilds provided voluntary health insurance for members, and to the Reformation, when friendly societies provided similar forms of sickness benefits and mutual aid throughout the continent, particularly in Northern Europe. By the 19th century, Belgium, Denmark, England, France, the Netherlands, and Sweden had taken measures to promote the societies, such as offering legal status and exemption from certain types of taxation, as long as they agreed to some degree of official supervision. This had led to more government support, more benefits, more participants, and more countries adopting such programs.

These developments provided the impetus for the modern welfare state and the basis for the socialist agenda, as more countries moved from voluntary private initiatives to compulsory public programs. Germany, the original welfare state, with compulsory sickness insurance for workers in 1883, an accident insurance plan in 1884, a comprehensive old age insurance law in 1889, and the first progressive income tax in Europe in 1891, had the largest socialist party on the continent by the early 1900s. Norway and the Netherlands introduced compulsory health insurance schemes in 1909 and 1913, respectively. Switzerland and Italy introduced similar but less ambitious programs in 1911 and 1912, respectively. A number of countries introduced old age insurance in the years before or after the war: Yugoslavia in 1909, Luxemburg in 1911, Rumania in 1912, Netherlands in 1913, Sweden in 1913, Portugal in 1919, Russia in 1922, Italy in 1923, Belgium in 1924, Bulgaria in 1924, and Czechoslovakia in 1924. Most countries on the continent provided some level of public coverage for accidents, invalidity, maternity care, sickness, and unemployment.

Even England, birthplace of modern conservatism, home to Burke and Disraeli, adopted old age pensions, a progressive income tax, a death tax, the gasoline tax, and deficit spending in the historic national budget of 1909, reflecting the rise of the Labor Party since winning its first seats in the House of Commons seven years earlier. "The maddest budget ever introduced," declared Sir Frederick George Banbury of the conservative House of Lords.[78] Then came the National Health Act of 1911, which introduced compulsory health insurance for workers as well as unemployment insurance.

During the Great War, European socialists made further gains in promoting their ideas if not their political fortunes. England implemented new infant and child care programs, free elementary education, and public housing programs, prompting Labour Party leader Ramsay MacDonald to observe that the conflict had done more for the social agenda of the left than 50 years of reform efforts.[79] France introduced minimum wages and medical services for workers.

By the 1920s, with wartime nationalism gone, socialists were everywhere in power or the main opposition to conservatives, promoting high upper income taxes and unemployment doles to end the old economic and social arrangements. In England, the Labor Party had increased its vote in the national elections of 1922 and 1923 and formed a government in 1924 through steady advances in industrial regions despite attempts by conservatives to appeal to the masses with unemployment insurance, military and civilian pensions, and nationalized electricity. Some 1.2 million permanently unemployed British workers received $1.5 million annually in public handouts. In Austria, Belgium, and Finland, socialists formed more than two-fifths of the legislatures. In Denmark and Sweden, they led the coalition governments. In Czechoslovakia, they shared power with the agrarians. In France, they formed the most active wing of the majority Radical-Socialist majority. In Germany, Social Democrats battled with breakaway elements and the Communists for primacy in industrial areas. In 1924 alone, some 20 million voters in England, France, Germany, Italy, and the Scandinavian countries had cast their ballots for socialists.

This had been foretold by Austrian economist Joseph Schumpeter in his 1918 essay, *The Crisis of the Tax State*, on how wartime taxes and revenue collection methods has established a new era of government finance. Before the war, no government had been able to raise more than a small fraction of national income, perhaps 5 percent, through taxes and borrowing. That had changed in 1914, especially in Eastern Europe, leading him to envision several possible scenarios: excessive taxation that would undermine economic growth, progressive income tax regimes that would undermine incentives to work, and popular demand for more public benefits that would lead to higher taxes, debt, and questions on the legitimacy of private property.

In the United States, social spending took place almost entirely at the state and local level. This distinction might be traced in part to the "rugged individualism" and self-support ethos that came from the settlers, immigration, and the westward push across the continent. There were other reasons. First, the country did not have a strong leftist party to induce conservatives into backing social legislation to retain votes from workers. Second, the federalist system of government put the onus on state and local governments to provide care for the needy, and set up an economic competition between the states that gave them an incentive to keep their taxes and spending in check.

* * *

Coolidge, flush from victory, turned full attention to his budget for the next fiscal year and reduced spending estimates by $59 million, including $26 million at the Department of Interior, $23 million at the Navy, and $8.6 million at the War Department. Ten days after elections he told reporters he wanted further tax reduction as long as the fiscal year produced a surplus six months hence, reiterating the policy he had established in his message to Congress in 1923 and repeated during deliberations on the tax bill in early 1924. "Then we will know what balance there is on hand and what provision could be made for further tax reduction," he said.[80]

In early December, he submitted his annual message to Congress, to be read by a clerk rather than delivered in person. Again he put the emphasis on economy:

> We have our enormous debt to pay, and we are paying it. We have the high cost of government to diminish, and we are diminishing it. We have a heavy burden of taxation to reduce, and we are reducing it.

Therein lay the origins of the ongoing prosperity and the hope for future prosperity as long as Congress kept appropriations within the budget. "The present estimated margin between public receipts and expenditures for this fiscal year is very small," he warned.[81]

The next day, in a publicized move to promote economy, Coolidge traveled to Chicago on a regular train to address the International Livestock Exposition, saving $1,700 in expenses as compared with what would have been paid on a special train. Every president since McKinley had taken special trains or special cars for security and privacy, but Coolidge, having preached economy to Congress, hoped to set an example despite Secret Service concerns for his safety. Initially he reserved a private car for $90 until he learned the railroad charged an additional fee of 25 fares. When he found out that only 10 persons could ride in the car, he said, "We'll pay no railroad fifteen extra fares when the fifteen extra persons can't be carried on the car paid for."[82] Accompanied by Grace, Mr. and Mrs. Stearns, Dr. James Coupal, and a dozen bodyguards, he sat in a regular compartment car, located between the diner and the observation car, and took a nap as passengers walked back and forth, pausing to observe the slumbering chief executive. Later the presidential party sat with other passengers in the diner, partaking of the standard $1.25 dinner.

After a day of speech-making in Chicago, the presidential entourage boarded a regular train back to Washington, 20 hours away. At Connellsville, Pennsylvania, Coolidge stopped to greet hundreds of well-wishers as a band played patriotic tunes and the master of ceremonies praised a group of girls for their campaign work. "They went around the district and converted many Democrats to the Republican cause," he said.

"Well, somebody did," Coolidge replied.[83]

A *Washington Post* columnist, amused by the publicity surrounding such a small savings, wrote, "Thank goodness, President Coolidge returns from Chicago without having fallen out of an upper."[84]

As the holidays approached, Coolidge tried without success to get his father to pass the winter in the White House with fireplaces and electric blankets, instead of his old stove-heated farmhouse. "I expect the observance of the holidays will be about the same as usual," Coolidge told reporters a week before Christmas, his voice trembling slightly. "The only difference, which will be apparent to all of you, is that three of us will be present rather than four, as in the past."[85] Two days later John returned from college and Frank and Emily Stearns arrived by train. The White House was decorated with holly wreaths on the windows, but no tree in the Blue Room because neither the president nor the first lady wanted one.

"I wish you a very Merry Christmas," Coolidge wrote his father on Christmas Eve. "If only Calvin were with us we should be very happy."[86]

That evening Grace had to convince him to walk to Sherman Square behind the Treasury to light the national Christmas tree, as planned weeks earlier. "I accept this tree and I will now light it," he told the crowd, leaving a short time later.[87]

Christmas Day he awoke early, retrieving his mail, greeting the police and bodyguards on duty, reading the newspapers, and working in his office. It was unusually cold outside, and the streets were quiet.

"Now John is home I miss Calvin more," he wrote his father.[88]

* * *

On the first day of 1925 he received a letter from William Jennings Bryan, the three-time Democratic presidential candidate and former secretary of state under Wilson, calling for the cancellation of the wartime debts. "The debts will never be paid, every day makes that more clear," he wrote; he had opposed and failed to stop the granting of private loans to England and France in 1915, as inconsistent with the neutrality of the United States, and he had resigned later that year in protest. Now, 10 years later, he proposed cancellation in return for an international disarmament pledge, which in turn would allow the United States to save money on military expenditures.

Coolidge wrote back right away: "Your interesting letter received. It has not seemed moral to me to cancel obligations. If you are in town some time I hope to see you."[89]

* * *

The "lame duck" session of the 68th Congress that winter dealt mainly with matters of minor or local importance, except for an attempt to override the seven-month-old presidential veto of the bill to increase postal salaries by $68 million. Coolidge invited numerous Republican senators to the White House to stress the need for economy and the national interest as a whole.[90] This would the first test of his mandate and his strength in the Senate since the election. The bill had bipartisan support and was seen as likely to pass.

In a theatrical scene on January 6, postal workers and other spectators filled the galleries to watch the Senate uphold the veto by a single vote as Democrat Nathaniel B. Dial of South Carolina crossed party lines to back the president. It was an administrative matter, more than a legislative matter, Dial told reporters.[91]

Otherwise, Coolidge devoted the final weeks of his abbreviated term to appointments and administrative issues. In early January, he named Attorney General Stone to fill a Supreme Court vacancy left by the retirement of Justice Joseph McKenna. Stone received widespread praise despite his pro-business views and the controversy over his role in a federal investigation and indictment against Democratic senator Burton K. Wheeler of Montana on charges related to his law practice, which some attributed to retaliation for his pursuit of Daugherty the previous year. The Senate Judiciary Committee endorsed the nominee, but Democrat Thomas Walsh of Montana convinced cohorts to return the nomination to committee for further review. Coolidge then took the unprecedented step of sending the nominee before the committee, where his five-hour testimony cleared the way for confirmation. As secretary of state, Coolidge chose former senator Frank B. Kellogg of Minnesota to succeed the retiring Charles Evans Hughes, without consulting Republican Senate leaders, as customary. For secretary of agriculture, he chose former educator and cowpuncher William M. Jardine of Kansas to replace interim appointee H.M. Gore, who had filled in since Henry Wallace died in October. The only cabinet member holdovers from August 1923 were Mellon, Hoover, Weeks, New, Davis, and Work.

Slemp, as planned, announced his retirement after the election, telling Dr. Boone he had protected the president long enough and was tired of dealing with Stearns and Butler, amateurs that they were: "Nothing else for me to do but resign."[92] The rumor that he would receive the next vacant cabinet position would prove untrue. Meeting with reporters on his way out, he said the president was in fine physical condition, sleeping well and having gained eight pounds since assuming what was supposed to be a "man-killing" job.[93] The new secretary was Indiana congressman Everett Sanders, who was born in a log cabin outside Terre Haute, Indiana, in 1882, the son of a Baptist preacher, tall, heavyset, and well-liked on Capitol Hill.

* * *

On Monday, January 26, Coolidge went to Memorial Continental Hall to address the semiannual meeting of the Business Organization of the Government with about 2,000 persons in attendance and a national radio hookup arranged with the NBC at no cost to the government, thanks to Director Lord, who agreed to keep proceedings to the standard one-hour segment. The cabinet was there. The first lady was up in a special box. Taking the rostrum, Coolidge restated his goal to produce an annual budget below $3 billion and stressed the need for economy to allow further tax cuts:

President Calvin Coolidge standing on the South Lawn at the White House, February 25, 1925, a week before his second inauguration, following a three-party election in which the Republican ticket won 54 percent of the popular vote and 72 percent of the electoral tally (National Photo Company Collection, Library of Congress).

> It is practical economy which I have in mind and which we must practice. I had rather talk of saving pennies and save them than theorize in saving millions and save nothing.

To achieve reductions, he needed support from every department and every manager in attendance:

> When you leave this meeting tonight carry with you a pledge to bond every effort to carry on your activities with less money. Take with you the determination to guard against each and every unnecessary expenditure. Take with you the determination to close the year with unused balances of appropriations.[94]

* * *

In planning for Inaugural Day, Coolidge wanted a modest, low-cost affair, with no official ball or fireworks, despite appeals from the local chamber of commerce for more elaborate plans. Newspapers praised him for abiding by his principles during a time of national debt reduction, but Washington businessmen feared the result would be smaller crowds than the usual 200,000 to 300,000 inaugural visitors, and less revenue. Normally the hotels along Pennsylvania Avenue raised their rates for rooms overlooking the inaugural parade route, but not this time.

"It looks like the simplest inaugural since Jefferson rode his horse from the White House to the Capitol, and tied him to a hitching-post," said one local proprietor.[95]

Coolidge encouraged his father to arrive early and stay a while in Washington rather than in snowbound Plymouth Notch, where drifts covered fence tops and temperatures dipped as low as 20 degrees below zero, leaving the village in isolation for long stretches without mail and other deliveries. The old gentleman was slow to commit, reluctant to leave his duties as deputy sheriff. Finally, six days before the inaugural, his son sent a melancholy note:

> Of course I want you to do what will give you most pleasure. If you do not feel like coming to the inauguration I am not going to urge you about it, or urge you to stay after you get here. You and John and I are all that is left. You have worked hard for me and I do not want to put any more burdens on you. The house is open and the invitation given; every medical or other attention are at your disposal.[96]

Colonel Coolidge proceeded to hitch up his horse and slog through deep snow to Ludlow, where he caught the train to Washington.

Chapter Six

Inaugural Address

Inauguration Day, March 4, broke cloudy with temperatures in the mid–30s. Up before seven, the president strolled the White House grounds and had wheat cakes and sausages with his wife, his father, his mother-in-law, his former law partner, the president of Amherst College, and a long-time friend from Northampton, while awaiting his son's arrival by train. Then he went to his office to review several bills and scan the newspapers, doubtlessly pleased by the lead editorial in the *New York Times*:

> President Coolidge begins his full term of office today with an unquestioned hold upon the confidence of his fellow-countrymen. They believe not only that he is safe but that he is sound. They approve of the personal quality which they have found in him. They endorse his main policies and hope for public benefit from them. Today, with the utmost good-will and with quite unusual obliteration of party animus, they cherish the hope that his extraordinary success, which he has taken without one trace of vanity, may continue through the next four years.
>
> Others had preached economy in the vague; President Coolidge urged it in the concrete and with one definite application after another. Others had talked of relieving tax burdens in general; this man attacked the problem in detail, struck his hand upon the spot and showed where savings could be made and that cut in taxation effected.[1]

Shortly before 11:00 the presidential party hastened to the motorcars lined along the White House drive, the president in striped, gray trousers, black cutaway coat, and a high silk hat, the first lady in a stylish "moonstone" dress, cut on a straight line, with a collar of gray fox, gray slippers, gray stockings, and a snugly fitting gray hat with a plume of burnt goose. They went up Pennsylvania Avenue, escorted by cavalry and a band of Civil War veterans, as high winds swept away the clouds and gave way to sunshine. The president raised his hat in response to cheers along the way, but did not smile.

Inside the Capitol, Coolidge sat at a long, green-covered table to review the final batch of bills approved by the 68th Congress that morning.

In barely 20 minutes he signed 71 into law, mostly minor in nature. The last bill was a provision to raise the annual salaries of legislators from $7,500 to $10,000 and that of cabinet members from $12,000 to $15,000, for a total cost of $1,367,000 a year. Congress had quietly put through the raise during an evening session, without a roll call, to limit debate and media attention. Coolidge was loath to intervene in a legislative matter but aware that such an expenditure would contradict his economy program and flout the results of the recent election. Leaning back, chin resting on his hand, long index finger pointing to his temple, face flushed, he called over Director Lord to discuss how the raise would affect the budget. As the clock ticked toward the noon deadline, legislators paused outside the room, peering through the door, asking one another whether he had signed the bill. Five minutes before noon he took out his watch, glanced at the clock to make sure his timepiece was correct, and requested a glass of water. Then, slowly rising from his chair, he walked across the room, returned, and, with a quick glance, affixed his signature to the bill. Sounds of applause filled the hallway. The end of the 68th Congress was at hand.

As Coolidge walked to the east portico of the Capitol, he received three trumpet flourishes from the Marine Corps Band and cheers from thousands of spectators on the lawn and several hundred more perched on the roof of the building. A battery of microphones arrayed on the main platform, linked to telephone wires, carried the proceedings to 24 radio stations from coast to coast. The American Telephone and Telegraph Company had taken precautions to prevent even the slightest disturbances to the circuit, checking for leaks on nearby power lines that might cause interference and placing engineers on duty to monitor volume and clarity. Three hundred photographers stood on a separate platform, many carrying "Big Bertha," a camera fitted with a telescope capable of taking close-up shots from a distance of 100 yards or more, in what would be the most photographed event in history, with 18 commercial planes waiting to rush the pictures to Baltimore, Philadelphia, New York, and beyond. Some photographs were transmitted over telephone wires, reaching as far away as San Francisco in seven minutes and making the early afternoon newspaper editions out west. A special train had been chartered to carry moving picture films of the ceremony to New York in what would be a record time of three hours and 40 minutes.

With an estimated 22.8 million persons listening by radio in all 48 states, Coolidge took the oath of office from Chief Justice Taft, who wore a black skullcap to keep warm, 16 years to the day he was sworn in as the 27th president during a blizzard that shut down rail and telegraph lines in the capital. Concluding with the words "I do," Coolidge kissed his Bible, opened to the first chapter of the Gospel of John, which, when he was six, he had read to his dying paternal grandfather. Then he began his 40-minute address, a proclamation of conservative values and faith toward mankind that he had written alone.

"We made freedom a birthright," he said, his Yankee intonations plainly audible through loudspeakers, even as his words bounced back from the wings of the Capitol in echoes that bothered listeners up front and prompted a South Carolina legislator to stand up and leave. Now, 150 years since the shots at Lexington and Concord, the country was unique in the annals of great nations in that it had no imperial ambitions, no interest in political alliances, and stood instead for arms limitations and the international arbitration of disputes.

Turning to domestic politics, he called for greater party loyalty in an appeal to Republican legislators after their gains in the 1924 elections:

> When the country has bestowed its confidence upon a party by making it a majority in the Congress, it has a right to expect such unity of action as will make the party majority an effective instrument of government. This Administration has come into power with a very clear and definitive mandate from the people.

That mandate, lest anyone be mistaken by divisions within the party, called for fiscal conservatism and government restraint:

> I favor the policy of economy, not because I wish to save money, but because I wish to save people. The men and women of this country who toil are the ones who bear the cost of the Government. Every dollar that we carelessly waste means that their life will be so much the more meager. Every dollar that we prudently save means that their life will be so much the more abundant. Economy is idealism in its most practical form.

On taxes, he warned about excessive collection and lauded the privilege and responsibility of living in a republic that held personal rights and property rights in the same regard:

> The collection of any taxes which are not absolutely required, which do not beyond reasonable doubt contribute to the public welfare, is only a species of legalized larceny. Under this republic the rewards of industry belong to those who earn them. The only constitutional tax is the tax which ministers to public necessity. The property of the country belongs to the people of the country. Their title is absolute. They do not support any privileged class; they do not need to maintain great military forces; they ought not to be burdened with a great array of public employees. They are not required to make any contribution to Government expenditures except that which they voluntarily assess upon themselves through the action of their own representatives. Whenever taxes become burdensome a remedy can be applied by the people; but if they do not act for themselves, no one can be very successful in acting for them.
>
> The time is arriving when we can have further tax reduction, when, unless

> we wish to hamper the people in their right to earn a living, we must have tax reform. The method of raising revenue ought not to impede the transaction of business; it ought to encourage it. I am opposed to extremely high rates, because they produce little or no revenue, because they are bad for the country, and, finally, because they are wrong. We can not finance the country, we can not improve social conditions, through any system of injustice, even if we attempt to inflict it upon the rich. Those who suffer the most harm will be the poor. This country believes in prosperity. It is absurd to suppose that it is envious of those who are already prosperous. The wise and correct course to follow in taxation and all other economic legislation is not to destroy those who have already secured success but to create conditions under which every one will have a better chance to be successful. The verdict of the country has been given on this question. That verdict stands. We shall do well to heed it.
>
> These questions involve moral issues. We need not concern ourselves much about the rights of property if we will faithfully observe the rights of persons. Under our institutions their rights are supreme. It is not property but the right to hold property, both great and small, which our Constitution guarantees. All owners of property are charged with a service. These rights and duties have been revealed, through the conscience of society, to have a divine sanction. The very stability of our society rests upon production and conservation. For individuals or for governments to waste and squander their resources is to deny these rights and disregard these obligations. The result of economic dissipation to a nation is always moral decay.[2]

Then came a simple 50-minute inaugural parade which the president watched from a stand built for the occasion, followed by a nap, a small dinner at the White House, and a reception with Massachusetts legislators at the Cairo Hotel, before retiring at 10:00 p.m., having put his son on a sleeper back to Amherst. It was announced that the inaugural committee would return $16,803 of the $40,000 that Congress had appropriated for the event.[3]

Chapter Seven

The Politics of Limited Government

The term began with confirmation hearings and allegations that attorney general-designee Charles B. Warren had violated antitrust laws as head of the Michigan Sugar Company. The evidence was weak, but the Senate turned him down by a single vote on March 10, the first such repudiation since 1866 and only the seventh in history, partly because he was at odds with Michigan Republicans, partly because Senate Republicans were upset that reporters knew about the appointment before they did, as with some previous Coolidge appointments. Vice President Dawes, representing the potential tying vote, was napping at the Willard because no one said his presence might be necessary. Coolidge blamed Senate Republican leaders for not lining up the votes. They blamed him for not taking a stronger personal role in promoting the nominee and pointed out that five presumably pro–Warren senators had been absent due to illness or travel. They recommended he not resubmit the nomination.[1] When he did anyway, the angry Senate rejected Warren by seven votes on March 16.

The next morning Coolidge submitted as nominee little-known Vermont lawyer John Garibaldi Sargent, to whom he then sent the following telegram: "Senate without opposition has confirmed your nomination to be Attorney General. Hope you can come at once."[2]

When Sargent arrived at Union Station, a Secret Service agent whisked him past reporters and photographers to a hotel to don a string bow tie and blacken his size 14 brown shoes for a swearing-in ceremony at Justice Department and a meeting at the White House. Coolidge, having known him since grade school but never having discussed with him service in the administration, greeted him as though nothing were unusual, asking about the weather back home and the trip down. Born on a farm near Plymouth Notch in 1860, Sargent had attended Black River Academy and Tufts University, practiced law in Ludlow with former Vermont Governor W.W. Stickney, served as attorney for Windsor County, and served as state attorney general. A shambling, bookish, pipe-smoking, trout-fishing, kindly man of Irish descent, with thick, unruly gray hair, standing six feet, three inches, 280 pounds, he was 11 years older than Coolidge and more conservative, having opposed the Sixteenth Amendment to sanction the income tax, the Seventeenth Amendment to initiate the popular election of senators, and the Nineteenth Amendment to allow female suffrage. This record went unnoticed during his 30-minute Senate confirmation hearing. "I feel like a cat in a strange garret," he told reporters.[3] With Mrs. Sargent tending to some newborn chicks on their poultry farm back home, he rented a room at the Willard on recommendation from the president.

The appointment came as a surprise. Newspapers portrayed him as a "country lawyer" when in fact he had represented large New England companies, achieved prominence at the regional level, and argued cases before the Supreme Court. Frank Stearns was delighted. "Nothing except your nomination and election has made me so happy for ten years as your appointment of Mr. Sargent," he wrote Coolidge, knowing the honest solicitor would serve the country well.[4] When Sargent learned Daugherty had appointed special attorneys in the territories of regular district attorneys, he immediately put an end to the waste by removing them from the payroll.

A columnist for the *Washington Post* observed, "It seems that after all no immediate changes in the cabinet are contemplated, but Vermont is ready!"[5]

* * *

Initial reports of a devastating tornado in the Midwest reached the White House on the afternoon of March 19. By evening Coolidge knew things were dire.[6]

The tornado had touched down in the rugged hill country outside Ellington, Missouri, appearing as a boiling mass of clouds rather than a widely visible funnel, without warning. It lasted three and a half hours, stretching almost a mile wide and 219 miles long across southern Illinois and Indiana, producing winds at nearly 300 miles per hour, snapping trees, and demolishing several towns along the way. A former war chaplain said the damage reminded him of a battlefield in France. An office clerk survived by squeezing inside a safe. One family survived by lying under their living room rug, another by lying beneath their car in their garage. Others survived by clinging to trees, fence posts, and the like, some suffering torn muscles and ligaments in their arms from the strain. Many in the path of the storm had struggled to breathe.[7] More than 800 miners emerged from the largest coal mine in the world, in West Frankfurt, Illinois, to find cars twisted into wreckage, homes flattened, and the local morgue filled with dead bodies, including their kin.[8] It was the worst tornado in the history of the country, killing 695 people, injuring 2,027 people, and causing $16.5 million in property damage.

Coolidge immediately put the resources of the Red Cross at the disposal of affected areas, providing doctors, nurses, volunteers, and supplies from chapters throughout the country. He also ordered the Army to provide assistance, resulting in 1,000 tents, 12,000 blankets, and thousands of cots and pillows. Donations arrived from across the country, reaching $2 million within a week and $3 million all together.

Neither the White House nor Congress gave any consideration to providing financial support to affected areas or taking responsibility for recovery and reconstruction. The Constitution did not mention natural disaster assistance as a federal power, so responsibility fell to states, localities, and nongovernment entities. The federal government did not have the administrative capacity to take full responsibility for the effects of natural disaster. It had never done so. In 1887, Cleveland vetoed a $10,000 appropriation granting free seed grain to farmers in drought-stricken Texas, for government had no right to do so. In 1889, Harrison perceived no federal role in response to the Johnston Flood in Pennsylvania that killed 2,209 people and destroyed thousands of homes. In 1900, McKinley responded to a devastating hurricane in Galveston that killed an estimated 6,000 residents and demolished 3,600 homes, the worst natural disaster in United States history at the time, by sending troops and limited funding for rescue efforts. In 1905, the Roosevelt administration refused to help New Orleans restrain a yellow fever epidemic until the city raised $25,000 in advance to cover expenses. In 1906, Roosevelt sent tents and temporary shelter to San Francisco following the massive earthquake that killed some 500 people and left more than 500,000 homeless, but local government, charities, and businesses paid for recovery and reconstruction. In 1921, Harding provided subsistence but no direct relief to Colorado flood victims. The following year, Louisiana declined to request federal support after a flood left some 50,000 people homeless.

The day after the tornado, Coolidge held a regularly scheduled press conference and took questions on a government railroad report, the prohibition commissioner, vacant positions in the administration, diplomatic negotiations, and a pending budget meeting. No one asked about what had been the worst natural disaster in the country since the Ohio floods of 1913.[9] It was not seen as the responsibility of the president or the federal government.

* * *

The end of confirmation hearings that week began a nine-month recess in Congress, as Coolidge ruled out a special session. Most recent presidents had convened them post-inauguration to enact certain bills or emergency measures, such as McKinley and the protective tariff of March 1897, Wilson and the war declaration of April 1917, and Harding and the tariff law of March 1921. There had been 21 such sessions since 1789 and seven since 1900. Conservative Republicans pressed Coolidge to call one for tax reform, but he decided to wait until the regular session in December. The problem with special sessions was that, once convened, they could stray beyond the main issue at hand to cover anything. To Coolidge, the country had gone through enough agitation during the past session of Congress and needed a respite.

"My own thought about the situation at the present time," Coolidge told reporters, "is that I would like it if the country could think as little as possible about the Government and give their time and attention more undividedly about the conduct of the private business of our country."[10]

Thus Washington settled into the quietest spring in years. "The Coolidges are less inclined to stir from their own fireside in the evening than any presidential pair within the last two or three decades," noted a *Washington Post* gossip columnist.[11] They had small dinner parties, but their main companion was Sargent, whom they invited to stay at the White House after he had trouble sleeping at the noisy Willard, ill accustomed as he was to hotel living and city traffic. He took the room normally reserved for Stearns, who was touring Europe that spring, hoping, if nothing else, to dispel the notion that he was an indispensable adviser to the president. "No, sir," he told reporters. "No living man knows what Mr. Coolidge will do three minutes ahead, and I have given up trying to guess."[12]

Among the dignitaries to call at the White House that spring was Will Rogers, who bet his senator escort $100 that he could make the president laugh. When the introduction was made, he cupped his hand to his ear and said, "Pardon me, but I didn't catch the name." To which Coolidge responded with a quiet chuckle.[13]

Easter week in mid–April brought balmy temperatures and large crowds as local sightseeing companies leased additional buses from Baltimore and Philadelphia to meet demand and city hotels filled to capacity. With the tulips, jonquils, hyacinths, magnolias, lilacs, delphiniums, forsythias, and cherry tree blossoms in bloom, the capital never looked prettier than in springtime, as tourists and students on spring break strolled about the Potomac Tidal Basin, the Lincoln Memorial, the Washington Monument, the Mall, the National Museum, the Capitol, the Library of Congress, the Tomb of the Unknown Soldier, the Zoo, and other sites. At the White House, Coolidge received a record 1,869 visitors at one handshaking session, what with travel agencies and rail lines across the country offering the chance to meet the president as an inducement to visit Washington, which had become the most popular spring break destination on the East Coast during the past decade or so. One advertisement ran: "See Washington. Climb the monument. Shake hands with the President."[14] Coolidge took pride in his handshaking prowess, averaging about one person per second and reaching a record 1900 one afternoon.[15] When someone asked how he could shake so many hands, he replied, "When I was boy I used to milk a herd of cows every day."[16]

The weather that spring was particularly pleasant. "These are glorious days here, fairly cool in the early mornings but very warm in the middle of the day," Grace wrote a friend back home. "I wish you might have seen the line of school children extending from the door of the executive office down the sidewalk opposite the State, War and Navy. There were hundreds of them and the President says their hands are dirty."[17]

On Easter Sunday, the sidewalks filled with churchgoers in their finest attire, men in top hats and swallow-tail coats, women in little flower hats, bright dresses, and initialed shoes in vogue that spring. Outside the First Congregational Church, the Secret Service could barely restrain 2,000 tourists when the president and first lady arrived for services. On Easter Monday, tens of thousands of children took part in the traditional egg roll on the south lawn of the White House.

The magazine editor who had spent a week with Coolidge in early 1924 came again. "The most noteworthy difference between the Coolidge of a year ago and the Coolidge of to-day is in his self-confidence," he wrote, for whereas the president had been feeling his way with the public back then, he now seemed at ease, having won his own term.[18]

Another visitor wondered how he handled the burdens of the presidency. "Oh, I don't know," he replied. "When I was mayor of Northampton I was pretty busy most of the time, and I don't seem to be much busier here."[19]

The White House employees, many of whom had been there two or three decades, were nonetheless struck by his habits and traits. "In his high shoes and his great galluses he was an odd sight in the White House corridors," noted his bodyguard.[20] Coolidge had his valet rub his hair with Vaseline at breakfast and told head usher Ike Hoover to put some hair on a portrait of John Adams in the Red Room. Hoover, a former employee of the Edison Company, had installed the first electric light system in the White House in 1891 and then accepted a permanent position because the servants and other employees were afraid to touch the lights and light switches. Back then the executive staff had consisted of 10 people, including doorkeepers and messengers. Now, 34 years later, he was working under his ninth president, though hardly his favorite. Peeved over having been denied a civil service grade promotion for which he was eligible, he considered Coolidge the most egotistical and clothes-conscious president of them all.[21] Housekeeper Elizabeth Jaffray also noted he had more clothes than any of the past five presidents.[22] Doorman John Meis gave Coolidge a haircut every other week, and when he accidentally nipped an ear on one occasion Coolidge ordered him to procure a pair of spectacles even though he had flawless vision. Meis had to keep the glasses in his pocket, slipping them on whenever he went to see the president for a haircut or to deliver a message on his silver tray.[23] Once Coolidge had him offer a shave to Charles Evans Hughes, staying as a guest while on break from a diplomatic assignment. As it turned out, Hughes had no interest in shaving the full beard he had kept for years, but each morning Coolidge sent Meis to his door with the same offer, much to his bewilderment.[24] In such pranks the president reviled, hiding from his bodyguard and trying to slip out the side door without notice for his morning stroll.

No one had a better look at the private Coolidge than young Dr. Boone. A Pennsylvania Quaker, he had served with the Marines in the war and earned the Congressional Medal of Honor, cleaning shrapnel wounds, treating mustard gas victims, combating gangrene, amputating limbs, closing wounds with safety pins sometimes, and trying to save lives without antibiotics or plasma at Verdun, Soissons, Belleau Wood, Meuse Argonne, Vierzy, and other battles. Now he saw the president twice daily and found him to be quirky, impatient, and headstrong. Boone tried to persuade him to reverse his evening routine of bathing, donning his tuxedo, and riding his mechanical horse at a trot while perspiring with exertion. It would have been healthier to bathe after riding, rather than dining in damp clothes, but that was his routine. It was a strange arrangement, with Coolidge summoning Boone over the slightest deviation in health, yet often determining his own treatment, such as taking a homemade tonic brewed by Miss Pierce in Vermont. Whenever he got seasick aboard the *Mayflower* he would retire to his cabin and instruct Boone to drop cocaine into the external canal of his ear. The doctor, though reluctant, "felt that if it helped him mentally, it would quiet his nervous system."[25] For indigestion, Boone provided Elixir Lactopeptin and supplemented its small alcohol content with additional alcohol. "I believe later on in his administration the doses of the fortification from alcohol were highly gratifying to him," Boone relates, "and we put enough into the Elixir Lactopeptin that it was a good substitute for a small cocktail." Coolidge, who before prohibition kept a flask or jigger of whiskey on hand, seemed to suspect but never asked.[26]

The president suffered from bronchial asthma, allergies, colds, and ear and throat infections in the low altitude of the capital. With his poor circulation—he had trouble staying warm in the drafty White House—he worried about his heart, closely monitoring his pulse and taking a daily electrocardiograph test.[27]

"He seemed to be quite a lonely figure so often," relates Boone, who watched him sit alone during movies shown on a rigged-up screen aboard the *Mayflower*, as Grace and guests laughed and enjoyed themselves.[28] Unaccustomed to living in intimate quarters with so many people, he probably longed for the privacy he had known at the Willard and, before that, the Adams House in Boston.

Stearns had a permanent suite at the White House and stayed weeks at a time. A teetotaler, five feet, six inches tall, with gray hair, a mustache, rimless glasses, a conventional black suit and black four-in-hand tie, a watch chain across his vest, and an ample waistline, he was 17 years older than Coolidge and semiretired from R.W. Stearns and Company, which he inherited from his father. The elder Stearns had gone into business in 1847, hiring agents to purchase yarn throughout New England and paying families on the South Shore and Cape Cod to produce specialty hand-knit goods and laces. A purveyor of quality merchandise, he and two other emporiums, George W. Warren and Company and C.F. Harvey and Company, helped establish the "one-price" system rather than the "trading" and "bargaining" that went on in stores across the country. When Frank took over in 1908 he moved the store to a seven-floor building at 140 Tremont Street, across from Boston Commons and a new subway station that brought in more customers for table linen, sheets, blankets, towels, silverware, luggage, hats, hatpins, hosiery, corsets, cameo brooches, pearl chokers, shoes, socks, satin gloves, and the like. "Make sure you have the best goods and yell," he liked to say.[29]

Stearns first met Coolidge in 1913 when he went to see him about a special legislative act that would allow their alma mater to connect to the local sewer system. The state senator had listened in silence for several minutes before standing up, walking over to a closet, unlocking the door, pulling out a chair, and motioning Stearns to have a seat. Then he listened some more, barely speaking, before wishing Stearns a good day and putting the chair back in the closet without saying whether he would support the act. Stearns considered him "strange" but months later received a handwritten note from Coolidge with a copy of the sewer bill he had put through the legislature.[30] So began a friendship between a rising young politician and an older businessman whose previous interest in politics consisted mainly of writing checks to Republicans and collecting Lincoln biographies. In his eyes Coolidge was a modern-day Lincoln with a similar simplicity, way with words, and backcountry shrewdness.[31]

"You know politics does not differ especially from anything else,"

Coolidge once told him. "In politics nothing is worth having unless you can have it in the right way."[32]

Now the dry goods merchant was practically living in the White House and sleeping in the Lincoln Bedroom at that. Morning-time he had breakfast alone or with his wife and took his exercise by pacing the upstairs hallway, smoking a cigar, and waiting for the president to call. Sometimes he went all day without seeing Coolidge. One afternoon he was summoned to the executive office to find the fatigued president sitting behind his desk, looking out the window toward the Potomac. Ten minutes passed in silence. Stearns sat in a chair. At last Coolidge turned and said, "That will be all."[33] After dinner they often sat in the study, smoking cigars and looking out the window with nary a word. "Two farm horses in a fence corner—haunch to neck—flapping flies with their tails, must have the same spiritual satisfaction that gave these two men their sparse delight," wrote one observer.[34] Stearns knew he was there to run errands and provide a familiar presence, dependable, trustworthy, without discussing government matters. When he had the temerity one evening to recommend someone for a judicial position, Coolidge advised him not to meddle in such matters: "You sell the cloth, Frank, and I'll take care of the politics."[35] When reporters portrayed him as an unofficial adviser to the president, he said no, he was "only a floorwalker."[36]

As time went on, Stearns could not help wondering about the man he had promoted for years. The way Coolidge treated his son was particularly disconcerting. Stearns, having resolved differences with his own son, who had converted from the Congregationalist faith to Catholicism and spurned the family business to become a librarian at the College of the Holy Cross, despaired that Coolidge was so impatient, so ornery, in relations with his lone surviving child, nitpicking over his clothes, grades, and activities. There was more. The slights that once seemed little more than eccentricities began to bother Stearns, as when Coolidge neglected to send a telegram to him and Mrs. Stearns before their trip to Europe, wishing them safe passage. At last he laid out his frustrations to Butler, who said anyone who had intimate associations with Coolidge was likely to get hurt, for he was inconsiderate. Sadly, Stearns came to conclude that Coolidge was not warmhearted, though a great man nonetheless.[37]

Dr. Boone once thought Coolidge was rude by nature but now understood his need to shut out the world while thinking through problems and policy options, which put a "nervous and emotional strain upon him." The physician could see, more than others, what a toll the office took on him, but thought he was better as a public man—genuine, subtle, politically sagacious—than in his personal relations.[38]

"Those who saw Coolidge in a rage were simply startled," wrote

Ike Hoover. "The older employees about the White House who had known Roosevelt used to think he raved at times, but in his worst temper he was calm compared to Coolidge."[39] Yet Coolidge was not one to brood or bear ill will against the subject of his wrath. "I never knew him to speak ill of anyone," observed Secretary Work.[40]

Frank W. Stearns (shown here ca. 1923), the Boston dry goods merchant who promoted Coolidge from his days as an obscure state politician and resided for months at a time in the White House, providing companionship but not political advice, he told reporters (Harris & Ewing Collection, Library of Congress).

Edmund Starling walked several miles a day with the president on the Mall or to F Street, where pedestrians recognized him and raised their hat in salutation. Lined with haberdashers, boutiques, candy stores, and the like, F Street had the best shopping in the area, for the new suburbs in Maryland and Virginia lacked department stores. Most people shopped downtown. Coolidge liked to look through store windows along the promenade, sometimes choosing a dress or hat for Grace, whose sizes he kept in a small notebook for reference. "He loved his wife deeply," Starling wrote. "He was, of course, a very sentimental man, and a very shy one. He loved a few people a great deal, and he was embarrassed about showing it. Gradually, as time went by, I found him to be so human and thoughtful that I came to the conclusion his outward reticence and aloofness were part of a protective shell." The tall, debonair, well-read bachelor had entered the service on Christmas Eve 1914 after working as a deputy sheriff and special agent for the railroads down south, carrying a six-shooter, solving dozens of robberies, and capturing the notorious "California Kid" to much acclaim. When he arrived at Washington he was told he was working for the Treasury Department, not the president, who could not order him to leave. Ten years had passed without serious incident despite one near-disaster. The first time Harding had returned home as president a reception committee engaged an old river steamboat for the homecoming, but Starling, inspecting the vessel, declared it "unsafe" and selected another boat for the president, to be placed beside the steamboat, on which 2,000 observers gathered to watch the event, causing the upper deck to cave in, killing several people. Now serving his third president, Starling, a Presbyterian from the hills of Kentucky, "could get along" with the Congregationalist from the hills of Vermont. As they walked, they discussed weather, literature, merchandise, history, politics, automobiles, farming, and other topics. Coolidge sometimes spoke of his mother: "I wish I could really speak to her. I wish that often."

They sometimes played a game in which Coolidge pretended his bodyguard was a secret drinker of bourbon, violating prohibition during off-hours. Starling went along with the routine, speaking in hushed tones of his latest encounters with bootleggers. In truth, Coolidge disliked prohibition. "Any law which inspires disrespect for the other laws—the good laws—is a bad law," he told the bodyguard.

One morning Starling arrived in a new brown suit with a green tie, receiving several sharp glances but, much to his surprise, no inquiries on where he bought the suit, how much he paid, and so on. Later Coolidge summoned him and handed him a small paper bag. "Here," he said. "Take this." Starling, returning to his station, opened the bag to find a brown tie.[41]

Those who knew Coolidge socially but not intimately, who saw him at his convenience, found him to be an easy companion. Bernard Baruch and Herbert Hoover found him almost garrulous at times, smoking cigars, resting his feet on his desk, discussing dogs, book publishing, history, philosophy, poetry, New England, social aspirants, higher education, among other topics. Will Rogers thought he had "more real, downright subtle humor than any one we have in public life."[42] Once he invited Coolidge to a performance to be held that evening at a downtown theater. It would not be much, he said, two or three hours of him talking, plus a quartet that sang. "Yes, I like singing," Coolidge replied.[43]

* * *

The long recess on Capitol Hill allowed Coolidge to concentrate on administration vice legislation. In the sphere of government regulation of business, he favored volunteerism over prosecution, partly to save money. At the Justice Department, the antitrust administrator and war hero William J. Donovan helped firms avoid trial by meeting with them in private to distinguish between legal and illegal activity, and by dropping charges if they agreed to halt any misconduct. These consent decrees terminated more than half of the antitrust suits under Coolidge and drew criticism from progressives even though 67 of the 111 decrees obtained since enactment of the Sherman Act in 1890 had been as such.

At the Federal Trade Commission—the FTC—sweeping reform was underway. Established in 1914 to investigate, publicize, and prohibit all "unfair methods of competition," it had struggled against conservative congressional opponents and adverse court decisions, achieving some success against trusts but taking two years to conduct cases and prompting companies to complain that false charges, recklessly brought by competitors, wasted resources and damaged reputations. Before 1925, Wilson appointees dominated the five-person commission. In February 1925, Coolidge had tipped the balance by replacing a term-expired Wilson appointee with former Republican congressman William E. Humphrey, who had once accused the FTC of being a "publicity bureau to spread socialistic propaganda," and who, combined with Harding appointee W.V. Fleet and Coolidge appointee C.W. Hunt, gave Republican appointees a three-to-two advantage over Wilson appointees.[44] That spring the commission announced several changes. First, it would pursue only specific allegations, not sweeping looks at entire economic sectors, as legislators often ordered under Section 6 of the Federal Trade Commission Act. Second, it would settle cases whenever possible by "stipulation" agreements with firms believed to be in violation of government-sanctioned trade practices. Third, it would give defendants the chance to present their case in a confidential preliminary hearing before pressing charges. Business interests praised the changes, liberals criticized them.

During the next six months, the FTC saved $500,000 by settling 184 cases through stipulation agreements, vice court orders. As Humphrey proudly told Coolidge, that amounted to more than $2,500 per case.[45]

The drive to reduce spending in Washington accelerated that spring with the president ordering through the Budget Bureau a review of all departments and budgets to meet his goal of getting the annual federal budget below $3 billion. "We must make each dollar sweat," said Director Lord, his investigative team attacking waste and inefficiency, his clearance unit matching purchasing needs with surplus supplies to prevent unnecessary orders, his aides replacing hundreds of government leases with one government-wide lease and consolidating hundreds of separate agency forms into 38 standard federal forms, reducing duplication and printing costs.[46] When a certain bureau ordered $35,000 worth of filing cabinets, he sent aides scrounging through government offices for spare or poorly used cabinets, lowering the bill to $3,974. No cost fell beneath his scrutiny: curtailing the distribution of free government publications, reducing telegrams, shortening letters, removing stripes from mail bags, replacing the red tape used to wrap official documents with regular white tape, turning grease into soap at a military hospital, lowering gas bills with early payments, narrowing the margins on money order blanks at an annual savings of $8,000, encouraging the switch from leaded pencils to mechanical ones at an annual savings of three cents per employee or $1,800 in total, combining government telegraph lines at an annual savings of $200,000, cracking down on the abuse of sick leave by post office clerks at an annual savings of $750,000, having government travelers reserve the less expensive upper berths in sleeper trains, and discouraging the "illegitimate use" of paper clips as toothpicks, ear reamers, bobbed hair holders, cuff links, pipe cleaners, watch chains, and toys. His statistician estimated that the "seven small and five large boxes" used to carry all the papers of the federal government from Philadelphia to Washington in 1800, would not hold sufficient paper clips to last 10 days in the current government.[47]

"If you can get people to economize on little things, they will get the habit on bigger things," Lord quipped.[48]

No expense was too small for Comptroller General J.R. McCarl and his dreaded blue pencil. The first to hold his position, as established by the Budget and Accounting Act of 1921, he was responsible for government finances, expenditures of appropriations, audits, and the settlement and adjudication of claims. Such claims came to more than 30,000 a year, including about 3,600 annually that went to him for decision. The mild-mannered, diminutive, Iowa-born attorney and former Republican congressional campaign manager was known as a stickler and the most disliked man in Washington or the watchdog of the Treasury by various accounts. He was the subject of much newspaper coverage. He was also untouchable in the sense that his term was 15 years and that no one in the executive branch could direct him or remove him by law. Nothing less than an act of Congress in response to a "grave offense" could remove him.

McCarl had clashed with the various departments since taking office in 1921, as they resisted what they perceived as meddling in their internal matters and challenged his decisions in court on numerous occasions. Never letting up, he and his team continued to tangle with senior managers and employees, challenging their accounts and claims, and issuing strict guidance on travel expenditures such as tips, laundry services, hotels, bathing facilities, taxi rides, and train rides. When General John J. Pershing, wartime hero, tried to claim reimbursement for train travel to Washington on official business, the accountants said no because he lost his ticket receipt.[49] When a government clerk in Panama lost a leg in a service-related accident and sent in a bill for a wooden replacement, they said no because the expenditure fell outside the "reasonable, medical, surgical and hospital services and supplies" allowed under the employee compensation law.[50] When the Bureau of Printing and Engraving ordered 37 pairs of wooden shoes, at $1.95 each, to protect employees from the acids that disintegrated the soles of their regular shoes, the accountants said no reimbursement for personal effects.[51] When the Navy sought funding for funeral wreaths for deceased sailors, at $15 each, the accountants said no.[52] When a clerk submitted a receipt for $1.50 spent on lunch during an official trip to Alexandria, Virginia, some seven miles from his office, they determined that the trip fell short of "traveling away from his post of duty," only to lose the case in small claims court.[53]

Such nitpicking brought ridicule from government employees and others. "Economy is a grand thing if a nation is rich enough to stand it," wrote a *Washington Post* columnist who often criticized McCarl and wryly noted that the cost of investigating small claims exceeded the savings from denying them. McCarl took guidance from the simple language in Article I, Section 9, of the Constitution: "No money shall be drawn from the Treasury but in consequence of appropriations made by law."[54] He would tell proponents of questionable expenditures to show him the law.[55]

The criticism was irrelevant to McCarl, who thought rules were rules and must be upheld to discourage others from going around them.[56]

The Coolidge administration would implement some 6,000 cost reductions that year. The Department of Treasury alone contributed more than 500 reductions, including saving $818,057 by eliminating 557 positions engaged in servicing the pared-down national debt, saving $48,670 by reducing linen content in securities certificates, saving $73,750 by switching from double sheets to single sheets of paper, saving $3,863 by replacing wax seals with paper seals on shipments of national bank currency, and saving $12,081 by switching from white rag to white sulphite writing paper for more than 18,000,000 income tax forms. The Department of Agriculture saved nearly $9,000 by changing the procedure for tuberculosis tests on cattle to reduce each one by more than a penny, and reduced spending on a biological survey out west by having employees sleep in tents rather than hotel rooms whenever possible. The Department of Commerce saved $20,000 by using employees rather than a contractor to move a large testing machine within the bureau of standards, including building a ramp and placement area for the machine. The Department of Labor saved $50,000 by moving alien deportations from New York to Galveston and using government-owned Merchant Marine ships rather than leasing privately owned ships. The Department of State saved $200 by canceling a clock-winder contract. Army doctors and surgeons saved $21,700 by reconditioning 500,000 yards of nonabsorbent gauze. The Veterans Bureau lowered its monthly telephone bill from $250 to $2.50 by ending nonessential long distance calls. The weather bureau in Los Angeles saved

$633 by purchasing tree stumpage from a recently burned-over area and cutting them into telephone poles rather than purchasing new poles. The postmaster at Canton, New York, saved $90 by turning up the edges on his frayed window shades rather than ordering new ones.[57]

The president, by personally reviewing all White House bills, kept expenditures below $1,000 a month for the first time in years. He changed the stationary from double sheets to single sheets, discontinued the tradition of providing complimentary pencils to reporters, halted the practice of 21-gun salutes for all but the most formal occasions, reduced the number of towels in washrooms, and limited the use of electric lights to cloudy days and evenings.[58]

"I should not be surprised to hear that the next great stroke for economy will be the placing of oars on the *Mayflower*," quipped one Democratic congressman.[59] Another inquired whether the president was subject to a $35 fine for breaking the sanitary regulations of the District of Columbia by substituting ordinary drinking glasses for paper cups at the White House water coolers.[60] As word slipped out that Coolidge rode a mechanical horse for exercise, complete with bridle and saddle, a Democrat chortled, "I shall not be surprised if soon it will be heralded to the people that the President is riding this wooden horse for the purpose of cutting down the oat bill at the White House stables."[61]

Coolidge liked to poke around the kitchen and pantry, inspecting the icebox and the larder, looking over the shelves, checking the menu, and asking the cost of milk, butter, meat, and other items from local markets. He had to pay for food except for state dinners and receptions, which were covered under a $25,000 special allowance.

"I don't see why we have to have six hams for one dinner," he said to the housekeeper one evening. "It seems like an awful lot of ham to me."

"But, Mr. President, there will be sixty people here," she replied, having done White House dinners since 1909. "These Virginia hams are small and we cannot possibly serve more than ten people with one ham and be sure of having an abundance."

"Well, six hams look like an awful lot to me."[62]

* * *

Coolidge, having accepted an invitation to honor the fallen dead at Arlington Cemetery on Memorial Day, May 30, took several days to prepare an address that went beyond the rhetoric usually associated with such occasions. The speech was to be broadcast by radio to millions of listeners, and he chose to deliver a message on the threat to freedom and self-government that had arisen from changes to the federalist system and the balance between the federal government and the states. For inspiration, he read through the Democratic Party platforms before 1896, most notably the one upon which Grover Cleveland successfully ran for election in 1884 as a proponent of limited federal government.[63]

"What we need is not more federal government, but better local government," Coolidge said at the podium that day, after paying tribute to Civil War veterans in attendance and others who had fought for their country. "Yet many people who would agree to this have large responsibility for the lapses of local authority."

He warned that state governments had become too dependent on Washington for law enforcement and financial aid in particular, putting the constitutional framework at risk. Take prohibition. The Anti-Saloon League had recently proposed the use of naval ships to impose a blockade against rum-runners. Coolidge opposed such a deployment, having already sponsored bilateral talks to halt illegal imports of alcoholic beverages and approved an additional $20 million for Coast Guard anti-smuggling efforts. Instead he encouraged state and municipal governments to do their part. The resources of the federal government had to be concentrated on important cases, such as intrastate racketeering. The federal courts could not handle police cases involving petty crimes or small offenders. The number of investigators and prosecutors was insufficient. Then he turned to a topic he had addressed on several previous occasions—federal subsidies to the states—in a more critical manner than before. This "insidious practice" encouraged states to spend money beyond their means and to increase their requests for aid, to receive as much as possible from Washington. The subsidies transferred money from state to state. They undermined the states as a whole and the principle of self-government, he said, in language that would have fit into the Democratic platforms from the 19th century and lent credence to remarks heard occasionally in the capital that he was in many respects a Grover Cleveland Democrat.[64]

Many in the audience that day remarked they had never heard Coolidge speak with such force or strong feeling.[65]

* * *

Three days later the first lady traveled to Mercersburg Academy for the unveiling of a portrait of Calvin the day before he would have graduated. To be with his former classmates on such an occasion, far from upsetting her, seemed to raise her spirits. "Never, for one moment have I felt a sense of separation from Calvin," she wrote. "When I am in places where he liked to be and with people whom he loved, I have a very keen sense of nearness to him."[66]

The president remained in Washington as temperatures exceeded

100 degrees, working at his desk in dark woolen suits and preparing for an address in Minneapolis at the centennial of the first Norse settlement. Newspapers and Republican leaders saw the trip as an indication he meant to run for reelection in 1928 by strengthening his position against radical third-party movements in the upper Middle West, where he struggled in 1924.[67] Coolidge told reporters he simply wanted to thank Minnesota voters for his narrow victory over La Follette, but an adviser added that the president did not regard his abbreviated term as a full term.[68] To promote economy, Coolidge requested a regular car in a regular train—like his trip to Chicago the previous year—but when the Secret Service and the train operators advised against repeating the risk, he told them to attach the presidential cars to a regular train rather than running a special. That way he and his party paid the regular fare rather than the charter fare, saving a total of $1,500 for the 30-hour trip. No thought went to flying from Chicago to Minneapolis to reduce the trip by eight hours. The Secret Service would have protested air travel for the president, had he been so inclined.[69]

The presidential compartment was kept cool with tubs of ice and electric fans as they traveled through the Middle West states and he waved to crowds at stations along the way, noticing most women wore silk dresses and many had silk stockings in a "general appearance of prosperity" thanks to strong crops, improvements in agricultural methods, and cooperative marketing.[70] In progressive Minneapolis, with 400,000 persons inhabiting what had been wilderness 45 years ago, he received an enthusiastic response during a motorcade ride from the station to the home of Frank Kellogg, where he rested before speaking at the Minnesota State Fair.

"Now we know why he appointed Kellogg Secretary of State—so he would have some place to stay while in Minneapolis," Will Rogers joked.[71]

* * *

The president continued to monitor negotiations with European countries on their wartime debt obligations. Finland, Hungary, Lithuania, and Poland had agreed to settlements during the past year, following the precedent set by England in 1922, with lower interest rates and longer payment schedules. The 12 other debtor countries had made minimal or no progress toward settlements. Algeria, Liberia, and Russia were unable or unwilling. Belgium, Czechoslovakia, Estonia, France, Greece, Italy, Latvia, Rumania, and Yugoslavia were somewhat recalcitrant. France had by far the largest debt among the holdout countries at $4.2 billion, including interest. The rest owed $2.5 billion all together and hoped that France would be able to negotiate better terms than England had received in 1922, thereby setting a precedent for their own negotiations.

This impasse led to a new policy in Washington during the late spring and early summer of 1925. The previous policy, established in 1921, had been to let debtor countries initiate talks on debt settlements. Now, Secretary Kellogg began to increase pressure on debtor countries by having ambassadors and ministers deliver simultaneously to Belgium, Czechoslovakia, France, Greece, Italy, Latvia, Rumania, and Yugoslavia a note stating the time had come to negotiate and reach agreement on repayment. Coolidge set a deadline of September 1 and put some clout behind this diplomacy by stating publicly that the administration would not look with favor on any loans by American bankers to countries which had not taken steps to pay their debt obligations to the United States. In doing so, he acknowledged the government had no legal authority to prevent such loans, but pointed out that banks usually consulted in advance with the Department of State, which in turn consulted with the Departments of Commerce and Treasury, providing an opening to discourage lending as appropriate.[72] This fell within his constitutional powers to conduct foreign relations, despite protests from Senator Borah and others on Capitol Hill. The new policy held up several loan requests and put immediate pressure on debtor governments, which had lost access to credit from the London banks as England returned to the gold standard with temporary restrictions on capital outflows. Coolidge was surely aware that his leverage to promote debt settlements would never be better.

France, which received a $100 million loan from J.P. Morgan and Company right before Coolidge revealed his new policy, secretly proposed a 110-year payment schedule, beginning with a 10-year moratorium on all payments, followed by 10 years of interest-free payments and 90 years of payments at an interest rate of 0.5 percent. When Mellon said no, Finance Minister Etienne Clementel proposed an 83-year payment plan with interest rates at 0.5 percent for the first 15 years and a maximum of 2 percent for the last 28 years, along with a "safeguard clause" that payments should be proportionately reduced in the event that Germany failed to meet its reparation payments, even though Congress had ruled out any such stipulation. Again Mellon said no. France then proposed a 68-year payment plan at an average interest rate of less than 1 percent. Again, no. This led Foreign Minister Aristide Briand to publicly acknowledge the validity of the debt, preparing his fellow citizens for the necessity of having to pay it and creating optimism in Washington that a settlement might occur.

Many other holdout countries began to move toward settlements. Belgium, in seeking a $50 million stabilization loan from J.P. Morgan and Company to help return to the gold standard, sent a commission to Washington to negotiate payment terms for its $480 million debt. Italy, in pursuing a $100 million loan from the same lender to support the imperiled lira, approached the Treasury Department to discuss a payment schedule for its $2.1 billion debt. Czechoslovakia, Estonia, Latvia, Rumania, and Yugoslavia asked to accelerate talks on their respective debt obligations.

A reporter for the *Washington Post* gave credit to Coolidge for producing a breakthrough with his "shrewd Yankee policy."[73]

* * *

On the first night of the summer of 1925, the president delivered his semiannual budget address to the Business Organization of the Government and used the occasion to reiterate his position linking budget surpluses and tax reductions. "The way has been prepared for further tax reduction," he said to the 2,000 or so attendees and a nationwide radio audience. "This I will recommend to Congress in the next budget message." This had been made possible by constructive economy, resulting in a federal budget that would end the fiscal year barely above $3 billion, within striking distance of the goal he had set during his early days in office. The surplus belonged to the people, he said, providing the opportunity to improve lives materially and spiritually across the country. He made sure to stress the link between spending and taxes: "Economy in the cost of government is inseparable from reduction in taxes. We cannot have the latter without the former."[74]

This familiar refrain was meant to undermine suggestions among some industry groups and politicians that tax cuts would effectively pay for themselves by stimulating greater economic growth and higher tax revenues. Coolidge would not make that assumption, however probable.

* * *

The following day, the president and Mrs. Coolidge and their entourage boarded a train to Massachusetts for a much longer "working vacation" than the two weeks they had taken the previous year, escaping the humidity and high temperatures, like most congressmen, ambassadors, ministers, and cabinet officers, who fled far and wide that summer. Hoover and Wilbur went to California, Sargent to Vermont, Weeks to Massachusetts, Mellon to Long Island, Kellogg to Minnesota, New to Michigan, Jardine to Kansas, Work to Wyoming, and Davis to Europe.

Inasmuch as Coolidge missed Plymouth Notch and wanted to be with his father, he needed more hotel rooms to accommodate his bodyguards, secretaries, and clerks, along with the 50 or so correspondents who followed him. So he had engaged an eleven-week lease at White Court, a seaside mansion at Swampscott, Massachusetts, beside the Stearns estate and within motoring distance of his father, who had heart trouble and an abscessed prostate gland. Friends of the president offered to purchase the mansion as his permanent summer vacation site, but he declined: "I might not like it."[75] The summer executive office was set up on the sixth floor of an office building in nearby Lynn, with telephone and telegraph lines to maintain contact with Rudolph Forster in Washington. The *Mayflower* was docked six miles away at Marblehead Harbor, creating a sensation along the North Shore of Massachusetts.

Coolidge seldom used the yacht that summer and shunned the swimming pool and private beach at White Court, unlike Grace who had taken to the water since learning to swim in her early 40s. Nor did he accept an open invitation at a local country club. "There is an art in holiday making," wrote an English lady correspondent dispatched to the scene. "I do not believe the President Coolidge knows what it is or how to acquire it."[76] Besides working mornings at his office, receiving visitors, and holding his twice-weekly press conferences, he walked about the estate, looked at the sea, watched the gardeners, smoked with Stearns, posed for photographers, and engaged in trips to Bunker Hill, Cambridge, Plymouth Plantation, Salem, and Quincy, to educate the public on the past. In Watertown, outside Boston, he visited the old Arlington Street Cemetery, stopping before two crumbling brown headstones that bore the names John and Mary Coolidge, his first ancestors in the country. They had emigrated in 1630 from Cottenham, England, with the Massachusetts Bay Company aboard the same ship as religious leader John Winthrop. John Coolidge had been elected town selectman in 1638 and reelected many times before his death in 1691, at 88. Mary Coolidge had passed on three months later at 88, leaving behind eight children. The president had descended directly from their second son, Simon, followed by Obadiah, Obadiah Josiah, John, Calvin, Calvin, and John.

When reporters asked Coolidge whether he was enjoying his vacation, he replied, "Oh, yes, very nice, I guess."[77] By way of amusement they made up humorous questions they wanted to ask him, such as why he had been a crank and when he would invite his mother-in-law to visit. The contest went on for weeks, each trying to come up with the most ridiculous question.[78]

Meantime, Coolidge became impatient with false press reports: that he expected an anthracite coal strike, that he planned to call a special session of Congress, that he was personally involved in debt negotiations with foreign diplomats, that he had witnessed evidence of rum-running at sea, that his spending cuts would force the army to dismiss as many as 10,000 men and 2,000 officers, that Secretary Weeks was about to resign after suffering a stroke. At last he angrily told reporters they ought to label their dispatches "Faking with the President."[79]

After Colonel Coolidge had emergency prostrate surgery in his parlor, observing the procedure with a handheld mirror under a local anesthesia while neighbors watched through the window, the president and first lady drove eight hours to see him. They found him feverish and wan, his hair showing flecks of gray for the first time. As father and son sat in the kitchen, Starling noticed, "They were shy with each other, but the deep bond of affection between them was apparent."[80] The village now had access to electricity through a power line from Ludlow, but the Colonel opted not to install it.

On the return to Swampscott, the president chose a scenic route and they got lost several times. When they arrived at a toll bridge across the Connecticut River, leading into New Hampshire, he handed a nickel to the female attendant, who failed to recognize him.[81] Later they stopped to have tea and toast at a little roadside restaurant at Gilsum, New Hampshire, where no one knew them.[82]

On Sunday, August 2, the president sent his father the following note:

> It is two years tonight since you woke me to bring the message that I was President. It seems a very short time. I trust it has been a great satisfaction to you. I think only two or three fathers have seen their sons chosen to be President of the United States. I am sure I came to it very largely by your bringing up and your example. If that was what you wanted you have much to be thankful for that you have lived to so great an age to see it.[83]

Three days later he wrote his son in quite another tone, imploring him to study harder:

> The world will pass and leave you and you will see many boys that you do not think are very smart going right by you and leaving you behind to be ignored, pitied, and despised. You will have to make the decision yourself. No one can make it for you. But unless you work, I do not propose to pay out money to let you idle around college.[84]

In early September, Coolidge invited his son back to Swampscott to celebrate his 19th birthday with cake but no presents, for they did not believe in making a fuss over anniversaries. In Washington, temperatures reached 100 degrees that weekend. In Swampscott, autumn was approaching with brisk temperatures, withered flowers, red-tinged maples, and shuttered-up cottages along the shore. Coolidge wore winter clothes on his morning walks. By the time he returned to humid Washington on September 10, he felt reinvigorated and ready to work after the longest presidential vacation since the halcyon days of Ulysses Grant.[85]

"Eleven weeks—with pay!" chimed a Washington Post columnist.[86]

* * *

The lead story that week involved sensationalist charges by Colonel William Mitchell, head of the Army Air Service, that gross negligence had left America ill prepared in aeronautics, with military orders virtually nonexistent since the war and passenger airlines hampered by fatalities, high ticket prices, hard wicker seats, cold interiors, and struggles to carry heavy luggage or get insurance coverage or fly at night. The United States was the lone power without an aeronautical policy. England, France, Germany, and Japan were developing large aerial forces with government subsidies covering 50 to 90 percent of operating costs. These countries perceived aviation from a military standpoint as vital to national defense. The United States did not. Colonel Mitchell, incensed by the recent destruction of the *Shenandoah*, a Zeppelin-type aircraft that U.S. naval authorities had ordered into a storm-swept area, accused the Army and Navy high command of incompetence and dereliction. Many newspaper editors and politicians accused him of false statements and called for court-martial hearings, but Coolidge kept clear of the controversy other than to announce the formation of a nine-person board to investigate the state of aviation in the country and make a recommendation on the need for an independent air force. He named Dwight Morrow as chairman of what became known as the "Morrow Board."

* * *

Of more interest to the president was whether his policy of deterring banks from floating loans to debtor countries would produce payment settlements with Italy and France, the main holdouts. On September 18, he told reporters that the press should stand by his policy and not encourage reduction or cancellation of the debts, in a rare attempt to intimidate newspaper coverage of his administration, revealing the importance he placed on the issue.[87] Negotiations with Italy began to move toward a settlement that autumn. Negotiations with France were a disappointment, however. The parties failed to agree on repayment terms and France continued to insist on a "safeguard clause" linked to German reparation payments, leaving Mellon livid and the informal loan ban in effect. French newspapers and politicians condemned "Uncle Shylock" for trying to turn a profit from the war, and Parisians harassed American tourists with insults, obscene gestures, and water balloons.

* * *

The last days of September found Coolidge straining to complete an address to the annual convention of the American Legion in Omaha, Nebraska, eager to make certain points that had been on his mind since the election, against the advice of some of his counselors.[88] Departing

Washington on October 4, his 20th wedding anniversary, accompanied by cakes and flowers, he and Grace dined in their private railcar and watched a movie from a projection machine.

Their wedding had been a small affair in the dark-shingled, Victorian-style Goodhue home at 312 Maple Street, Burlington, Vermont, with 15 guests and no invitations, photographs, or newspaper announcement. Mrs. Goodhue tried to postpone the event by asking Grace to come home for a year to learn baking and other homemaking skills, to which he replied they could buy bread. "We thought we were made for each other," he relates.[89] They shared vows in the parlor, in front of the bay window, on a rainy day, and departed on a honeymoon at Montreal and Niagara Falls before returning prematurely for a political campaign. Initially Grace had been stunned by his temper—how he sometimes lost his composure over nothing—but determined not to let him disturb her natural equilibrium, knowing such a tightly controlled person, dealing with the uncertainties of politics and elections, worrying about money, needed an outlet. It all went back to losing his mother at a young age, she thought, but when he went too far she would pull him back on a "tight rein."[90] As for Mrs. Goodhue, she "never liked that man from the day Grace married him."[91]

Now, 20 years later, they hurtled westward through the night as he read his speech with some displeasure. It was not a good speech, he told Edward Clark; he would like to have rewritten many parts.[92]

At the convention he received a rousing ovation from veterans seated in an amphitheater, braced against the cold as snowflakes fell from low-hanging clouds. Taking the podium, he praised their service, discussed foreign and military affairs, and decried attempts by certain military elements to manipulate public opinion—a clear salvo at Colonel Mitchell and others promoting a separate air force.

Then he spoke the words that would make newspaper headlines across the country—a plea for tolerance for all citizens:

> Whether one traces his Americanism back three centuries to the Mayflower, or three years to the steerage, is not half so important as whether his Americanism of today is real and genuine. No matter by what various craft we came here, we are all now in the same boat.

Noting that Americans of all races and religions had fought in the war without anyone questioning their patriotism, he spoke in earnest:

> If we are to have that harmony and tranquility, that union of spirit which is the foundation of real national genius and national progress, we must all realize that there are true Americans who do not happen to be born in our section of the country, who do not attend our place of religious worship, who are not of our racial stock, or who are not proficient in our language. If we are to create

> on this continent a free Republic and an enlightened civilization that will be capable of reflecting the true greatness and glory of mankind, it will be necessary to regard these differences as accidental or unessential. We shall have to look beyond the outward manifestations of race and creed. Divine Providence has not bestowed upon any race a monopoly of patriotism and character.[93]

This was perceived as a repudiation of the Ku Klux Klan, which had held a march of 40,000 or so persons in Washington a month earlier. Editorials in the *New York Times*, the *New York World*, the *Philadelphia Inquirer*, the *Chicago Tribune*, the *Cleveland Plain Dealer*, the *Richmond Times-Dispatch*, and other newspapers praised his message, and hundreds of congratulatory telegrams arrived at the White House.[94] In the fall elections the Klan would take a beating at the polls, losing contests in Kentucky, Michigan, New York, and Virginia, as its membership began to decline.

* * *

On October 25, Coolidge addressed the annual meeting of the National Council of Congregational Churches, in Washington, stating, "I have felt propriety in coming here because of my belief in the necessity for a growing reliance of the political success of our government upon the religious convictions of our people." To remedy lawlessness and other problems of postwar society, he believed in religion:

> I do not know of any source of power other than that which comes from religion.
>
> I do not know of any adequate support for our form of government except that which comes from religion.
>
> If there are general failures in the enforcement of law, it is because there have been failures in the disposition to enforce the law. I can conceive of no adequate remedy for the evils which beset society except through the influences of religion. There is no form of education which will not fail, there is no form of government which will not fail, there is no form of reward which will not fail.[95]

* * *

The following day he met with six governors who submitted a petition from 32 governors seeking the repeal of the federal inheritance tax to avoid double taxation with state inheritance taxes and unnecessary economic disruption. Coolidge agreed, having opposed the increase in the inheritance tax in 1924 and having recommended in a speech to a tax association in early 1925 that the federal government should gradually withdraw from the field all together. He also sensed an opening to restate his position on federal subsidies to the states, no doubt irked by a recent surge in spending on roads that appeared to go beyond the "post road" provision in the Constitution by supporting local road construction.[96]

In response to a question from reporters on the meeting with the governors, Coolidge said he agreed with their position, albeit with the stipulation that the federal government would simultaneously reduce subsidies to the states since they would have more money to pay for their own activities. "I think it would be better if the states get their own sources of revenue and make their own decisions about expenditures, rather than for Congress to undertake to say that the states ought to pay so much money and if they do why then the National Government ought to make quite a large contribution towards it," he said during a lengthy discourse on the need to reduce the centralization of government power in Washington.[97] This received widespread newspaper coverage and signaled that the administration would push to significantly reduce the rate on inheritance taxes and keep federal subsidies to a minimum.

* * *

On November 19, Coolidge addressed the annual dinner of the venerable New York Chamber of Commerce and a national radio hookup, lauding business conditions and practices throughout the nation, from factories to farms, from employer to employee: "It is the work of the world." In an age of unparalleled prosperity he called for friendly cooperation and understanding between government and business. The reform days of Roosevelt and Wilson were over. Business had shown the ability to "correct its own abuses," allowing government to concentrate on economy, tax reduction, debt reduction, and the flow of credit to domestic and foreign borrowers. "The financial strength of America has contributed to the spiritual restoration of the world," he said.[98]

This was too much for the *London Daily News*, which replied mockingly:

> The author of that prayer also thanked God he was not as other men are, and recorded with the smirking self-satisfaction his financial righteousness and his virtuous self-restraint. No rich parvenu can ever have addrest his humblest poor relation in a tone of more offensively oleaginous patronage than this.[99]

At home, Democratic newspapers and progressive periodicals chided the president for coddling "big business" and failing to see economic weaknesses such as stagnant commodity prices, speculation, and rising bank failures, even as stock market prices rose to record highs in October, with sales exceeding two million shares on 18 of 21 trading days that month. Republicans praised Coolidge for his speech, but on the whole he might have been more sanguine on the structure of the economy and the prospects for continued prosperity. Indeed he might have taken heed of the sharp decline in stock prices a week before the speech, after several Federal Reserve banks raised their rediscount rates from 3.5 to 4.0 percent, putting a damper on speculative trading and exposing potential volatility in the market.

* * *

All told, Coolidge delivered 28 speeches in 1925, more than any predecessor in modern times besides Wilson stumping for reelection in 1916, and continued to hold twice-weekly press conferences, demonstrating a command of administrative matters, appointments, budget estimates, crop prices, diplomatic negotiations, disarmament talks, economic trends, foreign debt settlements, foreign conflicts, immigration, labor, legal issues, legislative proposals, military needs, shipping, reparations, tariff rates, and other matters relevant to his responsibilities. This at a time when clerk Rudolph Forster estimated that the duties of the office were three times greater than when Roosevelt was president and five times greater than when McKinley was president, because of the addition of budget-making, tariff-making, and various new bureaus and commissions during the previous two decades.[100] "The duties of the President have increased in every way," said Joseph P. Tumulty, former secretary to Wilson.[101]

Coolidge, for all his sorrow, found the inner strength to press on, as when his mother died, as when his sister died. No doubt he was tormented by thoughts of young Calvin, of what might have been under different circumstances, had he not been president, but he was the sort to work through sadness and pain, a tough-minded, disciplined, conscientious man. The secretaries who worked by his side, day to day, perceived him that way. To Everett Sanders, he was "an exceptionally hard worker."[102] To Edward Clark, he kept the same routine through his presidency and "kept his emotions under control, not only on the surface, though it almost killed him."[103]

* * *

That autumn Coolidge worried about his father, who had to hire a secretary to handle correspondence and strained to accommodate visitors, fainting in front of a delegation from Rhode Island. The president sent a physician to examine him and invited him south for the winter, but he declined. As the elder Coolidge continued to suffer from "heart blocks" and poor circulation, he could no longer walk to the store to retrieve his mail and talk to neighbors. Immobile for the most part, he read the newspapers and listened to a recently bought radio set in his sitting room;

he liked to read the newspapers, he said, to keep up with the state of his health.[104] Louis Chamberlain, the stage driver between Bridgewater and Ludlow, stopped by twice daily, telling him the latest from the local hill towns and inquiring whether he needed anything. "Yes," the Colonel said, "a new pair of legs."[105] Dr. Albert W. Cram of Bridgewater called twice a day and advised against travel. As Christmas approached, the Colonel sat in his home while a snowstorm swept across the hills. From Washington he received a package of yuletide gifts and a letter from his son:

> All seems to be going fairly well with us.
>
> It is getting to be almost Christmas time again. I always think of mother and Abbie and grandmother and now of Calvin. Perhaps you will see them all before I do, but in a little while we shall all be together for Christmas.[106]

Three days after Christmas, Coolidge received word that his father was confined to bed after losing the use of his right leg to poor circulation. On the morning of January 1, 1926, as people lined up outside the White House for the traditional reception, the saddened president wrote:

> It is a nice bright day for the New Year but rather cold. I wish you were here where you could have every care and everything made easy for you but I know you feel more content at home. Of course we wish we could be with you. I suppose I am the most powerful man in the world but great power does not mean much except great limitations. I cannot have any freedom even to go and come. I am only in the clutch of forces that are greater than I am. Thousands are waiting to shake my hand today.
>
> It is forty-one years since mother lay ill in the same room where you now are. Great changes have come to us but I do not think we are any happier and I am afraid not much better. Everyone tells me how cheerful you are. I can well understand that you may be. So many loved ones are waiting for you, so many loved ones are daily hoping you are comfortable and are anxious to know about you.[107]

That month he had a telephone installed for his father, who at last agreed to the intrusion after being assured his number would not be made public. They began to speak daily, with the president simply picking up the receiver and calling Plymouth 5000.

* * *

The first session of the 69th Congress held Republican majorities of 55 to 40 in the Senate and 247 to 183 in the House, albeit with some of the same liberal spending blocs that had frustrated Coolidge since taking office. Both chambers had new leaders.

In the Senate, Charles Curtis of Kansas replaced Henry Cabot Lodge, who had died of a stroke in late 1924. The new majority leader fell short of his predecessor in intellect and stature but was more likely to stay in line with the administration. Born in a Kaw Indian village to a half–Indian mother and a white father in 1860, he had witnessed an attack by the Cheyenne at eight years old and helped save the village by slipping through the lines at night to inform authorities at Topeka, some 60 miles away. There he happened upon a fair with horse races and performed so well that a local stable hired him as a jockey. Returning home six years later he would have been content to stay had his maternal grandmother not convinced him to seek an education, leading to law and politics. A self-described progressive conservative, he agreed with the administration on most issues, with the notable exception of farm relief.

In the House, Nicholas Longworth of Ohio replaced the ineffective senator-elect Frederick Gillett. A Harvard man from the "naughty nineties," suave, wealthy, plump, bald, slightly cynical, with little apparent ambition, Longworth represented the silk stocking section of Cincinnati and, though married to the former Alice Roosevelt, had opposed his father-in-law and stayed loyal to the party in 1912. "If every statesman was as frank in arranging his hair as I am, there would be less deception in public life," he liked to say.[108]

Coolidge resumed his legislative breakfasts to promote good relations with Congress, but the combination of short-notice invitations and early servings limited their appeal. Ike Hoover was amused by all the excuses. Many pled sickness. One senator had his wife call to say a wheel had come off his car, another said his barn had burned down.[109]

One morning Senator Harry E. Hawes of Kentucky said, "Mr. President, this is an excellent breakfast. Probably there is only one better."

"Senator, what breakfast is that?" he replied in his nasal twang.

A Kentucky breakfast, Hawes said—a dog, a beefsteak, and a bottle of whiskey.

Coolidge did not smile.

"Of course, Mr. President, the dog eats the beefsteak."

At that the president chuckled and the room filled with laughter.[110]

The main issue in Washington again was taxes or how much to reduce them given the budget surplus and the national debt. As Will Rogers titled his second newspaper column of the year: "Taxes Is All There Is to Politics."[111]

The administration, led by Secretary Mellon, promoted that winter a $300 million tax reduction, the most that could be done without risking a budget deficit. The exemption upon single persons was to increase from $1,000 to $1,500 and upon heads of families from $2,500 to $3,500. This would eliminate taxes for about one-third of the 7.3 million taxpayers. The rest were to receive rate cuts: from 2 percent to 1.5 percent on the first $4,000 of taxable income, from 4 percent to 3 percent on the second

$4,000, and from 6 percent to 5 percent on $8,000 or more. Surtaxes were to be reduced to a maximum of 20 percent on incomes above $200,000. The inheritance tax, gift tax, luxury tax, and publicity provision of the 1924 act were to be repealed. The inheritance tax, Mellon said, should be reserved for the states, as they had requested several months earlier at the White House and before the House Ways and Means Committee.

Born in 1855, Mellon was old enough to recall holding a shotgun on the family porch in western Pennsylvania as Confederate troops swept across the area, looting and inciting panic, before meeting their match at Gettysburg.[112] At 17 he had entered the family bank and eventually made a fortune as a financier in oil, steel, aluminum, coal, glass, railroads, public utilities, insurance, distilleries, and other industries, becoming the third wealthiest man in the country behind John D. Rockefeller and Henry Ford; but such was his reticence toward publicists and newspapermen, following a bitter divorce from a young Irishwoman, who accused him of using listening devices and private detectives to investigate her alleged adultery, that people had known him by name only before Harding offered him Treasury in 1920. Now the eminence grise of Pennsylvania Republican politics and the most prominent secretary of the treasury since Hamilton, he remained a private, even reclusive, figure, shaking hands with his fingertips and speaking in a near-whisper. In the evening he could be seen walking home through Lafayette Square and up Connecticut Avenue, without a bodyguard, wearing a dark Edwardian suit and black tie, smoking a diminutive black-paper cigar, to his 12-room penthouse apartment at 1785 Massachusetts Avenue, adorned by Holbeins, Turners, Van Dycks, Rembrandts, El Grecos, and the Vermeer masterpiece, *The Girl in the Red Hat*. There he lived with his daughter, the glamorous Ailsa Mellon, when they were not at their summer home at Southampton, Long Island. This seigneur promoted the view that lower taxes would reduce nonproductive investments, such as tax-free, low-interest bonds, while creating economic growth and increasing the revenue base.

Coolidge shared the view that tax reductions would encourage individuals to invest in business rather than tax-free state and local bonds, leading to growth and jobs. Never had a president spoken with such conviction on the need to reduce taxes on the rich to help the poor:

> I am not disturbed about the effect of a few thousand people with large incomes because they have to pay high surtaxes. What concerns me is the indirect effect on the rest of the people. Let us always remember the poor.[113]

To win approval for the bill, Coolidge and Mellon had to overcome opposition from two camps. The first, Democrats and insurgent Republicans, favored a tax revision bill to restrict corporate tax-avoidance practices, such as paying stockholders dividends in stocks rather than cash,

Andrew W. Mellon, Secretary of the Treasury from 1921 to 1932, led the drive for income tax cuts during the Coolidge years on the condition that the federal government ran a budget surplus. Date unknown (Harris & Ewing Collection, Library of Congress).

or staggering distribution of payments to reduce tax liability in any one year. The second, mostly Senate Democrats, wanted to outdo Coolidge and Mellon with a $456 million tax cut by lowering the annual sinking fund payments of $253 million on the national debt, applying some $175 million in annual foreign debt payments to tax reduction vice debt reduction, and extending the debt redemption schedule from 25 years to 60 years. "I feel that we ought not to be forced, as we are now being forced by the administration, to pay off this indebtedness with undue rapidity," remarked Democratic Senator Furnifold Simmons.[114] Coolidge, in a private meeting with Chairman Smoot of the Senate Finance Committee, strongly opposed any such changes to debt redemption.[115] Hearings on Capitol Hill produced tax club spokesmen, economists, businessmen, and bankers, who, almost without exception, praised the benefits of lower taxes but opposed extending the debt payments for fear of disturbing the vast market for Liberty Bonds and other government securities. Senator Norris proposed an amendment to the bill that would steadily increase the tax on incomes above $100,000, peaking at a 30 percent rate on incomes above $1,000,000, but his colleagues voted him down.

With Coolidge holding firm for a $300 million reduction, the House approved a $327 million reduction and the Senate a $456 million reduction. This led to intense late-night negotiations as legislators sought to pass a bill before the federal income tax filing date of March 15. In the end they split the difference with a $387 million reduction, which passed the House by 390 to 25 and the Senate by 58 to 9.

Coolidge, disappointed by the amount, agreed to sign the bill after Mellon and Lord predicted the potential reduction in revenue would not cause a deficit as long as new appropriations were kept to a minimum. At the bill-signing ceremony on February 26, Mellon smiled in delight as reporters, photographers, and movie men packed into the executive office, but Coolidge seemed disinterested by the proceedings and annoyed when several legislators arrived 12 minutes late, putting him behind schedule. Quickly signing the bill, he shook hands with those present as photographers asked him to pose alone at his desk, holding the document.

"You never know when you have had enough," he snapped, in a rare display of anger at the press that underscored his concern about a looming deficit. "You are taking all my time."[116]

The Revenue Act of 1926 marked the most far-reaching tax reduction since the war. It raised the personal exemption to $1,500 for individual filers and $3,500 for families, exempting about one-third of the 7.3 million taxpayers. It reduced from 43 percent to 25 percent the maximum surtax, repealed the gift tax, increased from $50,000 to $100,000 the exemption from the inheritance tax, lowered by 50 percent the rate on inheritance taxes, reduced from 5 percent to 3 percent the excise tax on automobiles, and eliminated the tax on tires, cameras, lenses, film, jewelry, firearms, ammunition, and other items. It repealed the publicity provision of 1924.

In a message attached to the law, Coolidge warned that strict economy would be necessary to avert a possible $100 million deficit in 1927 and stated there would be no tax reductions in 1927 or 1928 because of mounting appropriations.[117]

* * *

In March, Colonel Coolidge suffered a heart attack as a snowstorm hit Plymouth Notch, leaving five-foot drifts in front of his house. A snowplow cleared most of the road from Ludlow before giving out on the hill to his village, as gangs of men with shovels and picks made a narrow path for Dr. Cram to get through on an old-fashioned "cutter" drawn by a horse. For several days Colonel Coolidge struggled to remain conscious, summoning neighbors and relatives to his sick-room to bid farewell, such as town selectman Arzo Johnson, town treasurer Ed Blanchard, town moderator Clarence E. Blanchard, ax-man George Frick, farmer Walter H. Lynds, farmer Thomas Moore, kinsman Herbert Moore, former sister-in-law Gratia Wilder, and storekeeper Florence Cilley. In Washington, the president fretted over what to do, wanting to see his father but waiting to ensure roads were passable for his entourage. The elder Coolidge encouraged him to stay put and attend to his duties.[118]

At noon, March 18, the president decided they were leaving in four hours, having received a telephone message that his father was rapidly sinking. He invited Sargent but not Stearns, who wanted to go.[119] They departed without a police escort and encountered rush-hour traffic on Pennsylvania Avenue, arriving late at Union Station and boarding a special five-car train. As they sped northward they stopped at Baltimore, Wilmington, and Philadelphia, to receive the latest bulletins from Dr. Cram. The president and first lady dined alone in silence and received the following telegram message in New York: "Condition unchanged. Your father very weak. Still sinking."[120] They retired for the evening outside the city.

Near midnight the train stopped at Bridgeport, Connecticut, where a messenger delivered the news that Colonel Coolidge had died in his sleep. Continuing on to White River Junction, Vermont, they transferred to the Woodstock line shortly before daybreak, climbing into the hills as the air became colder, the snowdrifts higher. At the end of the line they switched to a motorcar with chained tires until the snow-covered road became impassable at Bridgewater Corners, where a driver and horse sleigh waited to take them to the Notch with hot bricks and fur-lined robes to keep them warm as temperatures dipped below 10 degrees. The last few miles were slow and treacherous and they were nearly thrown from their sleigh more than once; their bodies ached all over from the hard trip, covering 500 miles. At the village they saw men hacking a path to the cemetery through four feet of snow. "It costs a great deal to be President," he wrote, disappointed he had been unable to say goodbye.[121]

To keep up the property, Coolidge retained Miss Pierce for a dollar a day and hired local farmer Lynn Cady.

* * *

Three days after returning from Vermont, the president read in the newspapers that in London the Chancellor of the Exchequer, Winston Churchill, had stood before the House of Commons to lambast the "wealthy and prosperous" United States for insisting on war debt payments from war-stricken Europe. England alone, he said, had to pay more than $500,000 daily for three generations, while France, Germany, Italy, and Poland had shown little ability or willingness to meet their obligations to his country.[122] The speech received much comment in the British press and among the British public, leading many to say the country should have gotten better terms than those signed in 1922, or waited and insisted on an all-round European debt settlement with the United States. This marked a dramatic turnaround from 15 months earlier when Churchill told Parliament that the Anglo-American debt had been settled one and for all.

Coolidge had no response to the hubbub, having taken the position long ago that the debts were to go through an established process and that his administration would react to formal proposals only, rather than statements. Mellon told reporters that cancellation would not be practical in any sense, given that the United States had to repay bondholders for the money that had been raised and loaned to Europe during the war.[123]

In the succeeding weeks, the Coolidge policy of pressuring governments to negotiate debt settlements by coercing Wall Street bankers to withhold loans produced more results as Congress approved agreements with Belgium, Estonia, Italy, Latvia, Rumania, and Yugoslavia. The terms included large reductions in interest rates, from as high as 5 percent to as low as 1 percent, to slash their overall payments by more than 50 percent. Then came a breakthrough with France, which, faced with the franc at an all-time low value against the dollar, agreed to a payment schedule that would begin at $30 million annually in 1927 and 1928 and increase to $125 million by 1944, without the controversial "safeguard clause" to tie French obligations to German reparation payments. The agreement, pending approval from the French Parliament, decreased interest rates enough to reduce the $4 billion debt by about 50 percent. In effect, France would repay an amount roughly equivalent to its postwar loans from the United States and thus be forgiven its war loans.

Coolidge praised the 13 settlements on some $22 million in debt, dating back to 1922, as one of the greatest financial transactions in history. He described the terms as liberal and fair for all sides, reflecting the ability to pay in debtor countries and providing them with an opportunity to improve their credit standing and rehabilitate their economies.[124]

The settlements were kept in a steel drawer in a secluded room at the Department of Treasury, stacked in a neat pile and weighted down by a .45-caliber revolver.

* * *

The president, having lowered taxes and accepted reductions in foreign debt payments, worked to limit appropriations against more than 5,000 legislative proposals that would increase spending by $7 billion, led by $2.8 billion for farm relief and $3.2 billion for highway construction, along with smaller items such as $200 million for loans to discharged soldiers, $100 million for gifts to former Confederate soldiers and their widows, and $40 million for an increase in Civil War pensions. No Congress in history had laid such a claim on the Treasury. Alarmed by this election-year extravagance, Coolidge publicly rebuked Congress and threatened to veto any bill that did not fall within budget parameters. In early May, the *New York Times* cited "close friends" of the administration as saying Coolidge would fight his own party in Congress, if necessary, and would take his position to the public.[125]

* * *

The following week found him absorbed in an address to be given on May 15 at the sesquicentennial anniversary of the Virginia resolutions of independence and the removal of the British flag from the state house. The address was to take place at the former colonial capital of Williamsburg, and he would use the occasion to encourage the states to hold on to their rights and privileges against federal encroachment, as he had done a year earlier in his acclaimed Memorial Day address. Indeed he looked forward to the trip as a chance to see some historic sites of great personal interest and to travel by boat down the Potomac to the Chesapeake Bay and then up the York River.[126] Captain Wilson H. Brown, his new naval aide, took command of the *Mayflower* and responsibility for the itinerary. Coolidge, meeting him in advance, asked whether he had been through the Naval Academy. "Yes, sir," he replied. "Well, I guess that'll keep you from tripping over the White House rugs," Coolidge drolled.[127]

Leaving Washington the day before the celebration, the presidential party stayed aboard the yacht that evening and disembarked the next morning at the dock at historic Yorktown before proceeding by motorcar for the last 10 miles to Williamsburg, accompanied by state police and greeted by cheering and singing along the way on a warm sunny day, as farmers came out from their huts and fields. Coolidge, riding with Governor Harry Byrd, noted the scarlet-tipped clover in bloom along the highway and voiced surprise that such a beautiful flower, resembling the forsythia, would grow in the wild in such abundance. Ever the storyteller, Byrd related a bit of local folklore that Lord Cornwallis and his troops inadvertently brought the seeds from England, inside the hay stacks to feed their horses.[128]

Arriving at Williamsburg, once "the cradle of the republic" and now a down-and-out southern town, they were met by a large crowd, representatives from the 13 original colonies, a 21-gun salute, and the ringing of the bell at Bruton Church on Duke of Gloucester Street, the same bell that rang out freedom on that historic day in 1776, six weeks before the ringing of the Liberty Bell in Philadelphia.

Coolidge took the stand behind the Christopher Wren building at William and Mary College to deliver what many anticipated would be a substantial address on the founding principles of the country. "No one who is interested in the early beginnings of America, or who is moved by love of our country, could come into these historic and hallowed surroundings without being conscious of a deep sense of reverence," he began, with a national audience listening by radio. After relating the events in which the Virginia colony and Virginians struggled for independence and created the new republic dedicated to individual rights and local self-reliance, he called on the states to assert their rights, and warned that the modern system of direct primaries and direct elections had given rise to vocal minorities and special interests that undermined party discipline and increased spending pressures in Congress. The federalist vision of the founders was at stake:

> If the Federal Government should go out of existence the common run of people would not detect the difference in their daily life for a considerable length of time, but if the authority of the States were struck down disorder approaching chaos would be upon us within twenty-four hours. No method of procedure has ever been devised by which liberty could be divorced from local self-government.
>
> No plan of centralization has ever been adopted which did not result in bureaucracy, tyranny, inflexibility, reaction and decline. Of all forms of government, those administered by bureaus are about the least satisfactory to an enlightened and progressive people. Being irresponsible they become autocratic, and being autocratic they resist all development. Unless bureaucracy is constantly resisted it breaks down representative government and overwhelms democracy. It is the one element in our institutions that sets up the pretense of having authority over everybody and being responsible to nobody....
>
> The Federal Government ought to resist the tendency to be loaded up with duties which the States should perform. It does not follow that because something ought to be done the National Government ought to do it. But, on the other hand, when the great body of public opinion of the Nation requires action the States ought to understand that unless they are responsive to such sentiment the national authority will be compelled to intervene.
>
> The doctrine of State rights is not a privilege to continue in wrong-doing but a privilege to be free from interference in well-doing. This Nation is bent on progress. It has determined on the policy of meting out justice between man and man. It has decided to extend the blessings of an enlightened humanity. Unless the States meet these requirements, the National Government reluctantly will be crowded into the position of enlarging its own authority at their expense.
>
> I want to see the policy adopted by the States of discharging their public functions so faithfully that instead of an extension on the part of the Federal Government there can be a contraction.[129]

* * *

By the time he returned to Washington two days later, sailing back up the river, the fight over farm relief was well under way. Before the Civil War, the supervision of agriculture had been a local and state matter. In 1862, the Republican Congress had established a modest Bureau of Agriculture with an annual appropriation of $80,000. In 1889, the Bureau had been converted into the Department of Agriculture with cabinet status and an annual budget of $1,134,480. By 1924, the budget had reached $85,061,453, more than the entire cost of the federal government in any year before the 20th century, exclusive of war costs. This covered activities such as animal husbandry, biological surveys, crop estimates, entomology, forests, home economics, insecticide recommendations, markets, plants, public roads, soil chemistry, and weather. Now proponents on Capitol Hill wanted the Department to take a greater role in addressing the protracted postwar slump in agriculture.

Simply put, farmers had borrowed too much during the war in response to expanding markets at home and abroad. With less competition from war-torn Europe, they invested in equipment and added more than 38 million acres of cropland between 1914 and 1919, increasing their debt levels. In 1920, they added another 10 million acres of cropland, even as farmers in Europe recovered from the war and those in Argentina, Australia, Brazil, and Canada started to increase output and compete in the global market. In 1921, the net income of American farmers dropped precipitously. Despite slightly better conditions from 1922 to 1924, the combination of stable commodity prices, global competition, debt, and high local and federal taxes, remained a barrier to prosperity.

"Well, farmers never have made money," Coolidge told R.A. Cooper, chairman of the Farm Loan Board. "I don't believe we can do much about it. But of course we will have to seem to be doing something; do the best we can and without much hope."[130]

The history of agriculture was marked by cyclical price patterns, giving rise to populist movements beyond the Alleghenies but minimal federal intervention. This time farmers in the Middle West were more insistent. First, the war had demonstrated the ability of the federal government to influence production and prices through the Lever Food Control Act of 1917, the War Industries Board, the War Trade Board, the Shipping Board, the Railroad Administration, the Fuel Administration, the Food Administration, and other emergency measures. Second, the federal government had expanded to the point that interest groups looked to Washington, rather than state governments, to intervene in the economy. Whereas the populists of the 1870s and 1890s regarded easy credit as the panacea, the new agriculturalist movement wanted to control surplus output.

Hence the farm bloc, a bipartisan group representing agricultural interests and promoting a distinct legislative program outside the two-party system for the first time in American history. This development may be traced to the decline of the parties following the Cannon revolt of 1910, the increase in the power of the committee system, the spread of the primary system, and the direct election of United States senators. All that created the conditions that led to a historic meeting in May 1921 between six Democratic and six Republican senators in the offices of the American Farm Bureau Federation. Now the bloc had 30 or so members in the Senate and nearly 100 in the House, pushing through legislation on credit, crop exporting, crop marketing, farm financing, and road subsidies. None of the previous blocs in history—the silver bloc, the tariff bloc, or the railroad bloc—had operated in such open defiance of the two parties. Nor had any been backed by such lobbies as the American Farm Bureau Federation, with offices in 40 states and nearly two million members, and the National Grange, with some 800,000 members.

Coolidge responded to pressure by promoting cooperative marketing, providing information on crops and prices, improving agricultural schools, and asking Congress to appropriate $230 million to the Farm Loan Board to lend to cooperatives to keep nonperishable crops off the market when surpluses threatened to lower prices. Such volunteerism at the local level had been undermined by nonparticipants in recent years, but Coolidge ruled out price-fixing and crop restrictions.

The farm bloc had a more radical solution in a bill cosponsored by two Republicans, Senator Charles McNary of Oregon and Representative Gilbert Haugen of Iowa, to stabilize prices through federal intervention. Originally promoted in 1922 in a pamphlet titled *Equality for Agriculture,* written by two employees of the Moline Plow Company and endorsed by the American Farm Bureau Federation, the American Livestock Association, the National Livestock Association, the American Wheat Growers Association, the National Agricultural Conference, and the Corn Belt Conference, the bill proposed levying a tax on certain agricultural products, to be dispersed into a fund as an "equalization fee." That is to say, a subsidy. The federal government in turn would purchase at a designated price all surplus quantities of corn, rice, swine, wheat, flour, wool, and other commodities for export, allowing farmers to raise prices enough to pay the fee. In theory. That designated price would be determined by a board, a fantastic task involving continuous estimates of feed costs, transportation costs, crop conditions, consumer demand, foreign competition, and other market conditions. Administrative costs were to be covered by a $375 million fund. Opposed by Coolidge and most legislators from the northeast and the south as the most ambitious proposal ever made to impose federal control over the law of supply and demand, the McNary-Haugen bill lost in the House by a 212–167 vote and in the Senate by a 45–39 vote, despite support from the entire Republican delegation from every state west of the Mississippi River. Indeed, Democrats opposed the bill more than Republicans did, by a 21–15 vote compared with a 24–23 vote.

The proposal was sure to reappear in the next Congress, however. The notion of using the federal taxing power to secure the economic security of an entire sector was taking hold out west where crop prices were more vulnerable than they were in the northeast and the south.

The other contentious issue that spring was federal regulation of aviation and radio. No one disputed the need for regulation, and few questioned the legality under the constitutional power to regulate interstate commerce. The commercial aviation industry lacked standards for pilot certification and airport safety. The 700-station radio industry was marred by crowded channels and frequency interference. At issue was whether to establish new commissions, as proposed in Congress but opposed by the White House. Coolidge took the position that commissions had a tendency to grow bureaucratically beyond their original intent. At a news conference in April, he enunciated that all regulatory work, outside the courts and interstate commerce, should be responsible to the president, either directly or through a cabinet officer, to restore the principle that every function of administration should be subject to executive power for supervision. He favored placing the regulation of aviation and radio under the Commerce Department.[131]

On aviation, the Morrow Board backed the president, resulting in the Civil Aeronautics Act of 1926. This authorized the Commerce Department to issue certificates of safety to companies whose pilots and crew passed a standard test, produce maps and flight charts, provide weather reports, investigate accidents, and construct more lighted airport runways. The new law was consistent with the power of the federal government to regulate interstate commerce. The close relation of intrastate and interstate commerce necessitated some federal control over intrastate commerce, such as rules of air traffic for all planes, but jurisdiction for matters outside the law fell back to the states.

On radio, Congress was divided between two bills. One, sponsored by Senator C.C. Dill of Washington, advocated the creation of an independent commission with complete regulatory powers. The other, drafted by Representative Wallace H. White of Maine, proposed a separate division in Commerce with the same powers, but which would be directly responsible to the secretary of commerce. This split was to carry into the next session.

In the final days of the 1926 session, Coolidge met almost daily with Chairman Martin B. Madden of the House Appropriations Committee, Chairman Bertrand H. Snell of the House Rules Committee, and Chairman Francis E. Warren of the Senate Appropriations Committee, to prevent late spending bills from reaching the floor and, if they did, to plot against their adoption. The result was to hold expenditures at 1925 levels despite the bonus and other initiatives, including a $350,000 bill to repair the White House roof, a $165 million bill to construct seven public buildings on 70 acres of land between Constitution and Pennsylvania Avenues, and a $19 million pension bill for Spanish War veterans to put them on par with Civil War veterans. Total appropriations were $6.8 million less than budget estimates for the year.

At the semiannual meeting of the Business Organization of the Government on June 21, Coolidge praised economy before a thousand or so managers and a nationwide radio hookup. "More work and better work for a smaller outlay of the money of the taxpayer is the real test of a progressive administration," he said. That was how he perceived his administration, and how the federal government could best serve the people during the high debt, high tax, postwar era. The fiscal year was ending with positive numbers. The $3.2 billion budget, while still above his goal, included a surplus of $390 million and a debt reduction of $836 million, exceeding expectations. The national debt had dropped below $20 billion for the first time since the war, finishing at $19.6 billion. The government had saved $100 million in interest payments. Yet he insisted that any talk of a tax cut was premature and that such action would hinge on whether the estimated surplus proved accurate. The idea that tax reduction could produce more revenue was still unproven in his opinion, pending the results of the recent tax bill.

> The correctness of the theory that reduction of tax rates economically applied will stimulate business and thereby increase revenue is being demonstrated. To what point further tax reduction may be carried cannot be stated until the new tax law has had sufficient opportunity to become fully effective and experience has shown what revenues it will produce.

Looking ahead, he warned that the paring-down of expenditures was near its limit and that the government would have to rely on lower interest payments to produce savings.[132]

The following day, Democrats in the House responded to the $390 million estimated surplus by submitting bills to cut personal income tax rates by 25 percent, repeal the automobile tax, and reduce the corporate tax rate from 13.5 percent to 10 percent. The White House was quick to oppose the bills and state the need to evaluate the new tax law for six months before considering any further reductions.

* * *

Later that week the NAACP adopted a resolution against segregation in the federal government: "We are astonished to note under President Coolidge and the Republican administration a continuation of that *segregation* of colored employees in the departments of Washington which was begun under President Wilson."[133] The following week, William Monroe Trotter and fellow delegates from the Boston-based National Equal Rights League called at the White House, carrying a petition against the odious practice, signed by thousands of citizens in nearly every state to mark the sesquicentennial anniversary of the Declaration of Independence. Twelve years earlier Trotter had made a similar appeal to President Wilson, only to be accused of rudeness and encouraged to leave. Coolidge said the work was being done gradually.[134]

* * *

To commemorate the historic anniversary, Coolidge accepted an invitation to speak on July 5 at the sesquicentennial exposition at Philadelphia, a massive event with halls and exhibitions spread across a thousand acres and 200 federal agents on hand to enforce prohibition. Much preparation went into the speech, seeking the right words to fit the occasion, to honor men such as his great-great grandfather, Captain John Coolidge, who fought at Lexington in 1775 and served five years in the Revolutionary Army before settling in Plymouth Notch in 1780. Leaving by train on the morning of the speech, the president and his party arrived three hours later at Broad Street Station, whence photographers surged toward him, snapping away with their cameras. Thousands of spectators lined the streets in a light rain, straining to catch a glimpse of the president and white-clad first lady inside their limousine as two bodyguards stood on the running boards of the vehicle and two others ran behind. At Municipal Stadium they arrived to a 21-gun salute and a capacity crowd of 35,000 spectators sitting in the wet bleachers. Millions of others listened by radio in a broadcast that included 22 stations and stretched beyond the Mississippi.

In a tone that matched the solemn skies that morning, Coolidge appealed for a return to the spiritual ideals of 1776 and the founding principles of the country, beginning with the religious faith of Colonial New England as spread through the writings and sermons of the Rev. Thomas Hooker of Connecticut, the Rev. John Wise of Massachusetts, and others. Therein lay the genesis of inalienable rights before Thomas Jefferson wrote the Declaration on a portable folding desk in a three-story lodging house at Seventh and Market streets, a few blocks away. At Amherst, Coolidge had written an award-winning essay on the American Revolution as a political struggle to preserve English constitutional liberties against the encroachments of King and Parliament. Now, 32 years later, he saw the fight for independence as mainly a moral and spiritual movement, not the culmination of Enlightenment thought from Europe but "profoundly American." More than a call for political and economic freedom:

In its main features the Declaration of Independence is a great spiritual document. It is a declaration not of material but of spiritual conceptions. Equality, liberty, popular sovereignty, the rights of man, these are not elements which we can see and touch. They are ideals. They have their source and their roots in the religious convictions. They belong to the unseen world. Unless the faith of the American people in these religious convictions is to endure, the principles of our Declaration will perish. We can not continue to enjoy the result if we neglect and abandon the cause.

We are too prone to overlook another conclusion. Governments do not make ideals, but ideals make governments. This is both historically and logically true. Of course the government can help to sustain ideals and can create institutions through which they can be the better observed, but their source by their very nature is in the people. The people have to bear their own responsibilities. There is no method by which that burden can be shifted to the government. It is not the enactment, but the observance of laws, that creates the character of a nation.

About the Declaration there is a finality that is exceedingly restful. It is often asserted that the world has made a great deal of progress since 1776, that we have had new thoughts and new experiences which have given us a great advantage over the people of that day, and that we may therefore very well discard their conclusions for something more modern. But that reasoning can not be applied to this great charter. If all men are created equal, that is final. If they are endowed with inalienable rights, that is final. If governments derive their just powers for the consent of the governed, that is final. No advance, no progress can be made beyond these propositions.

There was none of the bombastic rhetoric normally associated with Independence Day speeches, no visions of future glory. As the drizzle turned into a driving rain, he concluded:

We live in an age of science and of abounding accumulation of material things. These did not create our Declaration. Our Declaration created them. The things of the spirit come first. Unless we cling to that, all our material prosperity, overwhelming though it may appear, will turn to a barren sceptre in our grasp. If we are to maintain the great heritage which has been bequeathed to us, we must be like-minded as the fathers who created it. We must not sink into a pagan materialism. We must cultivate the reverence which they had for the things that are holy. We must follow the spiritual and moral leadership which they showed. We must keep replenished, that they may glow with a more compelling flame, the alter fires before which they worshipped.[135]

Afterward he visited Independence Hall and gravely looked at the Liberty Bell, reading the inscription and inspecting it from all sides. "Touch it, dear," Grace said with a smile.[136] That he did, running his finger along the rough edge of its famous crack. Among other sites, they viewed the gig in which Jefferson had ridden from Monticello to Philadelphia, and called at the Christ Church where Washington, Franklin, and other Revolutionary leaders had worshipped.

"That certainly was a great reception in Philadelphia," Stearns wrote Clark, who had stayed in Washington. "I have never been with the President anywhere where there was a reception to at all equal it. I am rather slow in estimating the value of a speech but I am coming to think that particular speech is the greatest speech the President ever made."[137]

* * *

The following day, with the speech receiving extensive newspaper coverage around the country, the president and first lady left for a two-month stay in the New York Adirondacks, 500 miles from Washington. Though relieved to escape the heat and humidity of the capital, Grace had hoped to return to Swampscott and dreaded her husband would be bored in the woods. Others shared her concern as they arrived at White Pine Camp, a secluded cluster of cabins that struck some as unpresidential.[138] The summer executive office was set up at a hotel three miles away, with a private telegraph line and six telephone wires providing communication to Washington. Coolidge told reporters that the area had fewer "hindering diversions" than Swampscott did, allowing them to concentrate on their work, which he surely thought would help promote his image and build public support for his policies.[139]

"Mr. Coolidge is Learning to Play," ran a *New York Times* article, as the president took up fishing twice a day.[140] Cleveland was an ardent fisherman and hunter, who now and then would venture into Chesapeake Bay for a long weekend or a week, shooting canvasback duck, snipe, and other game, during which time he could not be reached by mail or wire. McKinley took a vigorous daily walk and rode horses. Roosevelt was a hiker, a hunter, a naturalist, a wrestler, a boxer, and a tennis player. Taft and Wilson were golfers. Harding was a golfer and a fisherman. Coolidge previously engaged in no such activities, perhaps restrained by the knowledge that his father was watching back home and might disapprove of frivolous hobbies. The Colonel had always taken pride in telling reporters his son had not played much as a boy, which may well have discouraged the president from doing so as a man, when there was work to be done.

Newspapers portrayed him as a man at ease that summer, making the most of vacation, when in truth he soon became restless, trapped inside during frequent rain showers, bothered by black flies and mosquitoes. No one wanted to be around him, and Grace "looked badly" and seemed lonely and quiet to her physician, who looked forward to returning to Washington so the president would have more to occupy his mind.[141]

Arthur Brooks, the normally circumspect valet, complained to Boone that the president was nitpicky and inconsiderate. As he counted the days in the woods that summer, eager to return to his brick row house at 1302 S Street, Northwest Washington, he reminisced about happier days with Wilson and Harding. Wilson had been an exacting boss but a true southern gentleman who treated others with courtesy and respect. He had arrived in Washington with a few inexpensive, ready-made, ill-fitting suits before Brooks turned him into a natty dresser with tailor-made wool suits in winter and white pants and blue blazer in summer, while putting weight on his bony frame with a steady diet of oatmeal, chicken, steak, and Virginia country ham; alas, no one could get him to trim his ear hairs, for he wanted to appear as one of the people. Harding, ah Harding, a fine man in every respect, simple, natural, tall, handsome, broad-shouldered. One morning Brooks arrived at the White House to find him in a wide, blue-striped shirt and a bright tie. Scowling, the valet handed him a white shirt and a dark tie. No, no, no, Harding said, he was dressed for the day. To which Brooks replied, "A president cannot wear anything but a white shirt and the plainest kind of tie, no gaiety!" Harding relented and gave the shirt to Brooks as a present, since they wore the same size. As for Coolidge, he never required handling on sartorial matters, but was a difficult man, prickly, rude, failing to say good morning at times. Brooks was glad to receive permission in July to leave the camp early for health reasons.[142] Sadly, he passed away in September.

Three weeks into vacation, Coolidge took a short trip to Vermont on the third anniversary of the midnight inaugural. Miss Pierce was there to greet them, but the historic lamp, Bible, and pen had been removed to a place of safekeeping. An old weather-beaten salt bag, held in place with a safety pin, covered a rusted-out hole in the screen door. Content to be home, the president pruned an apple tree, replaced two rotten fence posts, talked to neighbors, and walked the hills, free from mosquitoes.

Young John Coolidge arrived for a short visit, now halfway through college and a source of tension between his parents, with his father criticizing his marks and threatening to pull him from school unless he improved. This suggests the president, having lost the son most like him in appearance and intellect, had become more set that John make the most of his opportunities and perhaps more intolerant of his shortcomings; having done much to help him academically, paying for tutors and summer school, without results. Perhaps he sensed John needed strong guidance to get through college after nearly flunking out last term and courting the daughter of Governor Robert Trumbull of Connecticut, a student at nearby Mount Holyoke. At White Pine Camp, mother and son took long walks and swam together. When she caught him having a Secret Service agent retrieve his tennis balls at practice one day, she scolded him for being like his father, never doing anything that he could get someone else to do for him.[143]

After the collegian returned to class, Coolidge sent a bodyguard to live with him and report on his progress. "I hope you are working hard," he wrote his son. "There is only a small difference between success and failure."[144] Rumor had it the bodyguard was to prevent an elopement with Miss Trumbull, after an intercepted letter at White Pine Camp hinted at a possible runaway marriage. "I am awfully sorry for him," Grace wrote of her son. "He labors under difficult circumstances."[145]

Scarcely a day passed that summer without dispatches on the president and his views on business conditions, disarmament, government finance, farm relief, foreign affairs, foreign debt negotiations, labor, tax cuts, and tariff rates, totaling some 1,275,224 words by telegraph wire. No president on vacation had ever received such publicity. With Congress in recess, he could dominate the news through his twice-weekly news conferences and by inviting persons prominent in various fields to his camp and posing for photographs. On taxes, he responded to Democratic calls for reductions in the coming legislation session by saying such talk was premature until the government knew how the most recent reductions would affect revenues. "If we should reduce taxes now when everyone recognizes that the country is prosperous and business is good, which makes a large income for the government, we would run into the danger of having to increase taxes in time of depression," he told reporters.[146] On spending, he summoned Director Lord to review the budget for fiscal year 1927 and reappeared 90 minutes later to reveal he had cut almost $100 million in proposed expenditures in what Democratic newspapers described as a staged event, the reductions selected in advance.[147]

The way he handled the farm issue was masterly. Rather than trying to undermine or isolate McNary-Haugen backers, he held interviews with numerous farm leaders and legislators to show the divergence of opinion on agricultural conditions and policies. Some thought the tariff on crops should be raised. Some thought the tariff on manufactured goods should be lowered. Others wanted price supports, credits, or a better cooperative system. This enabled Coolidge to appear as an impartial decisionmaker, telling reporters he would weigh the evidence and choose a policy that made the most sense for the most people.

There was every reason to believe he would be a candidate for president in 1928 despite controversy over the third-term issue. Several visitors that summer, from automaker Edsel Ford to former Ambassador Richard Washburn Child, emerged from private meetings with him to declare that the country would support another term. Republican leaders from Michigan, Illinois, Missouri, Indiana, North Dakota, South Dakota,

Minnesota, and other states assured him that his popularity was undiminished, despite reports he was "slipping" in the Middle West following the victories of insurgents Smith W. Brookhart and Gerald P. Nye in the Iowa and North Dakota primaries, respectively. Even his advisers thought he was using the visitors as a medium to serve notice he would run again.[148]

The day before leaving White Pine Camp, September 17, Coolidge gave a lengthy personal interview, not to the reporters who covered him all summer, swatting mosquitoes, writing fish stories and the like, but to the acclaimed writer, former wartime propagandist, and advertising man Bruce Barton, whose *The Man Nobody Knows* had been the best-selling bit of nonfiction in the country for two consecutive years, comparing Christianity to business and depicting Jesus as the most popular dinner guest in Jerusalem and a great executive who "picked up twelve men from the bottom ranks of business and forged them into an organization that conquered the world." A graduate of the Amherst class of 1907, Barton had written several flattering articles on Governor Coolidge after the police walkout, promoting him in subtly nativist terms as a Yankee of the purest type, standing firm against radicalism and representing the great silent majority. Since then he had advised on publicity, served as an unpaid political strategist, and arranged for publication a volume of Coolidge rhetoric called *The Foundations of the Republic* during the 1924 campaign. Invited to the Adirondacks by Amherst brothers Morrow and Stearns, he had sent his questions in advance and arrived as the temporary telegraph instruments were being taken away. The desk, chairs, and carpet were gone. The leaves were taking on red and yellow tinges. The ducks were flying south, and the summer people were leaving too. The two men sat on the porch, Coolidge in a green wicker chair and Barton on the wood-boards, notebook in his lap and a pencil in hand.

The interview began with Barton lamenting that more citizens could not meet their president in such circumstances. To which Coolidge replied that his work kept him from traveling about the country as much as he would like. "The supervision of the expenditure of nearly $4,000,000,000 each year is a very large task," he said, adding postal expenditures to the total. "It was only a few years ago that our expenditures were less than $500,000,000."

As the conversation turned to Vermont, Coolidge spoke of his father, now six months gone: "My father had qualities that were greater than any I possess. I cannot recall that I ever knew of his doing a wrong thing." Even now, 54 years old, president of the United States, he did not measure up to the man he had revered since childhood and who, but for a better academic education, might very well have gone beyond the local level in politics: "I have no doubt he is representative of a great mass of Americans who are known only to their local neighbors; nevertheless they are really great. It would be difficult to say that he had a happy life. He never seemed to be seeking happiness. He was a firm believer in hard work."

Asked what advice he would give young office-seekers, Coolidge recommended a separate livelihood, for, "Otherwise he loses his independence." He also suggested marriage and family life: "A man who has the companionship of a loving and gracious woman enjoys the supreme blessing that life can give. And no citizen of the United States knows the truth of that statement better than I."

As for college, he encouraged all youngsters to pursue opportunities afforded to them, no matter their aspirations: "A college education ought to fit a man or woman to be content in any occupation, because it enlarges the capacity for the enjoyment of the intellectual and spiritual side of life."

Continuing at ease with someone he had known and trusted for years, who had never asked a difficult question, Coolidge said he did not indulge in horseback riding because it took too long to change clothes, or frequent the theater because it made him tired the next day, or have time for books and magazines. Among poets, he liked Whittier, Scott, and Burns because they evoked memories of his youth, and considered *Snowbound* by Whittier "a complete description of what is best in rural New England life." For years he had read *Paradise Lost* before sleep. In the Bible he preferred the writings of St. Paul. Asked if the world was improving, he said, "Assuredly." There were more opportunities for young people than at any time in history. Business practices were more moral. International relations, on the whole, were stable and promising.

As the interview neared conclusion, they spoke of religion. "It would be difficult for me to conceive of any one being able to administer the duties of a great office like the Presidency without a belief in the guidance of a Divine Providence," he said. "Unless the President is sustained by an abiding faith in a Divine Power which is working for the good of humanity, I cannot understand how he would have the courage to attempt to meet the various problems that constantly pour in upon him from all parts of the earth."

So ended the interview, to be edited by Coolidge in his own hand, published in newspapers by arrangement with the Associated Press, and regarded as the beginning of his reelection campaign, meant to show the human qualities of a man aft described as austere, introspective, inscrutable. Never had a president been quoted at such length in the press. Few had been interviewed at all, other than Andrew Johnson with the *Cincinnati Commercial* and Grover Cleveland with the *New York World*. White House correspondents complained that whereas they had been prohibited from quoting Coolidge during the past three years, Barton had been allowed to do so. One quipped that, having written *The Man Nobody Knows* about Jesus, Barton had now provided the sequel.[149]

* * *

The presidential train back to Washington arrived near midnight on September 18, as telegrams and newspaper reports on a massive hurricane in Florida began to accumulate at the White House. The storm, stretching 60 miles from Miami to Palm Beach, reaching 180 miles per hour, had come without warning other than a bulletin from the U.S. Weather Bureau about a "very severe storm" less than 24 hours in advance. Boats had been sunk or smashed apart. Docks had been swept away. Bungalows constructed during the real estate boom of the middle 1920s had been shattered into pieces. Hotel windows had been blown out, sending glass pieces and shards flying onto the streets. Hundreds of people had died, many of whom were new to the state and had never been through such a hurricane, causing them to make fatal mistakes, like going onto the beaches or in the water during a lull in the winds.

The next morning Coolidge received further updates on what had been the most devastating hurricane in United States history, with 372 deaths, more than 6000 injuries, and at least $100 million in property damage. He approved a request from Florida Governor John W. Martin to have the Red Cross handle relief operations as donations from around the country began to arrive. The following day Coolidge issued a statement encouraging the public to support the Red Cross as it attempted to provide shelter, provisions, and medicines to tens of thousands of homeless people, and prevent the spread of typhoid and other diseases in response to the "overwhelming disaster."[150] This brought in $500,000 within hours and $3 million within several days. He also ordered the Army and Navy Departments to cooperate with state authorities wherever possible.

No one in Washington proposed federal funds to the state for emergency or rebuilding purposes. Nor did any editorials in the leading newspapers around the country. Nor did the White House correspondents ask the president a single question about the storm during his two press conferences that week or at any other time.[151] As with the Midwest Tornado of 1925, the country perceived states, localities, volunteers, and charity as responsible for responding to natural disasters.

* * *

The White House had been painted and updated during the summer, including a new electric refrigerator with copper-lined cooling coils and compress for a self-making ice plant, a far cry from the days of Adams and Jefferson when ice was cut from the Potomac and kept in deep trenches for use throughout the year. The first ice box had been installed during the Lincoln years, a simple device insulated with granulated cork and charcoal. It had been updated twice, with little improvement until now.

The manse also had a new housekeeper in Ellen Riley, a big-boned, curly-haired, bespectacled New Englander and former cafeteria manager at R.H. Stearns Company, who came on recommendation from Stearns and soon found ways to save $200 a month at the White House, while supervising 18 employees and walking the dogs. "The mud down here is horrid, red and sticky, not nice New England mud," she wrote home to Ipswich, Massachusetts.[152] Each morning she went to Center Market on Seventh Street for fresh provisions from the Maryland and Virginia countryside, buying butter by the tub, potatoes by the barrel, and fruit and vegetables by the cart, while riding in a horse carriage in a city that had one of the highest automobile ownership rates and some of the best roads for driving in the country. Various old-time residents preferred horses, such as Oliver Wendell Holmes of the Supreme Court, French Ambassador Jean Jules Jusserand, former Lincoln coachman Laurance Mangan, and Mrs. A.D. Addison of Q Street, who successfully challenged in court a city provision that banned horse carriages on stretches of Connecticut Avenue, Massachusetts Avenue, North Capitol Street, and 15th Street; but automobiles now ruled the broad streets and avenues of the capital, where the pesky flies and livery stables of the horse-and-buggy era were all but forgotten. Miss Riley was glad the first lady convinced the president to order a motorcar with the following note to Edward Clark: "The man, Webster, who drives the horses can also drive a car. It is no longer practical or efficient to do errands with horses."[153]

Assigned to a suite on the second floor of the mansion, above the front door, Riley became a family intimate. "The P. isn't nearly as solemn as he looks," she wrote home, noting his delight in watching movies with his dogs, encouraging them to chase any wild animal that appeared on the screen.[154] They shared affection for a pet raccoon who lived in a tree-house and often ventured inside the manse, tearing silk stockings, unscrewing light bulbs, and turning over plants. Inviting her mother to visit, Riley warned, "You may not see the P. at all. Or, perhaps he'll scare you to death looking into the room when you don't know he is there and he'll mumble something that you have no idea in the world what he says and look you all over as sharp as can be, and that will be all there is to it."[155]

* * *

With the second session of the 69th Congress to open in December, Coolidge promoted economy in what had become a rite of autumn under his administration. In press conferences he warned of impending spending pressures, led by farm relief, flood relief, harbors, roads, airports, and cruisers. "Now it is very important that this country keep down its expenditures," he said on October 1. "If it will do that, I think a great many other problems will solve themselves."[156]

Midterm elections were to be held in November, with Democrats seeking to take the initiative on taxes and create a wedge between Coolidge and voters on economy by proposing a $560 million tax reduction rather than using the $377 million surplus of 1926 and the estimated $185 million surplus of 1927 to pay down the debt. Democrats also advocated extending the debt redemption period from 25 to 32 years. Furnifold Simmons of North Carolina, ranking minority leader of the Senate Finance Committee, and John Nance Garner of Texas, ranking minority leader of the House Ways and Means Committee, led the campaign to convince voters that the administration was redeeming the debt too hastily.

Democrats suspected political motivations as well. "The Republicans are simply hoarding campaign material for the presidential campaign of 1928," said Senator William Cabell Bruce of Maryland.[157]

As voters prepared to select the 70th Congress, Republicans promoted their record on peace and prosperity but faced opposition from immigrants and farmers over immigration restrictions and the McNary-Haugen bill, in addition to historical realities. No administration since the Civil War had gained in midterm elections. Most had lost seats, including Arthur in 1882, Harrison in 1890, Cleveland in 1894, Roosevelt in 1906, Taft in 1910, Wilson in 1918, and Harding in 1922. Republicans held 28 of the 35 senate seats at stake that autumn, including several vulnerable candidates swept into office in the 1920 landslide. The seven Democratic seats at stake were from the Democratic solid south: Alabama, Arkansas, Florida, Georgia, Louisiana, North Carolina, and South Carolina. This discrepancy might be enough to give Democrats a majority or at least a nominal majority in league with Republican insurgents.

Coolidge, following precedent, did not participate in the campaign except to release to the public in late October a letter endorsing William Butler in his senate race against Democrat David I. Walsh, who stood to benefit from unemployment and industrial slackness in the textile area of Massachusetts. "This is not a campaign of purely local significance," Butler declared. "We are not only electing a Senator from Massachusetts, but we are passing judgment upon a national administration."[158] That went beyond what Coolidge wrote in his endorsement, but Butler was desperate. Newspapermen from as far as Kansas City arrived on the scene to cover the most interesting legislative race in the country.

On Election Day, Coolidge went to Northampton to vote, receiving praise for his commitment to civic duty, along with ridicule that he might have saved public funds by casting an absentee ballot with a two-cent stamp rather than traveling by train at nearly three cents a mile. By the time he returned to Washington at 10:00 p.m., the early returns on his desk showed Republicans losses in the East and Middle West. After receiving news from Boston around 11:00 p.m. that Butler was all but certain to lose, the president went to bed.

For Republicans the outcome was disappointing, their majorities cut from 60 to 39 in the House and from 16 to two in the Senate, where they lost tried-and-true regulars James W. Wadsworth of New York, Irvine L. Lenroot of Wisconsin, George W. Pepper of Pennsylvania, William B. McKinley of Illinois, Richard P. Ernst of Kentucky, O.E. Weller of Maryland, George W. Williams of Missouri, Ralph H. Cameron of Arizona, John W. Harreld of Oklahoma, Rice W. Means of Colorado, and Robert N. Stanfield of Oregon. This left Senate Republicans dependent on five to seven irreconcilable members who had consistently voted against the administration on farm relief, taxes, and other issues. To Democrats the results suggested Coolidge was slipping at last, even though few candidates had criticized him or attempted to make him an issue during the campaign. In fact, local issues had dominated most contests, including referendums on prohibition in California, Colorado, Illinois, Missouri, Montana, Nevada, New York, and Wisconsin. Democratic newspapers, such as the *Atlanta Journal*, the *Richmond Times-Dispatch*, the *Cleveland Plain Dealer*, the *Baltimore Sun*, and the *Minneapolis Star*, opined that anti-agriculture and pro-corporate policies were hurting the president, and Democratic national chairman Clem L. Shaver issued a statement declaring the elections to be "encouraging for 1928."[159] Coolidge took a long walk that morning and read a stack of newspapers and telegrams without comment. To aides he seemed no different than he did after his triumph in 1924.[160] To reporters he observed that the House races—the true national test—had demonstrated a Republican majority once again.[161]

* * *

As the "lame duck" session of the 69th Congress opened on December 6, Coolidge dispatched his annual message with the emphasis on economy once again. Noting the previous session had approved $100 million in new appropriations for veterans, public buildings, harbors, and rivers, he advised against further initiatives:

> Nothing is easier than the expenditure of public money. It does not appear to belong to anybody. The temptation is overwhelming to bestow it on somebody.[162]

No doubt he was thinking of the McNary-Haugen bill, which had picked up support in the south by including cotton and tobacco as commodities covered under the plan. In February 1927, Congress approved the bill with bipartisan support from the farm bloc, as 47 representatives and eight senators, mostly southerners, changed their vote from the previous session. All told, the bill was backed in the Senate by 52 percent of Republicans and 57 percent of Democrats, and in the House by about 52 percent from both parties. Vice President Dawes backed it. Majority leader Curtis backed it. Here at last was a farm relief measure with enough support to secure a majority in Congress despite opposition in the northeast. The delegations of Indiana, Iowa, Nebraska, North Dakota, South Dakota, Arizona, New Mexico, and Nevada voted unanimously for the bill. The delegations of Idaho, Kansas, Kentucky, Minnesota, Missouri, Tennessee, Washington, Wisconsin, and Wyoming were nearly unanimous.

The farm bloc braced for a presidential veto but hoped to avoid one. Lobbyists from the American Farm Bureau Federation met with Coolidge and made a strong plea. Thousands of letters and telegrams arrived at the White House requesting favorable action, far outnumbering those sent by opponents of the bill.

Coolidge responded several days later with a forceful, if repetitive, 27-page veto. He argued that the bill would favor growers of certain crops and result in higher prices at home, overproduction, soil erosion, mounting surpluses, and bureaucracy: "Instead of undertaking to secure a method of orderly marketing which will dispose of products at a profit, it proposes to dispose of them at a loss. It runs counter to the principle of conservation, which would require us to produce only what can be done at a profit, not to waste our soil and resources producing what is to be sold at a loss to us for the benefit of the foreign consumer." He warned that subsidized exports would provoke foreign governments to adopt antidumping laws and other trade restrictions, and that the bill would help food processors and agribusiness concerns more than family farms. Attorney General Sargent determined that two main features of the bill were unconstitutional. First, the price-fixing system violated antitrust laws. Second, the equalization fee was an unconstitutional form of taxation: "This so-called equalization fee is not a tax for purposes of revenue in the accepted sense. It is a tax for the special benefit of particular groups."[163] The veto was upheld, leading to tens of thousands of letters and telegrams to the president, more than anyone could remember at the White House on a piece of legislation and mostly favorable in an apparent reversal of public opinion.

No less contentious was the debate over releasing funds for construction of three of the eight cruisers authorized in the Naval Appropriations Act of 1924, amounting to $1.2 million. With their great speed and seaworthiness, their high gun platform and heavy guns, cruisers were essential to modern naval power, but Coolidge and supporters believed that such a construction would be construed as undermining efforts by the League of Nations to hold disarmament talks at Geneva, Switzerland, in April. Members of the House Naval Committee found that position unacceptable. They advocated the immediate construction of the last three cruisers and the authorization of 10 more to enter the talks from a position of strength and avoid a scenario by which the United States would slip to the fourth-ranked naval power by 1932, behind England, Japan, and France. These "big navy" enthusiasts accused rival nations of violating the Washington Five-Power Treaty of 1922, such as failing to scrap certain war vessels and exceeding their maximum naval strength under the 5–5–3 ratio, while increasing production of two vessel types outside the accord, submarines and cruisers. England had 54 cruisers built or under construction. Japan had 25. The United States had 15. As to why Coolidge would tolerate such imbalance, legislators suspected he was motivated by budgetary concerns and influenced by Director Lord. "But after all, it is the Congress and not the bureau of the budget that is responsible to the people of the United States," Speaker Longworth told reporters.[164] One congressman lambasted the president for imposing reckless penny-pinching on the Navy, while maintaining the "luxurious Mayflower" and 200 crewmen for his personal use at an annual cost of nearly $300,000, a cheap shot considering the yacht was used for training young officers.[165]

Coolidge, having been through three previous budget cycles, observed to Dr. Boone that the Navy annually started a war with "poor little Japan" to get more appropriations.[166]

Nonetheless, he offered a compromise by which Congress would appropriate preliminary funds for the construction of the three remaining cruisers but reduce new appropriations from 10 to seven cruisers. This led to a bill, signed on March 2, which cut the initial appropriation for the three cruisers from $1.2 million to $450,000, while postponing action on new cruisers.

The 69th Congress ended two days later without significant new appropriations. Coolidge approved the Dill-White Radio Control Bill, establishing a five-member commission within Commerce to institute federal control of licenses, and the McFadden-Pepper Banking Act, giving banks the right to open branch subsidiaries and extending their power with respect to loans on city real estate and purchases of investment securities. He also agreed to a two-year extension of the federal subsidy under the Sheppard-Towner Maternity Act of 1921, stating his opposition to making the program permanent. He and the Republican Congress ended the federal subsidy under the Chamberlain-Kahn Venereal Disease Act of 1918, the first modern grant-in-aid program to be terminated. The Democratic bill to reduce taxes by $560 million failed in committee hearings.

* * *

Heavy rainstorms in March and April led to flooding in the Mississippi Valley, breaking levees, drowning more than 200 people, causing property damage and livestock losses from Illinois to Louisiana, and covering some 26,000 square miles of the most fertile land in the world, comparable to the Egyptian plain of the Nile and the Babylonian plain of the Euphrates. Some river towns were as much as 15 feet under water. In Arkansas City, Arkansas, stores were flooded to the ceilings and more than 300 houses were torn from their foundations. In Greenville, Mississippi, some 10,000 survivors, mostly black farmers, found refuge on top of a levee, measuring eight feet across. In Louisiana, water covered the sugar cane fields, ruining the crop for the year. New Orleans was spared for the most part, but only because the Army Corps of Engineers wrecked a levee upriver, nearly annihilating the poor parishes of St. Bernard and Plaquemine. At the widest point, near Vicksburg, Mississippi, the river swelled to almost 100 miles across. It was the worst flood in the history of the Mississippi Basin, whether measured by volume of water, area of coverage, or economic loss. The Red Cross estimated direct economic losses at $246 million, including 41,487 ruined buildings, 162,017 flooded homes, and more than $100 million in destroyed crops and livestock.[167]

Coolidge declined to tour the disaster area despite appeals from newspapers and the governors of Mississippi, Arkansas, Tennessee, and Louisiana, probably because he thought a presidential visit would divert resources and distract from the work at hand. Instead he put Secretary Hoover in charge of a coordinated effort by federal, state, and local authorities, to rescue victims, subdue the flood waters, give shelter to 700,000 homeless persons in racially segregated tent towns, repair levees, set up temporary hospitals and commissaries, provide medical care, contain the outbreak of measles and mumps, lease boats, and facilitate low-interest commercial loans for reconstruction. Coolidge appealed to his fellow citizens to help the Red Cross raise $5 million for the victims in an unprecedented charity drive that took only nine days. Then he asked for another $5 million, which took eight days. When legislators and others called for direct public assistance, however, he declined. "I do not see any method by which resort can be had to the Federal Treasury for funds for relief work in the Mississippi Valley," he told reporters.[168] Instead he ordered the Army Corps of Engineers to conduct a survey of the Mississippi Valley and devise a plan to prevent disastrous floods from reoccurring, while making clear that the states, not the federal government, should lead reconstruction efforts.

Newspapers, legislators from both parties, and letters and wires from all over the country urged him to summon a special session of Congress that summer to prepare a flood bill so that levees would be built or rebuilt before the rainy season returned in springtime. Hoover and Smoot agreed, but Coolidge declined because the Army Corps needed at least six months to finish its investigation and flood control plan. White House aides suspected political motives at work and believed a special session would result in agitation against a third term and the formation of campaign issues for the year ahead. It "would be worse than the flood itself," Coolidge told cabinet members.[169]

* * *

The early months of 1927 brought more concerns abroad than at any time of the administration, led by Nicaragua, where trouble traced back a year to the withdraw of a longstanding Marine legation, followed by civil war and a coup d'etat by General Emiliano Chamorro. Secretary Kellogg condemned the takeover, refused to recognize the new regime, and rallied other Central American nations, prompting Chamorro to resign and the Nicaraguan legislature to tab conservative senator and ex-president Adolfo Diaz to be president under Article 106 of the Nicaraguan constitution. To help thwart Mexico-backed revolutionaries on the eastern coast of the country, led by former general Jose Maria Moncada and former vice president Juan Sacasa, Coolidge lifted an arms embargo against the country and dispatched 2,000 marines in early January 1927 to supplement the guard of about 100 marines in place since the revolution of 1912 and to restore order in the capital. When legislators criticized the deployment, he sent a special message to Congress, making the case for intervention on the grounds that Mexico was intervening in the internal affairs of Nicaragua, American lives and property were at risk, and American canal rights under the Bryan-Chamorro Treaty of 1916 were at stake. In response, Chairman Borah of the Senate Committee on Foreign Relations maintained that the war-making power lay with Congress.

Frustrated by opposition on Capitol Hill, Coolidge told reporters, "We are not making war on Nicaragua any more than a policeman on the street is making war on passers-by."[170] As fighting continued in eastern Nicaragua, he escalated the troop deployment to 5,500 marines and asked veteran diplomat Henry L. Stimson to pursue a settlement between the combatants. "If you find a chance to straighten the matter out," he said, "I want you to do so."[171] The result was a ceasefire on May 4, following a 30-minute talk between Stimson and Moncada under a black thorn tree near a dry river bed at Tipitapa. They agreed on amnesty for all persons in rebellion or exile, the return of all confiscated property, and free and fair elections in 1928.

In Mexico, trouble had been brewing since December 1925, when the legislature passed two antiforeigner laws. The first prohibited foreigners from owning land unless they renounced any right of protection by their home country. The second placed a 15-year limit on oil rights acquired in Mexico before 1917 and required foreign entities to apply for renewal of such rights by 1927 or risk losing them. More than $1.5 billion worth of U.S. interests were at stake, including oil concerns, mine owners, ranchers, and concession holders. At a press conference in January 1926, with tension mounting on all sides, the president appealed for mutual tolerance and understanding:

> We have to have a great deal of patience with that country. The government there has its difficulties and the people in this country ought to realize that Mexico is a different country from ours. The people have a different outlook on things. They have not had the advantage that we have up here, and there ought to be a general public expectation that we would in every way that we can be helpful to that country, and instead of trying to oppress them in any way or anything of that kind, that such actions as we take are taken with a view to being helpful.[172]

By January 1927, Coolidge had lost patience with negotiations and with Mexican intervention in Nicaraguan affairs. Amid rumors of a possible break in relations or even war, Mexico delayed implementation of the confiscatory laws and indicated a willingness to change them all together. After the U.S. Ambassador resigned that summer, Coolidge replaced him with Dwight Morrow, whom many thought would be the next secretary of state or receive a choice assignment in Europe. That Coolidge decided to dispatch such a confidant to Mexico City showed the importance he placed on U.S.-Mexican relations, even as critics on both sides of the border questioned the probity of sending the lead attorney from J.P. Morgan and Company to handle a sensitive economic dispute. "My only instructions are to keep us out of war with Mexico," he told his old classmate.[173] Morrow proceeded to help local authorities implement antiforeigner laws within the framework of international law and bilateral agreements by relying on Article XIV of the Mexican Constitution of 1917, which laid down the principle that no legislation should be retroactive, and some timely Mexican court decisions. The final agreement affirmed national ownership of the oil deposits but exempted firms that performed "positive acts" on their properties before 1917.

In war-wracked China, when Nationalist forces under Chiang Kai-shek threatened to violate the Boxer Rebellion of 1901 by closing the road from Peking to the sea, Coolidge allowed acting secretary of state Joseph Grew to warn all sides to keep the road open. As trouble in Shanghai threatened foreign lives in late January 1927, England mobilized troops outside the city and called on the United States for reinforcements before deciding to act alone, sending in hundreds of soldiers to restore order and protect its longstanding official concessions there. On March 24, Nationalist forces attacked foreign elements in Nanking and ransacked the American, British, and Japanese consulates, killing one U.S. citizen, and forcing several others to take refuge at the Standard Oil Company compound on Socony Hill, as U.S. and British warships pounded the city in retaliation. Coolidge ordered 1,500 Marines to prepare for action, followed by a note of protest demanding punishment of the officer responsible for the incident, a written apology from the head of the Nationalist army, and compensation for property damage and personal injuries, but not the sort of "punitive damages" that had offended China during the Boxer Rebellion two decades ago. The administration refused to sign a demarche by the Western powers threatening drastic action, including a blockade of the entire Yangtze delta. China proceeded to execute some officers, order the arrest of army propagandist Liu Tsu Han, express "profound regret" for the violence, and promise compensation for the destruction and injuries.[174]

China in turn hoped the United States would "express regret" at the bombardment of Socony Hill. The administration stopped short of an apology but noted how "deeply it deplores that circumstances beyond its control should have necessitated the adoption of such measures for the protection of the lives of its citizens at Nanking."[175] This helped produce a settlement that was generally accepted by all sides.

As signatories to the Washington Five-Power Treaty of 1922 prepared to meet at Geneva in June 1927, the Coolidge administration hoped for further naval limitations. The earlier treaty dealt with battleships and battle cruisers, most of which had become obsolete because of their vulnerability to attack from airplanes and floating mines. The new negotiations proposed to cover light cruisers, destroyers, and submarines, which would involve significant technical obstacles and have faint hope for success. There were many questions: What distinctions were to be made on cruisers of different sizes and types? What size guns could they carry? Were similar distinctions to be made with respect to destroyers and submarines? In holding talks without preliminary discussions on such issues, the administration badly misinterpreted the situation at hand. To make matters worse, France and Italy declined to participate in the talks. France had no interest in negotiations to limit the tonnage of auxiliary warships. Italy had to keep pace with France.

To be sure, Coolidge had a philosophical skepticism toward disarmament talks. "If the people want to fight, they will fight with broomsticks if they cannot find anything else," he said to Bernard Baruch one evening.[176]

To naval aide Wilson Brown, he admitted having little faith in arms limitations treaties as instruments of peace but felt he had to make the effort.[177]

The most positive foreign policy development involved a proposal by French premier Aristide Briand in April to pursue a bilateral agreement to outlaw war "as an instrument of national policy," whereupon Secretary Kellogg recommended broadening it to include all nations. By August 1928, 15 nations, including every military power except the Soviet Union, had agreed to the initiative, meeting in Paris to sign a treaty that renounced war and obligated signatories to pursue nonviolent settlements to all international disputes. Known as the Kellogg-Briand Pact, it lacked machinery to prevent violations and punish violators, but many saw it as a worthwhile endeavor to seize on widespread antiwar sentiments.

* * *

Per capita income in the United States reached a record in 1926, with Gross National Product increasing by an average of about 3 percent annually and wholesale prices dropping by an average of about 1 percent a year. Millions of families were buying their first refrigerators, washing machines, vacuum cleaners, hot irons, toasters, radios, cameras, sewing machines, phonographs, and automobiles, with the latter accounting for about one out of eight jobs in the country. Ford Motor Company alone was producing more cars in three months than Europe could make in a year, with advances in assembly line technology lowering prices. A car that would have cost $760 in 1920 was selling at $600 or less by the end of the decade. The French writer Andre Maurois came to visit for the first time and was struck by the youth and confidence of the people, the lack of class consciousness, and the number of workmen who owned new cars and arrived at factories for their shifts wearing soft hats or derbies.[178]

"I have only one criticism of America," he quipped, "and that is the fact that your telephone system works."[179]

Americans were saving, too. In fiscal year 1928, total savings deposits in banks hit a record high of more than $28 billion, an increase of 113.5 percent during the past decade. New England led the way with the highest per capita savings rate for the 16th consecutive year.[180]

Occupational trends revealed a modern economy in transition. From 1920 to 1927, the number of workers engaged in distribution, personal services, professional services, and transportation increased by more than 2.8 million, while the number of workers in agriculture, manufacturing, mining, and the federal government decreased by about 2 million. Automotive salesman, barbers, chauffeurs, garage employees, hairdressers, hotel workers, manicurists, radio dealers, truck drivers, and road workers were on the rise.[181]

One concern was whether consumption would be able to sustain the prosperity. Farm incomes remained stagnant and industrial wages increased slowly, as labor unions declined because of ethnic and racial rivalries, the emergence of company pension plans and profit-sharing schemes, the shift from manufacturing jobs to finance and service jobs, and several Supreme Court rulings, including one in 1923 that struck down a minimum wage law in the District of Columbia and had repercussions for similar laws in several states. The two largest firms in operation, Ford Motor Company and the United States Steel Corporation, prohibited union labor. Still, most workers paid lower federal income taxes or none at all—98 percent of the population was exempt by 1927—and worked fewer hours than they had during the Wilson years, as the eight-hour day and six-day week became almost standard in the industrial work force.[182] To socialist Norman Thomas, workers were "drunk with prosperity."[183]

The prosperity depended in part on rampant credit expansion and speculation. The currency in circulation fell from $3.68 billion to $3.64 billion during the 1920s, but credit expanded from $45.3 billion to $73 billion, as the U.S. Treasury, federal banks, private banks, and corporations combined to maintain the bull market.[184] Few experts seemed concerned that most motorcars and about one-seventh of all consumer goods in the United States were sold on installment plans by 1927, or that household debt more than doubled from $3.1 billion in 1922 to $6.9 billion in 1929.[185] Installment plans were essential to mass production, which in turn lowered prices on automobiles and other items. To Coolidge, they were better than the old system of running an open book account at the store, with no schedule of payments, as his father had done. For all his emphasis on economy in public expenditures—and in his personal life—he knew private debt was necessary for many families and crucial for driving economic growth.[186]

The rise of multidivisional corporations, led by Allied Signal, American Can, Du Pont, Jersey Standard, General Motors, Monsanto, Motorola, Otis Elevator, Sears, Singer, and Westinghouse, helped to boost the U.S. share of world manufacturing output from 35.8 percent before the war to 42.2 percent in the late 1920s, as England, France, and Germany fell from a combined 35.4 percent to 27.6 percent during that span. European firms were even losing share in their home markets, continuing a prewar trend.[187] This had many causes. European countries had higher debt, higher taxes, and smaller domestic markets than the United States. The continent had no agreement or customs union to promote trade, and many bilateral agreements from before the war were gone. In fact, trade barriers had increased since the war, including discriminatory taxes, duties, levies, regulations, and license requirements, driven by nationalism, postwar recessions, and new countries. The old Austro-Hungarian Empire had been replaced by eight countries, each with its own tariffs and other trade restrictions. Yet none of that, arguably, mattered as much as the modern U.S. corporation, marked by salaried professional managers, decentralized structures, diversified products, and research laboratories that came up with automatic switchboards, dial phones, teletype machines, power shovels, belt and bucket conveyors, pneumatic tools, concrete mixers, dump trucks, cellophane, rayon, and new refrigerants during the decade.

Business regulators continued to favor volunteerism over prosecution to save time and money. In February 1926, the FTC dismissed a complaint against a Chicago meatpacker whose secret control over a creamery company had been attacked as an unfair method of trade, when the meatpacker agreed to divulge its stake in the firm. In February 1927, the FTC dismissed a complaint against a Missouri disinfectant producer after it promised to stop paying premiums to purchasing agents and administrative officers as inducements to buy its products. In March 1927, the FTC dropped charges against a company that agreed to stop falsely advertising its product as United States Army boots. Such outcomes eliminated a backlog of cases and spared the cost of numerous trials, which undoubtedly appealed to the president. Critics argued that too many firms were allowed to atone for past wrongdoing by repenting rather than paying a fine.

The administration kept a hands-off stance toward Wall Street in line with traditional policy that trading in securities was not a form of interstate commerce, falling outside the jurisdiction of the FTC and the interstate commerce clause of the Constitution. As there were no federal or state laws on financial disclosure, most firms represented on the New York Stock Exchange did not publish statements on annual profits, debt, financial reserves, and other relevant data on their operations. Worse yet, more investors were buying stocks on the margin, paying a fraction of the purchase price, normally about 50 percent but as low as 10 percent, and putting the balance on credit or short-term call loans with high interest rates. If the value of the stock dropped below an amount equal to the collateral put down by the borrower, the lender could call for repayment at any time.

After *Washington Herald* editor and former White House clerk Judson Welliver showed Coolidge an article in the *Atlantic* by William Z. Ripley, Professor of Economics at Harvard, on how vast holding companies, created under lax state incorporation laws, raised millions of dollars through securities without issuing complete financial reports, the president invited the author to lunch in February 1926. Afterward Coolidge took him into the study where, feet on his desk, smoking a cigar, he heard about the "prestidigitation, double-shuffling, honey-fugling, hornswoggling and skullduggery" behind the booming stock market.

"Well, Mr. Ripley, is there anything that we can do down here?" he asked.

"No, it's a state matter," replied the professor.[188]

Two days later, following newspaper coverage of the Ripley-Coolidge meeting and the Ripley article, the New York Stock Exchange had its most precipitous decline of the Coolidge years, but the setback proved to be short-lived once it became clear the administration would not intervene with the internal operations of the market. "All of this is being done under the authority of state corporation laws," Coolidge told reporters.[189]

Coolidge liked to remark that the United States was one of the few great nations in history with separate capitals for politics and finance.[190] The division of power between Washington and New York reduced opportunities for one to corrupt the other. The New York Stock Exchange ran under a New York state charter and was a state matter for which the Governor of New York was responsible. In response to those who claimed the Federal Trade Commission had authority over securities trading, the administration looked into the matter and decided otherwise. There were limits to how much protection federal or state authorities could provide to investors, Coolidge told reporters, even with traditionally stable investments: "I think we all recall that Government bonds which were issued in time of war depreciated in market value quite a good deal."[191]

Similarly, Coolidge made no attempt to influence the easy money policy of the Federal Reserve Board that was partly to blame for the speculation. Established in 1913 to prevent panics in large banks, the board had two ways to manipulate the money supply: it could buy or sell government securities on the open market, which increased or decreased the cash reserves of member banks, or it could raise or lower the discount rate by which member banks could borrow money. With prodding from Benjamin Strong of the dominant Federal Reserve Bank of New York, the board kept the discount rate low during the postwar decade, partly to maintain growth, partly to make credit available to European nations trying to revive their economies and meet their debt obligations, partly to help England prevent currency outflows after returning the pound to its prewar gold equivalent in 1925. When the board tried to avert a slump in Europe and the United States by purchasing securities on the open market and reducing the discount rate from 4.0 percent to 3.5 percent in May 1927, member banks doubled their holdings of U.S. securities and broker loans increased by 24 percent during the last half of the year.[192] Yet the money behind such loans came mostly from nonbank sources over which the government had no authority, led by wealthy individuals, foreigners, and corporations, seeking to take advantage of the return rates of 7 percent or higher on call loans. Indeed commercial banks owned less than 1 percent of corporate stocks.

Asked at a news conference to comment on the policy of low discount rates, Coolidge replied:

> I think I have indicated to the conference a great many times that it is a board that does function and ought to function entirely apart from the Executive, acting almost entirely in the nature of a judicial position. I have sometimes made some comment on what they have done and the beneficial effect that I thought had accrued from it, but I do not recall that I have ever made any suggestion to the board as to any action that it ought to take.[193]

Chapter Eight

"I do not choose to run"

The debate over whether Coolidge would or should seek another term was well underway by early 1927, some 18 months before the election. At issue was whether his abbreviated term of 1923–1925 counted as a term. Coolidge thought not, but others pointed to Roosevelt, who, after taking office under similar circumstances in 1901, declared on his triumphant election night in 1904 that he would honor the two-term tradition by not seeking reelection, like Washington, Jefferson, Madison, Monroe, Jackson, and Cleveland. Washington thought the country in an emergency ought not be deprived of the services of any individual deemed best suited to lead, but his decision to refuse nomination for a third term, more personal than political, set the precedent. Jefferson declined renomination and advocated an amendment to enforce the two-term limit. Grant in 1880 and Roosevelt in 1912 pursued without success a third term after a four-year absence from office. Wilson in 1920 desired a third consecutive term but never received serious consideration because of his stroke.

Democratic and progressive publications took the position that Coolidge should not run. The *Birmingham Age-Herald*, the *Brooklyn Eagle*, the *Hartford Times*, the *Houston Chronicle and Herald*, the *Memphis Commercial Appeal*, the *New York Evening World*, the *Providence News*, the *St. Louis Post-Dispatch*, and others came out against a third term.

Republican newspapers, led by the *Albany Knickerbocker Press*, the *Grand Rapids Herald*, the *Manchester Union*, the *Minneapolis Journal*, the *New York Tribune*, the *Springfield Union*, the *St. Paul Press*, and the *Washington Star*, lined up behind the president. Many noted that he had had the shortest abbreviated term of any accidental president—19 months as compared with nearly four years for Tyler, Johnson, Arthur, and Roosevelt, and nearly three years for Fillmore.

The Hearst machine backed another term for Coolidge in a series of editorials from coast to coast, prompting critics, such as Willis Sharp in the *Atlantic Monthly*, to claim that newspaper financiers had been seduced by the Mellon tax cuts. Frank Kent, in *The Forum*, ridiculed Hearst and others for building a "Coolidge myth" around a man they knew to be mediocre in every respect, who, having been fortunate to inherit the office at a time of peace and prosperity, had accomplished little besides saving money on pencils, paper cups, and towels at the White House, a man lacking in magnanimity and grace, "thin in body, thin in mind, thin in spirit, thin in soul."[1] Such voices were in the minority, for Silent Cal had long since won the public trust with his simplicity of bearing, common sense, and emphasis on economy.

"He is nearly as good a politician as Lincoln," marveled Taft, who backed another term and considered the two-term tradition as applicable only to two elective terms.[2]

No man in memory had possessed such a popular hold on the people, said Chauncey Depew, the 93-year-old former United States senator from New York who backed Coolidge in 1928 without hesitation over the third term issue and predicted his reelection. Nothing was more statesman-like than to balance the budget, he said.[3]

* * *

Frank Stearns had no inkling what the president would do. In March, he and Mrs. Stearns took a two-week cruise to the Caribbean, inviting Dr. and Mrs. Boone and setting sail from New York on a British-registered ship happily unencumbered by prohibition, with stops in Cuba, Jamaica, Panama, and Costa Rica. They had a fine time, partaking in cocktails, sunning themselves, and hardly mentioning politics until, on the way home, Stearns let loose a barrage of opinions, stating that Coolidge was his own secretary of state, that Sargent was the second greatest man in the country, that the rest of the cabinet was feckless, and that Hoover was particularly unimpressive. Boone replied in a manner that struck Stearns as negative toward Coolidge, and then insisted he liked Coolidge but sensed frailties and weaknesses in him that were less apparent to others; for all his virtues as a public man, he was not warmhearted; he was curt, inconsiderate, and cruel at times, and probably would have been much worse without Grace. To all this Stearns listened without comment.

Later that evening Stearns was quiet during a discussion on whether Coolidge should seek reelection. Mrs. Stearns commented that the people were bound to tire of him and the type of president he was, if he served another term.[4]

* * *

All indications pointed to a Coolidge candidacy. Senator Fess of Ohio met with the president in March, following a trip out west, and told reporters that he was popular throughout the region and that the third term issue was a mere bugaboo.[5] Senator Willis of Ohio, not to be outdone, made a swing though the corn states and said they would back another term.[6] Charles D. Hilles, Chairman of the Republican National Committee, and others made similar statements.[7] Chairman Snell of the House Rules Committee visited the president in April and predicted afterward he would be the lone candidate in 1928, despite the formation of Lowden-for-president committees in the Middle West. "I have never seen him in better health," he told reporters.[8] Arguably the second most powerful figure in town, the upstate New York Republican had known Coolidge since their student days at Amherst and been his trusty ally on Capitol Hill since 1923, meeting with him twice a week to discuss legislation and control spending by burying certain bills in committee hearings. "Hard Boiled Snell," they called him, a short, broad-shouldered, former logger known to sharpen his pencil with a knife and say little inside the House chamber. He was closer to the president than any other legislator. That several supporters of the president would make such statements in short order seemed to suggest some coordination or consent from the White House. Coolidge, having seen Roosevelt struggle as a "lame duck" president during his second term, knew better than to reveal his intentions before he had to. Many thought he would postpone his announcement until 1928 to maintain leverage with Congress on taxes and other issues.

"Coolidge will not only run," wrote Will Rogers in a column, "but he will win by so much he won't even stay up to listen to the count over the radio."[9]

Most politicos predicted Democrats would nominate Governor Smith of New York despite his handicaps—his Catholicism, his affiliation with the Tammany Hall political machine, and his support of prohibition modification. The "wet" issue alone severely weakened his prospects.

In early May, Coolidge invited several cabinet officers and prominent Republican legislators to hear party chairman William Butler report on his fact-finding swing through Denver, Ogden, Salt Lake City, San Francisco, Los Angeles, Portland, and Seattle. They met over breakfast at 15 Du Pont Circle, where the president and first lady stayed that spring because the White House was under renovation. Butler, speaking in his clipped New England accent, relayed a "general satisfaction with the course of the government of Washington" and high hopes for the 1928 campaign. To one attendee, he appeared to be forecasting the "renomination and reelection of Mr. Coolidge by acclimation." The president listened without comment but seemed pleased.[10]

Nor did Coolidge respond to allegations that as a state senator in 1912 he signed an anti-third term petition against Roosevelt that stated: "No person who has held the office of President for two terms, or for any part of two terms, whether consecutive or otherwise, shall thereafter be eligible to be chosen to the office of President or Vice President."[11] True, he had supported Taft after Roosevelt broke from the party at the 1912 convention, but he refused to comment when reporters asked about the petition, even though a Massachusetts politician claimed to have a copy, complete with signatures. When reporters revealed Coolidge had not answered the question, he chastised them for violating the rules of the press conference.[12]

Two weeks later the White House announced the president would vacation that summer at a state-run lodge in the Black Hills of South Dakota, prompting speculation that he was trying to regain support he had lost out west by his veto of the McNary-Haugen bill, no less in the state scheduled to hold the first Republican presidential primary of 1928.

There was such speculation that even the most trivial occurrence drew attention as an indicator. When the White House released to the public an amusing letter from a 92-year-old Vermonter, newspapers dwelled on the last line in which he wrote he voted for Lincoln in 1860 and hoped to vote for Coolidge in 1928, taking that as a sign the administration was subtly preparing the public for a third-term announcement. At last the White House correspondents took the initiative by agreeing to each submit the same question at a press conference on an idle spring day: "Shall you run in 1928?" Coolidge, standing at his desk to greet them, read through the batch of 20 questions, tossing them on his desk, one by one, until he got to the end. "I have here a question about the condition of children in Poland," he said with a straight face, followed by a 10-minute discourse on a topic no one had brought up.[13]

The return of Charles A. Lindbergh from his historic New York-to-Paris flight on June 11 created a mania that temporarily swept aside politics in the city. No less than 21 special trains entered Washington that warm Saturday morning, carrying 25,000 passengers from New York, New Jersey, Pennsylvania, Delaware, Maryland, Ohio, West Virginia, Virginia, North Carolina, and South Carolina. Another 25,000 arrived by motorcar. All told, some 500,000 persons lined the streets as the pilot arrived at Washington Navy Yard aboard the USS *Memphis*, receiving a heroic welcome and a three-mile procession to the Capitol and the Washington Monument that matched any parade or presidential inauguration in history. Spectators filled the temporary wooden stands on Pennsylvania Avenue, or climbed trees or statues, shouting, "Lindy! Lindy!" One hotel let its first floor windows to a concessionaire who sold seats at 50 cents apiece. Women held up newspapers to protect themselves from the sun, but those with parasols were told to keep them down so everyone could see. The crowds were so dense that spectators needed assistance to remove their coats as the temperature rose. "The men have their coats off, with the permission of the ladies," a radio announcer assured his audience.[14]

Coolidge, having granted federal employees a rare early release from their normal half-day Saturday schedule to celebrate Lindbergh Day, arrived at the base of the Washington Monument at noon. There he stood on tiptoes atop a white makeshift platform to watch the approaching motorcade, while Mellon and Lord looked out their office windows several hundred yards away, taking a short break to observe the commotion. In greeting the young pilot, Coolidge was unusually demonstrative, though not nearly as much as his wife. In speaking to some 300,000 spectators and 30 million radio listeners over a record 50 stations from coast to coast, he noted that whereas Columbus took 69 days to cross the Atlantic, Lindbergh took only 33 hours; he praised the pilot for his pluck and achievement and presented him with the Distinguished Flying Cross "as a symbol of appreciation for what he is and what he has done."[15]

That evening the first couple hosted a reception for Lindbergh as politicians clamored to meet the new icon from Little Falls, Minnesota, 25 years old and previously an obscure air mail pilot who had survived two crashes before accomplishing what six other men had died attempting. He had flown across the ocean without radar or radio, sitting atop the fuselage in a wicker chair with the legs sawed off.

Two days later the first couple left for South Dakota with 80 persons, five canaries, their pet raccoon, and two collies for a two-day, 1,800-mile journey via Chicago and numerous little railroad depots where crowds waited to see Coolidge wave from the back car. Most wore plain clothes, without the knee-length dresses in vogue back east. As the train ran through Wisconsin and Minnesota at the standard speed of 37 miles per hour, Coolidge could see ankle-high corn stalks and a healthy wheat crop coming up in the fields, succulent and sweet. In South Dakota the grassland turned to rolling country as they crossed the Missouri and approached the Black Hills. At the train depot in Rapid City, the president received a boisterous welcome and spontaneously, rather uncharacteristically, picked up a little girl in his arms as he spotted her near the front of the crowd. "The campaign of 1928 may be regarded as formally opened," quipped a *Washington Post* columnist.[16] The presidential party then switched to motorcars for a 30-mile ride to their lodge. Since they arrived after sunset, the photographers and movie men could not record the event, but the publicity conscious president promised a reenactment the next morning.

The executive office was set up in a mathematics classroom at Rapid City High School, complete with typewriters, telephones, and a special telegraph wire to the White House. In preparation for the visit, Bell Telephone

Company had constructed a series of 13 copper circuits at a cost of nearly $500,000, allowing the president to make direct calls to Washington during business hours, nine to five, Monday through Friday. Workers had also run lines across the broken stretch of country between the lodge and the school, costing an additional $10,000. The other challenge was to deliver mail from Washington in a timely manner. The Air Mail Service had instituted a daily transcontinental run from New York to San Francisco in 1924, reducing delivery time by 22 hours, and had since added routes to other cities through contracts to private air companies. However, the nearest stop to Rapid City was several hundred miles away. That being unacceptable, Postmaster General New accompanied Coolidge out west and persuaded the Army Air Corps to transport official mail by special pouch for the final stretch into Rapid City.

No president had ever taken a vacation out west or in such a remote setting. McKinley, Roosevelt, Taft, and Wilson seldom varied their summer vacations. Harding never took one. Coolidge, in choosing a new destination for the fourth consecutive year, created unprecedented interest and newspaper coverage. He held press conferences at the school, took naps, rode horseback for the first time in years, shot at clay pigeons, went fishing for trout in a stream well stocked in advance by a local warden, spoke to farmers and cattlemen, and took two walks a day among the buffalo and elk that roamed the hills. He attended services in a small timber chapel, visited Sioux tribesmen, and hosted a barbecue for several hundred newspaper editors.

The third term issue continued to make headlines with Republican emissaries from Idaho, Kansas, Nebraska, Colorado, Wyoming, and Montana visiting the president and saying he could count on their states in 1928. Even potential rivals Senator Borah and General Wood predicted the region would back the president, as did many local newspapers and periodicals.[17] There was no denying his popularity out west that summer, despite the farm bill veto, despite the high tariff, despite claims that his appeal hinged on publicity stunts like attending rodeo shows, gold-panning, and donning a 10-gallon hat and cowboy chaps, which would be forgotten by the time voters went to the polls in a year, especially if corn and wheat prices slipped again.

"The people are not disturbed by talk of a third term," said Representative John Q. Tilson of Connecticut, Republican floor leader of the House, after touring the west and meeting with the president at the lodge.[18]

"The people do not care whether Mr. Coolidge serves one term or ten terms," Representative Madden told reporters, praising his record on economy.[19]

Politics aside, it was not much of a vacation. "It is really dreadful,"

Ellen Riley wrote home. "No one has a bit of privacy around here. The President and Mrs. C. get very tired of it all."[20] The lodge sat on a road, allowing hundreds of tourists to pull over in their automobiles and gawk or climb into trees with field glasses. Vacation travel, until recently an indulgence for the wealthy, had become commonplace thanks to mass production of the automobile and highway construction across the country. Many families took camping kits and went away for weeks at a time that summer. To take advantage of the tourist boom, rail operators placed 10 sleeping cars on a siding in Rapid City, local entrepreneurs established tourist camps and hot dog stands, and homeowners leased rooms. Newspapermen stood on the front lawn of the lodge all day, recording every movement and sending some two million words on the president that summer. The weather fluctuated wildly, from a hailstorm in June that broke 35 windows at Rapid City High School, tore shingles off houses, and punctured automobile tops, to a hot stretch with temperatures in the high 90s that made his 40-minute ride back to the lodge miserable. One afternoon he went so far as to discard his coat and sit shirt-sleeved on the front porch.

When Grace and her bodyguard failed to return from a 15-mile hike in time for lunch one day, the president, fearing she had been led astray or bitten by a rattlesnake, sat nearly motionless on the porch until she appeared, thirsty and apologetic. Inside the lodge, away from reporters, he lost his composure. Indeed he was so furious that he had the bodyguard sent back to Washington in what was shamelessly ascribed to a promotion as ill-founded rumors of a romantic tryst spread here and there. Grace, heartbroken with embarrassment and regret, stopped taking hikes and accompanied her husband to town for several days, shopping and waiting outside his office; to one observer she lost her "spontaneous gaiety" from that point on.[21]

All the while, Stearns was in Swampscott with Mrs. Stearns, who was recuperating from an illness and reluctant to travel 1,600 miles to South Dakota, having been told by Grace that it was an isolated place with yellow alkali dust blowing through every crevice.[22] Dr. Boone, staying with the elderly couple while the *Mayflower* underwent repairs at Boston Navy Yard, advised against such a physically demanding trip.[23] Edward Clark, on location with the president, also encouraged them to stay away, writing, "I am afraid you would both find it intolerably dull."[24] After a *Boston Post* reporter returned from temporary assignment in South Dakota and described it as "indescribably a terrible place," Stearns decided to stay home. This pleased Coolidge, for he did not want to be bothered about the election.[25]

* * *

The fiscal year ended on June 30 with federal expenditures at $2,974,029,674.62, minus debt reduction payments and postal expenditures. This was the goal he had set during his early weeks in office, to produce a budget below $3 billion for the first time since before the war. The surplus was an impressive $99 million.

* * *

Coolidge was at his plain mahogany desk one morning a few weeks later when Everett Sanders arrived for their daily appointment. The genial Middle Westerner had been with him for more than two years without quite understanding him or the New England temperament. To one reporter he seemed afraid of the boss.[26] Newspaper reports had him retiring and returning to Indianapolis to practice law.

Coolidge told him to have a seat. "Now—I am not going to run for President," he began, followed by a pause. "If I should serve as President again, I should serve almost ten years, which is too long for a President in this country."

Sanders, taken aback, replied, "I think the people of this country will be disappointed."

Coolidge pulled from his drawer a copy of the statement he would release to the public on the fourth anniversary of his succession to the presidency. It was a single sentence, written in blue pencil on a small piece of lined paper, three inches by five inches. Sanders thought the phraseology enigmatic and made a recommendation or two. Coolidge said he would release the statement on August 2, the fourth anniversary of his homestead inaugural. No one else knew.[27]

On August 1, Coolidge received Arthur Capper, the Kansas senator and farm periodical publicist who helped deliver the farm vote in 1924 despite opposing him on taxes, the bonus, and agricultural price supports. As they sat by the fireplace in a heavily beamed room with buffalo skins on the floor and antlers on the wall, Capper said most Republican legislators thought Coolidge should seek another term and most farmers would support him as long as he backed a revised McNary-Haugen bill in the next session. A recent questionnaire revealed that 121 out of 125 counties in Kansas favored another term for the president. Coolidge listened with intent.[28]

The following morning Coolidge barely spoke at breakfast, but turning to Grace on his way out, said, "I have been President four years today."[29]

At the high school, Sanders had a stack of documents ready to review that morning, but he began with a query: "Do you intend to make your announcement today?"

"Yes," Coolidge replied.

Sanders advised that he not do so at his morning press conference but that he wait until noon to avoid upsetting the stock market. Coolidge agreed.[30] Then he began to read through his papers and found a telegram from William Monroe Trotter in Boston stating that four black employees at the Pension Bureau in Washington had been segregated during a bureaucratic shuffle. He promptly sent a telegram to the commissioner of pensions: "Being advised that your Bureau has recently segregated four colored Examiners, the President directs you to revoke segregation at once." The commissioner complied but insisted his "reassignment" had been mistakenly "construed as segregation."[31]

At the press conference, Coolidge provided an update on naval reduction talks in Geneva, which were about to collapse over the cruiser issue. Ill-fated from the start, beset by technical challenges that should have been addressed in preliminary talks, the talks represented the most spectacular foreign policy failure of the administration. Japan wanted fewer but heavier cruisers to protect its Asian trade routes. England favored limiting cruisers to 7,000 tons with six-inch guns in accord with its fleet, but wanted to maintain at least 54 light cruisers and 25 heavy cruisers, far more than the other naval powers. The United States wanted smaller numbers of large cruisers with eight-inch guns to ply the vast Pacific Ocean, where refueling stations and naval bases were limited. After stating his "keen disappointment," the president sifted through the questions in a preoccupied way until he came across one asking what he thought was the greatest accomplishment of his administration. The reduction of the national debt by nearly $4 billion and the reduction of taxes would have to rank high, he replied.

"That answers the requirements of the day," he said. "If the conference will return at 12:00 I may have a further statement to make."[32]

This set the reporters a-tremble with speculation, for he had been leaving his office at noon each day and was not one to break with routine. They thought he might have an announcement on the naval talks.[33]

Alone, Coolidge took his pencil and wrote the same words he showed Sanders earlier, indicating they had been chosen with deliberation. Sanders then handed the 12-word statement to stenographer Erwin C. Geisser and requested 25 typewritten copies to be ready shortly before noon. Geisser, having typed the copies of the presidential oath in Vermont four years ago, felt his pulse rush as he looked down at the words, knowing he was about to witness history again. Shocked, he hammered out the message on ordinary typewriter paper and gave the copies to Sanders for delivery to the president. Coolidge read them over, took a pair of scissors from his desk, and cut the sheets into little slips, about five inches long and one inch deep.

At noon reporters returned to the mathematics room to find Coolidge standing beside his desk, a faint smile on his face. Sanders, Geisser, and Capper stood nearby. "If you will pass in front of me," Coolidge said, holding twice-folded slips of paper, "I will hand these to you." Sanders blocked the door to ensure no one left until everyone had a copy.

The statement read: "I do not choose to run for President in nineteen twenty eight."

The newspapermen were speechless, staring at their slips of paper and looking up at Coolidge, who stood behind his desk, hands clasped together.

"Is there any other comment?" asked a reporter from the *New York World.*

"None," he replied.[34]

With that the newspapermen left in a mad scramble for the nearest telephone and telegraph office, located several blocks away in a gray concrete building. Pedestrians thought a fire or some catastrophe had taken place as they saw the men sprint down the main street of the city or leap into automobiles. Several were nearly knocked down. Some followed behind, hoping to find out themselves. Coolidge donned a heavy overcoat and rode to the lodge with Capper in near-silence, looking out the window at the barren landscape, the reddish brown streams, and the rough dwellings lacking in blinds, shutters, shingles, and chimneys.

"The people have been talking about running me for president again," he said at one point. "I thought I would let them know how I felt about it. I guess they will understand it all right."[35]

At lunch he never said a word to Grace about the announcement, leaving Capper to break the news after he left to take a nap.

"Quite a surprise the President gave us this morning," he said, sitting in the living room in leather-covered rocking chairs.

Grace looked up from her knitting as he proceeded to describe what her husband had done.

"Now isn't that like him," she said.[36]

In Northampton, the *Daily Hampshire Gazette* had gone to press with its last edition at 3:30 p.m., when a wire service representative called with the dramatic news. Editors immediately altered the first page to include a headline story on the announcement for the city edition, since the suburban edition had already gone out. Readers were stunned. "I am sorry," said Jim Lucey. "I am sorry. I hoped he would run again. The country needs him."[37] Mrs. Goodhue had no comment when reporters arrived at 21 Massasoit Street except to say she knew nothing of the announcement.[38]

In Vermont, Attorney General Sargent had this to say: "I have no comment."[39]

In Boston, Stearns was stunned to receive the news by special wire and needed six days to think it over before writing as follows:

> I have tried every day since your announcement was made to write you a letter and each day I have backed off. I shall not make any thorough attempt now. I would rather talk with you some time. If I say that I am glad you made the statement, it might sound as though I have changed my mind about you as President. If I say that it leaves you in a wonderful position in case you are drafted, it might sound as if I questioned your genuineness in making the statement. Of course neither of these things is true. But the more I think about it, the surer I am the statement was wise, could not be improved upon in its wording, and was timely.[40]

Yet he and Butler and others conspired to ensure Coolidge would be in position to accept the nomination by acclimation, encouraged that he declined to elaborate on his intentions except to say at a news conference on August 5 that he did not expect to be in office after March 4, 1929. "I am not convinced he will not run if renominated," Butler told reporters.[41] Oulahan of the *New York Times* reported that Republican leaders planned to draft the president.[42]

To columnist Heywood Broun, the Black Hills statement had "magnificent swank."[43]

To Will Rogers, it was "the best worded acceptance of a nomination ever uttered by a candidate."[44]

White House usher Ike Hoover thought the statement was meant to move public opinion toward support for a draft movement in 1928.[45]

Porter H. Dale of Vermont, who had been at the Coolidge house on the fateful night four years ago, told reporters that Vermonters commonly use "choose" to mean "plan" or "intend." Its meaning was clear.[46]

Likewise, Ronald D. Sawyer of Massachusetts had known Coolidge two decades and often heard him use "choose" when he had made up his mind and did not wish to further discuss the matter in question.[47]

Several longtime associates insisted the president would never use the words "will not" because that would presume the party would want to nominate him.[48]

* * *

Director Lord arrived at Rapid City on Friday night, August 12, to discuss the preliminary budget estimates for fiscal year 1929, with faint hope to stay below $3 billion after achieving their long-stated goal the previous fiscal year, now six weeks in the past. Coolidge, noting that the estimates for fiscal year 1929 exceeded total appropriations for fiscal year 1928 and total expenditures for fiscal year 1927, reviewed the balance sheet and became frustrated by the figures for military spending. The Navy Department wanted $382 million, a 16 percent increase over 1928. The War Department wanted $451 million, a 22 percent increase. They combined for more than half of the increase in spending. He promptly dictated letters to the secretary of the navy and the secretary of war to protest their high estimates, to which the former blamed the need for a cruiser buildup following the failed Geneva talks and the latter the costs of the Mississippi River flood work. Coolidge instructed both departments to pursue cost-cutting options, which they did, reducing their estimates by $19 million and $50 million, respectively.

* * *

The ride back to Washington took two days and ran behind schedule as crowds gathered at stations, in response to the I-do-not-choose-to-run declaration, which had captured the public imagination. This spontaneous tribute moved Coolidge to appear on the rear platform of the train for several unscheduled stops and forced the conductor to slow down to five miles per hour at various other times. Upon arrival at Union Station at 10:00 p.m., September 11, they received cheers from a spontaneous crowd of some 500 persons. The White House was ready to be occupied after six months of renovation. The old roof of wood construction dating from 1817 had been replaced by one of steel, tile, and slate. The attic had been converted into a third floor with 21 new rooms, ample closets, and a sky parlor built on the flat part of the roof, slightly above floor level, with glass on three sides and a splendid view of the Mall, the Washington Monument, and the Potomac. There was still no central air conditioning, unlike in many hotels, stores, and cinemas across the city. When the temperature on Pennsylvania Avenue reached a year-high of 102 degrees several days later the president retreated to a room in the basement to stay cool. Dr. Boone found him in good health following his vacation, but walking less and taking on "a bit of a waistline" at 55.[49]

Coolidge spurned calls for a special session of Congress to provide relief to areas stricken by the Mississippi flood and instead approved the diversion of $2 million in river and harbor funds to repair some 225 levees compromised by the flood. The timing was urgent to have the levees ready before the next flood season in springtime. When Comptroller General McCarl ordered a halt to the transfer, determining that responsibility for the work lay with the states and subdivisions, barring an act of Congress, the administration found alternative funds from an undisclosed source.

"It's just being done," said a senior official when a reporter asked how that was possible.[50]

Herbert M. Lord (shown here in 1921), Director of the Budget Bureau from 1922 to 1929, led what he called the great economy crusade to reduce federal expenditures below $3 billion a year, the goal established by President Coolidge in 1923 and accomplished in 1927 (National Photo Company Collection, Library of Congress).

The work began at a frantic pace, 20 hours a day. Machines scooped up dirt from the river at a rate of 200 square yards a minute as workers inspected each load and removed any stick or other debris wider than a human wrist. This was necessary to prevent even slight crevasses that could turn into cracks or provide an opening for a crawfish or muskrat to burrow inside and cause damage to the structure. Other workers placed the dirt into position as engineers closely supervised them and tested the structures, which dated back as far back as 1717, built by French pioneers in response to early floods in New Orleans.

Meantime, the lull on Capitol Hill gave the administration time to prepare a flood relief bill and garner support for a $225 million tax cut to reduce corporate rates from 13.5 percent to 12 percent, lower rates on incomes between $18,000 and $70,000, and repeal the inheritance tax. That was the most Coolidge would allow under the budget estimate for fiscal year 1929. "I have said a great deal about tax reduction, of course, since I have been President," he told reporters, "but this always has to be borne in mind—that tax reduction is to be secured only as a result of economy."[51] When the United States Chamber of Commerce recommended a $400 million tax cut, based on recent surpluses, he derided the proposal as "absurd" during a press conference, his voice rising to a high pitch as he accused the group of always proposing tax cuts but never showing how to pay for them.[52] Indeed, the proposal failed to take into account that the government would receive less revenue in fiscal year 1928, compared with recent years, from the collection of back taxes and the receipts from the disposal of capital assets such as railroad securities, farm loan bonds, surplus war material and assets of the War Finance Corporation. Without these revenue streams, the government would have run a budget deficit in fiscal year 1923 and in fiscal year 1925.

The daily requests for proclamations and speeches went on, and Coolidge made news that fall by declining to issue a proclamation for American Education Week, as he had done the previous three years, for "to rephrase such sentiments tends rather to weaken them than otherwise."[53] When a large delegation came to the White House to ask him to make a speech to their group in the coming months, he glanced about the room and replied that since everyone seemed to be present, why not make the speech right then and save the bother of a trip.[54]

Similarly, he kept radio appearances to once a month, presumably to maintain public interest. With the increase in household radios, he could now speak to more than 50 million listeners a year, or almost half the population of the United States and more than the combined audiences of every president from Washington to Harding. A survey of more than 1,000 radio subscribers ranked him fourth in popularity behind three entertainers.[55] As to his effectiveness on the airwaves, White House aides noted that four-fifths of letters received following speeches indicated that the writers heard the president rather than read the transcript in the newspaper, and that the response increased proportionally to the number of stations carrying each address.[56]

* * *

The first week of November brought news of a devastating flood in Vermont caused by a two-storm convergence that dumped as much as 10 inches of rain in some places, following a wet October that had raised water levels throughout the state. An estimated 55 people were killed, including the lieutenant governor and an elderly woman whose car was surrounded by water for 24 hours on her way home from a medical appointment. Sarah Pollard told her nephew in the White House how people had been swept away by a wall of water rushing through a gorge in the Black River. Attorney General Sargent lost his house and nearly his wife. Some 10,000 people were homeless. Some 15,000 cows were drowned. More than 1,200 bridges were destroyed. The road from Ludlow to Rutland, leading to Plymouth Notch, was wiped out, as were countless others. All telephone and telegraph lines in southern Vermont were down. Total damage was placed at $25 million, the worst natural disaster in state history.

The disruption of rail lines precluded any possibility of a presidential visit, but Coolidge deployed troops to save lives and deliver medicine, and asked Hoover and Sargent to coordinate relief and reconstruction efforts with state leaders. "I have heard no single word of complaint," Hoover told reporters. "I have had no single request for help."[57] As with the Mississippi River flood, the Florida Hurricane of 1926, the Midwest Tornado of 1925, and the North Ohio Tornado of 1924, the Red Cross took responsibility for providing food, clothes, shelter, and medical assistance, while raising nearly $1 million in donations. A committee of New England bankers formed the New England Flood Credit Corporation, a holding company to sell $1 million worth of guaranty stock in the Vermont Flood Credit Corporation to make loans to Vermonters through Vermont banks, which agreed to accept character to supplement collateral.

Coolidge approved $2.6 million in federal assistance to supplement a state bond issue of $8.5 million, to repair roads and rail lines, but there would be no federal insurance or direct payments for victims despite the near-simultaneous Mississippi and Vermont disasters.

* * *

The most notable address he gave that autumn was to commemorate the founding of the Union League Club, in Philadelphia in 1862, as every other Republican president had done. Delivered to an audience of mostly industrialists on November 17, he praised the strong economy for promoting the general welfare and providing opportunities for a growing population, including millions of immigrants, many of whom had come to their new country without money or learning.

> To form all these people into an organization where they might not merely secure a livelihood, but by industry and thrift have the opportunity to accumulate a competency, such as has been done in this country, is one of the most marvelous feats ever accomplished by human society.

Yet he cautioned that the struggle to achieve national wealth, beset by recessions and other setbacks since the beginning, had given way to another struggle that would be endless.

> The test which now confronts the nation is prosperity. There is nothing more

> likely to reveal the soul of a people. History is littered with stories of nations destroyed by their own wealth.

The lesson, to Coolidge, was to limit government expenditures, maintain an annual budget surplus, and redeem the national debt on schedule. This would allow the country to consider more internal improvements, such as highway and road construction, flood control, a waterway system for the Mississippi Valley and its tributaries, a dam for the Colorado River, and infrastructure for commercial aviation into and from Latin America. "These will be some of the rewards of a judicious management of the national finances," he proclaimed in the first strong signal from his administration that the need and time to spend more money, for the people as a whole, was nearly at hand.[58]

* * *

Three weeks later, Coolidge sent his annual budget message and budget proposal to Congress, recommending a $225 million tax cut as the most the country could consider without a possible budget deficit. He described as "unthinkable" any further reduction, in what the press and political observers perceived as another attack on the United States Chamber of Commerce for its $400 million tax cut proposal.[59]

* * *

The press continued to speculate on the meaning of the now-famous Black Hills statement. Most papers took his statement as final, but some, such as the *Boston Herald*, the *New York Herald Tribune*, the *Wall Street Journal*, the *Philadelphia Inquirer*, the *Kansas City Star*, the *Richmond Times-Dispatch*, and the *Los Angeles Times*, took the position that he might be open to a draft, noting his choice of words. Roosevelt, by contrast, had stated in 1904 that "under no circumstances will I be a candidate for, or accept, another nomination."[60] A piece published in *Outlook* demonstrated that Coolidge, like most New Englanders, preferred direct, simple Saxon words, like choose, more than ornate Latin words. Having reviewed Coolidge rhetoric since 1914, the author described the statement as "so obvious that it seems mysterious."[61]

The use of choose or "chuse" to connote decision went back to Chaucer, Shakespeare, and other scribes of old England.

In Washington, opinion divided between those who thought Coolidge could be and would be drafted to take the nomination, those who thought he would not run under any circumstance, and those who thought he might accept the nomination in 1932 after four years of rest. Without a doubt he was the strongest Republican since Roosevelt.

Coolidge, well aware of the intrigue, added three sentences to a speech he was to make to the Republican National Committee on December 6 and asked Geisser to provide an advance copy to Stearns, who "cried brokenheartedly" at the following lines: "My statement stands. No one should be led to suppose that I have modified it. My decision will be respected."[62] Now 71 years old, with hypertension, obesity, and shortness of breath, the Bostonian became so upset watching Coolidge speak in the East Room that Dr. Boone thought he might have a cerebral hemorrhage.[63] No less perturbed, Butler left the scene glowering downward, chin tucked into his chest, hands thrust into his overcoat pockets, snapping at reporters, "I won't say anything."[64]

The president, by contrast, was in "a particularly happy frame of mind" and "very relaxed" that Christmas, laughing, joking, taking delight in gifts from the public, including turkeys, partridges, wild ducks, cheese, bread, honey, maple syrup, cakes, pies, and crates of oranges.[65] As Christmas fell on a Sunday, he gave federal workers a three-day holiday, albeit with a warning: "This order is not to be deemed as establishing a precedent."[66] Christmas Eve he worked alone in his office, while Grace handed out baskets at the Salvation Army headquarters and presents at a local theater. Later they attended the tree-lighting ceremony in Sherman Square, turning on the lights by pushing a button and returning to the White House for carols with 2,000 city residents, continuing the tradition they had set four years ago. Afterward he went to his office to write a message to the American people:

> Christmas is not a time or a season but a state of mind. To cherish peace and goodwill, to be plenteous in mercy, is to have the real spirit of Christmas. If we think on these things, there will be born to us a Savior and over us will shine a star sending a stream of hope to the world.[67]

The first Christmas message from a president, it was printed in newspapers across the country on Christmas morning.

The White House rang in 1928 with the traditional reception as a cold front from the Canadian Rockies swept through the capital, lowering the temperature to 10 degrees. Before prohibition, blood-warming rum had been dispensed on such occasions. Instead Grace ordered a departure from the usual itinerary by allowing callers to remain in the East Room to warm up rather than filing back outside right away. More than 3,000 men, women, and children shook hands with the first couple that morning as they began their last full year in Washington.

In the first press conference of the year, with the stock market boom hitting new heights, a reporter asked Coolidge for his view on the speculative nature of broker loans, which stood at $3.8 billion after nearly a $1 billion increase in 1927. Coolidge declined to answer on the spot but asked an aide to prepare a response.[68] On Friday, January 6, he told reporters that the loans did not appear to be excessive, but rather the result of increased security listings and bank deposits: "Now, whether the amount at the present time is disproportionate to the resources of the country I am not in a position to judge accurately, but so far as I indicated by an inquiry that I have made of the Treasury Department and so on I haven't had any indications that the amount was large enough to cause unfavorable comment."[69] This statement received wide newspaper coverage, but without any apparent effect on stock prices.

"If I were to give my own personal opinion about it," Coolidge told his cousin, H. Parker Willis from the *Journal of Commerce*, "I should say that any loan made for gambling in stocks was an excessive loan."

Willis replied, "I wish very much, Mr. President, that you had been willing to say that instead of making the public statement you did."

"Why do you say that?" Coolidge asked.

"Simply because I think it would have had a tremendous effect in repressing an unwholesome speculation, with which, I now see, you have sympathy."

Coolidge asserted: "Well, I regard myself as a representative of the government and not as an individual. When technical matters come up I feel called upon to refer them to the proper department of the government which has some information about them and then, unless there is some good reason, I use this information as a basis for whatever I have to say; but that does not prevent me from thinking what I please as an individual."[70]

A few days later, on January 11, the Federal Reserve Board decided not to raise the discount rate for borrowing. This led Benjamin Strong of the Federal Reserve Bank of New York to take separate action to restrain credit and stock market speculation by selling government securities to reduce liquidity in the banking system. Other regions within the Federal Reserve followed suit in early 1928, selling more than $400 million and slowly increasing the discount rate from 3.5 percent to 4.5 percent. The effect, however, was to hurt the domestic economy rather than to prevent a stock market bubble. New investment in construction and manufacturing leveled off and started to decline in a sign that the prosperity might be vulnerable.

The increase in interest rates meant higher returns on U.S. bonds and higher costs for European and other countries to service their U.S. debts, which put a damper on foreign lending from Wall Street and hurt international capital flows at a time when the world was more dependent on U.S. credit. Prospects for a global financial crisis began to accelerate in countless developments across markets that would be hard to assess or reverse as bankers, corporations, stock brokers, investors, and policy-makers struggled to respond amid a postwar world in which the United States had replaced England as the lead economic power and lender of last resort.

* * *

The country now drew unprecedented numbers of European travelers, arriving on ocean liners that could accommodate more than 2,000 passengers at once, make the trip in five days using turbine steam engines, and boast the latest safety features, including electronics to control the rudder, beacon signals to warn other vessels, and radio systems to maintain contact with coast guard patrols searching the sea lanes for icebergs floating down from Greenland. The liners predicted a banner year in 1928 thanks to tourism and business travel.

Emil Ludwig came over early in the year for a lecture tour on Bismarck, the subject of his latest best-selling biography or portrait as he described his works. The former wartime correspondent, novelist, and poet had written on various political, intellectual, and cultural figures, from Napoleon to Goethe, by interpreting their spirit or inner person, with attempts at psychoanalysis. This drew comparisons to Lytton Strachey in England and Andre Maurois in France as the leaders of a new form of biography, never mind that Plutarch had done the same thing 1,800 years earlier. Handsome, with dark eyes and heavy eyelids, 47 years old, Ludwig arrived at New York harbor to much acclaim, following his first trip across the ocean. As reporters surrounded him on the pier and inquired about his itinerary he seemed bemused. Speaking in a patrician Tyrolean German accent and a calm manner, he said he was more interested in the great bridges, skyscrapers, and industrial plants, than in art museums and libraries, and that he wanted to meet practical types during his visit. "Merchants, engineers, above all scientists," he said, Edison, Ford, Rockefeller, Wright, and that sort.[71]

Ludwig was soon struck by the fast pace of life, the poor writing in newspapers, and the emphasis on success rather than wealth among the people, who on the whole came across as modest, industrious, generous, and more humorous than Europeans. He was amused to see the elevator boy at his temporary residence in Manhattan continually check the stock market ticker, and disconcerted to watch his taxi cab driver turn the radio dial from station to station without possibly giving the attention necessary to truly enjoy or learn anything from the various music, drama, vaudeville, education, and sports programming available. When a correspondent for the *New York Times* approached Ludwig for his opinion on the state of the American worker and the lack of a social welfare apparatus in the country, like the one in Germany, he replied, "America is striving to make social welfare superfluous; to thwart or circumvent socialism by improving the condition of the laboring class."

To the intellectuals who lamented the materialism of the machine age, he posed a question: "Has a single poem, picture, opera or system been created in recent years which can be compared in importance with the fact that, when a ship is in distress at sea, it can now appeal for aid to every skipper within a thousand miles and this made rescue possible?"[72]

Invited to the White House, Ludwig told Coolidge that his next biography would be on Lincoln, prompting a discussion on Lincoln and Wilson as wartime presidents, the one revered by most, the other reviled by many. "It is difficult to decide," Coolidge said, "but think what a national hero Wilson would be today if in November 1918, he had been assassinated in this chair." Ludwig agreed that historical reputation depended in large part on how one leaves the public scene.[73]

The writer soon returned to bustling New York and then home to the pleasant shores of Lago Maggiore in the Italian-speaking part of southern Switzerland, where he had emigrated as a young man. Though his books had given him wealth and ease, he had long been skeptical about their permanent value, perhaps now more than ever.[74]

* * *

In mid–January, the president and entourage departed for the Sixth International Conference of American States in Cuba, hoping to promote goodwill and harmony following troubles in Nicaragua and Mexico. The agenda covered communications, legal reform, intellectual cooperation, and economic problems, but anti–U.S. outbursts were expected, in part because U.S. tariffs on sugar had hurt the Cuban economy. Traveling by special train to Key West and by battleship to Havana, he was accompanied by 86 persons, the largest presidential retinue in history and twice as many as Wilson took to Paris in 1919, mostly technical assistants, military men, and reporters, along with Secretary Kellogg, Secretary Wilbur, and Secretary Davis. Upon arrival they received a tumultuous reception with brass bands, church bells, and some 40,000 Cubans lining the streets, throwing flowers, blowing kisses, and waving from the balconies and rooftops of their brightly colored homes. Riding in an open sedan, Coolidge tipped his hat to the crowd and beamed in appreciation as women threw flowers and blew kisses. Oulahan of the *New York Times* had never seen him smile so much. The following morning he attended opening ceremonies of the conference and delivered an address to delegates from 17 governments, stressing their common origins, common heritage, and common destiny, without mentioning Nicaragua and Mexico. As the first president to speak in Latin America and to attend the conference, he received a generous response. Dr. Boone had "rarely seen him as happy."[75]

* * *

Back in Washington, Coolidge began to prepare his remarks for the semiannual meeting of the Business Organization of the Government, to be delivered on January 30 to a national radio audience, an opportunity to get across his message on spending and taxes before Congress sent bills for his signature in the coming weeks. "The great good which has come to this country from a balanced budget is too measureless, too far-reaching even to suggest any other course," he said that evening. "The nation is neither too weak nor too improvident to meet its obligations as they occur." The budget for fiscal year 1929, to begin on October 1, had an estimated surplus of $252,540,000. This modest figure would restrict what could be done on spending and taxes during the ongoing legislative session.

"It is far better to have no tax reduction than to have too much," he said in one of the most concise statements of his fiscal principles.

He went on to stress economy in expenditures as necessary to produce a balanced budget and a tax cut, in language that had become familiar to all by now. This time he delved more into the positive aspects of economy in a country with a growing population and economy. It was not "a policy of negation," he said. It made "ample provision for things that must be done," such as new public buildings, internal improvements, and national defense.[76]

* * *

In the early weeks of 1928, Stearns and Butler hoped Coolidge would submit to a draft movement, which they in turn would produce behind the scenes, and when Mellon conspired along the same lines, veteran political reporters suspected the president and his men were counting on a deadlocked convention to turn their way for one last hurrah. Many politicians and delegates thought Coolidge would be the nominee again, pointing to his curious choice of words in South Dakota and his apparent tolerance of draft movements in Connecticut, Illinois, New York, and elsewhere.

The speculation was erroneous. Grace, while visiting her mother in Northampton on March 4, called the White House and said, "Just wanted to remind you we have but one more year, Calvin."[77] So he began that morning to mark the fourth day of each month on his calendar as a milestone, a distance shortening each month until Inauguration Day, March 4, 1929. When several Republican state committees began maneuvers to place his name on their primary ballots, he sent word through Edward Clark that he would not be a candidate under any circumstances. He asked party leaders in Massachusetts, Connecticut, New York, Pennsylvania, and Wyoming not to place his name in nomination. "I never stated or formulated in my own mind what I should do under such circumstances," he wrote, "but I was determined not to have that contingency arise."[78] When congresswoman Edith N. Rogers said he could be renominated and reelected with ease, he replied, "But my health would never stand it."[79] *Time Magazine* noted that his skin had become much looser and more translucent than one would gather from photographs.[80]

The ordeal of speechmaking was reason enough to leave. In 1927, he gave 18 speeches, averaging more than 3,000 words each and requiring painstaking work. In 1928, he would give 20. As he sat in his library with the Italian-born portraitist Ercole Cartotto one evening, he pointed to a row of books containing his speeches: "Those are my works of art. Every word in them had to be considered much of a strain to do over again."[81]

The same health concerns held true for Grace, who contracted a serious and lengthy kidney infection in February, losing 20 pounds, suffering from swollen ankles, and receiving "animal inoculations" from the White House physicians.[82] "She has been a real sick woman," wrote Ellen Riley, noting her meals had to be prepared with great caution and disturbances kept to a minimum.[83] The demands of public life had taken a toll, leaving her worn and homesick, no longer taking a brisk daily walk to the Lincoln Memorial.

As to whether the president foresaw financial trouble for the nation, he made intimations along those lines to Starling and Clark, but the latter warns against the perception that he shrank from a coming crisis for which he had no answers. Coolidge, he said, felt his task had been to deflate the wartime government. That done, he was leaving because his work was complete, because he had given his best to the country, not because he saw a depression looming.[84]

"The basic fact remains that I do not want the nomination," he told Senator Watson. "I think I know myself very well. I fitted into the situation that existed after the war, but I might not fit into the next one."[85]

"I know how to save money," he told a cabinet officer. "All my training has been in that direction. The country is in a sound financial position. Perhaps the time has come when we ought to spend money. I do not feel that I am qualified to do that."[86]

The odds-on favorite to replace him was Herbert Hoover, who had turned the moribund Commerce Department into the most vital bureaucracy in Washington, promoting exports, research programs, industry standardization guidelines, and government-industry partnerships. Frank Lowden, Nicholas Longworth, James Watson, Charles Dawes, and Charles Evans Hughes were also possibilities, although the latter two had withdrawn their names from consideration. As the president walked with his bodyguard one evening, he ventured a prediction:

> Well, they're going to elect that superman Hoover, and he's going to have some trouble. He's going to have to spend money. But he won't spend enough.
>
> Then the Democrats will come in and they'll spend money like water. But they don't know anything about money. Then they will ask me to come back and save money for them. But I won't do it.[87]

Hoover soon had the support of 400 of the 1,089 delegates to the Republican National Convention, far more than any other candidate. Amid rumors that Coolidge secretly wanted another nomination, Hoover aides poured through lexicons on New England dialect to determine what the president meant by "choose" in his now-famous statement. Finally, Hoover took matters into his own hands, meeting with Coolidge in private and offering to influence his delegates to vote for the president for renomination.

Coolidge replied, "If you have four hundred delegates, you better keep them."[88]

Yet the prospect of Hoover as a potential successor seemed to annoy Coolidge, so much that when Secretary Jardine sought his backing for the Hoover campaign, he snarled, "That man has offered me unsolicited advice for six years, all of it bad!"[89] Harsh words considering Hoover provided valuable assistance during the anthracite coal strike of 1923, the California primary of 1924, and the Mississippi flood of 1927, but the sort of ill-tempered remark he made on occasion; perhaps he was vexed that one cabinet member was running for president and another assisting the campaign rather than tending to administration business. For a politician leaving the world-stage and seeing attention turn to a publicity-seeker like Hoover, who had hired several newspapermen as "private assistants" for promotional work, some resentment was natural. Stearns was downright hostile toward Hoover, complaining about his ingratitude and hasty pursuit of the nomination, even questioning his loyalty to the president, when in fact he had refrained from giving interviews during the campaign or hiring a campaign manager.[90] Coolidge no doubt thought Hoover would be too meddling, too solution-oriented, too engineer-like, lacking the political touch to be an effective president. Having lived most of his adult years overseas, away from the tumult of domestic politics, he had never worked for the party at the local level or held political office; he had no appreciation that every public issue involves party politics, no experience at handling the criticism and scrutiny of elective office-holding, no experience in the give-and-take of legislative politics, no abilities as a public speaker.

* * *

Of more concern to Coolidge were spending pressures in the first session of the 70th Congress, where Republicans held a 237 to 195 advantage in the House but only a 48 to 47 edge in the Senate, including five Republican insurgents who gave Democrats a nominal majority, threatening his fiscal program and proposed $225 million tax cut. "Prosperity and good times demand increased as well as new government functions," concluded the annual review of the Senate Appropriations Committee.[91]

Among the new proposals made that spring, prepared by the American Association for Old Age Security and presented by first-term House Democrat William I. Sirovich of New York, was to have the federal government provide grants to states for old age pensions, covering no more than one-third of total costs, with a limit of $1 per day for each individual recipient and $30 million per year overall. Two previous bills to provide a national old age pension, submitted in 1909 and in 1911, had failed to clear committee review and would have involved bureaucratic costs and legal challenges given the defined legislative powers under Article I, Section VIII, of the Constitution. This one took a different approach by emulating the federal subsidies to the states that had been in effect since 1914 and seen as constitutional since they were only appropriations, rather than programs, with optional participation. The states that stood to benefit immediately were Colorado, Kentucky, Maryland, Montana, Nevada, and Wisconsin, which during the past several years had passed statutes permitting county authorities to pay old age pensions from county funds. Many other states were considering such programs in response to increases in longevity, estimates that only about one in 10 workers were eligible to receive a company pension and that most such pensions were insolvent or even voidable, and changes in family structure and employment practices that made the elderly more vulnerable. Nonetheless, the proposed subsidy received little attention in the press or from either party, and remained buried in committee that spring, ending any consideration of old age insurance during the Coolidge years and ensuring that the United States would remain the lone industrialized country without such a benefit.

Coolidge, who had backed pensions during his years in Massachusetts politics, never said a word in public about the proposal and probably never gave the matter much thought, given that the sponsor was a first-term Democrat without any apparent support from Democrat leaders, the press, or the public. He had other proposals to worry about that spring.

"I am a good deal disturbed at the number of proposals that are being made for an expenditure of money," Coolidge told reporters, citing flood bill proposals at a minimum of $500 million, the McNary-Haugen bill at $400 million, the Boulder Dam bill at $125 million, the Muscle Shoals bill at $75 million, the postal salary bill at $20 million, the government salary bill at $18 million, a corn borer bill at $7 million to $8 million, and a vocational training bill at $6 million, among other initiatives, which on the whole threatened to produce the first $4 billion Congress. "The number and amount is becoming appalling."[92]

When reporters asked whether the proposals threatened tax reduction, he said, "If all these bills went through and became law I should think it would not only endanger tax reduction, but would make necessary the laying of additional taxes."[93]

Most troubling were developments related to the flood bill Coolidge had recommended to Congress in December 1927, based on a $296 million Army Engineer Corps plan to build levees and diversion channels known as floodways and spillways along the Mississippi River, pending contributions from local governments and property owners, who were to pay one-fifth of the cost, averaging a mere three cents per acre, per year, for 10 years. This proposal was consistent with 150 years of history, in which the federal government had made contributions toward surveys and navigation, but mostly left the states and local communities responsible for flood control on the Mississippi, such as setting up levee districts. In 1879, Congress had formed the Mississippi River Commission to improve navigation and, by implication, flood control, under the direction of army engineers. More recently, Congress had authorized about $10 million a year in federal funds to be spent on levees, pending local contributions, in the Flood Control Act of March 1923. Yet the responsibility for flood prevention and control had remained a local matter through local levee districts. Now the lower flood states claimed they were unable to contribute anything because 60 or so levee districts were bankrupt. Many politicians and newspaper editors believed the time had come to make Mississippi flood control a national issue, given the economic stakes, given that waters from 31 states ran into the river, including every river, bayou, creek, and brook between the Rockies and the Alleghenies.

Coolidge emphatically opposed the notion, as stated in his annual message to Congress:

> The Government is not the insurer of its citizens against the hazards of the elements. We shall always have flood and drought, earthquake and wind,

lightning and tidal wave, which are all too constant in their afflictions. The Government does not undertake to reimburse citizens for loss and damage incurred under such circumstances. It is chargeable, however, with the rebuilding of public works and the humanitarian duty of relieving its citizens of distress.[94]

As Congress began discussions on a program that would include $1 billion to $1.4 billion in federal funds without local contributions, Coolidge spoke at length in press conferences, trying to sway public opinion on an issue that had bedeviled engineers since the 18th century. The Senate soon passed by unanimous vote a flood bill that would commit Washington to an estimated $500 million to $700 million without local contributions. The House proposed a $473 million bill without local contributions. The two chambers agreed on a seven-member Mississippi Valley Flood Control Commission to implement improvements and a provision that would hold Washington responsible for flood damage along the lower Mississippi if federally built levees were to break.

Coolidge fought back with more tenacity than he had shown at any time in office. Privately, he derided the bill as "the most radical and dangerous bill that has had the countenance of the Congress since I have been President."[95] Publicly, he described it as "extortionate" and warned Congress that the people would not stand for such a raid on the Treasury by special interests and businesses seeking government contracts for dam construction, as "it has become a scramble to take care of the railroads and the banks and the individuals that may have invested in levee bonds, and the great lumber concerns that own many thousands of acres in that locality."[96] To Chairman Madden of the House Appropriation Committee, he said he would veto the bill as written.[97]

Madden, in failing health at age 73, met repeatedly with leaders from both parties to support the administration and tame the flood bloc, summoning his powers as the strongest House figure since "Uncle Joe" Cannon. Now in his 13th term from the hurly-burly first district of Chicago, the self-made millionaire had no tolerance for public assistance or public works, having overcome an impoverished childhood in which he lost an arm in a stone quarry accident to become head engineer and president of the firm that owned the quarry. Except for the Panama Canal, that is. In 1900, as a private citizen, he wrote the first Republican platform plank that favored building a canal. Five years later, as a freshman congressman on the House Appropriations Committee, he traveled to Panama at his own expense and determined that an expert commission appointed by Roosevelt had erred in proposing a sea-level canal. The engineer-turned-congressman convinced Roosevelt to hand the task to Army engineers and worked with them at the isthmus, paying his way and applying techniques he had learned in the rock quarries of the Des Plaines Valley. To Madden, the canal had been a worthy endeavor that only the federal government could pursue, but the Mississippi River, comprising the western boundary of his own state, was primarily a state and local matter. He would die at his desk of a heart attack later that month.

Chairman Snell of the House Rules Committee helped matters by keeping the flood bill off the House calendar. This gave Coolidge time to rally public opinion.

On April 10, Coolidge summed up his concerns with reporters, whom he urged to more fully review the issue:

> The flood control legislation is getting into a very unfortunate situation. I was afraid it would, when it became apparent that there was a great reluctance on the part of Congress to have any local contribution. Of course, as soon as that policy is adopted, then it becomes a bestowal of favors on certain localities and naturally if one locality is to be favored, all the other localities in the United States think they ought to come in under the same plan and have their floods taken care of.[98]

After weeks of press statements, negotiations, testimony, studies, and veto threats, Congress settled on a $325 million compromise bill, matching the maximum amount that Coolidge, in talks with Republican legislative leaders, said he would consider for approval. The bill, sponsored by Senator Wesley L. Jones of Washington and Representative Frank R. Reid of Illinois, and based on the Engineer Corps plan, included the construction of massive new levees and nonmonetary local contributions, such as spillways and rights of way for the levees, to protect some 13,465,000 acres. Coolidge, who had never been more involved in drafting a piece of legislation, summoned supporters of the Jones-Reid bill and reviewed its contents as they stood before his desk. Taking his pencil, he made three changes, placed the marked-up bill on his desk, and walked away to a window. First, he wanted to reduce the proposed engineering board from seven members to three members and make it temporary. Second, he wanted to ensure that the federal government would not be liable for any damage caused by flood waters arising in connection with the flood control work. Third, he wanted to stipulate that the federal government would not be required to buy the rights of way for rivers or channels that are natural floodways. The legislators agreed.

This momentous legislation ended more than 50 years of federal-state cooperation on Mississippi flood control by placing responsibility primarily in Washington. Coolidge had won on cost-savings and certain principles but lost on the larger issue. In signing the bill without ceremony on May 15, he said it should not be seen as a precedent.

The president proceeded to veto successfully three bills supported by his cabinet members and opposed by his budget director. The first, backed by Postmaster General New, proposed to increase pay for night work in the postal service at a cost of about $6,856,000 a year. Coolidge in his veto message stated that night work had always been part of employment in the postal service and that the service was already running a deficit of about $32,400,000 for fiscal year 1928. No doubt he was pleased, even amused, to learn that New was able to reduce the volume of night work by delaying the distribution of third-class mail, deposited late in the day, to the following day. The second bill, backed by Secretary Jardine, proposed to amend the Federal Aid Roads Act of 1916 by appropriating $3.5 million annually for three years to build roads in states with unappropriated or unreserved public lands, nontaxable Indian lands, and other federal reservations, without matching state funds since the lands fell outside state authority. Coolidge lambasted this "radical departure" from previous federal subsidies in that the proposed new roads would connect to state and local roads and provide widespread benefits to localities and states. The third bill, backed by Secretary Mellon, proposed to increase pay for certain low-grade employees in the Customs Service at a cost of $1,750,000 per year to boost recruitment and retention. Coolidge insisted that fiscal conditions would not allow any such additional expenditures and that the employees, like other federal employees, were due to receive a general raise later in the year.[99]

Attention turned to the new McNary-Haugen bill, much like the old one, with modifications to the controversial equalization fee, a $400 million administrative fund, a board to determine price levels for all pertinent crops, and bipartisan support outside New England and the south, despite White House opposition. After the bill passed the House, 204 to 121, and the Senate, 58 to 23, Coolidge responded on May 23 with the harshest presidential veto in decades, lambasting the "cruelly deceptive" provisions of the bill as "bureaucracy gone mad" and "delusive experiments" based on "preposterous economic and commercial fallacy" and "futile sophistries." He cited six problems in particular: the fallacy of price-fixing; the tax characteristics of the equalization fee; the need for a large bureaucracy for implementation; the increase in costs from middlemen and profiteering; the encouragement of overproduction; and the benefit to foreign farmers selling goods at lower prices.[100]

The Senate sustained the veto by a vote of 50 to 31, despite complaints among even some stalwart Republicans that Coolidge had used unnecessarily intemperate language. The Des Moines *Register* compared him to Italian dictator Mussolini for defying the legislature and the will of the people.[101]

All told, Coolidge vetoed 13 bills during the session, the most since Cleveland vetoed 116 bills in 1886. Although Congress overrode three Coolidge vetoes, they amounted to less than $15 million, including a postal salary increase of $9 million, a postal allowance increase of $2 million, and a retired officer pension increase of $3.5 million that violated the policy "to compensate service, not rank" and discriminated against enlisted men.

The money saved on vetoes allowed Coolidge to proceed with his third and final tax cut as the two parties maneuvered politically. House Democrats proposed to increase the tax cut from $225 million to $289 million, whereupon Mellon convinced Senate Republicans to defer consideration until tax returns arrived in March. Democrats then tried to regain the initiative by proposing reductions of $300 million to $400 million and accusing the administration of placing too much emphasis on debt reduction, vice tax reduction, noting that taxpayers had overpaid by an average of $5.99 each in 1927. "I feel that we ought not to be forced, as we are now being forced by the administration, to pay off this indebtedness with undue rapidity," said Senator Simmons, ranking minority member of the Finance Committee.[102]

The administration lowered its proposal to $201 million and rallied business and labor groups, as Coolidge threatened to veto any bill that might cause a budget deficit. In response, legislators approved the corporate and income tax cut, but not the elimination of the inheritance tax, for a net reduction of $222 million. The bill was approved on May 29.

The six-month session of Congress ended that day with two other notable developments. The Senate declined to pass a House bill authorizing the construction of 15 cruisers and one airplane carrier. The Senate also failed to pass the Boulder Dam bill because of an all-night filibuster, putting on hold an ambitious plan that dated back to 1922 to control the waters of the Colorado River and to promote irrigation and hydro-electric power in Arizona, California, Colorado, Nevada, New Mexico, Utah, and Wyoming, by building the highest dam in the world. "Regular order! Regular order!" shouted members as Senator Johnson of California tried and failed to save the bill by postponing the planned adjournment of the body at 5:30 p.m., nearly causing a fistfight over procedure on the Senate floor.

* * *

The farm bill veto caused a political maelstrom that Coolidge backers saw as an opportunity to make one last push for the 1928 nomination, what with Senator Norris threatening to run as an independent and Governor Adam McMullen of Nebraska calling for 100,000 farmers to march on the Republican National Convention in Kansas City and demand passage of McNary-Haugen and revision of the tariff. The dark horse candidacies of Frank Lowden and Charles Curtis, both of whom supported McNary-Haugen, hoped for a stampede in their favor. For Hoover the veto was ill-timed to say the least. Farmers, who blamed him for restricting their wartime wheat profits as U.S. food administrator, now blamed him and Mellon as the instigators behind the McNary-Haugen veto. Strangely enough, the veto appeared to hurt Hoover more than Coolidge, if only because the president was stronger in the East and better able to withstand setbacks in the Middle West. Indeed he would have won in 1924 without the 62 electoral votes he received in Idaho, Missouri, Montana, Nebraska, Nevada, New Mexico, North Dakota, South Dakota, Utah, and West Virginia. The specter of Hoover losing those states and having to win the East against likely opponent Governor Smith of New York worried Republican leaders. Yet Hoover remained the heavy favorite to secure the nomination, with about 500 delegates out of the 549 needed to win. That he would be nominated on the first ballot seemed almost certain, but, if not, he faced a possible deadlock and a Coolidge boom in which delegates would shift to the president.

The key state was Pennsylvania, led by Secretary Mellon, who wondered whether Coolidge would accept a draft nomination. "You know as much about it as I do," he told newspapermen.[103] Keeping his options open, he told the Hoover camp that their candidate came nearest to meeting the criteria as standard bearer of the party, but told his delegates to remain free at the convention. In truth he had doubts about Hoover. "He is too much inclined to have his own solution of problems, frequently unsound," the seigneur wrote in his diary, noting he never put an engineer in charge of any business enterprise because of their ineptitude in reacting to human elements.[104] The 79 delegates from Pennsylvania, combined with 60 uncommitted delegates from New York, 30 from Massachusetts, and 11 from Vermont, represented the basis of the possible Coolidge boom.

When Representative Snell told the president that a lot of his delegates wanted to draft him, Coolidge replied, "Hoover is a pretty good man, isn't he?"[105]

Ten days before the convention, Coolidge took a weekend cruise aboard the *Mayflower* with Stearns and Morrow, who turned to politics when their host went below deck to rest. Morrow, who believed the president should be offered the nomination as a courtesy, pressed Dr. Boone to issue a statement that Mrs. Coolidge was healthy and strong enough to serve four more years, if necessary. Appalled by the suggestion, Dr. Boone replied that she had a medical condition that could "progress into a very dangerous situation" and flatly refused to issue any such statement.[106]

After Dr. Boone returned to duty several days before the convention, following a trip home, he found the first lady overcome with fatigue. "Oh, Washington," she exclaimed.[107]

The president dispatched Sanders to Kansas City with instructions to tell several of the leaders of state delegations not to vote for him.[108] This message no doubt reached the chairman of the Hoover campaign, James W. Good, who dismissed a report that delegates would break to Coolidge when the balloting began in hopes of forcing him to issue a definitive statement on his availability: "He will not be renominated," Good told reporters.[109] The Coolidge draft movement began to unravel that evening when the boss of the Philadelphia political machine, William Vare, pledged his 15 delegates to Hoover on the first ballot. With other Pennsylvania delegates set to follow, Mellon bowed to the inevitable.

* * *

On that same day Coolidge learned his son had passed his spring-term courses and would be graduated. "Your mother and I wish to send you our congratulations and best wishes again for a pleasant commencement," he wrote, but since he was about to leave on vacation he had Stearns attend commencement exercises.[110] Grace was in no condition to appeal the matter.

* * *

Coolidge intended to leave Washington on the eve of the Republican National Convention to vacation in rural Wisconsin for two months. No modern president, except Roosevelt, had taken such lengthy vacations. Arthur, Hayes, and Cleveland made a point of never taking more than 30 days, like any other civil servant. McKinley and Taft kept their vacations to six weeks or less. Wilson took short vacations, usually less than three weeks and sometimes a long weekend. Harding took fewer vacations than any of them.

On the morning of departure—June 11—Coolidge was dismayed to learn Grace had taken ill with a cough and a high fever. "The President was in a highly excited, emotional state," relates Dr. Boone, who knew Grace was loath to leave with her mother ill in Northampton and suspected her sudden ailment was stress-related. As Coolidge paced about the mansion on a sore heel, Clark could see he was under a severe mental strain and, thinking a delayed departure would encourage speculation about a draft movement and worsen matters, pressed Boone to approve the first lady to travel.[111] If that were not enough, Boone knew the presidential entourage was preparing to go to Union Station, where a special train was to depart at nine that evening, complete with 60 soldiers, 10 Secret Service agents,

14 servants, 75 newspapermen, and wooden crates holding desks, chairs, typewriters, ink pens, paper, china, silver, linen, and other appurtenances.

It was no small matter to postpone such a trip. Local train schedules had been altered to avoid any chance of a collision. Every nut and bolt along the route had been inspected. Every switch had been inspected and placed under surveillance. Special emergency engines and crews were ready at each station, and guards with flashlights were deployed at bridges and rail sections eight hours ahead of the train, stretching well into the Maryland countryside. Various crews were on hand at the station: the engineer crew, the service crew, the telephone crew, the telegraph crew. A pilot train was fully manned and prepared to lead the way.

At seven that evening Coolidge went to Memorial Continental Hall for the semiannual meeting of the Business Organization of the Government. It was the eleventh time he had addressed the meeting; he had never missed one. Now he was to commence his last fiscal year in office, taking the podium with nearly 2,000 mangers in attendance and a nationwide radio hookup, amid speculation that he would use the occasion to make a statement on draft rumors in Kansas City. "I have rejoiced in keeping down the annual budget, in reducing taxes and paying off the national debt, because the influence of such action is felt in every home in the land," he said, Gladstone-like in his eloquence toward government bookkeeping. Contrasting the postwar depression of 1920–1922 with the ongoing prosperity, he praised the Budget Bureau for reducing expenditures and making possible tax cuts in 1921, 1924, 1926, and 1928, saving taxpayers some $2 billion annually, compared with what would have been collected under 1918 rates. Looking ahead, he estimated the fiscal year would end in 19 days with a surplus greater than $400 million. It would be his fifth consecutive surplus, preceded by $498 million in 1924, $250 million in 1925, $385 million in 1926, and $599 million in 1927. This marked the largest run of federal surpluses in American history, but he was concerned with preliminary estimates of a $94 million deficit in fiscal year 1929, based on legislation enacted during the recent session of Congress. "We must not have a deficit," he implored.[112]

When he returned to the White House, Boone made his recommendation: Mrs. Coolidge was in no condition to travel. The entourage at Union Station was instructed to disperse.

The following morning, June 12, Coolidge read in the newspapers that he remained a possible candidate to "stop Hoover" on the first ballot even though his staunchest supporters, Butler and Mellon, admitted such a scenario was unlikely. Telling physician James F. Coupal he had a case of "convention fever," Coolidge worked quietly at his desk and received periodic updates on his wife as she improved slowly but surely.[113] At noon he learned that Massachusetts and several other swing states had thrown their support to Hoover, bowing to the inevitable and ending prospects for a Coolidge stampede at the convention. Ike Hoover saw Coolidge emerge from his office, "visibly distressed," and retire to his bedroom, skipping lunch and remaining in seclusion for the rest of the afternoon. The usher surmised that he was devastated by the news.[114] More likely he was exhausted now that the ordeal was over, his nerves frayed by weeks of political intrigue before the convention and by Grace taking ill as events were culminating in Kansas City. Dr. Boone, who was with the president that day, noted his lack of interest in the convention once Hoover took command, but nothing more.

The following day was a scorcher in Washington with 90-degree temperatures as Grace continued to improve. That evening, the presidential party boarded the train at Union Station and left for Wisconsin with Coolidge declining to listen to the convention on a specially installed radio set in his railcar.

Arriving at a 5,000-acre retreat at Cedar Island on the Brule River, 35 miles from Superior, Wisconsin, the president was in a better frame of mind, though tired, as he and Grace took up residence in a one-story, 10-room bungalow hidden from public view except for tourists in rental canoes and airplanes that dropped low and circled overhead. Later that day he learned Hoover had been nominated on the first ballot in Kansas City, with 837 out of 1,089 votes, and invited the nominee to Wisconsin to discuss campaign tactics. "I did not realize how exhausted I was until I reached here," he wrote Stearns the following week, while struggling with allergies and asthma.[115] He worked half-days at a local high school, fished for trout, received visitors, conducted press conferences, and attended county and state fairs. When a reporter asked whether he would speak at one such event, he replied, "No, I am just going as an exhibit."[116] Indeed he went the whole summer without a public utterance, letting his press conferences and visitors make clear where his administration stood on the issues.

Grace slowly recovered her strength through rest and exercise. "The President and I have been improving each moment here, storing up strength and energy for the final pull," she wrote to Florence Irwin in Northampton.[117]

On the fifth anniversary of the midnight inaugural, Coolidge traveled by train to the Hull-Rust Mine in northern Minnesota, the largest open-pit ore mine in the world, providing some 10,000,000 tons annually for transport to the blast furnaces of the Middle West and Pittsburgh. The ore was used in skyscrapers, bridges, construction and harvesting machinery, automobile bodies, and innumerable other products around the world. Not even Erzberg, the legendary mountain of ore that financed the Austro-Hungarian Empire, had shifted the global balance of power to such a degree. Coolidge, stepping on to a platform built for the occasion, stood in silence for five minutes, overlooking a pit seven miles long and one and one-quarter mile across, watching steam shovels dig into the dull reddish brown earth and fill up a line of railcars. A man named Merritt, seeking gold and timber in the hinterlands, discovered the deposits in 1892, amid concerns of a dwindling global iron ore supply. Now the property of the U.S. Steel Corporation, the mine supplied about one-fourth of iron ore in the country and produced exports to distant points. It was on pace for a record year of production.

It was a "pretty big hole," Coolidge said at last.[118]

Back in Wisconsin, the president met with Director Lord, who arrived by train for an all-day budget meeting during which he reviewed the early figures for fiscal year 1929 and estimated a $100 million deficit that might be absorbed by rising revenue if the economy stayed strong. Afterward Coolidge told reporters that he would veto any spending bill that fell outside the income of the nation.

The White House mail arrived daily in a special pouch flown from Washington via New York, Chicago, St. Paul, and Superior, a 23-hour trip. Among the thousands of documents reviewed by the president that summer was a telegram from the 19th annual convention of the NAACP in Los Angeles, urging him to end segregation in the federal government, to which he replied in a noncommittal manner. This practice, while no longer present in the Agricultural Department, the Census Bureau, the Commerce Department, the Geological Survey, the Indian Office, the Labor Department, the Pension Office, the State Department, and the War Department, involved hundreds of federal workers. At the Treasury Department, 30 black clerks and a black supervisor within the Liberty Loan Division were placed in a separate room from white clerks, and black women in the registry were segregated from white cohorts. At the Interior Department, Miss Gretchen McRae was set apart from the stenographer pool, and five black clerks were segregated in a room on the fifth floor. At the Navy Department, 11 black clerks were segregated. The Veterans Bureau had 15 black clerks and a black supervisor in a separate room. The Bureau of Printing and Engraving had separate lockers and bathrooms for black and white employees. The Government Accounting Office had several rooms with segregated employees. Many departments had cafeterias with all-black tables, including Navy, Interior, the Government Accounting Office, the Government Printing Office, and the Post Office Building.

Why Coolidge failed to end segregation through executive order is unclear. He may have been swayed by the notion, put forth by government managers and others, that the victims of segregation did not mind separation. Many black civil servants were no doubt reluctant to complain, even to private NAACP investigators, for fear of losing their jobs.

* * *

The president and first lady returned to Washington in mid–September, tanned and healthy, but left a week later to visit her mother at a Northampton hospital en route to Vermont to tour the flood damage from 1927. As their train passed slowly through White River Junction, Bethel, Montpelier Junction, Burlington, and Rutland, they could see bridges, roads, telephone lines, barns, mills, fences, and farm implements that had been washed away, and repairmen at work. At each stop Coolidge waved to crowds from the rear platform, the last time he would see them as president. The leaves were already turning color. The sun had nearly set behind the hills when his train pulled into Bennington, the last stop and largest crowd of the day, some 5,000 persons. Stepping on to the platform, under the glare of the back light of the train, he smiled and bowed to applause. Thanking everyone, he described what he had seen, the damage and signs of recovery, before concluding with obvious emotion, speaking slowly without notes:

> Vermont is a state I love.
> I could not look upon the peaks of Ascutney, Killington, Mansfield and Equinox without being moved in a way that no other scene could move me.
> It was here that I first saw the light of day; here I received my bride; here my dead lie pillowed on the loving breast of our everlasting hills.
> I love Vermont because of her hills and valleys, her scenery and invigorating climate, but most of all, because of her indomitable people. They are a race of pioneers who have almost beggared themselves to serve others. If the spirit of liberty should vanish in other parts of the Union, and support of our institutions should languish, it could all be replenished from the generous store held by the people of this brave little state of Vermont.[119]

They arrived at Plymouth Notch in darkness. Miss Pierce met them at the door holding a kerosene lantern and set out dinner before they retired upstairs, worn by the trip. The next morning Coolidge awoke early to walk his property with caretaker Lynn Cady, who pointed out the large haystacks he had taken in. Coolidge asked about the 11 cows in the pasture. Cady said they were producing 75 quarts of milk a day, of which 60 quarts were sold to the cheese factory at nearly five cents a quart and the rest were sold in Woodstock at a good price. They went into the cornfield where several hired hands were cutting the crop. Then he drove up the hill to his 25-acre sugar grove, climbing over rocks and a fence to admire the red-leafed trees. As a boy he had helped during sugar season each spring, hammering spikes into the trees, placing buckets underneath, waiting for warm weather to push up the sap, and carrying the buckets home on a sled for the most crucial step—the boiling. "This was the most interesting of all farm operations to me," he wrote, for a mistake meant losing sap or ruining an expensive pan.[120] They would pour the sugar into tin cans for use throughout the year, amounting to hundreds of pounds annually.

Later that day the president and first lady boarded a Washington-bound train with less than six months to serve, traveling without public knowledge of their itinerary. In upstate New York, they stopped at a small station to switch tracks, and a local reporter, who happened to be there and observe the commotion among the workers, was astounded to learn the reason why. He spotted a Secret Service agent standing outside the entrance of the last compartment and asked whether he might possibly see the president. The agent checked his credentials, corroborated his identity with a station employee, slipped inside momentarily, and reappeared to say, "The president will see you." The reporter found him looking out the window, his chin leaning on his left hand, his elbow on the sill. Nervously, he asked whether the president would clarify his statement on the 1928 election.

Coolidge replied that he could not have been clearer. "I do not choose to run—and that's it."[121]

* * *

The first day of October brought news that French President Raymond Poincare had made a statement related to a committee of experts about to meet in Geneva to determine how much Germany could pay in reparations, now that most parties agreed that $33 billion was unattainable. Poincare, who had served previous terms in 1917 and 1922–1924, and who believed, like many French citizens, that England and the United States had reneged on their commitment in 1919 to provide a security guarantee and that the peace settlement had not prevented Germany from rearming, had taken office in 1926 after his predecessor failed to convince Parliament to approve the debt payment deal with the United States. France had still not signed the deal. No doubt perceiving the committee work in Geneva as an opportunity to revive a French position from years past, Poincare suggested at a war memorial dedication ceremony that any reduction in German reparation payments must be accompanied "by a corresponding cut in the interallied debts to the United States."[122]

Coolidge told reporters that the United States would not discuss any proposal to link the war debts to reparations and that he considered the "incident closed."[123]

Poincare, surprised by the quick response, insisted the newspapers had misconstrued his remarks.

This exchange lowered expectations for talks in Geneva. The consensus among diplomats and politicos was that the French public would never tolerate a reduction in German reparations without a reduction in French debt, and that neither Coolidge nor his successor, whether Hoover or Democrat Al Smith, would dare risk the wrath of the American taxpayer by using public funds to redeem some of the debt owed by the former allies.

* * *

In the presidential campaign that autumn, Coolidge followed tradition by avoiding partisan speeches. He thought Hoover would prevail amid decent crop prices and high industrial employment, despite joking with his usher, "The people have been so prosperous for eight years and have made so much money, they may wish to go on a spree and elect Governor Smith."[124] One afternoon in October, while Grace was visiting her mother, he and Dr. Boone came across a live radio address by Smith at the Missouri State Fair Grounds, ridiculing the much-publicized Coolidge economy as a "myth" based on "petty savings" such as removing stripes from mail bags, ordering the use of both sides of writing paper, turning off the White House lights at night, and rescuing from wastebaskets various pins, paperclips, and bits and pieces of pencils, even as the administration wasted paper to announce such reductions and approved $200 million in new departmental spending between 1924 and 1927. This latter assertion was grossly misleading. The actual increase was $29 million, to which Smith added postal expenditures, which were kept separate by law because they were met by postal receipts. Smith also claimed expenditures for the office of the president had increased by 100 percent from 1921 to 1928, neglecting to mention two unavoidable causes: $155,000 for extraordinary repairs to the White House and $86,000 for the White House police, which were formerly furnished by the District of Colombia. The administration was selling "eye-wash" to the public, he said.[125]

Coolidge became so irritated that he broke into a sweat and sent a note that evening to Director Lord requesting a list of cost-saving moves to rebut the Democratic candidate.[126] The following day Secretary Mellon issued a statement that described and defended the policy of economy.[127] Secretary Work and Charles Evans Hughes also made statements.[128] The president was not about to let anyone take away, or tamper with, what he saw as his greatest accomplishment in office.

On Election Day, Coolidge rode the train to Northampton to vote at Memorial Hall, after receiving late reports that Massachusetts was leaning

Democratic for the first time since 1912 when the Taft-Roosevelt split delivered the commonwealth to Wilson. By nine that evening the president and first lady were back in the White House, listening to returns as Hoover rolled to a victory of 444 to 87 in the electoral vote. He lost Massachusetts and Rhode Island in Republican New England, but won 40 out of 48 states and 58 percent of the popular tally. He even won in Florida, North Carolina, Texas, and Virginia, reaping eight years of party-building in the south, along with an anti–Catholic, anti-wet bias against Smith among predominately protestant populations. Those four states had been Democratic since Reconstruction. Florida could be explained by demographics, as more northerners had been migrating there in recent years, thanks to air conditioning. North Carolina had been veering Republican for a decade or so. Texas and Virginia were stunning victories. The southern vote allowed Republicans to balance losses in big northern cities among immigrant and black voters. In 1920, Harding had won all 12 cities with a population more than 500,000. Hoover lost five of them: New York, Cleveland, St. Louis, Milwaukee, and San Francisco. In 1920, Republicans had carried the 12 top cities by a combined 1,638,000 votes. Hoover lost them by 38,000 votes. Yet Republicans had gained support in up-and-coming southern cities, such as Atlanta, Birmingham, Dallas, Houston, and Memphis, particularly among native-born white voters.

"The success of our Party with your election to the Presidency and the endorsement of the administration are of great satisfaction to me," Coolidge wrote his impending successor. "With this endorsement I can now retire from office in contentment."[129]

To Oulahan of the *New York Times*, who had covered the White House since August 1923, Coolidge seemed relieved by the election, as though a burden had been lifted from his shoulders.[130]

* * *

The president and first lady took their first vacation in the south later that month, arriving at a place in the Blue Ridge Mountains of Virginia, with spectacular views of the Shenandoah Valley, and learning a short time later that their son and Miss Trumbull had announced their engagement. Thus began one of their happier vacations, walking, reading, and watching movies at night. On Thanksgiving Day, they went into Charlottesville, a historic town with brick architecture and sand streets, largely untouched by the war, home to Thomas Jefferson and his University of Virginia. At Amherst, Coolidge had described Jefferson in an essay as a "radical among radicals" who espoused state rights and nullification, while "declaring the Indians had the best form of government."[131] Now, having seen the triumph of Hamiltonian policies and the modern fiscal state, marked by the progressive income tax, monetary controls, subsidies to states, and other instruments of federal power, he better appreciated the Jeffersonian vision of limiting the role of the federal government, such as abolishing direct taxes and disbanding the internal revenue service, and leaving state and local governments responsible for the things that most affect the everyday lives of citizens.

Coolidge would later lament that public admiration toward the third president had become mostly sentimental:

> The trouble with us is that we talk about Jefferson but do not follow him. In his theory that the people should manage their government, and not be managed by it, he was everlastingly right.[132]

Chapter Nine

"Pretty good idea to get out when they still want you"

"No Congress of the United States ever assembled, on surveying the state of the Union, has met with a more pleasing prospect than that which appears at the present time," Coolidge began his final message to Congress, sent on December 4. The previous year had set record highs in employment and production output, helping to turn a feared deficit of $94 million into an estimated surplus of nearly $37 million. Yet Washington operated on a tight margin. The surplus represented less than 1 percent of federal expenditures:

> It is necessary therefore during the present session to refrain from new appropriations for immediate outlay, or if such are absolutely required to provide for them by new revenue; otherwise, we shall reach the end of the year with the unthinkable result of an unbalanced budget. For the first time during my term of office we face that contingency. I am certain that the Congress would not pass and I should not feel warranted in approving legislation which would involve us in that financial disgrace.[1]

The following day he provided further details in his final budget message to Congress, with estimated surpluses of $36,990,192 for fiscal year 1929 and $60,576,182 for fiscal year 1930. Increased spending on defense, aviation development, and flood control, in particular, had put the government on a tight budget for the next two years, assuming that revenues would remain steady. To protect the surpluses, he called for extreme economy and discouraged any thought of tax cuts for the year ahead.[2]

In a separate statement to reporters that week, Coolidge addressed an argument made repeatedly by politicians and scholars, at home and abroad, to encourage the United States to cancel the war debts owed by the former allies. "It is sometimes represented that this country made a profit out of the war," he said. "Nothing could be further from the truth." He estimated that the total costs of the war for the United States, including interest payments on the debt, had reached $36.5 billion, based on statistics from the Department of Treasury. The federal government was spending $500 million a year on disabled and dependent veterans, a figure that would increase for decades and potentially amount to $100 billion by the time the last recipient passed away. The additional cost in lives lost was incalculable.[3]

Two weeks later he signed the Boulder Dam bill, approved by the Senate as Congress opened session, at a cost of $165 million. Despite misgivings about federal involvement in what some said should be the responsibility of the states and private businesses, he foresaw regional economic benefits and thought the government would recoup costs in the sale of power and water in the coming decades.

* * *

At Christmas the president and first lady lit the national tree and heard several thousand carolers on the White House lawn before traveling by train and yacht to Sapelo Island, Georgia, where businessman Howard Coffin threw open his Spanish villa to his famous guests, two military aides, and a dozen Secret Service agents who had a temporary telephone line installed from the mainland to provide communication with Washington, if necessary. The island, a former haven for pirates, with ancient moss-covered trees, abundant fauna and flora, the ruins of a Spanish mission built in the 15th century, and a semitropical climate, was warm enough to walk at night without a hat or coat. English artist Frank O. Salisbury accompanied them to do their portraits and initially tried the president in a black suit that made him look like a parson. When Coolidge put on a light suit, Salisbury thought he looked distinguished. "This is a very distinguished suit," he replied. One afternoon Sanders interrupted a sitting to inform Coolidge that the New York dailies wanted photographs and film footage of him shooting a rifle to accompany stories of his turkey-hunting on the island that morning. Irritated, he put on his shooting clothes, complete with sombrero, leather jacket, breeches, and high-laced boots, to pose for pictures. No sooner had he returned than Sanders interrupted a second time. "Of course I am not going to go through the whole thing again," Coolidge snapped, but when told the gun shots sounds had not synchronized properly with the firing motion, he went back outside to reshoot the scene. This astonished and amused Salisbury, knowing that no English politician would ever go to such lengths to placate the press.[4]

* * *

On the first day of 1929 they returned to the White House for their final two months. A day later Wall Street rang in the New Year with the largest gain in six months, led by heavy buying in automobile, copper, electrical, public utility, rubber, and steel stocks, in response to positive earnings reports and volume orders. Shares for Allied Signal, General Electric, and 38 smaller companies finished the day at all-time high prices. Shares for American Can, Chrysler, General Motors, Mack Truck, Packard, Southern Railway, and Union Carbide were way up. Trading activity was so heavy that the ticker tape was 30 minutes behind the market all afternoon. Traditionally, company stocks sold at about 10 times their earnings. They were now nearing 50 times earnings.

"As goes the first day, so goes the year," was heard often that day.[5]

* * *

Among the first callers of the year was shoemaker Jim Lucey, who had waited five and a half years to visit the White House so as not to seem like an office seeker, he said with a wink; he had lunch at the manse and told reporters on the way out that the president had never looked better. That evening he stayed in town with his eldest son, a civil servant, only to be tracked down by Harold Brayman of the *New York Evening Post.* "Oh, you want to write a lot more nonsense about me," he said, having come to distrust reporters over the years. In 1923 they had flocked to Northampton to meet the philosopher-shoemaker who helped make a president, portraying him as a tobacco chewer when he actually had nails in his mouth and describing him as a cobbler as though he were some itinerant bungler rather than a skilled craftsman. One writer complained of hitting his head on the doorway to the shop, which, in fact, was seven feet high. Still, Lucey opened up to Brayman, talking at length about virtue, honesty, work, and religion, and quoting Conan Doyle, Bernard Shaw, and H.G. Wells. Virtue, he believed, was best seen in proportion to what a man resists, not necessarily in proportion to an absence of wrongdoing: "Some of the people we think are very good may never have had much inclination to be otherwise. Some of the most heroic virtue may exist in unseen and unknown people. We don't always know what a man has to resist and fight against. And therefore we should never be hasty to condemn a man for a little fault. We do not know what great one he has fought against successfully. The real virtue is like that of a bridge which may have been warped and twisted a little by a raging torrent, but stayed on its buttments, and not like the bridge so high it never felt the flood."[6]

At a White House reception that winter, a Washington lady said, "Mr. President, you have been very fortunate in your administration—no wars, no strikes, no panics."

"I never thought of it that way," he replied. "I did my duty as I saw it."[7]

At the semiannual meeting of the Business Organization of the

Government, on a frigid night in late January, with more than a thousand managers in attendance and a nationwide radio hookup of 30 stations, he delivered his last budget speech. Taking the rostrum, he lauded efforts since 1921 to reduce spending and cut the national debt from nearly $24 billion to $16.9 billion, saving nearly $1 billion in interest alone. On taxes, annual revenues had increased from $3.8 billion to $3.9 billion under his rate reductions and the burden had shifted toward the wealthy; persons making less than $10,000 annually paid only 2 percent of federal taxes, compared with 20 percent in 1921; persons making more than $50,000 paid 78 percent, compared with 44 percent in 1921. On spending, the Budget Bureau had helped to reduce cumulative department estimates by $2.6 billion since 1921. "I believe that the Federal Government today is the best conducted big business in the world," he said.

"In spite of all these remarkable achievements, much yet remains to be done," he continued. Congress was reviewing legislation that would exceed $1 billion in new expenditures, and local and state spending had doubled from nearly $4 billion in 1921 to nearly $8 billion in 1929, largely to pay for bonuses and highway construction. "It is a warning that should be heeded by everyone entrusted with the expenditure or appropriation of public funds," he said. "It is the reason that further commitments by the national government for any new projects not absolutely necessary should be faithfully resisted."

Then he turned the rostrum over to Director Lord, who similarly praised the hard work and vigilance across the government to hold down spending and highlighted fiscal year 1927 as the peak of retrenchment. "That 1927 figure of $2,974,029, 674.62 is the lowest expenditure level this government will ever see."[8]

Nine days later the Senate passed by a vote of 68 to 12 a bill to spend $274 million annually for the construction of 15 cruisers and one aircraft carrier by 1931, in response to cruiser buildups in England and Japan following the failed talks in Geneva. This would be the first construction since 1924 and the largest since 1916. Coolidge backed the number but not the timetable, which he thought would overburden the budget. Instead he favored building five cruisers at a time without a set schedule. To avert a veto, Republican legislative leaders insisted that bipartisan support for the bill was insurmountable and promised no further large appropriations during the session. Coolidge received the bill and a delegation of congressional leaders and committee chairmen, but rather than holding a traditional bill-signing ceremony, as expected, he impressed upon them that appropriations should be kept at a minimum for the rest of the session. Then, alone in his office, he affixed his signature a few minutes later.

He also signed the Migratory Bird Conservation Act, appropriating

$75,000 annually from 1930 to 1932, $1 million annually from 1933 to 1939, and $200,000 annually after 1940, to provide a system of sanctuaries for migratory birds. Conservationists had been promoting the system for years.

The pressure to spend money vexed Coolidge through his final days in office. Dr. Boone happened to be with him one evening as he reviewed the budget for fiscal year 1930, with estimated appropriations in excess of $3.8 billion. The flood work and cruiser bill had caused a sudden increase from his budgets of years past. The total appropriations approved by Congress during the session had exceeded budget estimates for the first time in his presidency. "Doctor," he said, "I do not know where in the world this nation is going to, how it is going to meet its expenses."[9]

* * *

On 17 February, Coolidge signed the last debt settlement bill of his administration, stipulating that Greece repay $18.1 million over a period of 62 years. The bill also provided Greece with a new $12 million loan, at 4 percent interest, for handling refugees.

These settlements had taken hard negotiations and threats, and gave reason for optimism that countries could return to a more stable fiscal basis from budget to budget. The cumulative effect of lower interest rates had been to reduce European debt obligations to the United States by 60 percent, ranging from 19 percent in the case of Latvia to 75 percent in the case of Italy, based on a "capacity to pay" policy. This meant European countries would owe $218 million in total payments during the coming year, compared with what would have been $544 million under the original loan terms and interest rates.

Many economists and political observers nonetheless predicted the debts would never be paid in full and should be reduced in principal or canceled all together. The $326 million reduction in payments for the coming year, due to the settlements, amounted to $2.67 per person in the United States at a time when per capita income was $748. Cancellation would have increased that figure to about $3.73 per capita. This figure, however small on an annual basis, compounded over a payment period of 62 years would have amounted to a considerable transfer of wealth from the United States to Europe. The Coolidge administration, working within the restraints imposed by Congress through the World War Foreign Debt Commission at a time when most Democrats and Republicans wanted the debts paid as much as possible, had achieved reasonable settlements with every debtor country except Armenia, Liberia, and Russia, which had been written off from a practical standpoint.

* * *

With less than a month left in office, Coolidge had to pack some 200 boxes of gifts, memorabilia, books, and other possessions, to be loaded onto four army trucks and transported to Northampton. "I am having rather more trouble getting out of the White House than I had getting in," he cracked to reporters.[10] When he found Grace packing her dresses, most of them bought in Washington, he asked what she would do with them back home. "Why I will put them in the cupboard," she said. Looking at the trunks strewn across the floor, he said, "You better put 'em in the rooms and we will live in the cupboard."[11]

As to what he would do next, he would not say. "I just found out, our Government does do something in the way of a pension for its ex-Presidents," he told Dwight Morrow. "We can send out our letters for nothing. The only thing about it is, nobody wants to hear from us then."[12]

On March 1, three days before the inauguration, Coolidge met with Director Lord to review the latest budget numbers and held his final cabinet meeting to thank officers for their dedicated service. The only holdovers from 1923 were Mellon, Davis, and New. That afternoon, at his final press conference, reporters asked him to state his main accomplishment in office. Minding his own business, he said.[13]

On Saturday, March 2, Coolidge worked a full day, reviewed 200 bills, and received from the local NBC station the microphone he used for most of his 37 radio broadcasts. At noon he held his final hand-shaking session with the public, drawing an estimated 553 visitors despite snow-sodden streets and sidewalks from a rare March storm. The scent of raw pine wood from crates and boxes filled the manse. Outside, workers rushed to complete the temporary stands along the inaugural route from the White House to the Capitol, double the amount installed for the low-cost Coolidge Inaugural.

"All set—facing north," Grace wrote Therese Hills back home. "I shall see you soon—almost follow upon the heels of this letter."[14]

Sunday brought Supreme Court Justice Harlan F. Stone, who ventured to hope his former schoolmate might return to public office, perhaps as a senator, as John Quincy Adams had done. No, Coolidge replied, the times had changed too much for an ex-president to reemerge in politics without being an awkward presence for his party leadership and the incumbent president. Stone agreed, saying he was wise to leave the White House because the country was about to experience the worst financial convulsion since 1873 and he had done enough service.

To which the president replied, "It is a pretty good idea to get out when they still want you."[15]

That evening—his last in the White House—he and Grace dined with the Hoovers as a lone carpenter, working by lantern light, hammered the last nails on the inaugural stands outside the mansion. Afterward Coolidge had the White House telephone operator summon his bodyguard from the Willard Hotel. Although tired from a long day of preparations for what was expected to be the largest, most festive inaugural since Wilson in 1913, with more than 100,000 visitors in town, nearly twice as many as in 1925, Starling hurried to the northeast gate of the mansion and upstairs to the president, who was still in a suit and tie. They had been together for five and a half years, walking each morning and traveling far and wide about the country. Now they were to part, possibly forever. Starling, still a bachelor, said he would leave the government soon to buy land out west. Coolidge suggested he move to New England so they could look for work together. They discussed fishing and hiking in remote places, and pulled out a map to look at South Dakota, Montana, Oregon, and Washington.

"Well, Colonel," Coolidge said at last, past midnight. "I guess you'd better get some sleep."

They shook hands. Starling, knowing better than to introduce any sentiment into their parting moment, struggled to find the right words.

"I'm sorry to see you go," he said, "but our best days are ahead of us."

The president removed his coat, revealing his broad, bright suspenders, which Starling thought would have been strong enough to hold up a chandelier.

"Goodnight," said the bodyguard.

"Goodnight, Colonel."

Starling heard the door close and the lock click as he reached the stairway. Instinctively he recalled seeing Woodrow Wilson emerge from his office late one snowy evening in 1918, thin and weary, worn out by the war and coal shortages and late nights on his typewriter, with only eight assistants to help with his many burdens. It seemed like a long time ago, Starling thought as he walked around the corner to the Willard, breathing in the brisk night air. Then the world had been teetering on the edge of destruction. Now it was calm, happy, and prosperous.[16]

Inauguration Day, March 4, the president woke up early and wandered through the mansion to make sure all of his possessions were packed. The forecast called for rain. "It always rains on moving day," he grumbled to Ike Hoover, who helped him search for a missing rubber.[17] No less than eight Secret Service agents laid aside their responsibilities to participate in the hunt once they heard he would not leave until it was found. Then he worked in his office, "business as usual," aides said as he reviewed a stack of measures, signing 53 of them, including one settling a Civil War claim of the state of Nevada, one establishing Teton National Park in Wyoming, and one making illegal entry into the country equivalent to a felony under certain circumstances.[18] He applied a "pocket veto" to 10 other bills, including the Dale-Lehlbach bill to increase maximum annuities from $1,000 to $1,200 for retired federal workers and a bill to establish a national park at Ouachita, Arkansas. This brought his total number of vetoes to 49, second only to Cleveland and more than twice as many as any other predecessor.

The president and first lady went downstairs to leave and found staff members near the door to say farewell in a scene in which he seemed afraid of showing emotion, observed one witness.[19] They rode to the Capitol as rain drops fell on the open limousine, and left soon after the ceremony to catch a train to Northampton. "Good-bye, I have had a very enjoyable time in Washington," he told the well-wishers and reporters waiting on the platform. "Good-bye folks," she said with a wave. As the train pulled from the station, they stood on the rear platform to cheering and popping camera flashlights. "Come on, now, three cheers for President Coolidge!" someone yelled out, producing the desired effect. "Three cheers for Mrs. Coolidge!" This brought an even louder response, an outpouring of affection and appreciation for the vivacious 50-year-old woman whose smile and great enthusiasm had won over the city.[20]

Chapter Ten

Citizen Coolidge

The train pulled into Northampton at half past one in the morning as two policemen stood watch and Coolidge slept in his railcar, 56 years old and a private citizen for the first time since 1910, without a bodyguard or pension but with some $300,000 in savings from his presidential salary. Later that morning the Democratic mayor came aboard to welcome them.

Three thousand people standing in the rain let out a cheer as they appeared on the rear platform of the train in fur-lined overcoats and hats. A band struck up "Home, Sweet Home" as they posed for photographs and slipped into a dark sedan, having told the city and the local chamber of commerce that they wanted a simple homecoming. Accompanied by three policemen on motorcycles, they went up Main Street, past the stores, the Hampshire County Courthouse, City Hall, Memorial Hall, Edwards Church, and the Academy of Music, greeted by scattered crowds along the way. At Smith College, students cheered along Elm Street, some bareheaded in the rain, others wearing brightly colored kerchiefs knotted gypsy-style over their hair. At the bottom of Round Hill, pupils from the Clark School waved flags. At 21 Massasoit Street, neighbors and Boy Scout troops stood outside their two-family frame house to welcome them back. A foot of snow lay on their patch of front lawn. A newspaperman standing on the sidewalk, waiting for further developments to fill out his story, thought the place drab in appearance, its paint stained and darkened by the rain.[1]

Not much had changed in eight years except they had switched from a two-party telephone line to a private one. The same furnishings were in place—a Morris chair, a sofa, some tables, a rug, an oak dining set, a piano in the hallway, and some pictures. The vegetable garden out back was still there, but overgrown. The rent had increased slightly to $32 a month. Newspaper reporters speculated about available properties that might interest them, from a white colonial on Elm Street to the Beeches estate across town, but they wanted to stay where they had raised their sons and knew their neighbors—a high school principal, a hardware merchant, a grocer, an optometrist, a streetcar official, a minister, a postmaster, and two elderly ladies.

"For most of us there is one spot on earth which is dearer than all others," wrote Grace. "For me it is here in this little nine-room cottage which could be set in the State dining room at the White House with some space to share."[2] They had to place dozens of trunks and boxes in storage, and move some 5,000 books to the Forbes Library in town.

The second day home Coolidge went to his former law office at 25 Main Street, a four-story, yellow-brick building across from the railroad station and two blocks from the courthouse, where his name remained on the door in gilt letters, partly eroded by years of window washing. Ralph Hemenway, whom he hired in 1915 and to whom he handed the firm in 1918 after his election as governor, greeted him inside his small, bright room with light green wallboard, a golden-oak desk with a glass top, a silver-topped glass inkwell, a telephone, a pot of ferns, several prints, some books, and the same swivel chair Coolidge had owned for 30 years. When reporters arrived at the scene, Coolidge motioned them inside and leaned back in his chair with a cigar, saying he was inclined toward a quiet retirement without speeches or trips abroad. Asked whether he planned to move, he said no, he liked his street.[3] After reading his mail, he left to find reporters lingering about his house. "And this is private life!" he exclaimed to Grace.[4] For several days he stayed in seclusion, unpacking, carrying things to the attic. On Sunday he and Grace returned to Edwards Church, sitting in their pew halfway down the aisle to the right.

Soon he took to writing an autobiography, which began as a series of articles completed during his final weeks in office and for which he received a handsome $65,000 advance. By mid–March he was writing 700 words a day, wandering about their cramped house, sometimes sitting in a brown rocker in the parlor, sometimes standing, with a pad of yellow paper, a pencil, and a piece of sole leather for a board. By late April he was done with the terse 247-page manuscript, to be typed by his secretary and published by the Cosmopolitan Book Company at $3 per copy. More a discourse on education, faith, thrift, hard work, perseverance, and public service, than an autobiography, it omitted key episodes of his presidency, including the Pennsylvania coal strike, Teapot Dome, the bonus bill, the Dawes plan, the second inaugural, the tax cuts, the Mississippi flood bill, the foreign debt talks, the Kellogg-Briand Pact, Nicaragua, Mexico, China, the overheated stock market, and race relations. "The only way I know to drive out evil from the country is by the constructive method of filling it with good," he wrote. "The country is better off tranquilly considering its blessings and merits, and earnestly striving to secure more of them, than it would be in nursing hostile bitterness about its deficiencies and faults."[5]

On weekdays Coolidge had breakfast at home before heading to his office, always in a suit and tie, a white shirt, and shiny black shoes, riding in the limousine he had purchased from the government, the presidential seal on the door and his former White House chauffeur at the wheel. At 25 Main Street he took the caged elevator to the second floor, tipping the operator a dime and greeting "Mr. Hemenway." It was still "Mr. Hemenway" and "Mr. Coolidge" after a dozen years. There he read letters and the conservative *New York Herald-Tribune* and *Boston New Bureau*, while smoking two or three cigars, which he lit by striking a wooden match on the sole of his shoe. No doubt he was pleased that President Hoover kept up his policy of economy, reducing military spending, maintaining the 1931 budget at 1930 levels, retaining Lord as budget director until his retirement at yearend, and selling the *Mayflower* in a much-publicized move to save $300,000 annually. When a visitor from Washington reported Hoover had gone so far as to give up the White House stables, the former president was skeptical.

"Where have the horses gone?" he asked.

"They've been sent back to Fort Meyer."

"Well, will they eat less hay there?"[6]

Coolidge did not practice law but sometimes advised local residents in disputes with local or federal agencies, such as helping a widow collect a pension of $30 a month for her late husband, a Spanish War veteran. By arrangement with a bookstore across the street, he charged one dollar to sign copies of his autobiography and donated the proceeds to the Missionary Society of the Edwards Church; whenever a messenger appeared with a book to sign, he dropped what he was doing and signed it. Once a month he traveled to Manhattan for meetings of the New York Life Insurance Company, which made him a director at $600 a year, plus expenses. He saw old friends such as Richard Irwin, Henry Field, and Jim Lucey, whose shop provided a sanctuary from pedestrians who interrupted his walks with friendly salutations and autograph requests.

At Plymouth Notch he planned an addition to the house, featuring a library, modern plumbing, and a hot water heater, but not a stair banister or handrail, or electricity, or central heating. The population of Plymouth township, including Plymouth Notch, Plymouth Union, Pinney Hollow, Tyson Furnace, Kingdom, Five Corners, Nineveh, and Frog City, had fallen by three-quarters during his lifetime, from 1,285 in 1870 to 331 in 1930, hurt, like most towns along the spine of the Green Mountains, by soil erosion, westward expansion, agricultural innovation, rail commerce, and declining wool prices caused by cheap imports and the postwar recovery of southern cotton. The cheese factory his father and neighbors had built 40 years ago was inoperable. Most of his childhood friends were gone. Ernest E. Moore was a judge in Ludlow. Henry Brown was a merchant there. Dell Ward had settled in Middlesex. The only relative Coolidge had left in town was his maternal aunt Gratia Wilder, who lived next door in a mustard-colored house with a chicken coop out back. Many farms lay fallow, stonewalls crumbled with neglect, fields turned to forests. The roads were better but little else had changed. The old elm still stood in the common, outside the store. As a boy, Coolidge knew a man who knew a man who had seen settler John Mudge plant the tree before the Revolution. Three lives. That was enough to span the history of his village and his country.

Grace, who preferred Plymouth Notch in "smaller doses," found contentment at home, gardening, knitting, walking, volunteering at church, promoting deaf-awareness, and seeing old friends like Therese Hills, who drove her around in a yellow-wheeled automobile.[7] Shortly before the Coolidge-Trumbull wedding in September she wrote John with loving advice:

> John, you are a son for a mother to be proud of and I want you to always feel that I am standing by ready to do anything for you and Florence. You two together should make something very beautiful of your lives.
>
> Just don't let little things be-cloud your vision and when the rough places have to be gotten over hold your chin up, throw your shoulders back and go forward—for it's the rough places which steady the feet and strengthen the muscles—life is so beautiful—never do anything which will mar the sweetness of it. So shall each year bring you new appreciation of it.
>
> Truly, how I love you—and now I want you to find in life all that is just and true and right and live it gloriously![8]

Then, lying awake at night, thinking of young Calvin on the fifth anniversary of his death, she wrote out the following lines of heartfelt longing:

> You, my son,
> Have shown me God.
> Your kiss upon my cheek
> Has made me feel the gentle touch
> Of him who leads us on.
> The memory of your smile, when young,
> Reveals his face,
> As mellowing years come on apace.
> And when you went before,
> You left the Gates of Heaven ajar
> That I might glimpse,
> Approaching from afar,
> The glories of his Grace.
> Hold, son, my hand

Guide me along the path,
That, coming,
I may stumble not,
Nor roam,
Nor fail to show the way
Which leaves us—Home.

The following day she sent the poem to the editor of *Good Housekeeping*, with a short note. "I have often received letters from mothers who have shared my experience and I hope that the poem might spread comfort," she explained, and she was published.[9]

At the wedding, held in Connecticut, she delighted for John and Florence but seemed a bit subdued as reporters and cameramen swarmed about the place, climbing up telephone poles and trees to record the event. The family found a microphone hidden underneath an oriental rug at the reception.

A month later, on October 24, Grace sat with her mother at Cooley-Dickinson Hospital in Northampton during her last moments.

That was the week the panic began on Wall Street with stock selloffs and declining prices. The following week was worse. On "Black Tuesday," October 29, investors traded 16.4 million shares at a record-setting loss. During a period of 60 trading sessions, the Dow-Jones industrial average fell from a high of 381.17 in early September to 198.69 in late November. As Coolidge had placed much of his savings in secure bonds and bank accounts, the crash did not affect him significantly.

In January 1930, the former first couple traveled by train, without bodyguards, to Florida, New Orleans, and California, where they visited Hollywood studios, lunched with Mary Pickford and Douglas Fairbanks, and stayed with William Randolph Hearst who served them wine from his private cellar. Crowds gathered everywhere they went. When Coolidge threw away a cigar butt in Los Angeles the result was a near-riot as men and women scrambled for the souvenir. When he emerged from taking a shower in his hotel room a reporter was waiting to ask whether he would consider running for president again. By the time he returned home in March he was done with traveling, although he never lost the longing.[10]

Dr. Plummer, the school principal next door, thought they might strike up a friendship, what with their common intellectual interests, but found Coolidge to be "by far the most reticent man I ever met." They hardly had an hour of conversation, even though their front porches abutted each other, divided by a slender piece of woodwork. The only difference he could see in Coolidge after eight years in Washington is he now smoked his cigars in an ivory holder.[11]

"A strange man," a neighbor said to his son as they watched Coolidge leave his duplex one morning, turning toward town. "A man of the people."[12]

Neighbors left the famous couple alone, but local hotels were only too willing to distribute maps marking the route to 21 Massasoit, resulting in a constant run of tourists and reporters, many of whom thought nothing of trampling across the lawn, peering through windows, and posing for photographs on the front porch. This procession sometimes tied up local traffic on the weekend. Dr. Plummer sat on his porch one Sunday afternoon and counted an average rate of 10 cars per minute, mostly tourists, some of whom mistook him for Coolidge, even though they bore no physical resemblance to each other.[13] Such curiosity-seekers were a constant bother as Coolidge sat on his sagging porch, 15 feet from the sidewalk, smoking a cigar or reading a newspaper, his straw hat tilted against the glare. "Well, isn't that a terrible place for the President of the United States to live!" he heard a lady exclaim as her limousine pulled up to the curb one morning.[14] At the White House he could stroll on the south lawn or through the gardens without being seen. Now he was continually under prying eyes. "You cannot realize how much I long for peace and privacy," he wrote *New York Sun* editor Henry L. Stoddard in April 1930.[15]

That spring they looked at properties in Northampton and settled on the Beeches estate, for which they paid $45,000 in cash to Mrs. Morris L. Comey, the widow of a former cotton mill supervisor. Built in 1914 by a Smith professor on Munroe Street, less than two miles from Massasoit Street, the house was set well beyond a pair of iron gates hanging between two stone pillars. Never again, Coolidge said impishly, could a policeman order him to shovel off his sidewalk. It was a gray-shingled, green-trimmed, three-story house covered with weather-stained sheet copper to blend with the beech foliage. The nine-acre property had a tennis court, a shallow swimming pool, and some 800 trees.[16]

On the last morning at 21 Massasoit he stood alone in an empty bedroom while Grace waited in the limousine with their remaining possessions.[17] That evening he wrote their landlord:

> I am sending you the key to the house. We have moved out everything except some things I have arranged with the new tenant to take. I have taken out the cable that I put in for the electric range but, of course, the connections are all there and if anyone wants power in the house it will be easy enough to put a cable in the cellar.
>
> I spent about fifty dollars last fall putting in new piping for the water which was running through pipes so filled with rust that there was no pressure. The only thing that needs immediate attention is a new wash bowl in the toilet room. That bowl has a large crack in it which leaks badly.

> This is the last check I shall send you and I wish to thank you for your constant kindness to me while I was living in your house.
>
> You will recall I spoke to you about the little pine tree that was set out by my boy who is gone and for that reason I would like to take it up some time.[18]

Moving into the Beeches, he fenced in the property to keep out reporters and sightseers, who left burned-out matchsticks on the lawn during their nocturnal visits, and replaced various old furnishings with wing chairs, thick upholstered sofas, electric lamps, and oriental rugs left behind by Mrs. Comey after he declined to purchase them. They kept Miss Reckahn to do the cooking and hired a live-in maid and caretaker to do the rest.

"Somehow, I feel that it is only a temporary house, like the Adirondacks or South Dakota—or even the White House—but then, they are all temporary," wrote Grace. "I sleep on an upper porch and get the air on three sides. It is at the east end of the house and I awake in the morning with the sun streaming in upon me and the birds twittering and chattering in the branches of the trees. Lovely, lovely world."[19]

Bruce Barton came by one afternoon and took a tour through the house. "The newspapers describe it as having twelve rooms," Coolidge said, "but there are four rooms we can't find." The living room was trimmed in old ivory enamel with walls done in steel-blue grass paper; at one end stood a stone fireplace and mantel, at the other a door leading to a solarium with window seats. The dining room walls were paneled and covered by sail cloth. In the library Barton paused to admire the well-filled bookcases, a steel engraving of George Washington over the caenstone fireplace, and an oil painting of the *Mayflower*. A pair of French doors led to a brick patio and a garden with purple iris beds, spiraea, hydrangea, and lilacs, followed by a pathway down a steep hillside covered by honeysuckle, clematis, and ivy. In the distance lay a sweeping view of the Northampton meadows and Mount Tom. Barton had never seen his friends so serene and happy. "You can't imagine how good it is," Grace said, wearing a little green beret and a simple frock as they sat down to lunch. Barton thought she looked years younger now that she was away from the strain of political life. After dining on crab-flake cocktail, soup, fried chicken, watermelon pickles, and preserved pears, Coolidge led his guest into the library for a smoke and a leisurely talk, pulling from his drawer two letters written by George Washington. The first, written to a friend who preceded him to the new capital along the Potomac, requested assistance in finding suitable living quarters until the executive mansion was built. Washington stipulated he could not accept private hospitality but would require a house in accordance with the dignity of his office. The second letter, written to an acquaintance late in his presidency, directed the purchase of two strong horses that could withstand the trip through the mud back to Mount Vernon; they had to be well-broken mares so he could use them later to breed mules; they should be purchased from a certain breeder at a certain price.

"He certainly thought things out in advance," Barton exclaimed.

Coolidge fell silent a moment and said, "He was the only man in American public life who never made a mistake."

"I met one of your fellow insurance directors the other day who says that you, also, are always right," ventured the writer.

"Send him up to talk to me," said Grace, entering the room.[20]

Many visitors sought advice. To a young politician being pressured to take a position on a controversial issue, Coolidge recommended letting the situation develop before taking action: "It seems to me public administrators would get along better if they would restrain the impulse to butt in or be dragged into trouble. They should remain silent until an issue is reduced to its lowest terms, until it boils down into something like a moral issue."[21] When Morrow ran for the United States Senate in New Jersey in 1930, he stopped by the Beeches, seeking the secrets of electoral success from his old classmate. "Talk as little as you can, but if you have to talk, talk about patriotism," Coolidge said. "They seem to like it."[22] Morrow won the election, but died 11 months later of a cerebral hemorrhage, exhausted and overworked. The sudden loss came as a shock to Calvin and Grace, who attended the funeral services in Englewood, New Jersey.

In July 1930, the McClure Newspaper Syndicate engaged Coolidge to write a short daily column titled "Calvin Coolidge Says," which paid a record $3.25 per word, ran in more than 100 publications, and took a nonpartisan, even nonpolitical, bland tone, unlike the highly charged articles written by Roosevelt in retirement. With help from former Associated Press correspondent Herman C. Beaty, who compiled clippings from newspapers and magazines, Coolidge chose a theme each morning, from the death of classical languages on campus to the secrets of individual success, and worked at his desk, writing, dictating, and sending his pieces by Western Union telegram. "I have not written on prohibition," he wrote Edward Clark. "Do not intend to."[23]

The former president had little to say, in person or in print, about the depression that followed the stock market crash, except to encourage unemployed workers to plant gardens and urge the wealthy to spend and invest money rather than hoarding. Always reluctant to propose solutions to problems beyond his control, he also felt deceived by an incident in the summer of 1930 when Hoover agreed to help him prepare his first article for the McClure Syndicate by allowing Secretary Mellon to brief him on the financial condition of the country. Mellon, serving his third Republican president, gave a generally optimistic message, resulting in an upbeat article. Afterward Edward Clark revealed that Mellon had been instructed to give a positive briefing and that Hoover had since decided to halt predictions on the contraction because they undermined public confidence in the administration. "I know it is perhaps impertinent of me to suggest such a thing," Clark wrote, "but I do hope that you will carefully avoid anything which resembles a hopeful prediction."[24] Coolidge from that point refrained from all serious discussion of the depression in his articles.

He opposed legislative proposals in 1930 and 1932 to appropriate $10 million in federal subsidies to the states for old age pensions, which were on the rise abroad and at home. Argentina, Australia, Austria, Belgium, Bulgaria, Canada, Chile, Czechoslovakia, Denmark, England, Finland, France, Germany, Greece, Greenland, Hungary, Iceland, Ireland, Italy, Japan, Latvia, Luxembourg, New Zealand, the Netherlands, Norway, Poland, Portugal, Rumania, Russia, Scotland, Spain, Sweden, Switzerland, South Africa, Uruguay, and Yugoslavia all had national pension or insurance programs, with contributions from at least two of the relevant parties, the state, the employer, and the individual. In the United States, public opinion and public policy were shifting away from the fundamentals of English poor law, prevalent since the 17th century, that government welfare for individuals should be limited to those unable to care for themselves, such as orphans, the blind, the deaf, and the mentally ill. California, Colorado, Kentucky, Maryland, Massachusetts, Minnesota, Montana, Nevada, New York, Utah, Wisconsin, and Wyoming had enacted "county-optional" pensions since 1923. They provided about a dollar a day, on average, to residents 65 years old and older, with strict residency requirements, payments reduced for those with other retirement incomes or large property holdings, and penalties in some cases for healthy children who failed to maintain their parents in old age. Nearly all these states converted to compulsory programs by the end of 1931, as Delaware, Idaho, Massachusetts, New Jersey, and West Virginia considered legislation along the same lines. Federal workers had received a pension in 1920.

Many saw public pensions as an appropriate response to an industrialized, urbanized society in which people lived longer, older workers struggled to earn a livelihood, and less than one in 10 retired persons received a private pension from a former employer. A 1930 study by the renowned Dr. I.M. Rubinow estimated that of citizens 65 years old and older, one million had enough savings to support themselves, one million were still working, two million were dependent on their children, one and a half million lived by begging or through marginal employment, and one million lived in poorhouses or other institutions.[25] The depression was overwhelming efforts by churches and charities to provide assistance, and state pensions were negligible. China, India, and Mexico were the only other populous countries without an old age pension.

To Coolidge, public pensions were bound to be disappointing:

> We try to reform ourselves on the outside when the only effective remedy is to reform ourselves on the inside.
>
> What a self-respecting people really needs is not a system of old-age pensions, but a population made sufficiently skilled by education and sufficiently self-controlled and well disposed by the help of religion so that old-age pensions would be a superfluity. Unless real reform comes from within the problem will never be solved.[26]

In 1921, Harding had let the postwar recession run its course, like other presidents beset by economic trouble, Van Buren, Buchanan, Grant, Cleveland, and Roosevelt. In late 1929, Mellon had offered similar advice to Hoover: "Liquidate labor, liquidate stocks, liquidate the farmers, liquidate real estate." The old financier even saw some benefit to the depression, asserting, "It will purge the rottenness out of the system."[27]

Hoover, by and large, remained committed to economy in expenditures as tax revenues fell. He took a voluntary pay cut from $75,000 to $60,000 annually. He saved $100,000,000 by closing 53 army bases and posts, and $51,000 by canceling the installation of a modern air conditioning system at the White House. He considered unemployment a problem for state and local government and opposed various bills in Congress to provide direct "dole" payments to unemployed workers. Yet he began to lose patience and take on the business cycle by more than doubling the amount of federal subsidies to the states, from $109 million to $234 million, and expanding such aid for welfare; channeling relief funds through banks; providing farmers with $600 million in price supports under the Agricultural Marketing Act of 1929; creating the pump-priming Reconstruction Finance Corporation to lend money to states and localities and businesses; and increasing nonmilitary federal expenditures by 259 percent during his term. With income tax and customs revenues declining from a combined $3 billion in 1930 to $2.2 billion in 1931, the federal government ran a deficit of $860 million, the first deficit in a decade. This amount doubled in 1932, even though the administration removed the expenditures of the Reconstruction Finance Corporation from the "ordinary" budget and placed them in a separate "emergency" budget in a bit of financial trickery without precedent. Hoover responded to the debt by signing the largest peacetime tax increase ever, raising the rate for high-income earners from 23 percent to 63 percent and breaking with the party platform of 1928, which had promised a continuation of low taxes. He did so against the advice of Mellon, who supported an increase to balance the budget, albeit a smaller one. The long-serving secretary had fallen from favor. Clark, now an executive at a pharmaceutical firm in Washington, D.C., kept in contact with Mellon and other top figures in the administration and sent regular updates to the former president. On Mellon, he wrote: "He is almost ignored on many occasions, but I am afraid the truth is that his advice is no longer as valuable as it was or that his mind is as alert."[28]

Even worse, Hoover backed the Smoot-Hawley Tariff of 1931, raising the duty on most imports despite hundreds of economists warning in a letter to the White House of retaliation abroad and reductions in international trade, which soon came to pass and undercut much of the positive aspects of the U.S. moratorium on foreign debt that summer. The depression only worsened, as did criticism of Hoover, who with his high collars, fat cheeks, and humorless countenance, was easy fodder for cartoonists.

Coolidge held his tongue except to quip, "President Hoover likes deep-sea fishing. I prefer the creeks."[29]

At last he could not resist mild criticism of his successor, who nearly tripled the White House staff from 40 to more than 100, including three secretaries. On agricultural price supports, Coolidge wrote: "In the general field of business, whether of industry or of agriculture, government interference in an attempt to maintain prices out of the Treasury is almost certain to make matters worse instead of better. It disorganizes the whole economic fabric. It is a wrong method, because it does not work."[30] Of the tax increase: "While there were other causes for the business depression, high taxes was an important one and is one of the main hindrances to a revival."[31] Instead he called on businessmen and wage earners to press their representatives for a tax cut. To maintain revenue, he advocated in July 1932 a national sales tax even though Mellon had long opposed the idea. "If we delegate the paying of our taxes we shall find we have delegated the control of our government," Coolidge wrote. "Nothing seems clearer than that if the people are to control the government they must pay the taxes to support it."[32]

Clark sent descriptions of the struggling president, how he worked evenings and Sundays, sometimes 18 hours a day, failing to connect with people, alienating the press, recalling his speeches from the printer as often as 15 times to make changes, and editing those written by cabinet officers. "No wonder he has to get up every night around one o'clock and work for a couple of hours," Clark wrote.[33]

As the months went by, the stories of bankruptcies and breadlines across the country had an effect on Coolidge, wearing away his optimism and wrecking his once-vaunted era of prosperity. In 1932, the Northampton Savings Bank collapsed. Hearing that Hemenway was among the victims, he walked into his office and placed a check for $5,000 on his blotter, saying quietly, "And as much more as you want."[34] Charity, not public spending, was his solution. "All that is needed is for us to give what we think America is worth to us," he wrote in a statement for the presidential commission on unemployment relief.[35]

Rumors of a Coolidge draft for president or vice president preceded the Republican National Convention of 1932 despite his efforts to discourage supporters. When he heard of an alleged plot by the House of Morgan and other Wall Street financiers to secure his nomination at the convention, he implored Clark to squash it, adding, "I am glad conventions do not come oftener than once in four years."[36]

That spring, with thousands of veterans marching on Washington to demand full and immediate payment of their 1924 bonus certificates, Coolidge hired a crew to install electricity in his old farmhouse. Now that renovations were complete—electricity, plumbing, hot water, oil stove, new floor planks, and a rebuilt foundation—he and Grace could live there at ease except for Miss Pierce cutting through their room on her way downstairs before daylight to make breakfast each morning. Neighbors thought he looked pale and thin, and storekeeper Herman Pelkey noticed that when he played horseshoes with local camp boys behind the store he had trouble reaching the pit. He took walks but had little interest in fishing or shooting. One morning he emerged with secretary Harry Ross and a Winchester rifle to shoot a woodchuck in the field. Returning 10 minutes later, gun in hand, Coolidge ran into Pelkey, who, having heard the shot resonate through the hills, asked whether he had hit anything. "You heard me shoot, didn't you?" Coolidge replied, barely breaking stride. Not even close, Ross whispered to the storekeeper as they watched him walk away, homeward bound.[37]

The family celebrated his 60th birthday on a rainy day, as he suffered a hay fever attack. When he received an invitation to represent Hoover at the opening ceremonies of the Summer Olympic Games at Los Angeles, he declined: "To attempt to go across the plains and through the field of blossoming vegetation would be extremely hazardous and probably land me on the coast totally unable to function at this season of the year."[38] As it was, he was waking up at night with breathing trouble and having to use a spray.[39]

Try as he might, he could not get away from politics. In July he asked former aides to thwart a rumored draft movement to nominate him for vice president. In August he declined an invitation to attend the notification ceremony for Hoover because of his hay fever. The following week Clark wrote that Hoover would appreciate a statement to the effect that his actions had prevented a banking shutdown in the country, to which

Coolidge replied that his throat hurt and "I find it terribly hard to know what to say."[40] When Clark suggested that he criticize Democratic nominee Franklin D. Roosevelt for proposing a bonus bill and other expenditures that would damage the national credit, Coolidge, having spent three decades in politics without resorting to such tactics, wrote back, "You know that I would not relish making any attack against the opposition candidate."[41]

In mid–August, *New York Sun* publisher and Republican stalwart Henry L. Stoddard came by on vacation and found Coolidge arranging books on the shelves of his new library, ashen in appearance, slow and timid in movement, and "strangely indifferent" to politics. They sat on the porch as tourists drove up at intervals, parking on the edge of the lawn 20 feet away, waving or bowing to Coolidge and admiring the scene from every direction, sometimes taking photographs. At least 300 people a day visited Plymouth Notch that summer and every summer since 1923. "I shall never understand why people want to crowd around to see me," Coolidge said.

The newspaperman returned in September to discuss a possible appearance at a party rally in New York. Coolidge was reluctant. "In politics, you know, you have to be wholly out or wholly in—and I have been wholly out," he said. "I intend to stay out." Besides he had nothing to say beyond his recent endorsement of Hoover in the *Saturday Evening Post*.

"I know how you feel," Stoddard replied, "but many others do not. That is why I am here." Republicans needed to hear from their former leader. The party was sure to lose in November, but he had to go down fighting like everyone else. The record had to show that.

Coolidge paused and replied, "I am always ready to share the fate of my party."

"Then you must make at least one speech."

Coolidge slowly reached for his cup of tea and took a sip. Looking straight at Stoddard, he agreed to a single speech in New York, not to exceed 30 minutes in length: "If you cannot get your argument across in half an hour, you might as well not talk at all."[42]

Yet he struggled with the speech, trying not to repeat what he wrote in the *Saturday Evening Post*, feeling out of touch with the administration and the campaign, lying sick in bed with asthma for a week. "The Presidency is a wearing job and takes its toll from any man who serves therein," Grace wrote an old friend. "Calvin was never set up as ruggedly as some and there are times when I feel those years took most of the reserve." She noticed he was continually taking his pulse and eliminating foods from his diet to alleviate chronic indigestion.[43]

"I do not intend during my lifetime ever to go through the agony of making another speech," Coolidge wrote Stoddard on October 3, eight days before the event.[44]

A week later he traveled to New York to deliver the speech before 15,000 spectators at Madison Square Garden. Stoddard noticed he looked better than he had in Vermont but had to sit during a short delay in the side room leading to the stage, fatigued by the commotion. The speech was a poor one, Coolidge said.[45] As he took the rostrum, dressed in a cutaway coat and pinstriped trousers, the spectators stood and cheered at such length that he took out his pocket watch, held it up, and pointed to the microphones, which had been rented from radio chains for a certain block of time at $170 per minute. "That's Cal," someone shouted. With the arena silent at last, he said, "I have come to reiterate my support of the President, and reassert my faith in the Republican party, the most efficient instrument for sound popular government ever entrusted with the guidance of a great nation." Without mentioning Roosevelt by name, he blamed the Democrats for obstructionism and called on their candidate to say whether he would veto the $2 billion bonus bill for veterans; however, many listeners seemed to lose interest and some laughed at lines not meant to be humorous; he had only to pause and look sideways at his audience through his horn-rimmed spectacles to incite an outburst of hilarity; his throat bothered him throughout the speech, nearly causing him to stop at one point.[46]

"I enjoyed it so much that I stood up all the time," someone told him afterward.

"So did I," he retorted.[47]

Motoring back to the hotel with Stoddard that evening, Coolidge discussed the prospect of a Roosevelt presidency, saying the Democrat had shown a "great fighting spirit" but predicting the burdens of office would wear on him, what with his physical disability. "The other part of the gamble is that I do not believe the people realize all that is in his mind as to policies; there is something about his speeches that makes me think he is going to try to overturn things. You cannot do that safely with a government in one term. Government is growth—slow growth. You cannot gamble with it—that is what I see ahead if Roosevelt is elected."[48]

Not only did Roosevelt win in a landslide with 54 percent of the popular vote and 472 electoral votes, but Democrats took control of Congress for the first time since 1916, breaking the northeastern-western alliance that had allowed Republicans to dominate national electoral politics since 1896. In the House, Republicans lost 103 seats, including longtime seats in Illinois, Indiana, Iowa, Kansas, Michigan, Missouri, and Ohio. In the Senate, the party lost 12 seats, 10 in the Middle West and western states. The newspapers were filled with articles on pending emergency measures, spending programs, and a brain trust of New York lawyers and social workers descending upon Washington.

Coolidge, though surprised by the lopsided result, took consolation in knowing the country benefited from competition between the two parties as he began an article for the *Saturday Evening Post* that praised the parties for consolidating public opinion on broad principles, allowing voters to vote on issues, and boosting accountability within government, despite their decline since their heyday in the 19th century. The first blows, delivered by civil service reformers, curtailed parties from distributing spoils to their supporters and deprived them of the right to print their own ballots. Then state laws stripped parties of their right, as private organizations, to control the process by which they nominate candidates for office. Thus legislators were more likely to appropriate money for particular categories of people or local purposes in response to pressure from interest groups. "These proposals make headway because legislators do not feel that their party organization is strong enough to support them in opposing such movements," he wrote.[49]

In mid–December he traveled to New York for a life insurance meeting and rang up Stoddard to meet at the Hotel Vanderbilt. "The election went against us much more heavily than I had anticipated," he said, lighting a cigar inside his suite. "I have been out of touch so long with political activities that I feel I no longer fit in with these times. Great changes can come in four years. These socialistic notions of government are not of my day. When I was in office, tax reduction, debt reduction, tariff stability and economy were the things to which I gave attention. We succeeded on those lines. It has always seemed to me that common sense is the real solvent for the nation's problems at all times—common sense and hard work. When I read of the new-fangled things that are now so popular I realize that my time in public affairs is past. I wouldn't know how to handle them if I were called upon to do so."

Yet he did not wish to criticize the incoming administration: "If they succeed the criticism fails; if they fail, the people find out about it as quickly as you can tell them."[50]

A few days after Christmas he went to see barber George Dragon, who had been trimming his hair since college. The barber thought he did not look well, the flesh sunken between the cords on the back of his neck. As they fell into conversation, Dragon ventured to ask a question the regulars had been pressing him to ask for some time now.

"Mr. Coolidge," he said, "how about this depression. When is it going to end?"

"Well, George, the big men of the country have got to get together and do something about it. It isn't going to end itself. We all hope it will end, but we don't see it yet."[51]

Two days later, December 31, Coolidge told Clark that he would not do commission work, much less run for president in 1936, returning to office like Grover Cleveland had done several decades ago:

> I should not want to serve on any bodies or commissions. The fact is that I feel worn out. No one can tell these days what a short time or three or four years may bring forth, but, of course, I know my work is done.
>
> I could not pick it up again. I imagine that was one trouble Cleveland had in trying to administer a second term. Any time you hear anybody talking of me, just tell them to stop it.[52]

On the first day of 1933, he wrote Starling, "I find I am more and more worn out."[53] Later that day he dined with former classmate Charles A. Andrews, who inquired about his health. "I am very comfortable because I am not doing anything of any account," he said, "but a real effort to accomplish anything goes hard with me. I am too old for my years. I suppose the carrying of responsibilities as I have done takes its toll. I'm afraid I'm all burned out. But I am very comfortable."

As to the depression, he said nothing endured except religion, the only reason for hope.[54]

Four days later, January 5, he awoke with indigestion and went to the office as usual. Weather conditions could hardly have been worse for someone with poor circulation and heart trouble. The temperature, after falling 60 degrees the previous day, rose dramatically that morning, which can cause blood vessels to contract and then enlarge, lowering blood pressure, restricting sufficient circulation to the head and limbs, and heightening the risk of sudden clotting in the coronary. At the office he read correspondence and newspapers, which reported modest gains in stocks, bonds, and commodity prices, in response to the first year-on-year increase in weekly railway traffic in more than a year. Then he told Harry Ross he wanted to go home. They arrived to see Grace leave for town in a frock and a floppy hat, arms swinging loosely by her side. Inside the house he talked about Plymouth Notch and wandered restlessly as he did whenever he had nothing to do, fetching a glass of water from the kitchen, watching the furnace being stoked in the basement, and looking in the library. Then he went upstairs to his dressing room where Grace found him a short while later, lying on his back in his shirtsleeves, the victim of a coronary thrombosis.

* * *

Within an hour the news reached Plymouth Notch by telephone. A neighbor walked to the Coolidge house and tapped on the door. "Calvin has just died," he told Miss Pierce, whose eyes filled with tears as she thanked him and closed the door.[55] The schoolhouse let out early and people went to the store to hear the radio reports.

The following morning the Mayor of Northampton announced he would not close the stores in honor of his late predecessor. "Every nickel counts," he said, the depression having caused a record number of bankruptcies and foreclosures in the city. "If the business places close they might lose sales and that is exactly what Calvin would not want." Nor did he drape the city in mourning other than to tie a flimsy piece of black crape outside City Hall. "Calvin was a simple man," he told reporters. "He would not want the people to go to all that expense."[56]

Funeral services took place a day later, a cold, rainy Saturday morning in Northampton. "I have never seen such weariness in a face," said one townsman, passing the casket at Edwards Church.[57] Following a simple 20-minute service, the procession headed north, black sedans behind a police escort, past people standing alongside the road or sitting in their horse-driven buggies, past Deerfield, Greenfield, Bernardston, North Bernardston, Guildford, Brattleboro, Putney, East Putney, Westminster, Bellow Falls, Rockingham, Bartonsville, Chester Depot, Gassets, Proctorsville, Ludlow, Tyson, Plymouth, and up to Plymouth Notch, where neighbors stood in a field beside the cemetery, huddled in a hailstorm. With dusk approaching, the body was laid to rest.

* * *

President-elect Roosevelt, having sent his wife and his son to the funeral services, finished a full day of meetings that afternoon and decided to cancel his daily press conference. Instead he slipped a comment to reporters on a proposal by Congressional Democrats to raise income taxes and impose a beer tax to help close an estimated $492 million budget deficit for fiscal year 1933. He was confident that legislators would be able to balance the budget, he said. He would leave the details to them.[58]

* * *

Grace Coolidge sold the Beeches in 1937 and had a house built near Smith College with a front porch, a doorknocker shaped like a human hand, a circular stairway, and a sunlit interior. The years were kind to her, bringing two granddaughters and good health to stay active in the Clark School, Edwards Church, and Pi Beta Phi, and take a long-awaited tour through Europe under the pseudonym "Mrs. Adams." During World War II, she helped the Red Cross and delivered food and gifts to local troops departing Northampton station. At home she listened to war reports and Boston Red Sox games on the radio; she later purchased a television but preferred radio. She walked as much as eight miles a day around town and through the nearby meadows and nature preserves. In September 1956, she attended the dedication of the Calvin Coolidge Memorial Room at the local Forbes Library, the last public appearance she would make. She passed away on July 8, 1957, at age 78.

* * *

John Coolidge started a firm in Connecticut in 1953 to produce business forms, later selling at a profit to concentrate on historical preservation at Plymouth Notch, restoring the family homestead to how it was in August 1923 and reopening the cheese factory. A staunch anti–New Deal Republican, he never ran for office but held several public posts before passing away on June 30, 2000, age 93.

* * *

Aurora Pierce continued to maintain the homestead, saving everything from papers to pincushions, and never using the telephone or electricity. In January 1953, neighbors invited her to watch the Eisenhower inaugural, the first time she saw a television. Three years later she had a stroke and was taken to a hospital where she passed away on June 12, 1956, age 87.

* * *

James Lucey died at home at 18 Gothic Street, on April 8, 1936, at age 81, leaving a widow, seven children, and eight grandchildren.

* * *

Richard Irwin passed away at home at Northampton on March 9, 1932, age 75.

* * *

Frank Stearns remained active with Amherst and philanthropic boards, but withdrew from politics for the most part. He died of pneumonia on March 6, 1939, at age 82, five months after his son was elected to the United States Congress from New Hampshire.

* * *

William Butler reappeared in newspaper headlines when his Hoosac Cotton Mills refused to pay $81,000 in processing taxes in 1935 and won a landmark case in *United States v. Butler* in 1936. This marked the first time the Supreme Court had given full consideration to government activity under the general welfare clause in the Constitution, despite much contention since the beginning of the republic, when Jefferson and Madison took a narrow interpretation and Hamilton took a broader one as long as expenditures went toward national, not local, purposes. The Court determined that the tax in the Agriculture Adjustment Act of 1933 was unconstitutional under Article I, Section VIII, Clause I: "It invades the reserved rights of the states. It is a statutory plan to regulate and control agricultural production, a matter beyond the powers delegated to the federal government." This effectively dismantled the controversial New Deal program, which traced back to the McNary-Haugen bills of the 1920s. However, the ruling provided the judicial opening for the Social Security Act of 1935 and other welfare programs by declaring that "the power of Congress to authorize appropriations of public money for public purposes is not limited by the direct grants of legislative power found in the Constitution." In doing so, the Court determined that the power of Congress to spend money "for the general welfare" was in addition to, not limited by, other powers granted by the Constitution.[59] This was what Madison had warned about: that if statutes could be passed under the general welfare clause, the legislative boundary between the federal government and the states would be eroded and the power of Congress to legislate would be unlimited. Indeed the Court would uphold the Social Security Act, the culmination of the federal grant-in-aid subsidies to the states and a new form of cooperative federalism to promote old-age pensions, unemployment insurance, maternal welfare, vocational rehabilitation, and public health, in *Helvering v. Davis,* in 1937. By a 7–2 vote, the Court took the position that any measure that improved the lives of some citizens was valid under the general welfare clause, as long as it operated throughout the country, and that the law did not violate the powers reserved to the states and to the people under the Tenth Amendment. This altered relations between individuals and the federal government and opened the way for Congress to adopt income redistribution schemes. Butler passed away that same year, on March 29, 1937.

* * *

Herbert M. Lord retired as budget director in July 1929 but never recovered from his hard seven-year stint in the position, suffering an attack of influenza and a nervous breakdown in short order. He died in Washington on June 2, 1930, age 71.

* * *

John Garibaldi Sargent returned home to practice law in Ludlow. He lived until March 5, 1939, age 78.

* * *

Andrew Mellon returned to private life and was charged with income-tax fraud in a politically motivated case. After a grand jury declined to indict him, the Roosevelt administration responded with a civil suit that led to the notorious "Mellon Tax Trial" of 1935–1936. Mellon insisted on his innocence and persisted with plans to create a national art gallery on the Washington Mall, offering to pay construction costs, donating his $50 million art collection, and meeting with Roosevelt to secure support. The Board of Tax Appeals cleared him of wrongdoing in December 1937, four months after his death at age 82.

* * *

Charles Dawes, after serving in various capacities in the Hoover administration, including as Director of the Reconstruction Finance Corporation in 1932, returned to Chicago as a banker and pursued his interests as a pianist and composer, glad to be done with politics. He died at home in Evanston, Illinois, on April 23, 1951, at age 85.

* * *

Edward Clark stayed in Washington as a consultant on legislation, customs, and tariff matters. He died on December 5, 1935, at 57.

* * *

C. Bascom Slemp remained active in Republican politics and founded the Institute of Public Affairs at his beloved University of Virginia. He died on August 7, 1943, age 72.

* * *

Everett Sanders resigned as chairman of the Republican National Committee in 1934 under pressure from anti-Hoover forces. He practiced law in Washington and lived until May 12, 1950, age 68.

* * *

Edmund Starling was promoted to head of the Secret Service in 1935 and was married for the first time a year later at age 61, forsaking plans to move out west. Instead he retired to Florida in November 1943, after traveling more than a million miles in support of presidential trips from Wilson to Roosevelt. "I'll never tell all," he said as he began his memoirs.[60] Less than a year later, on August 3, 1944, he succumbed to pneumonia at age 69, before *Starling of the White House* went to print.

* * *

J.R. McCarl filled out his term as Comptroller General until 1936 and proved a nemesis to the Roosevelt administration and the Democratic Congress as he regularly challenged expenditures based on the often vague legislation and loose administrative practices of the New Deal. When the administration tried to use relief funds to build low-income housing in the District of Columbia, he ruled the expenditure illegal. When Secretary of the Interior Harold Ickes established a housing corporation with a $100 million budget for slum clearance, McCarl ruled it unconstitutional in a widely publicized decision. When Congress set aside $500 million for drought relief, he denied the use of $15 million to finance a drought-prevention project in the Great Plains as outside the parameters of the original appropriation. On the final day of his term, he sent a farewell message to employees at the General Accounting Office, imploring them to combat the "powerful and resourceful" forces seeking "broader administrative discretion and wider latitude in the spending of public monies."[61] Three months later he appeared on a nationally syndicated radio program to condemn the deficit spending of the Roosevelt administration and the "deplorable state" of public finances, breaking his silence since leaving office.[62] He remained in Washington, practicing law, issuing negative comments on the New Deal on occasion, and dying suddenly at his office on August 2, 1940, at 60 years old.

* * *

Harlan Fiske Stone became part of the liberal faction of the Supreme Court that backed the New Deal agenda during the 1930s, taking the position that state participation in the federal programs was voluntary and that legislative bodies should be free to regulate commerce and experiment with social programs as long as they did not interfere with individual liberties. The contrary viewpoint is best demonstrated by the payroll tax that Congress levied on workers in 1935. The tax included a rebate of 90 percent to employers in states that established unemployment compensation schemes in line with federal requirements, effectively penalizing states that declined to participate and underscoring the taxing powers of the federal government to coerce states into certain actions. President Roosevelt named him as Chief Justice in 1941, and he remained in that capacity until his death on April 22, 1946.

* * *

Wilson Brown continued to serve as naval aide to Presidents Hoover, Roosevelt, and Truman, all distinct from Coolidge and from one another in temperament, leadership traits, and political philosophy. Once Brown happened to mention to Roosevelt a four-volume biography on former Chief Justice John Marshall, who had been born in a log cabin in Virginia and had led the highest court from 1801 to 1835, through historic rulings to protect property rights and contracts in line with the Constitution and the Bill of Rights. The biography, written by Albert Beveridge, had won the Pulitzer Prize in 1920, and when Coolidge had seen Brown reading a volume while leaning against a fence in Plymouth Notch in the summer of 1926, he had praised the aide for putting his time to good use. Not so Roosevelt, who dismissed the work as "fusty volumes that thought only of property rights and worried little about human rights and public welfare."[63] Brown went on have a quiet retirement in Connecticut, writing his memoirs and living until January 2, 1957, nearly through the first term of Republican president Dwight Eisenhower, who, despite pressure from old guard party elements to roll back the New Deal, expanded Social Security, increased the minimum wage, and created the Department of Health, Education, and Welfare, in what was called Modern Republicanism.

Chapter Notes

Source Abbreviations

CCMF: Calvin Coolidge Memorial Foundation.
FL: Forbes Library.
LC: Library of Congress.
PCCSHS: President Calvin Coolidge State Historic Site.

Introduction

1. Address at the Seventh Regular Meeting of the Business Organization of the Government, June 30, 1924, CCMF.
2. James D. Richardson, *Messages and Papers of the Presidents* (Washington, D.C., 1950), p. 9723.
3. Inaugural Address, March 4, 1929, CCMF.
4. *New York Times*, January 31, 1928.
5. *Frothingham v. Mellon*, 262, U.S. 447 (1923).
6. *Washington Post*, June 22, 1926.
7. Calvin Coolidge, *Autobiography* (New York: Cosmopolitan Books, 1929), p. 229.

Chapter One

1. Vrest Orton, *Calvin Coolidge's Unique Vermont Inauguration* (Plymouth, Vermont: CCMF, 1970), p. 47.
2. Coolidge, *Autobiography*, pp. 173–174.
3. *Wall Street Journal*, August 2, 1923.
4. Inauguration scene: Orton, *Calvin Coolidge's Unique Vermont Inauguration*, pp. 50–51, 60–62, 84; *New York Times*, August 4, 1923; *Boston Herald*, August 4, 1923; *New York Times*, September 9, 1923; *American Heritage*, Vol. 15, No. 1 (December 1963).
5. Cameron Rogers, *The Legend of Calvin Coolidge* (New York: Doubleday, Doran, 1928), p. 166.
6. Ira Chamberlain to Sarah Coolidge, September 17, 1862, Coolidge family papers, Document 215, Folder 23, Vermont Historical Society.
7. *Literary Digest*, September 5, 1925.
8. *Literary Digest*, September 5, 1925.
9. Edward C. Lathem, ed., *Your Son, Calvin Coolidge: A Selection of Letters from Calvin Coolidge to His Father* (Montpelier: Vermont Historical Society, 1968), p. 80.
10. Joe Curtis, *Return to These Hills* (Woodstock, Vermont, 1940), p. 81.
11. *Washington Post*, August 4, 1923.
12. Benjamin F. Felt diary, Misc. File 5.9, FL.
13. *New York Times*, August 4, 1923.
14. Claude M. Fuess, *Calvin Coolidge: The Man from Vermont* (Boston: Little, Brown, 1940), p. 320.
15. Fuess, *Calvin Coolidge*, p. 311.
16. Coolidge, *Autobiography*, p. 76.
17. *Saturday Evening Post*, September 20, 1924, and October 25, 1924.
18. *Literary Digest*, September 5, 1925.
19. Fuess, *Calvin Coolidge: The Man from Vermont*, p. 93.
20. *Outlook*, April 9, 1924; Edward C. Lathem, ed., *Meet Calvin Coolidge* (Brattleboro, Vermont: The Stephen Greene Press, 1960), p. 41; *Daily Hampshire Gazette*, March 10, 1932.

21. Ishbel Ross, *Grace Coolidge and Her Era* (New York: Dodd, Mead, 1988), p. 22.
22. Lathem, ed., *Your Son, Calvin Coolidge*, p. 118.
23. Lathem, ed., *Your Son, Calvin Coolidge*, p. 121.
24. Alfred Pearce Dennis, *Gods and Little Fishes* (Indianapolis: Bobbs-Merrill, 1924), p. 133.
25. Ronald D. Sawyer, *Cal Coolidge, President* (Boston: Four Seas, 1924), p. 98.
26. CC to Benjamin F. Felt, November 17, 1913, Misc. File 5.9, FL; R.M. Washburn, *Calvin Coolidge: His First Biography* (Boston: Small, Maynard, 1923), p. 82.
27. *Women's Home Companion*, March 1920.
28. Lathem, ed., *Your Son, Calvin Coolidge*, p. 117.
29. Calvin Coolidge, *Have Faith in Massachusetts* (Boston: Houghton Mifflin, 1919), pp. 3–8.
30. *National Geographic*, October 1965, p. 570.
31. Robert A. Woods, *The Preparation of Calvin Coolidge* (Boston: Houghton Mifflin, 1924), p. 60.
32. Lathem, ed., *Your Son, Calvin Coolidge*, p. 132.
33. William Allen White, *Puritan in Babylon* (New York: Macmillan, 1938), p. 140.
34. *Boston Evening Transcript*, January 3, 1919.
35. Fuess, *Calvin Coolidge*, p. 186.
36. Fuess, *Calvin Coolidge*, p. 188.
37. Coolidge, *Autobiography*, p. 128.
38. *Boston Herald*, January 6, 1933.
39. *Boston Evening Transcript*, September 12, 1919.
40. *Boston Herald*, September 13, 1919.
41. Coolidge, *Have Faith in Massachusetts*, pp. 222–224.
42. *Literary Digest*, November 15, 1919.
43. Lathem, ed., *Your Son, Calvin Coolidge*, pp. 160–161.
44. Robert H. Ferrell, *The Presidency of Calvin Coolidge* (Lawrence: University of Kansas Press, 1998), p. 16; Fuess, *Calvin Coolidge*, p. 236.
45. Boston *Sunday Herald*, June 13, 1920.
46. Lathem, ed., *Your Son, Calvin Coolidge*, p. 166.
47. *Boston Sunday Post*, June 27, 1920.
48. *New York Times*, April 4, 1923.
49. *Boston Evening Transcript*, April 3, 1923.
50. *New York Times*, April 7, 1923.
51. Sobel, *Coolidge: An American Enigma* (Washington, D.C.: Regnery, 1998), p. 227.
52. Joel T. Boone autobiography, chapter 21, p. 502, Boone papers, LC.

Chapter Two

1. *Wall Street Journal*, August 8, 1923.
2. Coolidge, *Autobiography*, p. 179.
3. *Current Opinion*, January 1924.
4. *New York Times*, July 7, 1927; Taft to Clarence Kelsey, September 29, 1923; Taft to Horace Taft, September 29, 1923; Taft papers, LC.
5. Fuess, *Calvin Coolidge*, p. 314.
6. *Wall Street Journal*, August 14, 1923.
7. *New York Times*, August 16, 1923.
8. *New York Times*, August 17, 1923.
9. Joel T. Boone autobiography, chapter 21, p. 728, Boone papers, LC.
10. Calvin Coolidge, Jr., to CC, August 12, 1923, CCMF.
11. CC to Calvin Coolidge, Jr., August 14, 1923, Personal Files of President Calvin Coolidge, LC.
12. *Wall Street Journal*, December 14, 1923.
13. Grace Coolidge *Grace Coolidge: An Autobiography*, eds. Lawrence E. Wikander and Robert H. Ferrell (New York: Norton, 1992), p. 62.
14. White, *Puritan in Babylon*, p. 247.
15. Frederick W. Dallinger to CC, August 5, 1923, the Presidential Papers of Calvin Coolidge, LC.
16. Press conference on August 28, 1923, CCMF.
17. Donald R. McCoy, *Calvin Coolidge: The Quiet President* (Lawrence: University of Kansas Press, 1967), p. 175.
18. *Barron's*, October 1, 1923.
19. CC to Gifford Pinchot, September 7, 1923, the Presidential Papers of Calvin Coolidge, LC.
20. *New York Times*, January 6, 1933.
21. *New York Times*, March 2, 1929.
22. John Hays Hammond, *The Autobiography of John Hays Hammond* (New York: Farrar and Reinhart, 1935), p. 752.

23. *New York Times*, September 16, 1923.

24. *Washington Post*, September 7, 1901.

25. Herbert Hoover, *The Memoirs of Herbert Hoover: The Cabinet and the Presidency* (New York: Macmillan, 1952), pp. 55–56.

26. *Washington Post*, January 29, 1928.

27. Boone autobiography, chapter 21, p. 734, Boone papers, LC.

28. *New York Times*, April 22, 1927.

29. Ellen Riley to mother, May 27, 1927, Riley correspondence, PCCSHS.

30. C. Bascom Slemp, *The Mind of the President* (New York: Doubleday, Page, 1926), p. 5.

31. Lathem, ed., *Meet Calvin Coolidge*, p. 77.

32. *World's Work*, April 1924, pp. 579–590.

33. Coolidge, *Autobiography*, p. 196.

34. Edmund Starling, *Starling of the White House* (New York: Simon & Schuster, 1946), p. 209.

35. White, *Puritan in Babylon*, p. 257.

36. *Saturday Evening Post*, February 28, 1931.

37. Bruce Barton, "The President Shouldn't Know Too Much," *The Real Calvin Coolidge*, Issue 2 (Plymouth Notch, 1984).

38. Jules Abels, *In the Time of Silent Cal* (New York: Putnam, 1969), p. 31.

39. Bernard M. Baruch, *Baruch: The Public Years* (New York: Holt, Rinehart and Winston, 1960), pp. 191–192.

40. Robert H. Ferrell and Howard H. Quint, eds., *The Talkative President: The Off-the-Record Press Conferences of Calvin Coolidge* (Amherst: University of Massachusetts Press, 1964), p. 14.

41. CC to Frank A. Munsey, December 27, 1923, Personal Files of President Calvin Coolidge, LC.

42. Boone autobiography, chapter 21, p. 38, Boone papers, LC.

43. Grace Coolidge, *An Autobiography*, p. 65.

44. GC to Ivah Gale, September 28, 1923, CCMF.

45. M.E. Hennessy, *Calvin Coolidge: From a Green Mountain Farm to the White House* (Boston: G.P. Putnam's Sons, 1924), p. 55.

46. Coolidge, *Autobiography*, p. 79.

Chapter Three

1. *Barron's*, July 23, 1923.

2. *Nation's Business*, May 1927.

3. *New York Times*, August 30, 1925.

4. *The Federalist*, No. 10.

5. *Pollock v. Farmers' Loan & Trust Co.*, 157 U.S. 429, 607 (1895).

6. *Wall Street Journal*, November 4, 1926.

7. *New York Times*, October 11, 1925.

8. *Washington Post*, December 28, 1924.

9. Andrew Mellon to CC, October 23, 1923, the Presidential Papers of Calvin Coolidge, LC.

10. *Saturday Evening Post*, January 6, 1923, pp. 30, 52–53.

11. *Colby Alumnus*, Vol. 18, No. 2, Winter 1929, p. 117.

12. David T. Zuckerman, "Are We Redeeming Our National Debt Too Hastily?" *Political Science Quarterly*, Vol. 40, Issue 2 (June 1925), p. 254.

13. *New York Times*, January 25, 1925.

14. *Budget Address to Congress*, December 3, 1923, the Presidential Papers of Calvin Coolidge, LC.

15. H.R. Rep. No. 68-313 (1924), p. 4; *New York Times*, May 20, 1924.

16. *New York Times*, November 14, 1923; February 4, 1924; March 21, 1924.

17. *New York Times*, January 28, 1924.

18. *New York Times*, November 19, 1923.

19. Boone autobiography, chapter 21, p. 50, Boone papers, LC; Lathem, ed., *Meet Calvin Coolidge*, p. 70.

20. Horace Green, *The Life of Calvin Coolidge* (New York: Duffield and Company, 1924), pp. 191–192.

21. *First Annual Message to Congress*, December 6, 1923, CCMF.

22. *The World's Work*, April 1924.

23. *New York Times*, November 18, 1923.

24. *New York Times*, December 7, 1923.

25. *Washington Post*, November 21, 1926.

26. *New York Times*, December 8, 1923.

27. Boone autobiography, chapter 21, p. 854, Boone papers, LC.

28. Lathem, ed., *Your Son, Calvin Coolidge*, p. 194.

29. *Washington Evening Star*, January 22, 1924.

30. Ferrell and Quint, *The Talkative President*, p. 59.

31. *New York Herald Tribune*, January 27, 1924. The appointments of Strawn and Gregory were withdrawn because of their previous association with oil interests. They were replaced by Republican Owen J. Roberts and Democrat Atlee Pomerence, who, after determining that Fall received some $400,000 in cash from Sinclair and Doheny, charged all three men with conspiracy to defraud the federal government and indicted Fall and Doheny on the additional charge of bribery.
32. *American Magazine*, June 1929.
33. Richard Irwin to CC, February 5, 1924, Personal Files of President Calvin Coolidge, LC.
34. Elihu Root to William H. Taft, September 17, 1926, Root papers, LC.
35. Boone autobiography, chapter 21, p. 144, Boone papers, LC.
36. Marian C. McKenna, *Borah* (Ann Arbor: University of Michigan Press, 1961), p. 202.
37. McCoy, *Calvin Coolidge*, p. 217.
38. H.L. Mencken, *A Carnival of Buncombe: Writings on Politics* (Chicago: Vintage, 1980), p. 125.
39. Boone autobiography, chapter 21, p. 144, Boone papers, LC.
40. *New York Times*, March 30, 1924.
41. McCoy, *Calvin Coolidge*, pp. 273–274.
42. Lathem, ed., *Meet Calvin Coolidge*, p. 111.
43. Boone autobiography, chapter 21, pp. 26–27, Boone papers, LC.
44. Boone autobiography, chapter 21, p. 289, Boone papers, LC.
45. Coolidge, *Autobiography*, p. 44.
46. *Wall Street Journal*, April 11, 1924.
47. Press conference on February 26, 1924, CCMF.
48. *Washington Post*, January 30, 1923.
49. *Washington Post*, May 20, 1924.
50. Message to the House of Representatives Returning Without Approval a Bill Providing for Adjusted Compensation for War Veterans, May 15, 1924, CCMF.
51. *Congressional Record*, 68th Congress, 1st Session, Volume 9, p. 8661.
52. *Veto of S 5*, May 3, 1924, CCMF.
53. Lathem, ed., *Your Son, Calvin Coolidge*, p. 94.
54. *Time Magazine*, May 26, 1924.
55. Harry Barnard, *Independent Man: The Life of Senator James Couzens* (New York: Charles Scribner's Sons, 1958), p. 172.
56. *New York Times*, June 9, 1924.
57. Richard E. Neustadt, "Presidency and Legislation: The Growth of Central Clearance," *The American Political Science Review*, Vol. 48, Issue 3 (September 1954), pp. 644–647.
58. Herbert M. Lord to CC, May 29, 1924, the Presidential Papers of Calvin Coolidge, LC.
59. *New York Times*, June 8, 1924.
60. *St. Louis Globe Democrat*, June 4, 1924.
61. *Washington Post*, April 16, 1924.
62. *Time Magazine*, June 16, 1924.
63. *Washington Post*, May 10, 1924.
64. *New York Times*, December 2, 1923.
65. Elmer E. Cornwell, Jr., "Coolidge and Presidential Leadership," *Public Opinion Quarterly*, Volume 21, Issue 2 (Summer 1957), p. 271.
66. *American Mercury*, August 1924.
67. *New York Times*, March 17, 1935; *Washington Post*, July 12, 1931.
68. *Washington Post*, September 15, 1929.
69. *Good Housekeeping*, May 1935.
70. Boone autobiography, chapter 21, p. 49, Boone papers, LC.
71. *New York Times*, April 23, 1924.

Chapter Four

1. *New York Times*, December 4, 1924.
2. World War Foreign Debt Commission, Combined Reports, pp. 341–42.
3. Merlo J. Pusey, *Charles Evans Hughes* (New York: Macmillan, 1952), p. 579.
4. *New York Times*, January 1, 1925.
5. Press conference on December 28, 1923, CCMF.
6. Press conference on January 15, 1924, CCMF.
7. *Washington Post*, March 19, 1924.
8. Louria, Margot, "The Boldness of Charles Evans Hughes," *The National Interest*, No. 72 (Summer 2003).
9. Elizabeth Johnson and Donald Moggridge, eds., *The Collected Writings of John Maynard Keynes* (Cambridge: Royal Economic Society, 1978), p. 234.
10. *American Magazine*, June 1929.
11. Press conference on January 22, 1924, CCMF.

12. Lathem, ed., *Meet Calvin Coolidge*, p. 178.
13. *Washington Post*, June 27, 1925.

Chapter Five

1. William H. Taft to Elihu Root, June 9, 1924, Root Papers, Box 66, LC.
2. Diary of Theodore Roosevelt, Jr., June 10–12, 1924, LC.
3. White, *Puritan in Babylon*, p. 297.
4. White, *Puritan in Babylon*, p. 298.
5. *New York Times*, June 10, 1924.
6. *New York Times*, June 10, 1924.
7. *Literary Digest*, September 8, 1923.
8. *Literary Digest*, December 10, 1927.
9. *Boston Globe*, June 5, 1924.
10. *Washington Post*, June 11, 1924.
11. Joe Martin, *My First Fifty Years in Politics* (New York: McGraw Hill, 1960), p. 145.
12. Republican Party Platform of 1924, the American Presidency Project, UC Santa Barbara.
13. *New York Times*, June 9, 1924.
14. *New York Times*, June 13, 1924.
15. Lathem, ed., *Your Son, Calvin Coolidge*, p. 189.
16. *American Magazine*, June 1929.
17. Boone autobiography, chapter 21, pp. 177–178, Boone papers, LC.
18. Boone autobiography, chapter 21, p. 853, Boone papers, LC.
19. Boone autobiography, chapter 21, p. 186, Boone papers, LC.
20. Lathem, ed., *Your Son, Calvin Coolidge*, p. 190.
21. *Ladies Home Journal*, April 1924, p. 17.
22. *New York Times*, August 29, 1924; *Ladies Home Journal*, April 1924.
23. *New York Times*, June 22, 1924.
24. Address at the Seventh Regular Meeting of the Business Organization of the Government, June 30, 1924, CCMF.
25. Boone autobiography, chapter 21, pp. 200–201, Boone papers, LC.
26. Lathem, ed., *Your Son, Calvin Coolidge*, p. 190; *New York Times*, July 5, 1924; *Washington Post*, July 5, 1924.
27. GC to John Coolidge, July 17, 1932, CCMF.
28. Boone autobiography, chapter 21, p. 213, Boone papers, LC.
29. *Washington Post*, July 9, 1924.
30. Boone autobiography, chapter 21, p. 216, Boone papers, LC.
31. GC to Therese Hills, August 3, 1924, Misc. Files, FL.
32. Boone autobiography, chapter 21, p. 216, Boone papers, LC.
33. Coolidge, *Autobiography*, p. 190.
34. *New York Evening Post*, March 2, 1929.
35. Boone autobiography, chapter 21, pp. 107–108, Boone papers, LC.
36. *Time Magazine*, August 4, 1924.
37. Lathem, ed., *Meet Calvin Coolidge*, pp. 139–141.
38. *Washington Post*, October 25, 1936.
39. Geoffrey Perrett, *America in the Twenties* (New York: Simon & Schuster, 1982), p. 189; *New York Times*, July 13, 1924.
40. *Wall Street Journal*, November 7, 1924.
41. Press conference on July 18, 1924, CCMF.
42. Ferrell and Quint, *The Talkative President*, p. 39.
43. *Washington Post*, August 24, 1924.
44. *Washington Post*, September 24, 1924.
45. J.J. Watts to CC, September 17, 1924, the Presidential Papers of Calvin Coolidge, LC.
46. Charles G. Dawes, *Notes as Vice President* (Boston: Little, Brown, 1935), p. 24.
47. *New York Times*, August 17, 1924.
48. *Wall Street Journal*, August 20, 1924.
49. CC to John Coolidge September 25, 1924, Personal Files of President Calvin Coolidge, LC.
50. Starling, *Starling of the White House*, p. 224.
51. *Washington Post*, September 7, 1924.
52. *American Magazine*, June 1929, p. 94.
53. C. Bascom Slemp to Joseph Branin, September 3, 1924, the Presidential Papers of Calvin Coolidge, LC.
54. Holy Name Society: Authority and Religious Liberty, September 21, 1924, CCMF.
55. Will P. Banning, *Commercial Broadcasting Pioneer: The WEAF Experiment, 1922–1926* (Cambridge: Harvard University Press, 1946), p. 174.
56. James E. Watson, *As I Knew Them* (Indianapolis: Bobbs-Merrill, 1936), p. 239.
57. Religion and the Public, October 15, 1924, CCMF.

58. Ferrell and Quint, *The Talkative President*, p. 10.
59. Boone autobiography, chapter 21, p. 501, Boone papers, LC; *New York Times*, September 18, 1924. Newspapers obtained a copy of the speech and published its contents, leading to much comment.
60. *New York Times*, September 15, 1924.
61. Arthur Capper to CC, October 26, 1924, Personal Files of President Calvin Coolidge, LC.
62. William Allen White to CC, August 22, 1924, Personal Files of President Calvin Coolidge, LC.
63. *New York Times*, October 26, 1924.
64. John D. Hicks, *Republican Ascendancy* (Berkeley: University of California Press, 1960), p. 91.
65. *New York Times*, November 1, 1924. These figures do not include small donations during the last several days of the campaign.
66. *New York Times*, June 21, 1925.
67. *Washington Post*, November 2, 1924.
68. Lathem, ed., *Your Son, Calvin Coolidge*, pp. 194–195.
69. Ferrell and Quint, *The Talkative President*, p. 11.
70. *Washington Post*, October 24, 1924.
71. *Washington Post*, October 27, 1924.
72. Press conference on October 28, 1924, CCMF.
73. *Washington Evening Star*, November 4, 1924.
74. *Washington Post*, November 5, 1924.
75. *The Literary Digest*, LXXXIII, November 22, 1924.
76. Richard Irwin to CC, November 22, 1924, Personal Files of President Calvin Coolidge, LC.
77. Henry F. Pringle, *The Life and Times of William Howard Taft* (New York: Farrar and Reinhart, 1939), p. 968.
78. *New York Times*, April 30, 1909.
79. Bruce D. Porter, *War and the Rise of the State* (New York: Free Press, 1924), p. 8.
80. Press conference on November 14, 1924, CCMF.
81. Second Annual Message to Congress, December 3, 1924, Miller Center, University of Virginia.
82. *New York Times*, December 5, 1924.
83. *New York Times*, December 6, 1924.
84. *Washington Post*, December 6, 1924.
85. Ferrell and Quint, *The Talkative President*, p. 40.
86. Lathem, ed., *Your Son, Calvin Coolidge*, p. 197.
87. *Washington Evening Star*, December 25, 1924.
88. Lathem, ed., *Your Son, Calvin Coolidge*, pp. 198.
89. William Jennings Bryan to CC, January 1, 1925; CC to William Jennings Bryan, January 4, 1925, Personal Files of President Calvin Coolidge, LC.
90. *New York Times*, January 7, 1925.
91. *New York Times*, January 7, 1925.
92. Boone autobiography, chapter 21, p. 303, Boone papers, LC.
93. *Washington Evening Star*, March 4, 1925.
94. Address to the Business Organization of the Government, January 26, 1925, the Presidential Papers of Calvin Coolidge, LC.
95. *Literary Digest*, February 28, 1925. In truth, Jefferson walked from his boarding house to Capitol Hill that morning, but the horseback myth persists.
96. Lathem, ed., *Your Son, Calvin Coolidge*, p. 201.

Chapter Six

1. *New York Times*, March 4, 1925.
2. Inaugural Address, March 4, 1929, CCMF.
3. *Washington Post*, March 8, 1925.

Chapter Seven

1. *New York Times*, March 12, 1925.
2. CC to John Garibaldi Sargent, March 17, 1925, the Presidential Papers of Calvin Coolidge, LC.
3. *New York Times*, March 22, 1925.
4. Frank Stearns to CC, March 17, 1925, the Presidential Papers of Calvin Coolidge, LC.
5. *Washington Post*, March 25, 1925.
6. *New York Times*, March 20, 1925.
7. *New York Times*, March 20, 1925.
8. *Washington Post*, March 20, 1925
9. Press conference on March 20, 1925, CCMF.
10. Ferrell and Quint, *The Talkative President*, p. 127.
11. *Washington Post*, March 29, 1925.
12. Boone autobiography, chapter 21, p. 1232, Boone papers, LC.

13. *Washington Post*, March 8, 1925.
14. *New York Times*, February 27, 1927.
15. Coolidge, *Autobiography*, p. 201.
16. *Time Magazine*, April 27, 1925.
17. GC to Therese Hills, April 8, 1925, Misc. File 19.8, FL.
18. *World's Work*, June 1925, p. 162.
19. Wilson Brown, *American Heritage*, Vol. 6, Issue 2 (February 1955).
20. Starling, *Starling of the White House*, p. 207.
21. Irwin H. Hoover, *Forty-Two Years in the White House* (Boston: Houghton Mifflin, 1934), p. 232.
22. *Cosmopolitan*, April 1927.
23. Boone autobiography, chapter 21, p. 563, Boone papers, LC.
24. Boone autobiography, chapter 21, p. 564, Boone papers, LC.
25. Boone autobiography, chapter 21, p. 186, Boone papers, LC.
26. Boone autobiography, chapter 21, p. 869, Boone papers, LC.
27. Boone autobiography, chapter 21, pp. 241, 646–47, 721, Boone papers, LC; Sobel, *Coolidge: An American Enigma*, p. 308.
28. Boone autobiography, chapter 21, p. 241, Boone papers, LC.
29. *Boston Evening Transcript*, February 9, 1929.
30. Boone autobiography, chapter 21, p. 8, Boone papers, LC.
31. *New York Times*, August 9, 1923.
32. Lathem, ed., *Meet Calvin Coolidge*, p. 27.
33. *New York Times*, August 10, 1924.
34. White, *Puritan in Babylon*, p. 141.
35. *Boston Herald*, January 7, 1933.
36. *Boston Evening Transcript*, February 9, 1924.
37. Boone autobiography, chapter 21, pp. 703, 720–727, Boone papers, LC.
38. Boone autobiography, chapter 21, pp. 181 and 370, Boone papers, LC.
39. Hoover, *Forty-Two Years in the White House*, p. 233.
40. *Good Housekeeping*, June 1935.
41. Starling, *Starling of the White House*, pp. 204, 208–212, 261, 265, 206–207, 211–212. Dr. Boone also claims Coolidge was personally opposed to prohibition (Boone autobiography, chapter 21, p. 731, Boone papers, LC).
42. *New York Times*, May 17, 1929.
43. Lathem, ed., *Meet Calvin Coolidge*, pp. 145–146.
44. G. Cullom Davis, "The Transformation of the Federal Trade Commission, 1914–1929," *Mississippi Valley Historical Review* 49 (December 1962), p. 448.
45. W.E. Humphrey to CC, November 21, 1925, the Presidential Papers of Calvin Coolidge, LC.
46. *Literary Digest*, July 3, 1926; *New York Times*, June 28, 1925.
47. Lawrence Sullivan, "The Great American Bureaucracy," *The Atlantic Monthly*, February 1931, p. 142.
48. *Literary Digest*, July 3, 1926.
49. *Time Magazine*, August 12, 1940.
50. *Washington Post*, December 1, 1925.
51. *New York Times*, March 15, 1926.
52. *Nation's Business*, February 1926.
53. *Time Magazine*, August 31, 1925.
54. *Washington Post*, July 3, 1926.
55. *Washington Post*, January 12, 1930.
56. *Nation's Business*, February 1926.
57. *Washington Post*, August 30, 1926.
58. *Time Magazine*, March 2, 1925.
59. *Daily Hampshire Gazette*, February 13, 1925.
60. *New York Times*, March 2, 1925.
61. *Time Magazine*, February 23, 1925.
62. Elizabeth Jaffray, *Secrets of the White House* (New York: Cosmopolitan Books, 1927), pp. 104–105.
63. *New York Times*, June 1, 1925.
64. The Reign of Law, May 30, 1925, CCMF.
65. *Washington Post*, May 31, 1925.
66. GC to Joel T. Boone, June 4, 1925, Boone papers, LC.
67. *Washington Post*, June 7, 1925.
68. *New York Times*, June 7, 1925.
69. *New York Times*, June 7, 1925.
70. Press conference on June 8, 1925, CCMF.
71. *Washington Post*, June 21, 1925.
72. Press conference, March 31, 1925, CCMF; *New York Times*, May 17, 1925.
73. *Washington Post*, June 21, 1925.
74. Address at the Ninth Regular Meeting of the Business Organization of the Government, June 21, 1925, CCMF.
75. *Time Magazine*, July 6, 1925.
76. *New York Times*, August 8, 1925.
77. *New York Times*, July 19, 1925.
78. Boone autobiography, chapter 21, pp. 459–469, Boone papers, LC.
79. *Time Magazine*, August 3, 1925.
80. Starling, *Starling of the White House*, p. 233.

81. *Washington Post*, July 1, 1925.
82. *New York Times*, July 1, 1925.
83. Lathem, ed., *Your Son, Calvin Coolidge*, p. 211.
84. CC to John Coolidge, August 5, 1925, Coolidge family papers, Vermont Historical Society.
85. *New York Times*, September 7, 1925.
86. *Washington Post*, September 10, 1925.
87. Press conference on September 18, 1925, CCMF.
88. *New York Times*, October 8, 1925.
89. Coolidge, *Autobiography*, p. 93.
90. Boone autobiography, chapter 21, pp. 50–51, Boone papers, LC.
91. *Time Magazine*, May 31, 1926.
92. Edward Clark to Frank Stearns, October 8, 1925, Clark papers, LC.
93. *American Legion: Toleration and Liberalism*, October 6, 1925, CCMF.
94. *New York Times*, October 8, 1925.
95. Address of President Coolidge before the Annual Council of the Congregational Churches, October 25, 1925 (Washington, D.C.: Government Printing Office, 1925), p. 1.
96. Press conference on October 16, 1925, CCMF.
97. Press conference on October 27, 1925, CCMF.
98. New York Chamber of Commerce: Government and Business, November 19, 1925, CCMF.
99. *Literary Digest*, December 5, 1925.
100. *Time Magazine*, August 13, 1923.
101. *New York Times*, August 5, 1925.
102. *Saturday Evening Post*, December 20, 1930.
103. *Washington Post*, January 6, 1933.
104. *New York Times*, November 29, 1925.
105. *New York Times*, March 11, 1926.
106. Lathem, ed., *Your Son, Calvin Coolidge*, p. 215.
107. Lathem, ed., *Your Son, Calvin Coolidge*, p. 219.
108. *New York Times*, December 6, 1925.
109. Hoover, *Forty-Two Years in the White House*, p. 127.
110. Harry E. Hawes to Cyril Clemens, March 22, 1934, Misc. File, FL.
111. *Washington Post*, January 10, 1926.
112. Burton Hersh, *The Mellon Family: A Fortune in History* (New York: William Morrow, 1978), p. 56.
113. *New York Times*, August 15, 1924.
114. Arthur W. Macmahan, "American Government and Politics," *The American Political Science Review*, Vol. 22, Issue 3 (August 1928), p. 662.
115. *New York Times*, February 21, 1926.
116. *New York Times*, February 27, 1926.
117. *Wall Street Journal*, February 27, 1926.
118. *Washington Post*, March 13, 1926.
119. Boone autobiography, chapter 21, p. 514, Boone papers, LC.
120. *New York Times*, March 19, 1926.
121. Coolidge, *Autobiography*, p. 192.
122. *New York Times*, March 25, 1926.
123. *Wall Street Journal*, March 26, 1926.
124. *New York Times*, May 5, 1926.
125. *New York Times*, May 3, 1926.
126. Press conference, May 7, 1926, CCMF.
127. *American Heritage*, February 1955.
128. *Washington Post*, May 16, 1926.
129. Address at William & Mary College, May 15, 1926, CCMF.
130. White, *Puritan in Babylon*, p. 344.
131. Press conference on April 27, 1926, CCMF.
132. Address at the Thirteenth Regular Meeting of the Business Organization of the Government, June 10, 1927, CCMF.
133. NAACP, Annual Report, 1926, p. 32.
134. *Washington Post*, July 3, 1926.
135. The Inspiration of the Declaration, July 5, 1926, CCMF.
136. *Philadelphia Inquirer*, July 6, 1926.
137. Frank Stearns to Edward Clark, July 8, 1926, Clark papers, LC.
138. Boone autobiography, chapter 21, pp. 568–569, Boone papers, LC.
139. Press conference on June 1, 1926, CCMF.
140. *New York Times*, August 1, 1926.
141. Boone autobiography, chapter 21, p. 591, Boone papers, LC.
142. Boone autobiography, chapter 21, pp. 70–71, 580–582, Boone papers, LC.
143. Boone autobiography, chapter 21, pp. 576–624; Boone diary, August 13, 1926, Boone papers, LC.
144. CC to John Coolidge, October 8, 1926, Personal Files of President Calvin Coolidge, LC.
145. GC to Therese Hills, October 12, 1926, Misc. File 17.11, FL.

146. Press conference on September 14, 1926, CCMF.
147. *Literary Digest*, August 28, 1926.
148. *New York Times*, July 30, 1926.
149. *New York Times*, September 23, 1926.
150. *New York Times*, September 21, 1926.
151. Press conferences on September 21, 1926, and September 28, 1926, CCMF.
152. Ellen Riley to mother, undated, PCCSHS.
153. GC to Edward Clark (undated), Clark papers, LC.
154. Ellen Riley to mother (undated), PCCSHS.
155. Ellen Riley to mother, April 3, 1927, PCCSHS.
156. Ferrell and Quint, *The Talkative President*, p. 107.
157. *Congressional Record*, 69th Congress, 2nd Session, vol. 68, p. 3208.
158. *New York Times*, October 31, 1926.
159. *New York Times*, November 4, 1926.
160. *New York Times*, November 4, 1926.
161. *Wall Street Journal*, November 6, 1926.
162. Fourth Annual Message to Congress, December 7, 1926, the American Presidency Project, UC Santa Barbara.
163. Message to the Senate Returning Without Approval S.4808—The McNary-Haugen Farm Relief Bill, February 25, 1927, CCMF.
164. *Washington Post*, February 10, 1927.
165. *Congressional Record: Proceedings and Debates of the Second Session of the Sixty-Ninth Congress*, Volume LXVIII, Part I (Washington, D.C.: Government Printing Office, 1927), p. 1098.
166. Boone autobiography, chapter 21, p. 721, Boone papers, LC.
167. *New York Times*, November 8, 1928.
168. Press conference, April 29, 1927, CCMF.
169. Boone autobiography, chapter 21, p. 756, Boone papers, LC.
170. *Washington Post*, April 26, 1927.
171. Elting E. Morison, *Turmoil and Tradition: A Study of the Life and Times of Henry L. Stimson* (Boston, 1960), p. 271.
172. Ferrell and Quint, *The Talkative President*, p. 234.
173. Fuess, *Calvin Coolidge*, p. 413.
174. *New York Times*, April 4, 1928.
175. The notes were made public by the State Department in a press notice dated April 3, 1928.
176. Baruch, *Baruch: The Public Years*, p. 192.
177. *Good Housekeeping*, May 1935.
178. *New York Times*, February 19, 1928.
179. *New York Times*, December 4, 1927.
180. *Wall Street Journal*, December 13, 1928.
181. Laurence B. Mann, "Occupational Shifts Since 1920," *Journal of the American Statistical Association*, Vol. 24, No. 165 (March 1929), pp. 42–47.
182. Ferrell, *The Presidency of Calvin Coolidge*, pp. 170 and 174.
183. *Nation's Business*, May 1926.
184. Johnson, Paul, *Modern Times: From the Twenties to the Nineties* (New York: HarperCollins, 1983), p. 233.
185. Ferrell, *The Presidency of Calvin Coolidge*, p. 183.
186. *Nation's Business*, March 1926.
187. Derek H. Aldcroft, *From Versailles to Wall Street, 1919–1929* (Los Angeles: University of California Press, 1927), p. 300.
188. Perrett, *America in the Twenties*, p. 286; White, *Puritan in Babylon*, pp. 336–338.
189. Ferrell and Quint, *The Talkative President*, p .130.
190. New York Chamber of Commerce: Government and Business, November 19, 1925, CCMF.
191. Ferrell and Quint, *The Talkative President*, p. 391.
192. Ferrell, *The Presidency of Calvin Coolidge*, p. 177.
193. Ferrell and Quint, *The Talkative President*, p. 135.

Chapter Eight

1. *The Forum*, January 1927.
2. Claude Fuess, *Calvin Coolidge: Twenty Years After* (Worcester, Massachusetts, 1954), p. 6.
3. *Washington Post*, May 14, 1927.
4. Boone autobiography, chapter 21, pp. 700–710, Boone papers, LC.
5. *New York Times*, April 18, 1927.
6. *New York Times*, April 13, 1927.
7. *New York Times*, April 21, 1927.
8. *New York Times*, April 5, 1927.

9. *New York Times*, April 23, 1927.
10. *Washington Post*, May 7, 1927.
11. *Washington Post*, May 14, 1927.
12. *New York Times*, May 18, 1927.
13. Fuess, *Calvin Coolidge*, p. 390.
14. *New York Times*, June 12, 1927.
15. *Lindbergh: Welcoming Home Speech*, June 11, 1928, CCMF. Coolidge, having promoted legislation to improve the airline industry, sent an inquiry to the Department of Commerce asking whether the designer of the plane that Lindbergh flew should receive a medal as well. William P. MacCracken, Assistant Secretary of Commerce, replied that if that happened, they would also have to honor the inventor of the earth inductor compass that Lindbergh used and the inventors of other various gadgets on the plane.
16. *Washington Post*, June 15, 1927.
17. Literary Digest, July 21, 1927.
18. *New York Times*, June 24, 1927.
19. *Time Magazine*, July 4, 1927.
20. Ellen Riley to mother, July 13, 1927, Riley correspondence, PCCSHS.
21. Boone autobiography, chapter 21, pp. 839–841, 844, 849, Boone papers, LC; *New Republic*, August 6–13, 1927; *Washington Post*, June 30, 1927.
22. Boone autobiography, chapter 21, p. 810, Boone papers, LC.
23. Boone autobiography, chapter 21, p. 809, Boone papers, LC.
24. Edward Clark to Frank Stearns, June 29, 1927, Clark papers, LC.
25. Boone autobiography, chapter 21, p. 807, Boone papers, LC.
26. Boone autobiography, chapter 21, p. 575 and 552, Boone papers, LC.
27. *Saturday Evening Post*, December 6, 1930.
28. *Washington Post*, August 2, 1927.
29. Sobel, *Coolidge: An American Enigma*, p. 369.
30. *Saturday Evening Post*, December 6, 1930.
31. Everett Sanders to Winfield Scott, August 2, 1927; Acting-Secretary Finney to Everett Sanders, August 2, 1927, the Presidential Papers of Calvin Coolidge, LC.
32. Ferrell and Quint, *The Talkative President*, p. 75; *Washington Post*, August 3, 1927; *New York Times*, August 3, 1927.
33. *Saturday Evening Post*, December 6, 1930.
34. *Saturday Evening Post*, December 6, 1930; *New York Times*, August 3, 1927; Fuess, *Calvin Coolidge*, pp. 393–395.
35. Cyril Clemens, Box 2, File 2.5, FL.
36. Grace Coolidge, *An Autobiography*, p. 64. The timing may have surprised her, but not the decision; she had been stitching since March 1925 a coverlet for the Lincoln bed that gave the dates of the Coolidge presidency as August 1923 to March 1929.
37. *Daily Hampshire Gazette*, August 3, 1927.
38. *Daily Hampshire Gazette*, August 3, 1927.
39. *Washington Post*, August 3, 1927.
40. Fuess, *Calvin Coolidge*, p. 339.
41. *New York Times*, August 5, 1927.
42. *New York Times*, August 5, 1927.
43. *Time Magazine*, August 15, 1927.
44. *Washington Post*, August 4, 1927.
45. Hoover, *Forty-Two Years in the White House*, p. 177.
46. *New York Times*, August 4, 1927.
47. *New England Quarterly*, June 1945.
48. *Washington Post*, August 4, 1927.
49. Boone autobiography, chapter 21, p. 867, Boone papers, LC.
50. *Washington Post*, September 17, 1927.
51. Ferrell and Quint, *The Talkative President*, p. 110.
52. *New York Times*, November 11, 1927.
53. *New York Times*, October 13, 1927.
54. *Wall Street Journal*, March 22, 1927.
55. Sobel, *Coolidge: American Enigma*, p. 302.
56. *New York Times*, September 4, 1927; April 17, 1927.
57. *New York Times*, November 27, 1927.
58. *Address before the Union League of Philadelphia*, November 17, 1927, CCMF.
59. *New York Times*, December 8, 1927.
60. *New York Times*, November 9, 1904.
61. *Outlook*, August 17, 1927.
62. Boone autobiography, chapter 21, p. 902, Boone papers, LC.
63. Boone autobiography, chapter 21, p. 838, Boone papers, LC.
64. *Washington Evening Star*, December 6, 1927.
65. Boone autobiography, chapter 21, p. 893, Boone papers, LC.
66. *Washington Post*, December 17, 1927.
67. *Washington Evening Star*, December 26, 1927.
68. Ferrell and Quint, *The Talkative President*, pp. 137–138.

69. Ferrell and Quint, *The Talkative President*, pp. 137–138.
70. White, *Puritan in Babylon*, p. 391.
71. *New York Times*, January 11, 1928.
72. *New York Times*, January 22, 1928; March 4, 1928; June 3, 1928; October 21, 1928.
73. *New York Times*, February 9, 1930.
74. Felix E. Hirsch, "Memories of Emil Ludwig," *Books Abroad*, Vol. 23, No. 2 (Spring 1949). Ludwig, whose books were burned in Nazi Germany because of his Jewish faith, moved to the United States in 1940 and wrote anti-fascist propaganda during World War II.
75. Boone autobiography, chapter 21, p.917, Boone papers, LC.
76. *Address at the Fourteenth Regular Meeting of the Business Organization of the Government*, January 30, 1928, CCMF.
77. Boone autobiography, chapter 21, p.954, Boone papers, LC.
78. Coolidge, *Autobiography*, pp. 243–244.
79. *Boston Evening Transcript*, January 6, 1933.
80. *Time Magazine*, February 20, 1928.
81. Lathem, ed., *Meet Calvin Coolidge*, p. 130.
82. Boone autobiography, chapter 21, p. 930, Boone papers, LC.
83. Ellen Riley to mother, February 28, 1928, Riley correspondence, PCCSHS.
84. *Boston Evening Transcript*, January 6, 1933.
85. Arthur M. Schlesinger, Jr., *Crisis of the Old Order, 1919–1933* (Boston: Houghton Mifflin, 1957), p. 88.
86. *Good Housekeeping*, May 1935.
87. Starling, *Starling of the White House*, p. 263.
88. Hoover, *Memoirs*, p. 193.
89. White, *Puritan in Babylon*, p. 400.
90. Boone autobiography, chapter 21, p. 797, Boone papers, LC.
91. *Congressional Record*, Appendix, June 7, 1928, p. 10907.
92. Ferrell and Quint, *The Talkative President*, p. 111.
93. Ferrell and Quint, *The Talkative President*, p. 112.
94. Fifth Annual Message to Congress, December 6, 1927, Miller Center, University of Virginia.
95. CC to General Jadwin, April 6, 1928, the Presidential Papers of Calvin Coolidge, LC.
96. Press conference on April 10, 1928, CCMF.
97. Ferrell and Quint, *The Talkative President*, pp. 80–84; *New York Times*, April 18, 1928.
98. Press conference on April 10, 1928, CCMF.
99. Harry S. New to Herbert Lord, May 14, 1928; New to Lord, May 15, 1928; Lord to Everett Sanders, May 16, 1928; William Jardine to Lord, May 15, 1928; Andrew Mellon to Lord, May 26, 1928; the Presidential Papers of Calvin Coolidge, LC.
100. *Washington Evening Star*, May 24, 1928.
101. *Time Magazine*, June 4, 1928.
102. Congressional Record, Seventieth Congress, 1st Session, vol. 69, p. 9704.
103. *New York Times*, May 27, 1928.
104. Burton Hersh, *The Mellon Family* (New York, 1978), p. 288.
105. Bertrand Snell to Cyril Clemens, January 8, 1944, Misc. Files, FL.
106. Boone autobiography, chapter 21, p. 994–995, Boone papers, LC.
107. Boone autobiography, chapter 21, p. 999, Boone papers, LC.
108. Coolidge, *Autobiography*, p. 244.
109. *New York Times*, June 10, 1928.
110. CC to John Coolidge, June 8, 1928, Personal Files of President Calvin Coolidge, LC.
111. Boone autobiography, chapter 21, pp. 1102–1109, Boone papers, LC.
112. Address at the Fifteenth Regular Meeting of the Business Organization of the Government, June 11, 1928, CCMF.
113. Boone autobiography, chapter 21, pp. 1102–1109, Boone papers, LC.
114. Hoover, *Forty-Two Years in the White House*, p. 176. It should be noted that Hoover begrudged Coolidge for not re-grading him to a higher rate on the Civil Service pay schedule and seemed intent at times in casting the president in the worst possible light.
115. CC to Frank Stearns, July 24, 1928, Personal Files of President Calvin Coolidge, LC.
116. Ferrell and Quint, *The Talkative President*, p. 18.
117. GC to Florence Irwin, August 28, 1928, Misc. File 1.5, FL.
118. *New York Times*, October 8, 1939.

119. Vermont Is a State I Love, September 21, 1928, CCMF.
120. Coolidge, *Autobiography*, p. 26.
121. Donald S. MacNaughton, *Milwaukee*, Volume 64, Issue 2 (April 2002), pp. 64–66.
122. *Washington Post*, October 2, 1928.
123. *Washington Post*, October 3, 1928.
124. Hoover, *Forty-Two Years in the White House*, p. 179.
125. *New York Times*, October 18, 1928.
126. Boone autobiography, chapter 21, p. 1072, Boone papers, LC; CC to Lord, October 16, 1928, the Presidential Papers of Calvin Coolidge, LC.
127. Statement by the Secretary, October 18, 1925, Coolidge papers, LC.
128. *New York Times*, October 18, 1928, and October 25, 1928.
129. *Washington Post*, November 8, 1928.
130. *New York Times*, December 23, 1928.
131. *Saturday Evening Post*, October 25, 1924.
132. Coolidge, *Autobiography*, p. 214.

Chapter Nine

1. Sixth Annual Message to the Congress of the United States, December 4, 1928, CCMF.
2. *Wall Street Journal*, December 6, 1928.
3. *New York Times*, December 2, 1928.
4. Lathem, ed., *Meet Calvin Coolidge*, pp. 125–127.
5. *New York Times*, January 3, 1929.
6. *New York Evening Post*, January 12, 1929.
7. Fuess, *Calvin Coolidge*, p. 438.
8. Address at the Sixteenth Regular Meeting of the Business Organization of the Government, January 28, 1929, CCMF.
9. Boone autobiography, chapter 21, p. 1205, Boone papers, LC.
10. Ferrell and Quint, *The Talkative President*, p. 18.
11. *American Magazine*, June 1929.
12. *American Magazine*, June 1929.
13. *Washington Post*, March 2, 1929.
14. GC to Therese Hills, March 2, 1929, Misc. File 18–12, FL.
15. *Good Housekeeping*, November 24, 1934.
16. Starling, *Starling of the White House*, pp. 275–281.
17. *New York Tribune*, March 5, 1929.
18. *Washington Post*, March 2, 1929.
19. Abels, *In the Time of Silent Cal*, p. 282.
20. *Washington Post*, March 5, 1929; *New York Times*, March 5, 1929.

Chapter Ten

1. *Boston Globe*, March 7, 1929.
2. Grace Coolidge, *An Autobiography*, p. 103.
3. *Boston Globe*, January 7, 1929.
4. Grace Coolidge, *An Autobiography*, p. 158.
5. Coolidge, *Autobiography*, p. 185.
6. *Washington Post*, October 10, 1929.
7. GC to Maude Trumbull, November 18, 1932, CCMF.
8. GC to John Coolidge, June 19, 1929, CCMF.
9. Susan Webb, "Grace Goodhue Coolidge," *The Real Calvin Coolidge*, Issue 10 (Plymouth Notch, 1994).
10. Lathem, ed., *Meet Calvin Coolidge*, p. 183.
11. Lathem, ed., *Meet Calvin Coolidge*, p. 166.
12. Woods, *The Preparation of Calvin Coolidge*, p. 63.
13. Lathem, ed., *Meet Calvin Coolidge*, p. 164.
14. Recollections of Edwin L. Olander, Misc. File 3.17, FL.
15. Henry L. Stoddard, *It Costs to Be President* (New York: Harper Brothers, 1938), p. 134.
16. Lathem, ed., *Meet Calvin Coolidge*, p. 221.
17. Memoirs of Howard D. French, Misc. File, FL.
18. CC to James W. O'Brien, May 28, 1930, Misc. File, FL.
19. GC to Joel T. Boone, June 26, 1930, Boone correspondence, LC.
20. Lathem, ed., *Meet Calvin Coolidge*, p. 190; American Magazine, March 1931.
21. Wilfred E. Brinkley, *American Political Parties* (New York: Alfred A. Knopf, 1945), p. 350.
22. Harold G. Nicolson, *Dwight Morrow* (New York: Harcourt, Brace, 1935), p. 353.
23. CC to Edward Clark, June 13, 1932, Clark papers, LC.

24. Edward Clark to CC, July 1, 1930, Clark papers, LC.
25. William H. Wandel and Birchard E. Wyatt, *The Social Security Act in Operation* (Washington, D.C., 1937).
26. *Washington Post*, January 26, 1931.
27. *Cosmopolitan*, May 1930; Charles P. Kindleberger, *Manias, Panics, and Crashes: A History of Financial Crises* (New York: Wiley, 1989), p. 154.
28. Edward Clark to CC, November 11, 1931, Clark papers, LC.
29. *Washington Post*, February 18, 1930.
30. *Literary Digest*, January 10, 1931.
31. *New York Times*, March 23, 1932.
32. *New York Times*, July 15, 1932.
33. Edward Clark to CC, November 11, 1931, Clark papers, LC.
34. White, *Puritan in Babylon*, p. 431.
35. *Washington Post*, November 8, 1931.
36. CC to Edward Clark, June 17, 1932, Clark papers, LC.
37. *Vermont Sunday Magazine*, June 30, 1985.
38. CC to Edward Clark, July 7, 1932, Clark papers, LC.
39. Lathem, ed., *Meet Calvin Coolidge*, p. 210.
40. CC to Edward Clark, September 26, 1932, Clark papers, LC.
41. CC to Edward Clark, October 12, 1932, Clark papers, LC.
42. Stoddard, *It Costs to Be President*, pp. 136–141.
43. GC to Ivah Gale, September 28, 1932, CCMF.
44. CC to Stoddard, October 3, 1927, Personal Files of President Calvin Coolidge, LC.
45. Lathem, ed., *Meet Calvin Coolidge*, p. 205.
46. *Washington Post*, October 12, 1932; *New York Times*, October 12, 1932.
47. *New York Times*, January 6, 1933.
48. *The New York Sun*, January 6, 1933.
49. *Saturday Evening Post*, October 6, 1934.
50. Stoddard, *It Costs to Be President*, pp. 136–141.
51. *International Tribune*, January 7, 1933.
52. CC to Edward Clark, December 31, 1932, Clark papers, LC.
53. Starling, *Starling of the White House*, p. 302.
54. Lathem, ed., *Meet Calvin Coolidge*, p. 216.
55. *Boston Herald*, January 6, 1933.
56. White, *Puritan in Babylon*, p. 441.
57. Fuess, *Calvin Coolidge*, p. 465.
58. *Washington Post*, January 8, 1933.
59. *United States v. Butler*, 297 U.S. 1 (1936).
60. *Washington Post*, August 9, 1944.
61. *Washington Post*, July 2, 1936.
62. *Washington Post*, October 1, 1936.
63. *American Heritage*, February 1955.

Bibliography

Books

Abels, Jules. *In the Time of Silent Cal.* New York: Putnam, 1969.

Aldcroft, Derek H. *From Versailles to Wall Street, 1919–1929.* Los Angeles: University of California Press, 1927.

Banning, Will P. *Commercial Broadcasting Pioneer: The WEAF Experiment, 1922–1926.* Cambridge: Harvard University Press, 1946.

Barnard, Harry. *Independent Man: The Life of Senator James Couzens.* New York: Charles Scribner's Sons, 1958.

Baruch, Bernard M. *Baruch: The Public Years.* New York: Holt, Rinehart and Winston, 1960.

Booraem, Hendrik V. *The Provincial: Calvin Coolidge and His World, 1885–1895.* Lewisburg, PA: Bucknell University Press, 1994.

Boyce, Robert. *The Great Interwar Crisis and the Collapse of Globalization.* New York: Palgrave Macmillan, 2009.

Brinkley, Wilfred E. *American Political Parties.* New York: Alfred A. Knopf, 1945.

Carpenter, Earnest C. *The Boyhood Days of President Calvin Coolidge.* Rutland, Vermont: Tuttle Company, 1925.

Carter, Paul. *The Twenties in America.* Hoboken: Wiley Blackwell, 1968.

Cogan, John F. *The High Cost of Good Intentions: A History of U.S. Federal Entitlement Programs.* Stanford: Stanford University Press, 2017.

Coolidge, Calvin. *Autobiography.* New York: Cosmopolitan Books, 1929.

Coolidge, Calvin. *Foundations of the Republic.* New York: Charles Scribner's Sons, 1926.

Coolidge, Calvin. *Have Faith in Massachusetts.* Boston: Houghton Mifflin, 1919.

Coolidge, Calvin. *The Price of Freedom.* New York: Charles Scribner's Sons, 1924.

Coolidge, Grace. *Grace Coolidge: An Autobiography.* Edited by Lawrence E. Wikander and Robert H. Ferrell. New York: Norton, 1992.

Curtis, Joe. *Return to These Hills.* Woodstock, Vermont, 1940.

Dawes, Charles G. *Notes as Vice President.* Boston: Little, Brown, 1935.

Dennis, Alfred Pearce. *Gods and Little Fishes.* Indianapolis: Bobbs-Merrill, 1924.

Ferrell, Robert H. *The Presidency of Calvin Coolidge.* Lawrence: University of Kansas Press, 1998.

Ferrell, Robert H., and Howard H. Quint, eds. *The Talkative President: The Off-the-Record Press Conferences of Calvin Coolidge.* Amherst: University of Massachusetts Press, 1964.

Fleser, Arthur F. *A Rhetorical Study of the Speaking of Calvin Coolidge.* Lewiston, NY: Edwin Mellen Press, 1990.

Fuess, Claude M. *Calvin Coolidge: The Man from Vermont.* Boston: Little, Brown, 1940.

Garraty, John A. *Henry Cabot Lodge: A Biography.* New York: Alfred A. Knopf, 1968.

Gilbert, Robert E. *The Tormented President: Calvin Coolidge, Death, and Clinical Depression.* Westport, CT: Praeger, 2003.

Green, Horace. *The Life of Calvin Coolidge.* New York: Duffield and Company, 1924.

Greenberg, David. *Calvin Coolidge.* New York: Henry Holt/Times Books, 2006.

Hammond, John Hays. *The Autobiography of John Hays Hammond.* New York: Farrar and Rinehart, 1935.

Hard, Walter R. *Vermont Vintage*. Brattleboro, Vermont: Stephen Daye Press, 1937.

Hennessey, M.E. *Calvin Coolidge: From a Green Mountain Farm to the White House*. Boston: G.P. Putnam's Sons, 1924.

Hennessey, M.E. *Four Decades of Massachusetts Politics*. Freeport, NY: Norwood Press, 1971.

Hersh, Burton. *The Mellon Family: A Fortune in History*. New York: William Morrow, 1978.

Hicks, John D., *Republican Ascendancy*, Berkeley, California: University of California Press, 1960.

Hoover, Herbert *The Memoirs of Herbert Hoover: The Cabinet and the Presidency*. New York: Macmillan, 1952.

Hoover, Irwin H. *Forty-Two Years in the White House*. Boston: Houghton Mifflin, 1934.

Jaffray, Elizabeth. *Secrets of the White House*. New York: Cosmopolitan Books, 1927.

Johnson, Paul. *Modern Times: From the Twenties to the Nineties*. New York: HarperCollins, 1983.

Kahn, Johnathan. *Budgeting Democracy: State Building and Citizenship in America, 1890–1928*. Ithaca: NCROL, 1997.

Kindleberger, Charles P. *Manias, Panics, and Crashes: A History of Financial Crises*. New York: Wiley, 1989.

Lathem, Edward C., ed. *Meet Calvin Coolidge*. Brattleboro, Vermont: The Stephen Greene Press, 1960.

Lathem, Edward C., ed. *Your Son, Calvin Coolidge: A Selection of Letters from Calvin Coolidge to His Father*. Montpelier: Vermont Historical Society, 1968.

Lockwood, Allison. *A President in a Two-Family House*. Northampton, MA: Northampton Historical Society, 1988.

Martin, Joe. *My First Fifty Years in Politics*. New York: McGraw-Hill, 1960.

Mason, Alpheus. *Harlan Fiske Stone: Pillar of the Law*. New York: Viking Press, 1956.

McCoy, Donald R. *Calvin Coolidge: The Quiet President*. Lawrence: University of Kansas Press, 1967.

McKenna, Marian C. *Borah*. Ann Arbor: University of Michigan Press, 1961.

Morison, Elting E. *Turmoil and Tradition: A Study of the Life and Times of Henry L. Stimson*. Boston: Houghton Mifflin, 1960.

Murray, Robert K. *The Harding Era*. Minneapolis: University of Minnesota Press, 1969.

Murray, Robert K. *The Politics of Normalcy: Governmental Theory and Practice in the Harding-Coolidge Era*. New York: W.W. Norton, 1973.

Nicolson, Harold G. *Dwight Morrow*. New York: Harcourt, Brace, 1935.

Noggle, Burl. *Teapot Dome: Oil and Politics in the 1920s*. New York: W.W. Norton, 1962.

Orton, Vrest. *Calvin Coolidge's Unique Vermont Inauguration*. Plymouth, VT: Calvin Coolidge Memorial Foundation, 1970.

Perrett, Geoffrey. *America in the Twenties*. New York: Simon & Schuster, 1982.

Pietrusza, David. *Calvin Coolidge: A Documented Biography*. Church & Reid Books, 2013.

Pringle, Henry F. *The Life and Times of William Howard Taft*. New York: Farrar and Reinhart, 1939.

Pusey, Merlo J. *Charles Evans Hughes*. New York: Macmillan, 1952.

Rogers, Cameron. *The Legend of Calvin Coolidge*. New York: Doubleday, Doran, 1928.

Ross, Ishbel. *Grace Coolidge and Her Era*. New York: Dodd, Mead, 1988.

Russell, Francis. *The Shadow of Blooming Grove*. New York: McGraw-Hill, 1978.

Sawyer, Ronald D. *Cal Coolidge, President*. Boston: Four Seas, 1924.

Schlesinger Arthur M., Jr. *The Crisis of the Old Order, 1919–1933*. Boston: Houghton Mifflin, 1957.

Shlaes, Amity. *Coolidge*. New York: Harper Collins, 2013.

Slemp, C. Bascom. *The Mind of the President*. New York: Doubleday, Page, 1926.

Sobel, Robert. *Coolidge: An American Enigma*. Washington, D.C.: Regnery, 1998.

Starling, Edmund. *Starling of the White House*. New York: Simon & Schuster, 1946.

Stoddard, Henry L. *As I Knew Them*. New York: Harper Brothers, 1927.

Stoddard, Henry L. *It Costs to Be President*. New York: Harper Brothers, 1938.

Washburn, R.M. *Calvin Coolidge: His First Biography*. Boston: Small, Maynard, 1923.

Watson, James E. *As I Knew Them*. Indianapolis: Bobbs-Merrill, 1936.

Weed, Clyde P. *The Transformation of the Republican Party, 1912–1936*. Boulder: Lynne Rienner, 2012.
White, William Allen. *Puritan in Babylon*. New York: Macmillan, 1938.
Wooddy, Carroll H. *The Growth of the Federal Government: 1915–1932*. New York: McGraw-Hill, 1934.
Woods, Robert A. *The Preparation of Calvin Coolidge*. Boston: Houghton Mifflin, 1924.

Articles

Alsott, Anne L., and Ben Novick. "War, Taxes, and Income Redistribution in the Twenties: The 1924 Veteran's Bonus and the Defeat of the Mellon Plan." *Tax Law Review*, Vol. 59, Issue 4 (Summer 2006).
Amenta, Edwin, and Bruce G. Carruthers. "The Formative Years of U.S. Social Spending Policies: Theories of the Welfare State and the American States During the Great Depression." *American Sociological Review*, Vol. 53, No. 5 (October 1988).
Arneson, Ben A. "Federal Aid to the States." *The American Political Science Review*, Vol. 16, No. 3 (August 1922).
Bailey, Thomas A. "The West and Radical Legislation, 1890–1930." *American Journal of Sociology*, Vol. 38, No. 4 (January 1933).
Bates, J. Leonard. "The Teapot Dome Scandal and the Election of 1924." *The American Historical Review*, Vol. 60, Issue 2 (January 1955).
Benton, E. Maxwell. "The War Debts Policy of the United States." *Social Science*, Vol. 9, No. 1 (January 1934).
Black, John D. "The McNary-Haugen Movement." *The American Economic Review*, Vol. 18, Issue 3 (September 1928).
Black, John D. "The Progress of Farm Relief." *The American Economic Review*, Vol. 18, Issue 2 (June 1928).
Blair, John L. "A Time for Parting: The Negro during the Coolidge Years." *Journal of American Studies*, Vol. 3, No. 2 (December 1969).
Blakey, Roy G. "The Revenue Act of 1924." *The American Economic Review*, Vol. 14, Issue 3 (September 1924).
Blakey, Roy G. "The Revenue Act of 1926." *The American Economic Review*, Vol. 16, Issue 3 (September 1926).
Bogart, Ernest L. "An Examination of the Reasons for Revision of the Debt Settlements." *The American Economic Review*, Vol. 18, Issue 1 (March 1928).
Boswell, James L. "Some Neglected Aspects of the World War Debt Payments." *The American Economic Review*, Vol. 21, No. 2 (June 1931).
Boyden, Roland W. "Relation Between Reparations and the Interallied Debts." *Proceedings of the Academy of Political Science in the City of New York*, Vol. 12, No. 4 (January 1928).
Boyden, Roland W. "The United States and the Dawes Plan." *Proceedings of the Academy of Political Science in the City of New York*, Vol. 11, No. 2 (January 1925).
Bradford, Gamaliel. "The Genius of the Average: Calvin Coolidge." *The Atlantic Monthly* (January 1930).
Bradley, Phillips. "The Farm Bloc." *Journal of Social Forces*, Vol. 3, No. 4 (May 1925).
Buck, A.E. "The Development of the Budget Idea in the United States." *The Annals of the American Academy of Political and Social Science*, Vol. 113 (May 1924).
Bullard, Arthur. "Russia in the Fabric of International Finance." *The Annals of the American Academy of Political and Social Science*, Vol. 100 (March 1922).
Burlingham, Charles C. "Harlan Fiske Stone." *American Bar Association Journal*, Vol. 32, No. 6 (June 1946).
Burtin, Oliver. "The History of Veterans' Policy in the United States." *Historical Social Research*, Vol. 45, No. 2 (2020).
Burton, Theodore E. "Indebtedness of European Nations to the United States." *Advocate of Peace through Justice*, Vol. 88, No. 11 (November 1926).
Chepaitis, Joseph B. "Federal Social Welfare Progressivism in the 1920s." *Social Service Review*, Vol. 46, No. 2 (June 1972).
Comstock, Alzada. "Reparation Payments in Perspective." *The American Economic Review*, Vol. 20, No. 2 (June 1930).
Cornwell, Elmer E., Jr. "Coolidge and Presidential Leadership." *Public Opinion Quarterly*, Vol. 21, Issue 2 (Summer 1957).
Corwin, Edward S. "The Spending Power of Congress. Apropos the Maternity Act." *Harvard Law Review*, Vol. 36, No. 5 (March 1923).

Corwin, Edward S. "The Passing of Dual Federalism." *Virginia Law Review*, Vol. 36, No. 1 (February 1950).
Costigliola, Frank. "The United States and the Reconstruction of Germany in the 1920s." *The Business History Review*, Vol. 50, No. 4 (Winter 1976).
David, W. Jefferson. "The Radio Act of 1927." *Virginia Law Review*, Vol. 13, No. 8 (June 1927).
Davis, G. Cullom. "The Transformation of the Federal Trade Commission, 1914–1929." *The Mississippi Valley Historical Review*, Vol. 49, Issue 3 (December 1962).
Dodds, H.W. "The United States and Nicaragua." *The Annals of the American Academy of Political and Social Science*, Vol. 132 (July 1927).
Dopp, Lloyd H. "A Summary of the Relations of the United States and Mexico Since 1919." *World Affairs*, Vol. 98, No. 3 (September 1935).
Douglas, Paul H. "The Development of a System of Federal Grants-in-Aid I." *Political Science Quarterly*, Vol. 35, No. 2 (June 1920).
Douglas, Paul H. "The Development of a System of Federal Grants-in-Aid II." *Political Science Quarterly*, Vol. 35, No. 4 (December 1920).
Ekelund, Robert B., Jr., and Mark Thornton. "Schumpeterian Analysis, Supply-Side Economics and Macroeconomic Policy in the 1920s." *Review of Social Economy*, Vol. 44, No. 3 (December 1986).
Essary, J. Frederick. "President, Congress, and the Press Correspondents." *The American Political Science Review*, Vol. 22, Issue 4 (November 1928).
Fairchild, Henry Pratt. "The Immigration Law of 1924." *The Quarterly Journal of Economics*, Vol. 38, Issue 4 (August 1924).
Falkus, M.E. "United States Economic Policy and the 'Dollar Gap' of the 1920s." *The Economic History Review*, Vol. 24, No. 4 (November 1971).
Felix, David. "Reparations with a Vengeance." *Central European History*, Vol. 4, No. 2 (June 1971).
Hamilton, Earl J. "Origin and Growth of the National Debt in Western Europe." *The American Economic Review*, Vol. 37, No. 2 (May 1947).
Harris, Joseph P. "Federal Financial Participation in Social Work as a Permanent Policy." *Social Service Review*, Vol. 9, No. 3 (September 1935).
Hathorn, Guy B. "C. Bascom Slemp: Virginia Republican Boss, 1907–1932." *The Journal of Politics*, Vol. 17, Issue 2 (May 1955).
Haynes, Fred E. "The Significance of the Latest Third Party Movement." *The Mississippi Valley Historical Review*, Vol. 13, No. 2 (September 1926).
Holcombe, Randall C. "The Growth of the Federal Government in the 1920s." *Cato Journal* (Fall 1996).
Horn, James J. "Did the United States Plan an Invasion of Mexico in 1927?" *Journal of Interamerican Studies and World Affairs*, Vol. 15, No. 4 (November 1973).
Johnson, Hugh. "Vested Interests in Government Spending." *The Academy of Political Science*, Vol. 17, No. 4 (January 1938).
Keller, Robert R. "A Macroeconomic History of Supply-Side Fiscal Policies in the 1920s." *Review of Social Economy*, Vol. 42, No. 4 (October 1984).
Keller, Robert R. "The Role of the State in the U.S. Economy during the 1920s." *Journal of Economic Issues*, Vol. 21, No. 2 (June 1987).
Kemmerer, Edwin Walter. "The Burden of Germany's Obligations under the Dawes Plan." *The Annals of the American Academy of Political and Social Science*, Vol. 120 (July 1925).
Leffingwell, R.C. "An Analysis of the International War Debt Situation." *The Annals of the American Academy of Political and Social Science*, Vol. 102 (July 1922).
Leffler, Melvyn. "The Origins of Republican War Debt Policy, 1921–1923: A Case Study in the Applicability of the Open Door Interpretation." *The Journal of American History*, Vol. 59, No. 3 (December 1972).
Leland, Simeon E. "Federal, State, and Local Governmental Relationships in Re Public Welfare." *Social Service Review*, Vol. 7, No. 3 (September 1933).
Lohof, Bruce A. "Herbert Hoover, Spokesman of Humane Efficiency: The Mississippi Flood of 1927." *American Quarterly*, Vol. 22, Issue 3 (Autumn 1970).
Louria, Margot. "The Boldness of Charles Evans Hughes." *The National Interest*, No. 72 (Summer 2003).

Lutz, Karl B. "The General Welfare Clause: Does It Authorize a Welfare State?" *American Bar Association Journal,* Vol. 36, No. 3 (March 1950).

Macdonald, Austin F. "Recent Trends in Federal Aid to the States." *The American Political Science Review,* Vol. 25, No. 3 (August 1931).

Macmahon, Arthur W. "First Session of the Seventieth Congress." *The American Political Science Review,* Vol. 22, Issue 3 (August 1928).

Macmahon, Arthur W. "First Session of the Sixty-Ninth Congress." *The American Political Science Review,* Vol. 20, Issue 3 (August 1926).

Macmahon, Arthur W. "Second Session of the Seventieth Congress." *The American Political Science Review,* Vol. 23, Issue 2 (May 1929).

Macmahon, Arthur W. "Second Session of the Sixty-Ninth Congress." *The American Political Science Review,* Vol. 21, Issue 2 (May 1927).

Maddox, Robert James. "Keeping Cool with Coolidge." *The Journal of American History,* Vol. 53, Issue 4 (March 1967).

Mann, Laurence B. "Occupational Shifts Since 1920." *Journal of the American Statistical Association,* Vol. 24, No. 165 (March 1929).

Marks, Sally. "The Myths of Reparations." *Central European History,* Vol. 11, No. 3 (September 1978).

Marx, Fritz Morstein. "The Bureau of the Budget: Its Evolution and Present Role." *The American Political Science Review,* Vol. 39, Issue 4 (August 1945).

McCleary, G.F. "Health Insurance in Europe." *The Milbank Memorial Fund Quarterly,* Vol. 12, No. 1 (January 1934).

McKee, Oliver, Jr. "Lobbying for Good and Evil." *The North American Review,* Vol. 227, No. 3 (March 1929).

McKee, Oliver, Jr. "Lobbyists Extraordinary." *The North American Review,* Vol. 229, No. 1 (January 1930).

Mehrotra, Ajay K. "The Intellectual Foundations of the Modern American Fiscal State." *Daedalus,* Vol. 138, No. 2 (Spring 2009).

Miller, A.C. "Responsibility for Federal Reserve Policies: 1927–1929." *The American Economic Review,* Vol. 25, No. 3 (September 1935).

Murname, M. Susan. "Selling Scientific Taxation: The Treasury Department's Campaign for Tax Reform in the 1920s." *Law & Social Inquiry,* Vol. 29, No. 4 (Autumn 2004).

Myers, William Starr. "The Republican Party and The Tariff." *The Annals of the American Academy of Political and Social Science,* Vol. 141 (January 1929).

Neustadt, Richard E. "Presidency and Legislation: The Growth of Central Clearance." *The American Political Science Review,* Vol. 48, Issue 3 (September 1954).

Newcomer, Mabel. "Fifty Years of Public Support of Welfare Functions in the United States." *Social Service Review,* Vol. 15, No. 4 (December 1941).

Niefeld, S.J. "The Development of the Budget System of the United States." *Public Finance Analysis* (1951/52).

Odegard, Peter H. "Lobbies and American Legislation." *Current History,* Vol. 31, No. 4 (January 1931).

Patterson, Ernest M. "Tax Revision in the United States." *Weltwirtschaftliches Archiv* (1926).

Pell, John. "The Enigma of Calvin Coolidge." *The North American Review* (May 1930).

Perrott, George St. J., and Mountin, Joseph W. "Voluntary Health Insurance in Western Europe: Its Origin and Place in National Programs." *Public Health Reports,* Vol. 62, No. 21 (May 23, 1947).

Phillips, Orie L. "Constitutional Limitations on Social Legislation." *Proceedings of the Academy of Political Science,* Vol. 16, No. 4 (January 1936).

Post, Russell L. "The Constitutionality of Government Spending for the General Welfare." *Virginia Law Review,* Vol. 22, No. 1 (November 1935).

Quadagno, Jill S. "Welfare Capitalism and the Social Security Act of 1935." *American Sociological Review,* Vol. 49, No. 5 (October 1984).

Ratchford, Benjamin U. "History of the Federal Debt in the United States." *The American Economic Review,* Vol. 37, No. 2 (May 1947).

Robinson, Marshall A. "Federal Debt Management: Civil War, World War I, and World War II." *The American Economic Review,* Vol. 45, No. 2 (May 1955).

Rogers, Lindsay. "First and Second Sessions of the Sixty-Eighth Congress." *The*

American Political Science Review, Vol. 19, Issue 4 (November 1925).
Rogers, Lindsay. "The Second, Third, and Fourth Sessions of the Sixty-Seventh Congress." *The American Political Science Review*, Vol. 18, Issue 1 (February 1924).
Roseman, Alvin. "Old-Age Assistance." *The Annals of the American Academy of Political and Social Science*, Vol. 202 (March 1939).
Ross, Stanley R. "Dwight W. Morrow, Ambassador to Mexico." *The Americas*, Vol. 14, No. 3 (January 1958).
Saldin, Robert P. "World War I and the 'System of 1896,'" *The Journal of Politics*, Vol. 72, No. 3 (July 2010).
Schmidt, Emerson P. "The Present Impasse of Old Age Pensions." *Social Science*, Vol. 5, No. 2 (February, March, April 1930).
Seligman, Edwin R.A. "Comparative Tax Burdens in the Twentieth Century." *Political Science Quarterly*, Vol. 39, No. 1 (March 1924).
Shelton, Fred DeWitt. "The Lobby System at Washington." *Social Science*, Vol. 4, No. 2 (February, March, April 1929).
Smiley, Gene. "A Note on New Estimates of the Distribution of Income in the 1920s." *The Journal of Economic History*, Vol. 60, No. 4 (December 2000).
Smiley, Gene, and Richard H. Keehn. "Federal Personal Income Tax in the 1920s." *The Journal of Economic History*, Vol. 55, No. 2 (June 1995).
Smith, Harold D. "The Budget as an Instrument of Legislative Control and Executive Management." *Public Administration Review*, Vol. 4, No. 3 (Summer 1944).
Snyder, Carl. "The Increase of Long-Term Debt in the United States (from 1880)." *Journal of the American Statistical Association*, Vol. 29, No. 186 (June 1934).
Spencer, Frank. "The United States and Germany in the Aftermath of War: 1918–1929." *International Affairs*, Vol. 43, No. 4 (October 1967).
Strout, Richard Lee. "Our Budgetary Raree-Show." *The North American Review*, Vol. 235, No. 2 (February 1933).
Sullivan, Lawrence. "The Great American Bureaucracy." *The Atlantic Monthly* (February 1931).
Thompson, Walter. "The Trend toward Federal Centralization." *The Annals of the American Academy of Political and Social Science*, Vol. 113 (May 1924).
Thorndike, Joseph T. "The Fiscal Revolution and Taxation: The Rise of Compensatory Taxation, 1929–1938." *Law and Contemporary Problems*, Vol. 73, No. 1 (Winter 2010).
Vandervelde, Emile. "Ten Years of Socialism in Europe." *Foreign Affairs*, Vol. 3, No. 4 (July 1925).
Walker, Thomas F. "The Joker in the Constitution: A Basis for the Welfare State." *American Bar Association Journal*, Vol. 38, No. 6 (June 1952).
Wallace, Jerry L. "Calvin Coolidge's Third Oath." *The Real Calvin Coolidge*, Number 19 (2001).
Wallis, John Joseph. "American Government Finance in the Long Run: 1790 to 1990." *The Journal of Economic Perspectives*, Vol. 14, No. 1 (Winter 2000).
Watkins, Myron W. "The Federal Trade Commission: A Critical Survey." *The Quarterly Journal of Economics*, Vol. 40, Issue 4 (August 1926).
White, R. Clyde. "The Social Insurance Movement." *Journal of the American Statistical Association*, Vol. 38, No. 223 (September 1943).
Williams, C. Fred. "William M. Jardine and the Foundations for Republican Farm Policy, 1925–1929." *Agricultural History*, Vol. 70, No. 2 (Spring 1996).
Williams, John H. "Reparations and the Flow of Capital." *The American Economic Review*, Vol. 20, Issue 1 (March 1930).
Withers, William. "Our Mounting Government Debt." *The Annals of the American Academy of Political and Social Science*, Vol. 214 (March 1941).
Woodburn, James A. "Western Radicalism in American Politics." *The Mississippi Valley Historical Review*, Vol. 13, No. 2 (September 1926).
Young, Evan E. "The Attitude of the United States Government Towards the Soviet Regime." *The Annals of the American Academy of Political and Social Science*, Vol. 114 (July 1924).
Zieger, Robert H. "Pinchot and Coolidge: The Politics of the 1923 Anthracite Crisis." *The Journal of American History*, Vol. 52, Issue 3 (December 1965).
Zuckerman, T. David. "Are We Redeeming

Our National Debt Too Hastily?" *Political Science Quarterly*, Vol. 40, Issue 2 (June 1925).

Collections

Calvin Coolidge diary, President Calvin Coolidge State Historic Site (Plymouth, Vermont).
Coolidge family papers, Vermont Historical Society (Barre, Vermont).
Coolidge papers, Calvin Coolidge Memorial Foundation (Plymouth, Vermont).
Coolidge papers, Forbes Library (Northampton, Massachusetts).
Edward T. Clark papers, Manuscript Division, Library of Congress (Washington, D.C.).
Ellen Riley collection, President Calvin Coolidge State Historic Site (Plymouth, Vermont).
Everett Sanders papers, Manuscript Division, Library of Congress (Washington, D.C.).
Frank W. Stearns collection, Amherst College (Amherst, Massachusetts).
Frank W. Stearns papers, College of the Holy Cross (Worcester, Massachusetts).
Joel T. Boone Papers, Manuscript Division, Library of Congress (Washington, D.C.).
The Personal Files of Calvin Coolidge, Manuscript Division, Library of Congress (Washington, D.C.).
The Presidential Papers of Calvin Coolidge, Manuscript Division, Library of Congress (Washington, D.C.).

Index